The author of *Cat Confidential* and *Cat Detective,* Vicky Halls is one of the UK's leading cat behaviour specialists. She is currently working on a major television series on this subject. She lives in Kent.

Critical acclaim for *Cat Confidential*:

'*Cat Confidential* is definitely a superior work'
Sunday Express

'A useful book full of practical advice on a whole range of common cat problems, as well as some more unusual ones'
Daily Mail

'Ms Halls is pleasantly free of mawkishness . . . and is an excellent story-teller'
Sunday Telegraph

'Practical and often hilarious guide'
You Magazine

'The Mary Poppins of the feline world'
Mail on Sunday

'Packed with anecdotes and tips, this is a must for any cat-lover'
Woman & Home

'This wise and entertaining book is a must have for all cat lovers'
My Weekly

www.rbooks.co.uk

Also by Vicky Halls

CAT CONFIDENTIAL
CAT DETECTIVE

and published by Bantam Books

CAT COUNSELLOR
VICKY HALLS

BANTAM BOOKS

LONDON • TORONTO • SYDNEY • AUCKLAND • JOHANNESBURG

TRANSWORLD PUBLISHERS
61–63 Uxbridge Road, London W5 5SA
A The Random House Group Company
www.rbooks.co.uk

CAT COUNSELLOR
A BANTAM BOOK: 9780553817621

First published in Great Britain
in 2006 by Bantam Press
a division of Transworld Publishers
Bantam edition published 2007

Addresses for Random House Group Ltd companies outside the UK
can be found at: www.randomhouse.co.uk
The Random House Group Ltd Reg. No. 954009

The Random House Group Ltd makes every effort to ensure that the papers used
in its books are made from trees that have been legally sourced from well-man-
aged and credibly certified forests. Our paper procurement policy can be found
at: www.randomhouse.co.uk/paper.htm

Typeset in 12/15.25 Cochin by
Falcon Oast Graphic Art Ltd.

Printed and bound in Great Britain by
Cox & Wyman Ltd, Reading, Berkshire.

2 4 6 8 10 9 7 5 3 1

This book is dedicated to the memory of
Joan and Eric Pattle, my mum and dad.

CONTENTS

Acknowledgements   11
Introduction   13

Chapter 1: A Love–Hate Relationship   21
With information relating to:
   History
   Religion
   Art
   Cat lovers (and haters), superstitions and proverbs

Chapter 2: Can Cats Share?   40
With case histories and advice relating to:
   Multi-cat households
   Redirected aggression
   Behavioural changes

Chapter 3: Where Do You Go To, My Lovely?   84
With case histories and advice relating to:
  Territory
  Dependency
  The law

Chapter 4: Cats and All Things Furred, Feathered
    and Finned   116
With case histories and advice relating to:
  Multi-species households
  Inter-species relationships

Chapter 5: The Eternal Triangle   138
With case histories and advice relating to:
  Living (or not) with your partner's pet
  An honest confession

Chapter 6: How To Love Your Nervous Cat   160
With case histories and advice relating to:
  Nervousness (inborn, achieved or thrust-upon)
  Rehabilitation of feral cats
  Changing the cat/human relationship to tackle
    nervousness

Chapter 7: How To Love Your Aggressive Cat   192
With case histories and advice relating to:
  Cat terrorism
  Women who love (cats) too much
  Changing the cat/human relationship to tackle
    aggression

Chapter 8: How To Love Your Dependent Cat   234
With case histories and advice relating to:
   Dysfunctional relationships
   Cats' dependency on their owners (and vice versa)
   Acquired dependency
   Changing the cat/human relationship to tackle
     dependency

Chapter 9: Why *Do* We Love Cats So Much?   278
With advice relating to:
   Why women love cats
   How men love cats

Chapter 10: The Relationship Survey   296
With results and analysis and the last word

Epilogue   327
Index   333

ACKNOWLEDGEMENTS

I would like to thank Mary Pachnos, my wonderful agent, and Francesca Liversidge, my editor at Transworld, for their continued support, advice and good humour. Tamzin Barber, a brilliant cat counsellor in the making, helped me so much with research, as did Sharon Cole, Robin Walker, Vicki Adams, Rozanna Malcolm and Clive Butler. My clients, as always, have been consistently wonderful and every one has contributed in some way to this book. I would also like to thank Peter, who continues to look after Lucy, Annie and Bink in Cornwall. I couldn't do the work I do without his input and support. Last but not least are Mangus and Charles, the other two sides of my own eternal triangle. Thank you, Mangus, for sitting by my computer constantly and keeping me sane. Thank you, Charles, for just being you.

INTRODUCTION

For some years now, as a cat behaviour counsellor, I
have trekked around the country visiting owners and
their cats. All the cats have one thing in common. They
are behaving in such a way as to cause a great deal of
angst and distress to their owners. They may be attacking next-door's Persian, biting the postman or pooing
on the duvet. The problem in question can be just about
anything, even 'my cat loves me too much' or 'my cat
doesn't love me enough'. My job is to unravel the
mystery, identify the underlying issue and, God willing
and with a *lot* of cooperation from the client, put it right.
It is such a bizarre way to earn a living (cat psychiatry

was never discussed by my school's career adviser) that it is almost inevitable that a certain amount of objective analysis must take place. After all, I do spend a great deal of time driving around the country with nothing better to do than muse on the vagaries of my profession. Are cats getting more stressed? Are there more problems now than in the past or are we just more amenable to discussing them? Have we crammed too many cats onto this tiny island of ours? Are they getting stressed by each other? Are we expecting too much of them? Is this our fault? Is seven hours really a reasonable amount of time to get from Kent to North London? (Sorry. The driving in this job can be unbearable.)

I recently produced some statistics to illustrate particular points being made in a seminar for pet behaviour counsellors. My quest was merely to break down the workload of three consecutive years to see what percentage of cases each common problem represented. As I crunched the numbers I started to disappear down a completely different avenue quite by accident. I was vaguely searching through my copious notes for answers to the question 'Are there any common causes here?' and I found something quite astonishing. Fifty per cent of the problem behaviour was exhibited as a direct result of something specific to the owner/cat relationship. The remaining 50 per cent was exacerbated by the same thing. Now this in itself may not seem like such a revelation but, believe me, it is. Think about it. If you have read *Cat Confidential* and *Cat Detective*, my two previous books, you will know by now that cat behaviour counselling is all about changing the environment and changing the way the owner interacts with the cat. I don't train the cats or force my will upon them. I work around them and, as if by magic, they reform. I have avoided for many years apportioning blame for the cats' misdemeanours; this is never productive and certainly not a positive way to get the owner on your side. Maybe that's why I've never actually looked at the facts this way round before. I've always known that owners can greatly influence the behaviour of their cats but I don't think I ever sat down and really thought about what a significant and widespread issue it really is. Not that I want to imply in any way that owners with messed-up cats are bad owners. Quite the contrary; they are usually good, loving, caring and intelligent people trying desperately to do the right thing. Cats unfortunately can lead us up the garden path sometimes with their enigmatic ways, and loving them as much as we do can be a problem.

I have a confession. Recently I succumbed to enormous pressure and agreed to adopt a cat to live with me in my flat in Kent. My other cats, as many of you will know, live in my lovely rural house in Cornwall and they are blissfully happy spending their days hunting, exploring and roaming freely. I always said I would never keep a cat indoors but when confronted with this poor little mite in need of the right home I couldn't refuse. I felt it would be a great way to experiment with all my environmental enrichment ideas to stimulate the bored house cat. Selfishly, I also felt that Mango (now called Mangus), the cat in question, would be great company whilst I bashed away at my laptop . . . which she is. At first, I endeavoured to maintain control of the relationship and frequently ignored her when I was busy, encouraging her to be self-reliant. That worked for a while but I admit to letting my guard down (she is incredibly sweet). She saw the chink in my armour, went in for the kill and now rules the place completely. She takes up more of my bed than I do, dictates my every movement, and protests loudly, as anyone who telephones my office will testify, if I dare to stop tickling her whilst discussing a patient.

This is what we are up against. This is how they shape our behaviour and we in turn shape theirs. I would like to think, with my experience, that I can see the warning signs and will never allow my relationship with Mangus to become dysfunctional. Sometimes when she looks at me I am not so sure . . .

Having experienced this epiphany about the true extent of the influence of our relationships with our cats, I want to pass the knowledge on. Understanding what is appropriate or inappropriate will potentially enhance your well-being and de-stress your cat.

Accepting that cats are a different species with minimal social requirements and no fundamental need for a relationship of any sort is difficult since it flies in the face of everything we have ever believed about our unique bond with them. Whatever we specifically demand of them socially and emotionally, there must be something in the owner/cat bond that gives them pleasure too. I have absolutely no intention of destroying good, fun, happy kinships between cat and human. I am, however, suggesting that many of us, particularly if our cats are exhibiting problem behaviour, should review the relationship honestly and possibly tweak it a little before condemning the cat.

I don't want this book to be full of warnings and foreboding about loving your cat too much. Half the fun of having cats is the fact that, if you are very lucky, they can be extraordinarily tolerant of stroking, squeezing and kissing. I would prefer to think of *Cat Counsellor* as a journey of discovery about what your cats want from you and from each other, and what you, fundamentally, want from them.

In order to truly understand the origins of the feline/human union I felt it was important to see how the relationship has grown over the centuries. The first chapter is therefore devoted to looking at a potted history of the domestic cat. I'm sure you've all heard much of it before: the cat as a deity in ancient Egypt in stark contrast with its vilification and persecution in the

Middle Ages. Rather than dwell on the historical chronology, I want to explore the attitude of those people who worshipped or feared the cat to see if it sheds any light on our current obsession. I've also indulged myself by including a number of old cat superstitions and proverbs just to illustrate the significance of this tiny but enigmatic creature to many nations throughout the world.

In the subsequent two chapters I will focus on the cat's relationship with its own species. So many of us now keep more than one cat; this section of the book will show us how best to handle the stresses and strains of cohabitation for the fundamentally antisocial feline (they really aren't small dogs). And, although some of the problems you may experience are purely 'a cat thing', we are a nation of animal lovers and many of us embrace all species. Chapter 4 gives general advice about helping your cat to live harmoniously with all things furred and feathered. The rest of the book is devoted to exploring the complications of the human/cat relationship and how we should behave to get the best out of our cats. Most intriguing of all (I think) are Chapters 9 and 10, where I reveal the results of a national survey establishing why women find cats so incredibly alluring but also suggest a slightly controversial personal theory that differs somewhat from the more traditional ideas. Definitely a voyage of discovery for me!

I haven't written *Cat Counsellor* as an instructional manual. It does contain advice on various subjects but there is no point going over ground that has been covered already by *Cat Confidential* and *Cat Detective*. Many of the stories in the chapters illustrate important points without actually offering solutions. Such is the nature of the beast that some problems are unfixable, however much of a pickle human beings get themselves into by trying. I hope that *Cat Counsellor* will give you a personal insight into what goes on in these special relationships. Whether you are a model with a moggy, a secretary with a Siamese or an artist with an Abyssinian I hope it helps you in some way to understand your cat better.

CHAPTER 1

A Love-Hate Relationship

Every day I experience examples of the extraordinary relationship that mankind has developed with the domestic cat. I marvel at the depth of my feelings for my own cats, Lucy, Annie, Bink and Mangus, and witness acts of incredible love and devotion during my typical working day as a cat behaviour counsellor. I have often suggested this to be a modern-day phenomenon, but in fact the human/cat bond has been around for thousands of years. We may currently express it differently in our insular western society but the allure of the feline is common to many races and has been for a very long time.

The origins of the relationship are probably best viewed by going back to ancient Egypt, circa 4000 BC, when cats were employed to keep mice and rats away from grain stores. For a long time this was considered to be the earliest reference to domestication, but a grave found in Cyprus in 1983, dating from 7500 BC, contained the skeletons of a human and a type of immature cat. Cats are not native to Cyprus so this discovery does rather suggest that cats were tamed or maybe even domesticated as early as that. Statues from Anatolia (the Asian part of Turkey) created around 6000 BC depict women playing with domesticated cats, so I have every suspicion that further evidence of a pre-Eygptian inter-species relationship is waiting to be uncovered. I doubt very much that cats were 'backward in coming forward' once they saw the obvious advantages of getting to know humans.

It is easy to see from history how the symbiotic nature of the human/cat relationship arose. Traditional nomadic lifestyles ceased so storage of crops was essential. The grain attracted quite a bit of interest from mice, rats and (inevitably) African wildcats. The cats were encouraged to stay around by the Egyptians, who fed them scraps by way of inducement. The presence of an abundance of food, both scavenged and caught, and the absence of predators or human deterrence meant that feline colonies soon formed.

All grain was stored in royal granaries, and as these large concentrations of goodies attracted huge quantities of mice it was essential that the Pharaoh had access to as many cats as possible to protect the precious commodity. It would have been extremely difficult to confiscate everyone's personal cats so in an obvious stroke of genius the Pharaoh made all cats demigods. A mere human couldn't own a demigod (only a god could do that) but they could look after them. Egyptians brought their fostered cats to work at the granary overnight and picked them up in the morning. For this service they received a tax credit and were able to claim their cats as dependants even though all cats were technically the property of the Pharaoh. It sounds great in theory, but can you imagine taking your cat to work at the local granary and then picking him up again in the morning? For one thing, he would have left of his own accord before the whistle blew because he'd had enough; for another, as soon as he realized he was supposed to work with a bunch of other cats you wouldn't see him for dust; alternatively, you'd get him there once but never see him again as he'd immediately move in with someone more sympathetic. I cannot imagine how the system worked but it is well documented; were African wildcats so compliant? One thing is certain: the Egyptians would not have risked incurring the wrath of their Pharaoh so they were probably uniquely persistent.

The cats were always put first in the Egyptian household. After all, people were only human; cats were demigods. (Is it just me or is this equally true today?) When a cat died the family who housed it went into ritualistic mourning, shaving off their eyebrows and pounding their chests to show their grief at the loss. The cat's body was wrapped and brought to a priest to make sure the death was natural (killing or injuring a cat was a capital crime). It was then embalmed. Not surprisingly, people came to believe that cats had a direct influence on their health, and their fortunes.

Cats and religion

The ancient Egyptians regarded cats as embodiments of the fertility goddess Bast, also known as Bastet. Bastet was originally lion-headed, but she became depicted as a cat or a cat-headed woman as the appeal of the domestic cat grew. The ancient Egyptian symbol Ru (referring to, amongst other things, the symbolic transition from the spiritual plane to the material one) appeared in many magical texts at a time when cat and woman were worshipped as one and is shaped like the half-dilated pupil of a cat's eye. Egyptian art shows myriad images of cats in domestic situations, often sitting under the wife's chair to symbolize an enhancement of her fertility by association with Bastet. Cats were clearly doing what comes naturally, catching rodents and birds; humans were depicted as encouraging the behaviour or, at least, somehow facilitating it. Already the mighty cat had learnt the art of training humans.

It was not just the Egyptians who worshipped cats. The Roman goddess Diana, in her role as moon goddess, was linked with the cat and also with the feline-friendly number nine. Nine is a mystical number and can frequently be seen in various mythologies. It followed that Diana, long associated with the cat, should endow the animal with its proverbial nine lives. Freya, the Viking goddess of fertility, love and war, was strongly associated with cats also. Her chariot was driven by two large cats, Bygul and Trygul; and kittens were often given in her name to brides to ensure good fortune in love and romance.

The European faiths transferred many of the attributes of Bastet to their own deities, so the early Christian Church actively absorbed cult festivals. The Virgin Mary became the symbol of the virgin-mother goddess. The connection between the female and the cat even features in early Christian imagery, where a cat is seen giving birth in the manger where Mary cradled the baby Jesus. In a Leonardo da Vinci sketch of the Holy Family, Jesus is shown cradling a cat. The Copts, the original Christians in Egypt, believed that when the Holy Family fled to Egypt to escape Herod's infanticide they stayed for a while in Bubastis, where Bastet's temple was the centre of cat worship, at a time when the latter was at its height. In the Jewish Gospel of the Holy Twelve there is a tale of Jesus remonstrating with a crowd of ne'er-do-wells who were tormenting a cat; I'd like to think that He had a particular affection for felines!

The cat is highly respected in Islam because of tales that the prophet Muhammad was a cat lover. One story tells of a cat that saved Muhammad from being bitten by a deadly snake. In another tale, when Muhammad was called to prayer, his cat Muezza was asleep on the sleeve of his robe. Rather than disturb his cat, the prophet cut off the sleeve. He used water from which his cat had drunk to wash himself and his wife ate from the dish from which Muezza had eaten, such was their devotion.

In Burma and Siam people believed that the souls of the departed lived in the bodies of cats before moving on to the next life. In Japan religious ceremonies were held for the souls of departed cats. According to Chinese myth cats were supernatural creatures who could detect ghosts and evil spirits; the cat god, Li Shou, is said to ward off evil spirits of the night. Agricultural deities in China were also often depicted in the form of cats. It is hard to find a culture or religion without references to cats as symbols of fertility, wisdom, protection or good fortune.

All the great cat goddesses such as Bastet and Diana, with their link to the moon, combine both feminine and feline attributes. Since time immemorial, women have been thought to possess the ability to be mediums, soothsayers and clairvoyants. Intuition too is deemed to be a female attribute. Cats have an enigmatic quality that makes them appear wise and 'knowing'. They are often described as 'old souls' – I've done so myself – and the attraction of women to cats could be seen to represent a link to an ancient part of the human soul. This may seem fanciful but thousands of years of cat history, myths and legends amount to a powerful influence on modern-day thinking. Any animal that has been the subject of a massive swing in human reaction from deification to persecution to deification again (we do worship them, let's face it) in the space of a few thousand years must be fairly special. Even today, when the domestic cat is experiencing unprecedented popularity as a pet in the western world, people seem to be divided between cat lovers and cat haters. Such is the influence of Sooty, Ginger and Tigger that there appear to be very few fence-sitters.

Cats spread throughout the world

Cats were routinely kept on ships for rodent control and viewed as important members of the crew (even

Nelson had a cat called Tiddles who saw quite a bit of nautical action before dying in battle). There are numerous stories of heroic cats including that of Able Seaman Simon, a black and white moggy who was badly injured on the Royal Navy frigate HMS *Amethyst* in 1949. He was treated along with the injured sailors and, as he recovered, he patrolled the sick ward and gave comfort to the men. He was promoted to Able Seaman for his services to morale. Sadly he died in quarantine when he got back home but it was he who received the most media attention upon his return to Plymouth.

In the early days, it wasn't long before journeys across the Mediterranean enabled cats to populate other continents and, you might be forgiven for thinking, start their strategic planning for world domination. Wherever they arrived they were obviously received with good grace; they performed a useful role in vermin control but also became willing pets and companions. By the fourth century AD word of the cat's usefulness as a rodent deterrent had spread throughout the Roman Empire, whose occupation of much of Europe and parts of North Africa and the Middle East enabled more homes to play host to the domestic cat. In the 1700s cats were imported into the New World from Europe when colonies of settlers were overcome by plagues of rats, and they charmed yet another continent into permanent cohabitation. Rodent eradication was undoubtedly the initial key to their success but there are clues every-where to show that their predatory skills were only half the story.

Cats in art

Art is a useful indicator in the exploration of social history, and early paintings and pottery from Greece, Rome, China and Japan, for example, depict children playing with pet cats in their homes. A mosaic panel dating from Roman times in the Naples museum shows a domestic tabby cat with its paw on a bird ready to devour it. Small cats kept as household pets appear on works of Greek art of the fifth and fourth centuries BC. Silver coins show naked youths playing with, or accom-panied by, tiny felines. Several versions show the cat leaping for a bird held in the boy's hand or pouncing in pursuit of a ball. House cats are portrayed playing with balls of wool on vases in the British Museum. The Chinese and Japanese depicted the cat in delicate watercolours; clearly indicating that the cat was im-portant in the oriental way of life also. The air of equanimity which surrounded the cat and its aura of inner wisdom were qualities with which Buddhists could empathize. Many compositions in ancient art include a toy, so I am sure my obsession with a fishing-rod contraption with a feather on the end is hardly new.

It is interesting to see that the cat's early role in human society consisted of what comes naturally: hunting prey. There was no manipulation through selective breeding to change the status quo. All that man succeeded in doing was enabling the cat to see the obvious advantages of human dwellings and the entertainment value of the inhabitants. We have been at their beck and call ever since; clever animals!

The persecution of the cat

Unfortunately there was a period in history when cats didn't get their own way. They had for centuries been revered for their apparently supernatural abilities, and their tendency to be rather independent further accentuated that air of mystery. However, as time went on they developed a more cultish status and came to be associated with various religious rituals. In medieval France cats were sacrificed to ensure a successful harvest, and were seen as the familiars of witches. The Catholic Church demonized cats in the thirteenth century when their association with the pagan goddess Freya led them to be regarded as the manifestation of the devil. Hundreds of thousands of cats were tortured, burned at the stake or roasted alive and cat numbers plummeted by over 90 per cent. The cat population was also affected by the plague, as they were erroneously blamed for carrying the disease and therefore culled on sight. Ironically, when so many humans were dying from the plague that there was no one to spare to cull the cats, they were able to kill the rats *truly* responsible for the spread of the disease.

However, even during this darkest period in their history, there were still people who loved and cherished cats. Many farmers would not give up their cats because of their obvious contribution to pest control; and there must have been countless old women (in the Middle Ages this category would have included anyone over the age of forty) who, ignored by a male-oriented society that had no further use for them, lonely and isolated while the younger family members were working, would turn to the company of a hungry feral cat, thus reinforcing the popular association between the 'witch' and her cats originally suggested by the historical and religious woman/feline link. Unfortunately, if any misfortune occurred, old women were often blamed, together with their cats, who were seen as willing accomplices. I just thank goodness I wasn't around at the time. The finger of suspicion would undoubtedly have pointed at me!

Cats continued to be ritualistically slaughtered or casually tortured well into the nineteenth century in various parts of Europe. Unlike dogs, cats were seen as elusive, independent and highly resistant to human influence and domination. In a male-oriented society it would not have been appropriate to consort with an animal with such a 'feminine' quality; it would surely render any man susceptible to the charge of weakness and – by extension – impotence. In the circumstances I am amazed that the cat ever made a comeback.

It is extremely hard to understand the mentality of humans at a time when an animal's life was considered worthless. We are blessed with a society now that largely abhors cruelty to any living creature and many people will campaign tirelessly for their welfare. However, I think it's important to remember that in those days mere survival was still the key motivation. There can have been little room left for compassion for animals if those animals did not represent livelihoods and food. In twenty-first-century Britain we take subsistence for granted and pursue other things instead: happiness maybe, or entertainment, or material possessions. It is far easier for us to spare a thought for animals; our very survival is no longer uppermost in our minds.

The revival of the cat

Such is the nature and influence of the cat, however, that make a comeback it did. It was reluctantly agreed that cats had helped to reduce the spread of the plague and they began to creep back into favour, but this process was not fully established until well into the nineteenth century, when the Christian churches finally stopped persecuting 'witches' and their familiars. Attitudes towards animals in general became more caring and in 1824 the Society for the Prevention of Cruelty to Animals was founded, later given the royal seal of approval by Queen Victoria in 1840. The expansion of towns and cities in Britain meant that feral cats far outnumbered the house variety in Victorian times. The mood of the nation was changing, however, as I have said, and in 1871 the first cat show took place; the organizer's aim was to encourage public perception of the cat as a household pet. By 1887 the first national cat club of Great Britain was established and the cat has gone from strength to strength ever since. In 1927 the Cats' Protection League was founded, solely to promote the welfare of cats in the UK.

Initially the intention of Harrison Weir, the organizer of the first cat show, was also to promote the care and welfare of the cat. He had seen the neglect and abuse that they had been subjected to and, as a genuine cat lover, he wanted to publicize their true nature and educate people away from their ill-treatment. Sadly he gave up judging at cat shows twenty-one years later because he was disillusioned with the results of his efforts. He felt that the breeders and members of the cat club were more interested in winning prizes than in promoting cat welfare. In *Cats And All About Them*, a book written by a breeder of Persians (Frances Simpson) in 1902, it is quite apparent that her good-natured advice is geared towards encouraging cat fanciers to breed for both pleasure and profit. (Seeing old photographs of pedigrees does focus the mind on the current obsession with extremes; the breeds of one hundred years ago are merely gentle variations on nature's own perfect specimen.) Throughout this book and others of its time it is clear that 'cat lovers' are people with a living, breathing hobby whose ultimate aim is to forge friendships with other 'cat lovers' and win prizes, just as Harrison Weir lamented. The enthusiasts of this era obviously had an interest in cats but they were, after all, only cats.

Leaping forward to publications of the 1960s (my first decade on this planet and therefore my own first personal experience of the human/cat relationship) we find that there is a distinct change in mood. There is a constant sense of anthropomorphism and interpretation of behaviour in a very human context. It is clear that the 'pet' part of the relationship is changing subtly into something more emotional. In one publication called *Cats' ABC* by Beverley Nichols, for example, there is an interesting subtext that shows a strong regard for 'feline people' and a dismissive snarl at all those guilty of a 'non-feline' persuasion. These 'us' and 'them' camps are still very much in evidence today.

In my opinion cinema and television have played a major role in changing our perception of the nature of the cat. They may just have been reflecting the mood and beliefs of the time but they are certainly significant in reinforcing our perceptions. Cartoon characters such as Felix the Cat, Tom and Jerry, Sylvester and Tweety Pie, Top Cat and Garfield show cats that exhibit human traits. Many even talk, whilst still retaining feline characteristics. Are these cartoons and similar representations guilty of creating an imaginary concept of the human/cat hybrid that is buried somewhere in our subconscious? Johnny Morris (a great hero of mine) has a lot to answer for when it comes to giving a voice to animals. The 1960s children's programme *Animal Magic* showed him as the zookeeper discussing various species and, undoubtedly to make the information more accessible, providing a 'voice-over' of the animals talking back and joining in the narrative. *Animal Magic* obviously got to me as, in 'conversations' with cats, I will often give my own verbal interpretation of what they are saying using a form of primitive ventriloquism, just as Johnny did. This has amused many of the vets and nurses I have worked with over the years, but it is easy to see how you might start to believe that cats are capable of complex reasoning. They really are *not* small people in zip-up furry coats. I think it is just as easy (and better for them) to love cats for being cats.

So our quick overview of the historical background

to our relationship with our cats has reached the present day. Books about cats now have titles such as *Yoga for Cats*, *Psycho Pussy* and *Do Cats Need Shrinks?* We board our pets in hotels when we go away on holiday and carry their photograph to show anyone who is interested. Cat ownership is a multi-million-pound business; we spend a fortune on medical bills, toys, food and videos to entertain them when we are out. It is even technically possible to make a diamond out of the cremated ashes of our dearly departed cat or clone them using their DNA as the ultimate memorial. However, just before we get down to the brass tacks of cat relationships and how to survive them, here is a plethora of trivia!

Famous ailurophiles (cat lovers)

As if we didn't know already, there have been many famous and noteworthy cat lovers including Sir Winston Churchill, Abraham Lincoln, Charles Dickens, Theodore Roosevelt, Ronald Reagan, Nostradamus, the Duke of Wellington, Queen Victoria, Sir Isaac Newton, Florence Nightingale, Beatrix Potter, Sir Walter Scott, Renoir, Monet, William Wordsworth, Horatio Nelson, Thomas Hardy, Victor Hugo . . . (an impressive list, I'm sure you will agree) and more recently Bill Clinton, Halle Berry, Billy Crystal, Warren Beatty, Yoko Ono, Rolf Harris,

Ann Widdecombe MP, the Osbournes, Ricky Gervais, Jonathan Ross . . .

Interestingly, famous ailurophobes (cat haters) include Napoleon, Mussolini, Hitler and Genghis Khan . . . need I say more?

To further enhance the story of the significance of the cat in just about every nation's culture there are numerous superstitions and proverbs bestowing incredible powers to our feline friends.

Superstitions from around the world

- A tabby cat is considered lucky, especially if it takes up residence in your home of its own accord. This is a sign that money is coming to you.
- The British believe that if a black cat crosses your path, good luck follows; Americans believe that it is bad luck.
- Touching a cat causes loss of memory.
- A cat sneezing is a good omen for everyone who hears it.
- A three-coloured cat will keep the house safe from fire.
- If you dream of a tortoiseshell you will be lucky in love.

- If you dream of two cats fighting it foretells illness or a quarrel.
- If you kick a cat, you will develop rheumatism in that leg.
- Letting a cat look into a mirror will cause you trouble.
- On every black cat there is a single white hair which will bring wealth or love to the person who removes it without the cat's scratching them (don't try this at home).

Proverbs from around the world
- In a cat's eyes all things belong to cats – England
- Beware of people who dislike cats – Ireland
- All cats are bad in May – France
- After dark all cats are leopards – New Mexico
- I gave an order to a cat and the cat gave it to its tail – China
- You will always be lucky if you know how to make friends with strange cats – Colonial America
- Happy is the home with at least one cat – Italy
- The cat's a saint when there are no mice about – Japan
- If you play with a cat you must not mind her scratch – Yiddish origin

I would like to think that I have put a good case forward for the cat although I feel I am probably preaching to the converted. They are now populating our homes by the millions and, almost without exception, are an important member of the family. The fact that 'the family' is no longer an exclusive club for humans can have quite far-reaching implications. In order to be a social unit in the proper sense we have to understand the nature of cat relationships to make it work to the benefit of everyone. That's only fair.

CHAPTER 2

Can Cats Share?

I spend a lot of time telling people that multi-cat house-holds don't work, but I think it's important to recognize that there is another perspective. I work with cats that don't get on; without exception the problems I see in multi-cat households are related to overcrowding in the house or the territory. For some cats two is a crowd so I can't even blame owners for unreasonable cat acquisition (here speaks a woman who has lived with seven); this really is a cat thing. However, for many cats, living with a feline companion is reassuring and entertaining and the exchanges between them look, to all intents and purposes, like genuine affection. For example, my friend's cats Whiskey, George and Lady have been together for many years. Only the other day I visited to find Whiskey and George curled up together in an impossibly small cat basket with their paws entwined round each other's bodies. Every now and then George washed Whiskey and Whiskey washed George and then both settled down with contented sighs to sleep in each other's embrace. They share a litter tray, food bowls, laps and beds and demonstrate the perfect example of domestic bliss. It's very unlike the behaviour of the cats I spend my working life with but probably a common scenario in many lucky households throughout the land. It was only when all three cats collectively jumped when the cat flap rattled that I realized their sociable natures hid the innate suspicion of others that dwells within all domestic felines to some degree.

Whatever relationships are forged within the home (or even with Tigger next door) it is no coincidence that so many cats are behaving badly and developing stress-related illnesses. There are a lot of cats in some areas and this spells trouble for the average moggy stuck in the middle of so many overlapping territories. Many of the cats I visit live in places chosen specifically for them. Owners seek out culs-de-sac, unmade roads and quiet streets in order that their cherished pets do not fall victim to speeding cars. However, all the neighbours in this cat-friendly haven had exactly the same idea. Therefore, what you end up with is a bunch of cats (without a fractured pelvis between them) putting each other through hell fighting for rights of passage in a vastly overcrowded territory. How ironic that our best intentions can have such a disastrous effect.

The next few case histories illustrate some of the potential pitfalls of a multi-cat household. The first two stories in this chapter discuss the most potentially difficult social dilemma – introducing number two cat to number one. Single cats may look lonely and bereft of feline company but the truth is often quite different. Any socializing that the cat might crave can be satisfied by a quick foray into the garden next door for some eyeballing with the ginger tom. If you are really fortunate the interaction may involve a quick game, a little mutual grooming and various other pleasant activities. Do not, however, be fooled into believing that this obvious kinship would be quite so evident if the ginger tom came through your cat flap; certain things are sacrosanct. The two cases I illustrate here did not stem from any conscious effort by either owner to provide company; the situation was thrust upon them as something of a fait accompli. Nevertheless, if you decide that your cat is genuinely lonely when you are out at work and you cannot resist adding to your feline family then there is advice below that may limit the risk of a complete disaster.

Paddy and Butch – the cats that put an end to the ironing

There is nothing worse than having a cat fight in the tranquil surroundings of your own home. My great friend and colleague Robin Walker refers to this as 'the war on the living-room floor' and he couldn't be more accurate in his description. Whenever this happens there is an enormous temptation to intervene. We want to punish, we want to console and generally get involved in something that is, fundamentally, a cat thing. How many times have you sat stroking one of your cats whilst contorting yourself in an attempt to give attention to the other one at the same time to avoid jealousy? How many times have you plunged into the middle of your two cats to remove the aggressor? Trust me, avoid pulled muscles and ripped flesh in the future. It doesn't work like that. Paddy's and Butch's owners found this out the hard way.

Sally and Megan were sisters. They had both divorced within a couple of years of each other and decided that living alone in two properties just didn't make any economic sense. They had always been great friends so decided to pool their resources and buy a house together. Sally had an eight-year-old tabby moggy called Butch and Megan had an ex-stray of indeterminate age called Paddy. They each knew and loved the other's cat so it didn't really occur to them that

Paddy and Butch wouldn't feel the same. Of course they would get on. The day of the move came and Sally and Butch arrived first, closely followed by Megan's furniture and then her cat. The sisters decided, once settled, that the best idea would be to let the cats out in the living room and allow them to explore and get to know each other. Both cat baskets were opened at the agreed time at opposite ends of the room and Sally and Megan sat back to witness the introduction. Paddy and Butch stared at each other with low rumbling growls and the occasional hiss for good measure from the safety of their cat carriers. Just as Megan was about to say 'Oh well, it could be worse', Butch launched himself like a rocket at Paddy's basket. At the same moment Paddy threw himself sideways and disappeared behind the sofa to avoid the imminent attack. Sally and Megan each screamed 'NO' and instinctively rushed to her own cat to administer whatever reassurance was necessary to prevent bloodshed. Unfortunately it's difficult to reason with a cat consumed with evil intent and both Sally and Megan became fearful for their own safety. The fight continued but eventually, with the aid of a chair and a large cardboard box, Butch was steered into the kitchen and the door shut behind him. Paddy was retrieved from the bottom of the television cabinet where he had sought refuge.

Sally and Megan were in a state of tearful shock. How could this have happened? How could they have totally failed to predict their cats' behaviour? I got the call some weeks later after they had spoken to their vet. The long days since their move had been difficult. Both Sally and Megan had spent all their time at home following the cats around in a low crouch with out-stretched arms to herd them about the house and prevent fights. Occasionally they were not vigilant enough and the two cats met nose to nose. Paddy would usually spit in Butch's face and that would start the fur flying. Megan and Sally would then rush from their respective locations and dive into the fray. Sally had already sustained some painful scratches to her head during one of these rugby tackles.

Both cats had previously lived alone and obviously thoroughly enjoyed it. Butch had always been territorial in his garden and surrounding area but a soft teddy bear at home. He wasn't quite so cuddly when I saw him as he clearly knew Paddy was nearby and ripe for a good squashing. His brow was furrowed, he was rather tense and he didn't like being confined or the atmosphere in the house. Paddy had also enjoyed life as a singleton, but only for the past couple of years. Prior to that it was anyone's guess what he had endured. He might have been wrong-footed when Butch launched his pre-emptive strike but I was sure that, given a little more warning next time, he would be equally keen to establish his own set of rights.

I listened to the sisters explaining how they were

very proactive in their cats' disputes. Every move they made was governed by the behaviour of their cats. For example, Paddy felt safer in a high place so every time Megan got the ironing board out he would jump on top before she even switched the iron on. Needless to say both sisters' clothes were looking a little creased; nothing was getting ironed. They also spoke in urgent whispers and moved around the house in quiet slow motion; the air just reeked of tension. I soon found myself whispering too, it was so contagious. This had to stop!

I explained to Sally and Megan that pussyfooting and whispering weren't conducive to a relaxed environment. All their actions, despite their intentions, were fuelling the fires of hatred between Butch and Paddy. The cats were sensing their owners' anxiety and feeling justified in their perception of threat and danger. After all, if Sally and Megan were that scared then the cats had every right to be on red alert.

We devised a battle plan that would take the heat out of the situation. I didn't want to make the proposed therapy programme too structured or formal; I rather hoped that changing the way Sally and Megan behaved would have a big enough impact. I had a strong sense that the fighting was motivated to a large extent by the atmosphere of tension in the home. I asked Sally and Megan to create some new areas indoors purely for the cats: shelving to allow them to view each other from high vantage points and secret private areas for escape and time out. This would enable Paddy to use structures other than the ironing board to get away from Butch and both cats would benefit from rest in secluded places where they felt they were out of danger. The most important part of the programme involved changing Sally and Megan's behaviour. I asked them to stop worrying and start relaxing. I tried to convince them that the fighting would cease if they chilled out. No more refereeing or furtive whispering; bring on the yoga and whale song.

A series of emails ensued that detailed the progress made over the next few weeks. My hunch was right and almost immediately Sally and Megan saw the results of their newfound calm. After the first five days of little or no response to their cats' altercations Sally noticed that Butch and Paddy touched noses without serious repercussions. This was indeed a triumph and it encouraged them to continue with their policy of ignoring the cats whilst appearing incredibly relaxed. It took their pussy pugilists a while to discover the network of shelving throughout the house but the secret hideaways under the bed and in the cupboard were found immediately and used regularly. By the end of the eight-week period Sally and Megan had become almost cocky, wondering what all the fuss had been about. Butch and Paddy were not exactly bosom buddies (I never promised that) but they seemed to have agreed to disagree. They would still scrap, growl and hiss at each other from time to time but the most this elicited from Sally or Megan would be the rather gentle reprimand of 'Language, Butch/Paddy!'

It was great to be able to turn the corner for Butch and Paddy by changing the owners' behaviour but it isn't always that straightforward. Most human intervention will make things worse but there are often measures that can be taken environmentally that will also reap rewards.

Chloe and Lay-by Laddie – the marriage made in hell

Throughout my working life I get to meet the most extraordinary people but some really stick in my mind. It could be because they are particularly charming or conscientious with their behaviour programme or just plain barking. However, Bill and Irene will always have a place in my heart as probably the most stubborn, determined and kind-natured couple you could ever wish to meet. They also have the dubious honour of being part of the longest behaviour therapy programme I have ever undertaken. Let me explain why.

Bill was a long-distance lorry driver and he spent many days away from home. During one of his stints 'up north' he found himself on a dual carriageway in need of a rest. As he scanned the road for suitable parking he passed a small lay-by. He had already dismissed it as too small for his artic but something about the rough piece of ground made him look twice. There, sitting on the edge of the busy main road, was a scruffy black cat, his fur rippling and his little body leaning back with the force of each juggernaut as it thundered past. Bill was confused; he'd seen many cats sitting on verges but they were always focusing on some poor rodent in a hedge. Surely this one wasn't planning to cross the road? Bill was a great cat lover; he even had a picture of his beloved tortoiseshell, Chloe, in his cab (and one of his wife, Irene, of course). He couldn't possibly drive on without checking that the little black cat was safe. He soon found a large parking area and left his truck to return to the lay-by. He fully expected the black cat to be gone or flattened but, to his great relief, the little fellow was still sitting by the side of the road being blown about by the traffic. As Bill approached he started to talk softly to the cat and crouch down; he didn't want to scare him into the path of a speeding car. The cat remained still and watched Bill as he crept towards him. Suddenly Bill realized that the little black cat wasn't right at all. He was sitting upright, but awkwardly, and as he moved towards Bill's outstretched hand to sniff his fingers he dragged himself forward by his front legs without getting up. Bill knew immediately that the cat was injured and probably paralysed. He removed his jacket and very carefully placed the little black cat in this makeshift stretcher and carried him back to the lorry. A few phone calls later Bill was making a detour to the local veterinary surgery where they awaited his arrival. As Bill drove he was moved to see the little black cat lying next to him, purring and gazing into his eyes. He promised him that everything would be done to fix him and make him more comfortable.

Six weeks and £2000 later little 'Lay-by Laddie' was recovering well. He had suffered a fractured pelvis and broken leg; the vet was amazed at his resilience since it was clear the injuries had been sustained some days before his meeting with Bill. During his extensive hospital treatment Bill had returned home to Irene and Chloe but he monitored Lay-by Laddie's progress on a daily basis and always visited him when he was driving in that part of the country. He also paid the extensive bills without a second thought as no owner had been found, so it was evident where Laddie would be going once he was back on his feet.

Chloe, a delicate tortoiseshell and white cat, had always been rather shy and retiring. Irene and Bill loved her dearly but the relationship felt a little one-sided. They spoke to her, they stroked her, they gave her all the love she could possibly want but she remained steadfastly under the bed or in the wardrobe 90 per cent of the time. How wonderful it would be for her to have a companion, they mused, who might just bring her out of herself. Secretly they both admitted that bringing Lay-by Laddie home was just as much about their needs as about Chloe's. With a little tender loving care, castration and a lot of good food he had become a handsome and affectionate cat, charming all the nurses at the vet's surgery and winning Bill over completely. He was definitely going to be the sort of cat who would take any amount of hugging and squeezing. So, with a little bag of goodies from the staff, he left the hospital to start the journey to his new home.

Bill and Irene knew that it was important to make a gentle introduction between the two cats. They were not overly concerned as they felt sure Chloe would welcome Lay-by Laddie with open paws once she saw what a little charmer he was. When he got home he was placed in the dining room with his own bed, litter tray, food and water and a selection of toys. This would be his den for a couple of days until it was time to 'meet and greet' his new companion.

That weekend they decided to let Lay-by Laddie out of the dining room to explore the rest of the house. Chloe had already shown some interest in him by sniffing under the door but she always walked away looking seriously unfazed. It was bound to be fine. As he took his first steps out into the hallway, Chloe watched casually from the worktop in the kitchen. Lay-by Laddie sauntered past her and drank a little water from her bowl before sitting down under the kitchen table and washing his paw. Domestic bliss; all was apparently well. For the next three days the two cats cohabited without any friction, and then came Tuesday morning. Chloe was sitting once again on the work surface in the kitchen as Irene opened a tin of cat food for their breakfast. Lay-by Laddie heard the telltale sound of impending grub and rushed into the kitchen with great excitement. Chloe was spooked and jumped backwards off the worktop; Lay-by Laddie then decided (rather ill-advisedly) to bash her round the head for her trouble. Chloe screamed and retreated upstairs followed by Lay-by Laddie followed by Irene. A huge storm of flying fur later Lay-by Laddie was once more confined to the dining room and Chloe was being comforted by a rather stressed owner. It was soon apparent that things had gone disastrously wrong. Lay-by Laddie and Chloe could not be left alone together. He wasn't fighting with her or bullying her every time; sometimes he wasn't doing anything more than looking at her. She would see him, get the screaming ab-dabs and rush under the bed for the rest of the day. He could almost be seen sniggering as he wound round his owners' legs: 'What'd I say? What'd I do?' This was not a marriage made in heaven.

Bill and Irene realized that a stalemate had been reached and they called me for help. I listened to their story and, when I visited, I was also bowled over by

Lay-by Laddie's cute nature and gentle ways. However, I wasn't fooled. Here was that typical case of entire (in Lay-by-Laddie's case recently entire) stray tomcat (very affectionate) being adopted and moving in with the resident cat. All is well for a while as he susses the opposition and then, WHAM! He sees that the other cat is a wimp and all he has to do is look in her general direction to bring about complete disintegration. She dissolves in a heap and the tomcat takes over her home whilst, every now and then, beating her up mercilessly just to prove a point. Sadly, Lay-by Laddie had adopted this strategy and poor Chloe was absolutely terrified. By the time I visited she hadn't come downstairs for ten days.

There are occasions when, with the best will in the world, some cats should not be kept together. I listened to Bill's story and I listened to Irene's concerns and I found it hard to say anything constructive or positive about the future for Lay-by Laddie and Chloe as an item. However, I can never just walk away from even the worst scenario with an 'Oops, sorry, can't help you' (unless of course it involves seven cats from Singapore; more of that later) so I discussed a plan of gradual re-introduction for Chloe and Lay-by Laddie. I asked Bill to construct a wooden frame covered with chicken wire that would fit inside a doorway, working on the principle that the cats should have sight and smell of each other before allowing direct contact. We also ensured the home had plenty of cat goodies around to avoid the need for competition. Lay-by Laddie would be given access to the house on a timeshare basis with Chloe safely ensconced behind the chicken-wire frame in her favourite bedroom hideaway. On alternate occasions Lay-by Laddie would be in the dining room (now definitely his domain) and Chloe would venture forth and stretch her legs. Every few weeks Irene and Bill attempted to mix them and each time it ended in tears.

After eight weeks I had to talk seriously to Bill and Irene about the future. It wasn't working and they had two seriously fed-up pussies on their hands. Would they consider finding a lovely new home for Lay-by Laddie? The answer was, not surprisingly, a resounding no. It had to work. So that is how I embarked on the longest behaviour therapy programme known to man. We persevered and maintained the exposure without direct contact whilst rotating the cats through various rooms. Lay-by Laddie was introduced to the garden and both cats enjoyed timeshare out there too. Every week over the next nine months Irene phoned to give me a progress report. I was astonished by her resilience. Bill was often away driving his truck and the full responsibility fell on her shoulders most of the time, but she didn't give up. She didn't even falter.

During the ninth month something happened. It appeared that Irene and Bill had at last broken Lay-by Laddie's resolve. He seemed to breathe a huge sigh of resignation and reluctantly agree to disagree. Chloe, on seeing that her adversary had become passive, returned to her normal everyday existence. She stayed under the bed and he stayed in the dining room or rubbed round Irene's legs. The chicken-wire frame was taken down and peace reigned at last. I missed those phone calls so I was delighted to hear from Irene and Bill some months later. Tragically the news wasn't good. Lay-by Laddie had gone out one day and not returned. He never seemed to venture much further than the garden but, for some reason, he didn't come in for his tea that night and was never seen again. They contacted rescue catteries, vet surgeries, the council, put up posters, but all to no avail. He had been gone ten days when they called me and is still missing to this day. It is tragic when things like this happen; there is nothing worse than losing a cat in this way without any understanding of their fate. It seemed particularly sad for Irene and Bill, given their determination to make things work for Chloe and Lay-by Laddie. I'd like to think that somebody somewhere is currently benefiting from his company.

Rhubarb and Hazel – the day the volcano erupted

Many cat households exist in an atmosphere of rumbling discontent that is difficult for owners to appreciate without knowing what to look for. It is easy to presume that all is well if there is no fighting. However, tension between cats can simmer like an active volcano and any sudden trauma or challenge can cause a massive eruption. Anxiety and stress reach fever pitch and previously tolerable relationships can be broken for ever.

This next case was a first for me: the only time I have left a consultation taking the patient with me. It also has a claim to fame as the case about which I wrote the fewest notes (five sentences to be exact). However, I remember it all as if it were yesterday. It started with yet another tearful and distressed telephone call early one morning. Elizabeth was distraught: one of her cats, Hazel, had visited the vet two days ago for dental treatment. When she had been brought home that evening she had been attacked viciously by her companion, Rhubarb. Elizabeth was deeply shocked by this and the next two days had been a nightmare. Hazel was shut in a tiny room and whenever Elizabeth had let her out *she* had attacked Rhubarb! They were now permanently separated and Elizabeth was a shadow of her former self; she desperately needed help to return things to normal. I had seen many cases of this kind. Two cats live together but feel little if any genuine affection for each other. One goes to the vet, comes back smelling different, and an attack is launched. All their previous pent-up emotions and social issues come to the fore and they can never return to normality again; a genuine irretrievable breakdown of a relationship that was dodgy in the first place. I had an idea that I would be merely consoling Elizabeth and recommending she rehomed one of her cats.

I reserved judgement but didn't expect to find such a dreadful situation. Elizabeth lived alone in a two-bedroom (rather cramped) maisonette. She kept Rhubarb and Hazel indoors because she was frightened of losing them. She went out to work all day and the cats were left to their own devices. She didn't allow them in her bedroom so they had the run of a small sitting room, kitchenette, hallway, stairs and boxroom upstairs. When she was at home they were with her all the time, crying and looking for attention. This was their life and Elizabeth couldn't see anything wrong with it whatsoever; they were loved and that was all that mattered. After all, they seemed happy enough. When I visited, Hazel was shut into the boxroom (I could hear her scratching at the door and crying). Rhubarb was behind the sofa, peering out from time to time looking rather forlorn. After some discussion with Elizabeth I decided to attempt a controlled meeting between the two cats. Elizabeth was borderline hysterical at this point but I reassured her that all would be well; I had to see the extent of their emotional response. (Can I just say that this was a lesson well learnt for me: namely, if the owner is against such exposure between two cats, don't do it!)

Elizabeth reluctantly collected Hazel from the box-room and carried her downstairs. I sat on the floor, in between the door and Rhubarb's hiding place, armed with a tapestry cushion. Elizabeth put Hazel down in the hallway and as she burst into the room I remember wishing I had armed myself with something a little more robust. She immediately wailed like a banshee and launched herself in the direction of Rhubarb, who had been peering round the edge of the sofa in sheer terror. He immediately ran round to emerge from the other side of the sofa as Hazel did a quick change of direction and I fell flat on my face having rugby tackled the speeding aggressor and missed. A major scuffle followed as the two cats connected and their screaming was only surpassed by that of Elizabeth. I had completely lost my dignity at this stage and my only mission was to stop the fighting and pray that neither cat was injured. I plunged into the fray armed only with panic and the tapestry cushion (don't try this at home) and managed to scruff Rhubarb and pull him away. I rushed into the hallway, slammed the door and released a very shaken Rhubarb with a stroke and profuse apology. He immediately disappeared into the depths of the boxroom, not to be seen again that evening.

I returned to the sitting room, having regained a degree of composure, and sat down with Elizabeth to discuss what to do next. One good thing that came from this unfortunate encounter was an understanding that there was no way forward for Elizabeth. She told me that she was suffering from depression, anxiety and stress, and was on constant medication. She could not bear to cope with this situation for another moment so one of the cats had to leave. I totally agreed with her but probably for other reasons. These cats were confined in a small and non-stimulating environment. Their proximity was causing some distress but fighting had previously not been an option because of the lack of availability of escape routes. Where could either cat go when retreating? There was nowhere to hide but the tension between them was growing. The sudden adrenalin rush that occurred when Hazel returned from the vet's surgery was the trigger to attack in a 'kill or be killed' response to imminent danger. It was probably as excited and intensely emotional as either cat had ever been and they had become destined to repeat the behaviour as a dramatic release of all their pent-up frustrations. I would have been delighted if she had agreed to rehome *both* the cats.

After several hours Elizabeth agreed that Hazel would have to go. She was the less nervous and clingy of the two cats and more likely to appeal to a new owner. Once Elizabeth had decided to give up her pet she wasn't prepared to wait. Her emotions were at fever pitch and she pleaded with me to take the cat there and then. I very reluctantly made a call to her vet and they agreed to take her in that night and attempt to find a new home for her. I left that house taking the patient with me. I thought the only lesson to be learnt from this experience was that keeping cats indoors in a cramped and confined environment without any appropriate stimulation was a recipe for disaster. Any perceived danger would potentially lead to this sort of aggression and any tolerable relationship would be destroyed. I was wrong; that wasn't the only lesson I learnt. I had a phone call from the vet the following day to say that they had heard from Elizabeth. She wanted Hazel back; she had decided to keep her but asked the vet to put Rhubarb to sleep because it wouldn't be fair to rehome him because he was so shy. I wrote to Elizabeth and left a message for her to contact me but she never returned my call. I didn't pursue the matter. It is too easy for pet behaviour counsellors to become emotionally involved in every case, which can only be to the detriment of their own health and that of future patients. I know the veterinary practice involved and I am sure they would have used all their persuasive skills to reassure Elizabeth that there was a future for Rhubarb. I would like to think of him sunning himself somewhere in a small garden without a care in the world. I hope Hazel and Elizabeth are happy too.

❖ ❖ ❖

I see several cases of redirected aggression of this kind

every year; I give advice on many others over the telephone. The problem always seems more intense and intractable in households where the cats are kept exclusively indoors like Hazel and Rhubarb. In my experience the most serious scenarios involve two cats only, shortly after the onset of social maturity (around the age of two). If, however, the cats have lived together without too much grief for six or seven years you have a sporting chance of getting things back to normal. This next case will give you some ideas if you are experiencing a similar dilemma.

Buttons and Beau – the battling Birman brothers and the broken bones

Katie left several messages on my answerphone in the office in the space of four hours; I realized things were obviously urgent when I returned her call that evening. The most dreadful thing had happened and it had left her reeling. It had also put her in hospital. She proceeded to explain. Buttons and Beau were eight-year-old brothers, gorgeous Birmans, and Katie was besotted with them. They had been adopted four years previously from a local sanctuary where they had found themselves after a marriage breakdown. They lived with Katie and her husband Phil as indoor cats. After careful consideration Katie felt their coats were too high-maintenance to justify sending them out into an environment full of mud, slugs and twigs.

They had lived in harmony (allegedly) until four days ago, when the dreadful thing happened. Buttons hadn't been too well recently and the vet had diagnosed laryngitis. Shortly afterwards there had been a fight on the landing between the brothers, centred round the water bowl that was traditionally located there. Beau hadn't been looking himself either recently and a visit to the vet the following day confirmed that he too had succumbed to the same infection. When Katie brought Beau home that morning she was not prepared for the nightmare that ensued. She put the cat carrier down in the hallway and opened it as Buttons came sniffing towards Beau to investigate all the challenging smells his brother had brought home with him. Katie expected a 'Phew, it's great to be home' sort of reaction from Beau but instead he launched himself out of the cat basket directly towards his brother. The resulting fight was as intense as anything you would see on a Tom and Jerry cartoon. The two cats became a ball of tumbling fur and flailing legs but the worst thing of all was the noise. Katie could not believe that domestic animals, particularly her own babies, could sound so fierce. She threw herself towards them, with little regard for her own safety, but unfortunately tripped on a doorstop and fell head first into the melee. Her head hit the hall table, her hand hit the wall and the cats swiftly moved their fight upstairs. As Katie lay dazed the screaming stopped: Buttons had sought refuge under a chest of drawers in an impossibly narrow gap. Two broken fingers and a black eye later Katie still couldn't put the boys together without a rerun of this explosive encounter. Phil was devastated (and somewhat bemused) that his wife had incurred such dreadful injuries and insisted that one of the cats (at least) would have to go. At that point Katie remarked that Phil was more likely to go than either of the two cats if she had her way, but I wasn't sure this was necessarily the best option in the circumstances. I reassured her that it might not have to come to that and, without guaranteeing success, agreed to visit her to establish whether we could restore normality.

I arrived, as a matter of urgency, later that same week and sat opposite a very sorry-looking Katie to discuss the situation. Her right eye and cheek were swollen and two of her fingers were strapped up on her right hand. That really was some rugby tackle. Beau sat with us, showing great interest in my 'magic bag', and Buttons was sulking somewhere private upstairs. In the eight days since the accident Katie had become confident enough not to resort to shut doors during the day to separate the two cats. She did, however, keep them apart at night and the daytime was full of vigilance and measures designed to prevent a repeat performance. There was, though, according to Katie, a great deal of posturing and swearing between the two. Beau was definitely the instigator of the aggression; Buttons hardly responded at all. Katie thought he looked rather bemused by the whole thing. He would occasionally chase Beau if he got fed up, apparently, but that was all.

I let Katie talk for a while (at last she had found someone who truly understood) but soon steered her towards a more thorough history of their lives prior to the events of the previous week. She described a typical adult sibling relationship. The two boys did their own thing, occasionally resting in the same room together but mainly coexisting rather than enjoying each other's company. Probably an accident waiting to happen, but I did not hear anything particularly alarming until she started to talk about the last six months. She said that Buttons had become quite distressed by a series of decorating projects, both outside and inside the house. He had suffered from a couple of bouts of cystitis and inappropriate urination on the front doormat as a result, followed soon afterwards by a period of fur loss on his belly, described by the vet as 'probably stress-related'. Just as this problem seemed to be resolving itself he went down with an extremely high temperature and the laryngitis.

I put it to Katie that there was a possible link between the upheaval at home and the subsequent falling out between the brothers. The relationship had probably never been that brilliant once the siblings reached maturity. It simmered just like the one between Rhubarb and Hazel. Indoor cats have very predictable lives but any changes to their environment (their entire world, really) can potentially be quite distressing. I think Buttons bore the brunt of this, so his stress levels increased, his immune system was compromised and his health suffered as a result. Stress works in layers, and the combination of changes, ill health and an annoying brother may have pushed him over the edge. He needed that water bowl on the landing and his brother muscling in to relieve his own sore throat was probably too much to bear. Beau then visits the vet, returns to see an approaching Buttons and decides a pre-emptive strike is probably advisable given the events of the previous day. The perfect recipe for a relationship breakdown.

As if on cue Buttons came downstairs and entered the room. Katie visibly stiffened and her voice became urgent and mildly frantic: 'What do I do, what do I do?' I asked her to focus on me and stop worrying, but as Beau hissed at Buttons, who continued to approach unperturbed, she said she couldn't cope and she had to intervene. She picked up Beau, who grumbled rather but continued to watch his brother. Buttons examined my bag, sniffed round generally, then went back into the hallway to use the litter tray. Beau remained under the table, breathing rapidly and nervously licking his lips. Buttons definitely had the upper paw here but the balance was so precarious I wasn't convinced it would stay that way.

I was keen to find out if either cat had injured the other during their fights. Katie replied that no physical harm appeared to have been done. In answer to several more of my questions, Katie was painting a picture of competition, passive aggression and guarding of strategic areas. The only difference pre- and post-apocalypse was that the aggression was more overt as their antagonism had reached a new level; it was finally all out in the open.

I was extremely pleased to see that the cats could at least be in the same room, but there was still a great deal of tension between them. More significantly, Katie was tense, and that had to stop. Owners understand-ably get very concerned when previously placid cats turn on each other. Unfortunately their anxiety adds to the feline tension, as I have said so many times before. It is easy to appreciate the significance of that in theory but another matter altogether for an owner to try to change and feel relaxed under these circumstances.

I gave Katie a programme to follow that increased the number of resources within the home to a level that should eliminate the need for Beau and Buttons to be so competitive. The often recommended 'one per cat, plus one, in different locations' is a good formula for all cat resources from litter trays to scratching posts and toys to water bowls. The house was rather short of private hiding places and high perches so we looked at various ways that Katie could enhance the ability of the the cats to get away from each other. Now came the important bit: how would Katie cope with changing herself? I bartered a little with her; after all, it's pointless asking someone to do something they honestly believe is beyond them, and we eventually agreed that she would try to relax, ignore the hissing and growling and (if really desperate to get involved) only employ distraction techniques such as moving across the room, talking to Phil or dragging a piece of string in front of the combatants. In no circumstances was she to scoop one up, reprimand the other or generally get involved in a complicated feline dispute. I also suggested, should the very worst happen, that she used my favourite technique of placing a cushion or pillow between the cats rather than a part of her body.

I awaited the first report with some trepidation but I really shouldn't have worried unduly. Katie was determined to make it work and, despite her husband's being pretty annoyed about the sudden abundance of litter trays, water bowls and scratching posts, she had approached her tasks with relish. She was *not* going to give up one of her boys no matter what it took to set things right again. Over the next few weeks she learnt to ignore the hissing by chanting a mantra in her head that went something like 'it's a cat thing, it's a cat thing'. I had tried to explain to her that a certain amount of aggressive posturing or noise was all part of everyday cat life and we really ought to let them say what needed to be said. It must have struck a chord because it was this thought that allowed her to relax sufficiently to see a significant improvement by the end of the two months. Beau and Buttons never really got back to normal (as far as I know) but Katie was happy enough and she realized she had been very fortunate to avoid the terrible decision to split them up.

❊　❊　❊

Whilst Hazel's and Beau's troubles started after a visit to the vet, it doesn't always happen that way. Redirected aggression can cause breakdowns too. Seeing a cat outside, fireworks, mail coming through the letterbox, a picture falling from the wall . . . there are so many sudden unexpected events that can make the adrenalin pump and cause your feline to release its pent-up emotions on the nearest available moving object. It is seldom something you can prevent, but following general guidelines about multi-cat living will limit the odds of your ever having to face it.

There are many potential problems associated with multi-cat living, the most common of which have been discussed in great detail in both *Cat Confidential* and *Cat Detective*. One such situation occurs when one member of the cat group dies. I have experienced this myself when three of my cats, Zulu, Puddy and Bln, tragically died within five months of each other. Cat groups usually have a deep respect for hierarchy and when one member is no longer there a shift in the balance of power almost always takes place. There is usually one of three possible responses from the remaining cats, irrespective of how their 'rank' changes: they grieve, they blossom or they appear oblivious. This is often a good indication of the true relationship when the deceased cat was alive. Add the owner's emotions to this equation and things can get very complicated.

Tilly – the 'grieving' cat

Every now and then we meet a cat who rocks our world. Pookah was such a cat for his owners, Diane and Nick. I visited Diane only a few weeks after their beloved pet had passed away. Pookah had been diagnosed with cancer two years previously and he had valiantly coped with chemotherapy and operations during that period. He clearly had a wonderful person-ality; he was affectionate, demonstrative and larger than life. As Diane described her relationship with him it was apparent that she was finding it difficult to talk without breaking down and weeping. I saw photos and listened to her stories and began to feel that I really would have liked to meet this cat, such was her distress at his passing. The reason for my visit was a small ginger female, Tilly, who was hiding behind a table in the corner of the room. Tilly had been Pookah's constant companion throughout his life. Diane described the relationship between the two cats as 'one of tolerance rather than affection'. Tilly used to play a very secondary role, always in the background and never really part of the family. Pookah slept on the master bed and Tilly slept on the landing. Pookah sat on his owner's lap and Tilly sat on a cushion under the dining room table. Diane admitted that she was not a particularly rewarding cat to have around compared with Pookah.

When Pookah died both Diane and Nick were devastated. They had devoted such time and emotional energy to him and they missed him dreadfully. However, their grief was interrupted by Tilly's un-expected reaction. Suddenly she howled at night and paced and searched; she became a thing possessed. Diane was clearly affronted by this since she felt that Tilly, having shown no great affection for Pookah during his life, should not overindulge herself in demonstrative mourning rituals. I was shocked at the depth of her feelings about this; she even said at one point that she resented Tilly and wished it had been she who had passed away. Tilly continued to pace and howl until suddenly she committed the most heinous of crimes: she tried to take the place of Pookah in her owners' affections. Diane was furious, Tilly was confused and Vicky was asked to visit to make sense of it all. I tried, very gently, to explain to Diane what changes were taking place in Tilly's world.

Cat relationships are complex and often elements of personality expressed to human companions differ greatly from those shown to other cats. It was clear from the history that Pookah was more assertive than Tilly. He controlled access to his owners, the best seats in the house and the master bed. Tilly withdrew to a safe distance as a successful ploy to prevent bloodshed or, even worse, psychological warfare. She accepted defeat and was relatively content to live her life in the shadow of the dominant Pookah. When he died she was left with a real dilemma. Suddenly she was on her own. Where was he? What sinister strategy was he employing to further intimidate her? The distressed pacing and searching may well have been her attempt to restore the status quo; after all, better the devil you know. After a while, though, the scent profile of the home changes and surviving cats realize that their tormentors are no longer there. Tilly became more vocal, affectionate and interactive because she now had access to her owners without incurring the wrath of her companion. She wasn't trying to take his place as such; she was merely enjoying her new-found freedom of expression. This phenomenon became apparent after I conducted research into the subject in the Elderly Cat Survey in

1995. Many people reported that cats blossomed after the death of a companion. Unfortunately it doesn't sit particularly comfortably with many owners, Diane and Nick included.

Diane was a caring and sensible lady and, when confronted with this new angle on the proceedings, she suddenly felt rather guilty. How could she have thought so ill of the little ginger cat? We talked about Pookah and grief and the loss of a beloved pet. We also discussed the possibility that Diane and Nick could develop a new relationship with Tilly without feeling guilty or imagining that it would in some way detract from the memory of dearest Pookah. I spoke to Diane the week after my visit and she reported a great improvement in her relationship with Tilly. The little ginger cat had relaxed enormously and now found that her approaches were received with love and kindness instead of hostility. I hope they are still enjoying each other's company.

Siobhan and her seven Singapore strays

I cannot resist including a story that illustrates so vividly the limitations of cat behaviour counselling! It may be an extreme example but it happened and it will probably make essential reading for those contemplating an exotic holiday in a place where feral cats are rife. I am not suggesting for one moment that we ignore their plight. We have all at some stage in our lives felt our heartstrings pulled by a skinny, scabby puss whilst on holiday. How many of us have returned to a certain spot time and again with food when we have seen a starving mite hanging around the back of the local hotels and restaurants? Occasionally the more determined cat lovers have gone just one step further and ended up paying high vet bills and even higher transport costs to take the little darling home. One such lady took this progression to another level.

Siobhan had lived for some years in Singapore with her husband. She was passionate about all things feline and she devoted her workless days to roaming the streets looking for waifs and strays. Or it certainly appeared so, as after five years she had acquired seven Singapore street cats of varying shapes and sizes, all of which were contained within the spacious surroundings of her air-conditioned apartment. They coexisted in relative harmony (or so she said when we met back in England some time later) but she actually described something quite different. It sounded to me as if the cats spent all day hiding in various dark areas until food was provided at night and the apartment was quiet. They didn't fight but I was suspicious that they had merely created a small feral colony in the confines of a beautiful airy apartment and dealt with the dissent in the group by shutting down. They urinated and defecated in several litter trays, if Siobhan was very lucky, or on the marble floor in various corners if she wasn't. I bet Siobhan's husband was thrilled.

The cats varied in their sociability with people but they all seemed to trust the lady who had 'saved' them from an uncertain fate. However, Siobhan had some reservations when it was decided that the couple would return to England. How would her babies cope with quarantine? Would they settle? Would they adjust to life outdoors or would they run away? By the time I met Siobhan she had been back in England for seven months and the cats were out of quarantine. Her husband had purchased a huge rambling Elizabethan pile in the middle of a wooded area in Sussex. It was full of exquisite period features and loads of nooks and crannies for seven Singapore street cats to get lost in. Surely they would be happy?

What I saw when I visited that house defied belief. Siobhan was so stressed and tense that she made me feel uptight within the first five minutes. She oscillated between tearful, hysterical and aggressive in a matter of seconds. I didn't know whether to pass her a tissue, sympathize or duck. The whole process was exhausting and not helped by the screams of various cats and a young Swedish girl who had been employed specifically to 'nanny' the warring felines and prevent bloodshed. The surreality was Monty Python-esque and I was completely perplexed about what I was supposed to do with this tragic situation. I was feeling a bit of a challenge coming on.

I have seen many imported cats over the years, all of which have been 'saved' from a life on the streets. There is only one problem with this rescue strategy. These are cats used to living on their wits; they may become friendly and gooey with their new human companions but their response to other cats is often another matter. You can take the cat out of Singapore but you can't take Singapore out of the cat, you could say in this particular case. Each of these cats was warring with the other six. Some were displaying active aggression and others were adopting various defence strategies to avoid being attacked. The ferocity of all of them was intense, as their world had become so terrifying they felt it was a case of kill or be killed. They were all surviving on red alert and I cannot even begin to contemplate how wretched they must have felt. Siobhan's histrionics were merely fuelling the fire, and the poor Swedish student must have felt that everyone in England was mad. They even employ cat behaviour counsellors!

There were at least three of the cats, particularly the eldest male, who needed to be rehoused. They found the concept of sharing impossible to grasp and made the situation extremely difficult for the whole group. 'Maybe if they were taken out of the equation it would be possible to work with the remaining four?' I tentatively suggested. Siobhan was adamant. They stayed together because she loved them and they loved her and no one would look after them as well as she did. Well, that just about put the icing on this particular fruit cake so I gave her a programme to follow and bade her farewell. What a nightmare.

I received an abusive phone call the following morning. At least, that's what I thought it was initially until I realized the tirade of profanities was coming from Siobhan. One of the recommendations I had given her was to stop interfering so heavily in the cats' altercations except when they actually injured each other. She followed my advice, apparently, and one of the less confident cats had been attacked and chased out of a small window by the assertive male. She hadn't been seen since despite the Swedish nanny's doing several laps of the surrounding woodland with a bag of cat biscuits, a basket and a pair of stout gloves. This was clearly all my fault. In a strange way my heart went out to Siobhan that morning. She had acted with great compassion, albeit misplaced, when she 'rescued' her seven Singapore cats. She truly believed that she could provide them with a wonderful alternative to the misery of life as a feral. Had she stuck to one cat, probably the eldest male, the relationship might well have blossomed and she would have been rewarded for her generous act a thousandfold. Unfortunately poor Siobhan thought her cats had been happy in her previous home and she would have been devastated to hear that their not fighting in the apartment was more a survival strategy than a sign of contentment. Rescuing no fewer than seven cats was seen by Siobhan as a symbol of her love for the species. When it all went horribly wrong back in England she was extremely distressed and she desperately needed to blame someone, anyone, for the disaster. I just happened to be in the firing line on that particular occasion.

The little cat was found some weeks later but there was no common ground between Siobhan and me. I gave her a programme to follow but it was eventually agreed that she would create two distinct units within her home, three cats to be housed on one side of the barrier and four on the other. It struck me as a ridiculous way to live when the alternative solution of splitting the group up would have been in the best interests of the cats. Unfortunately poor Siobhan couldn't see anything beyond keeping the cats together. We never spoke again but I hope the cats are OK and have reached some sort of compromise. If this story prevents even one group of cats from suffering a similar fate it has been well worth relating.

Gallons of urine and rubber sheets

I would like to end this chapter with a story about a case I never saw. It came to my attention during a book-signing event in a store in Devon whilst I was promoting my last book, *Cat Detective*. These evenings are always great fun: the store closes, the wine flows and cat lovers come from far and wide to enjoy a lively evening of feline facts and advice. We usually have a lengthy and often hilarious question-and-answer session during which we discuss everything from cat flaps to overgrooming and all subjects in between. The audience are almost always armed with reams of paper covered with questions and a good time is had by all. And there will always, always be a gem of a question. If you didn't know otherwise you could easily presume that these people are planted in the audience, such is the nature of their comments.

All was going well during the evening in Devon and there was a great deal of laughter and banter and general high spirits. I had just finished a short session on keeping cats indoors and I was encouraging the audience to move on to another topic. In the middle of the room a gentleman had been sitting with his wife. I always like to check everyone out and I was pretty sure this chap had something on his mind. He had that slightly smug look on his face as if to say 'know that; know that too' so I was quite delighted when he raised his hand; I wanted to hear this one. I knew it was going to be a corker when he started with 'I've had cats for fifty-five years'. I nodded at him with an air of expectancy I could barely contain. He continued, 'I currently have thirty-five cats but have owned as many as forty in the past and they have always all got on well together.' Now I could have launched in there by challenging his statement most vehemently but it would have led nowhere. Let's just say I begged to differ with his appraisal of his cats' apparent happiness but I managed to contain myself with a wide-eyed expression and a quick 'Wow!' The audience were still buzzing as members continued various spin-off conversations but the room soon fell silent as our conversation progressed. He looked at his wife and she gave an encouraging nod as he said, 'The problem we have is that some of the cats are peeing on our bed at night.' Without showing any hint of I-told-you-so, I said, 'I see; how many of them are doing this?' He replied, 'We're not sure but we think it's about six of them.' I showed no emotion and no sign of surprise but the audience gasped. I continued, 'How often is this happening?' to which he replied, 'Every night.' Completely hooked, I casually asked, 'How long has this been going on?' He thought for a while, conferred with his wife, and then said, 'About four years.' You could have cut the atmosphere with a knife as I said quietly, 'Mmm, that's a lot of urine.'

I then acknowledged the audience's reaction by explaining to them that, unfortunately, it was the easiest thing in the world to find oneself in such a dreadful situation. Problems start and advice is followed, suggestions are made, litter trays are added and duvets are laundered. Suddenly, four years down the line, you are swimming in urine and your morning routine of washing duvets and wiping down rubber sheets comes as naturally as brushing your teeth. When he added that most of the urination on the bed took place when he and his wife were in it many of those present could not contain their disgust as an audible 'ergh' went round the room. The man asked if I would offer some advice or even consult in his home, but not before adding several priceless caveats: namely 'my cats aren't stressed; there's nothing wrong with their bladders; I'm not rehoming any and I think twelve litter trays are quite enough, thank you.'

I said 'Call me' and moved on to another question. He hasn't done so as yet but I have a horrible feeling that one day he will.

The secrets of a harmonious multi-cat household

- Start with two cats from the outset if you feel you want a multi-cat household; this is always easier than introducing 'No. 2' to 'No. 1'.
- Choose compatible individuals to share your home such as littermates, preferably brother and sister. Two equal-age same-sex siblings may dispute

the hierarchy when they mature socially.

- Avoid extreme characters when choosing kittens, for example extremely nervous, confident or active. These may potentially be difficult cats to live with or find others difficult to live with.

- If you want to adopt an adult cat, choose an individual that shows a history of sociability with other cats. Avoid those that have been given up for adoption because of behavioural problems in a previous multi-cat environment.

- There is no particular benefit in keeping kittens from your own cat's litter. Once the initial rearing process is complete the mother will naturally be ready to say goodbye.

- Keep an appropriate number of cats for your environment. This is particularly relevant if your cats are kept exclusively indoors.

- If there are many cats in the neighbourhood this fact will impact on your household too. Stick to two; if you have more cats in these circumstances it could increase the sense of overcrowding in your own group.

- Even if your cats have access to outdoors it is still advisable to provide indoor litter facilities. Then if there is any bullying going on outside your cats will always have the choice to toilet in comparative safety indoors.

- Avoid too many highly intelligent and sensitive

pedigrees in the same household. Although most are the perfect pets, they can be extremely territorial or sensitive to inter-cat issues, particularly breeds such as Burmese, Bengal and Siamese.

- Remember your household will always have a 'one cat too many' threshold and you may push your luck if you keep increasing the numbers. If you have a harmonious foursome, for example, why not leave it that way!

- Social issues become important at the onset of maturity between eighteen months and four years of age. This is when you may experience problems between cats who have previously been friendly.

- Don't get too involved in your cats' disputes; it is impossible to ensure you are reinforcing the right message. Some things need to be said between them but it doesn't always look nice.

- If you lavish constant attention on your cats you will yourself become a valuable resource. This can be dangerous and make your cats aggressive towards each other when you are around.

- Food, water, beds, hiding places, high perches, toys, scratching posts and litter trays should be provided in sufficient number to prevent competition. 'One per cat plus one in different locations' is the magic formula!

- Provide plenty of high resting places to enable any individuals to observe activity from a safe area.

- Private places are also extremely important; every cat, no matter how sociable, needs 'time out' to enjoy moments of solitude.
- Provide dry food for 'grazing' throughout the day or divide it into several smaller meals to avoid any sense of competition if food is only available at certain times. (Cats with a history of feline lower urinary tract disease or chronic cystitis should be fed a wet diet so ad lib dry food would not be appropriate.)
- Water is an important resource and positioning bowls away from food will encourage cats to visit them more frequently.
- Ensure there are plenty of scratching posts to protect your furniture. Cats will scratch for both claw maintenance and territorial reasons and there will be an increased need to signal to others in a multi-cat environment. These scratching posts should be located near entrances, exits, beds and feeding stations to ensure an appropriate surface is available in areas of potential competition.
- Studies have shown that the likelihood of urine-spraying indoors increases in direct proportion to the number of cats in the household. You have been warned!

CHAPTER 3

Where Do You Go To, My Lovely?

If your cat has access to the great outdoors then you know there is a huge chunk of his activity about which you know very little. How many people can honestly say they know exactly what their cat is doing once he exits the cat flap in the morning? Wouldn't it be great if all our cats could be fitted with tiny cameras so that we could get a true understanding of their feline 'day at the office'?

There are some things we do know, through research on feral colonies and house-cat territories conducted by biologists such as Roger Tabor. This shows us that a cat's world is divided into three recognized areas:

- the 'core' area or den
- the territory
- the home range.

The core area

This is the area within which your cat feels most secure. This is where he sleeps deeply, plays, eats and enjoys all the benefits of cohabiting with humans. It is such a safe place to be that any prey he catches during his hunting forays will often be brought back there so he can enjoy it without being disturbed. As we represent such an element of security, the core area is almost automatically the home itself; however, if there is an established opening or cat flap into the property this may create a rather blurred picture of what represents the safe den. The core area may then be, for example, the first floor (it's always safer to go 'up' in your cat's mind) or it may be the room where the family congregates most frequently. Disputes in multi-cat households may also affect the perception of the core area for less confident individuals.

The territory

Whilst the core area forms the hub of the territory there

is a whole other world that is included for the cat with access outside. The territory is defined as that area the cat actively defends against invasion by others. The size of this area will vary greatly with each individual and depend on season, level of confidence, sex, density of population and many other factors. Your cat may take Sooty's face off if he dares to venture onto the patio but not flick a whisker if he sees him further down the garden. Cats don't respect their owners' boundaries as a representation of defendable property; they are not governed by fences, hedges and walls. Territories often include roads, waste land, other people's gardens and anything in between.

The home range

This includes the territory but describes the total area over which your cat will roam. I have seen many 'feline-friendly' streets where some poor cats are lucky to call the bottom of the garden their own. In Roger Tabor's 1976–78 study in East London he found that those females included had a home range of the garden plus any further space that their confidence and the density of population would allow. A typical home range in a densely populated area is 0.05 acres for a neutered female, although neutered males often roam further.

❀   ❀   ❀

Your cat will spend his day patrolling; scent marking using his face, body and paws and generally checking to see who's about. The type of encounter with other cats outside will vary depending on how territorial your cat is, how territorial the other cat is and where the eyeballing takes place. Many cats can be seen sitting within a respectful distance of each other in apparent harmony and yet the same two cats will be fighting tooth and claw the next day in another location. Your cat will also be spending time hunting (if so inclined), sunning himself, sleeping in secret dense bushes and hopefully staying out of trouble. Sadly some don't and they spend time breaking into other people's houses and terrorizing their cats, getting shut in garden sheds, fighting, killing birds or playing chicken with the traffic. It's not hard to understand why so many cat lovers want to keep their pets at home where they can see them.

I won't be dwelling on the theoretical stuff of the great outdoors in this chapter because I want to focus on the sorts of problems that arise as a result of giving your cat his freedom. I certainly don't want to put anyone off making the decision to let their cat outside. This is by far the most natural lifestyle and cats who can behave normally are more likely to be mentally healthy. However, there are a lot of other cats, people and cars out there, and some issues and quandaries are common to many owners.

Returning to a previous home

One subject I get many calls on throughout each year is the problem of cats returning to previous homes. This can be extremely distressing since they often have to cross busy roads to get there. There seem to be some common elements to most of the cases, such as:

- the cat had previously spent a great deal of time outside
- the cat was considered to be territorial on his 'patch'
- the cat lived with at least one other, often a sibling
- the house move was within a mile of the previous home.

This is a difficult situation as the cat in question is voting with his paws. It is entirely likely that his bond was with the environment and not the family and that the house move was confusing and highly undesirable. The cat might well have spent so much time outdoors as a result of a poor relationship with his or her sibling, and the prospect of being confined in a strange place with someone it dislikes is too much to bear. Navigation in these circumstances is astonishing but highly achievable for cats. Owners of such wanderers report that after several days they will receive a phone call from an ex-neighbour saying that the cat is hanging round the garden of the old house, crying pitifully. In my experience these cats rarely come 'home' to their new abode on their own; the owner collects them only to face exactly the same thing when the cat is next let outside. I am often asked if the cat should be confined indoors for prolonged periods to get acclimatized to the new house. This is a dangerous strategy since it may only fuel his desire to escape at the next possible opportunity.

Unfortunately there is no easy solution to this problem. A product called Feliway (synthetic feline pheromones) is available from your vet practice and a useful addition to the new property. It can be purchased in a plug-in form and the scent message that it emits may give your cat a better perception of the new house as home. Small frequent tasty meals can sometimes be helpful, together with plenty of opportunities indoors to get away from other cats. Persistence in retrieving the wanderer from your old house is the key, with the aid of a cooperative ex-neighbour, together with strict instructions to everyone not to feed him. If the relationship between your cats is really not good (and the new occupiers of the old property are amenable) it may be in his best interests to let him stay there.

The wanderer exposed

Some wandering cats are not necessarily returning to previous homes and favoured stamping grounds.

Consider the opportunistic cat who cannot resist the chance of commandeering as many homes as possible within a given area. A cat with four owners travels between each one depending on his own personal whims; each owner believes they are having an exclusive monogamous relationship with their cat and he just goes off 'hunting' from time to time. This cat may well be seriously over-vaccinated and even registered twice with the same vet in one village (under different names, of course). I have received hundreds of letters over the years detailing problems but many owners just want to tell me their stories; fascinating. One letter I read back in the early nineties is particularly relevant.

We acquired Marmalade with this house, which we purchased two years ago. The previous owners had taken him on in the same way, as had the owners before him. Marmalade is well known (notorious) in the neighbourhood. He has obviously, in the past, roamed over most of this valley. He is known to be eighteen years old, and is thought to be considerably older. He has only one ear and his back legs are skinny and bent with age. His tongue is usually hanging out because the few teeth he still has are at the back of his mouth. He doesn't seem to be able to miaow any more, but can and does purr very loudly. His old owners told us that he often went missing for several days at a time, and then reappeared; they put this down to hunting trips. Sure enough, this pattern continued for several months after we moved in. Then the girl next door came to tell us she was moving out and would we please look after her little ginger cat, which was very old and went hunting for days at a time!

This is just another illustration of our complete gullibility when faced with a loving cat in apparent need of a good home; we never really *own* cats at all, do we?

The next few cases illustrate the complexity of the concept of territory. It is safe to say that situations of this kind could happen to any one of us.

Billy Bob – the reluctant defender

Billy Bob and Joey were two Orientals who had a great relationship. They adored each other and they adored their owner, Jackie, and this triangular love-fest continued for twelve glorious years. Jackie became the sort of owner who believed that cats loved other cats and feline company was everything because they enjoyed the experience. Billy Bob used to follow Joey and go on great adventures with him through the adjoining gardens. They had a cat flap and they came and went as they pleased. It was a perfectly balanced and enjoyable existence for all until Joey became ill. He was diagnosed with a tumour and over a period of four weeks he deteriorated until the time came for him to be peacefully put to sleep at home. Jackie chose this option to ensure that Billy Bob understood that Joey had died and wouldn't be coming back. She was quite surprised by Billy Bob's reaction on the day; he seemed relatively unmoved. After Joey's body was taken away, however, he began to display his grief. He paced, he wailed like a banshee, he searched and, when he wasn't doing all that, he clung to his owner. His distress was palpable. He stopped eating and poor Jackie didn't know what to do to ease his suffering. Worse was to come when Billy Bob jumped up on Jackie's bed one morning and urinated all over her pillow. This isn't a wake-up call that any cat owner relishes but she cleaned up after him and forgave him his indiscretion. After all, he was in mourning and he had been behaving out of character since Joey's death. Unfortunately it wasn't a one-off and several incidents later Jackie contacted me for my help and guidance at a very difficult time.

When I met Billy Bob I was overwhelmed by his tension and distress, and his behaviour towards Jackie was extraordinary. He watched her all the time, he touched her whenever he could and every time she sat down he jumped all over her. If he could have unzipped her skin and climbed inside he would have done. I asked Jackie whether this was normal for him and she reported that his clingy behaviour had only started since Joey's demise. Prior to that the two cats had appeared relatively self-reliant, merely spending evenings curled up on her lap whilst she watched television. She had never previously found it difficult to move around the flat because of a cat at her feet. She had certainly never found it hard to leave her house either, unlike now, when every excursion had to be carefully planned to take the minimum amount of time. Every time she returned she dreaded the sight of a urine-stained duvet or pillow.

In order to understand this apparent change in personality it was necessary to look again at the relationship between Billy Bob and Joey. The apparent affection between the two cats was actually something rather more dysfunctional. What had appeared to be a sociability born of a desire to spend time with each other was actually a dependency. Their relationship was based on need not want and Billy Bob was suffering from the symptoms of withdrawal from his addiction to Joey.

Over many years breeders have attempted to create the ultimate sociable cat. Many breeds are described by their 'dog-like' behaviour. I suppose the fact is that we want pets for emotional reasons and we expect a relationship to develop that gives back what we put in. Dogs are ideal for this purpose but many of us work and cannot devote the necessary time and energy to their care. So we develop a cat that behaves like a dog and, hey presto, we have the perfect compromise. Or do we? I often wonder whether trying to improve on nature is truly in the best interests of the species we profess to love so much. Are we really creating a sociable pack animal in the body of a territorial solitary predator with absolutely no adverse consequences, or are we actually achieving something else entirely?

I explained to Jackie that I had felt for some time that many apparently sociable cats, either with people or with each other, were merely exhibiting a dependency. Susceptible individuals find self-reliance too difficult to achieve and they learn very quickly that clinging to another provides the security they crave. Whilst this is great all the time the two parties are together it poses a dreadful dilemma when one isn't there any more. Billy Bob had reached this point and transferred his dependency to Jackie. The only problem with this arose when it came to defending the territory against invading cats. This had always been Joey's job and he had patrolled the area fearlessly (with Billy Bob several paces behind), keeping all potential adversaries at bay. The word had soon got out that Joey was no more and the more daring and opportunistic members of the local community had started to investigate what exactly it was that Joey had been defending so vehemently. What they found was Billy Bob, a nice bit of garden, a cat flap and loads of food. His garden was no longer the safe fortress it used to be and toileting in the flower bed became fraught with danger. Billy Bob just wasn't equipped to do Joey's job and he wallowed in a mire of insecurities and phobias. No amount of vocalizing to his owner was getting the point across that danger was present; I'm positive that Billy Bob thought Jackie pretty useless when it came to defence of their castle. When he needed to urinate desperately he found the soft yielding surface of his owner's bed and the strong positive scent message too much to resist, so voided his bladder in this safe location. Given his character and circumstances I would defy anyone to do otherwise. I felt an equal amount of sympathy for both Billy Bob and Jackie; this was a difficult situation.

It is impossible to get into the head of the scared and insecure cat and tell him to 'pull yourself together'. I wish it was that simple. Billy Bob had lost the plot and everything frightened him. He had turned to Jackie for support and guidance at a time when she was least able or willing to give it. Not only was she grieving for Joey, but Billy Bob was peeing on her bed! I had to devise a plan that would return the relationship to one with a more manageable level of interaction and, somehow, restore a little confidence in Billy Bob so that he could at least function relatively independently. It was an extremely difficult problem to address because there were so many complications and practical consider-ations. If we blocked up the cat flap and stopped the invading forces from entering and terrorizing Billy Bob we would merely push him further into the arms of his owner. He would become totally reliant on her to give him entry and exit to the home. This would reinforce his insecurities tenfold and make him even less able to function as a fully fledged cat. If, however, we didn't shut the cat flap his adversaries would continue to gain entry and he would undoubtedly continue to pee on Jackie's duvet.

The added complication I have not mentioned until now was Billy Bob's complete aversion to all things resembling litter trays. This made it impossible for us to confine him indoors for any period of time without risking an assault on the pillow. We did try to give him every type of tray and litter known to man (even soft incontinence pads) but he wasn't fooled by any of it and retained urine to bursting point rather than pee anywhere but his owner's bed.

Lateral thinking, as always, saved the day in this particular case. Both Jackie and I were at our wits' end and rehoming had been mentioned several times. Part of me felt this was an option worth considering but I knew that Jackie, deep down, would do anything to get things back to how they used to be when Joey was alive. I came up with a plan. Billy Bob wasn't going anywhere very much these days. He would patrol outside somewhat reluctantly but avoided any temptation to go beyond the relatively predictable space of his own back yard. The surrounding fencing was high and the whole area lent itself to the concept of a 'secure garden'. We therefore agreed that any holes in the fence would be repaired and a series of inverted pillars and netting would be attached to the top of the fence to make the space safe from future invasions.

The process was watched with great interest by Billy Bob and it was soon time for him to explore his fortified domain. I asked Jackie to wash the patio and soak the plants and turn over the soil to provide a 'blank canvas' of scent for Billy Bob to explore. Within the first day Jackie was delighted to report that she had observed Billy Bob urinating under the pyracantha. What a result!

Poppy and the girls – the curse of the cat flap

Anyone who has read my previous books will know I am not a big fan of the cat flap. I do, however, understand that they are a necessary evil since many cats would be deprived of the opportunity to go outside if they didn't have one. None the less I cannot resist offering a cautionary tale just in case your cat flap has become more of a curse than a blessing.

Rachel and her boyfriend lived with four female moggies, Poppy, Smudge, Angel and a rather petite cat called Belle. The first three were all around the same age, ten or eleven, and Belle was the baby at the tender age of three. They lived in a pleasant cul-de-sac of semi-detached houses in Surrey and they hadn't had a care in the world with their feline family until a couple of months before Rachel called me. All four cats seemed to get on really well; they came and went and had complete freedom. So why, suddenly, had Belle started spraying urine in the house and Smudge peeing on the carpet? This was a terrible shock for Rachel and she was desperately trying to understand what was happening. She felt either it was something she was doing or her cats had inexplicably decided to become dirty.

I visited Rachel to put her mind at rest about the whole 'dirty protest' thing and to get to the bottom of the recent dramatic changes in behaviour. Poppy, Smudge, Angel and Belle did indeed have complete freedom to come and go via a cat flap in the wall of the spacious lounge/diner leading to the back garden. When I sat talking to Rachel I was surrounded by a 'posse comitatus' of felines, arranged strategically in various positions in the room. Belle was crouched by the cat flap, Poppy was on the table in the dining area, Smudge was on the arm of a chair and Angel was on the window sill. They were trying to look relaxed and casual about the whole thing but I had a sense that they were coiled springs waiting to act at the first sign of trouble. The fact that they were all facing towards the cat flap didn't go unnoticed either.

As I suspected, there had been a new neighbour's cat coming in through the flap and stealing their food recently. Rachel, like so many owners, felt this wasn't such a big issue since all four cats had witnessed the invasions at one time or another and only one, the diminutive Belle, had offered any challenge. Rachel was more concerned about the behaviour between the 'four girls' as she called them. A tension had arisen among them and she was positive that the innocent-looking Belle was behind it all. She had taken to sitting in front of the cat flap and guarding it. As Belle's unsuspecting victim entered the perceived safety of the home she was bopped heavily by a small but powerful paw. The recipient of the blow would then scream and either reverse out again or vanish to the sanctuary of a wardrobe to ponder on the whole unpleasantness. Poppy, Smudge and Angel were, however, taking some revenge for this display of thuggery, according to Rachel. All four cats had previously slept on their owners' bed at night (I often wonder if the increasing sale of oversized beds is anything to do with this sort of sleeping arrangement?) but recently the older three had found one companion conspicuous by her absence. Belle had taken to sleeping in the living room alone. Was this a defensive measure or something Belle had decided of her own free will? There had also been a number of scraps between the four cats; Angel had taken to disappearing off to a quiet corner, poor Smudge had started voting with her bottom and urinating in the corner of the bedroom and Belle had been seen several times spraying urine in various locations in the living room and kitchen. Poppy seemed rather ill at ease too and something was clearly not right.

Whilst I could clearly see the animosity I wasn't convinced that the girls' deteriorating relationship was the primary cause of the problem. My finger of suspicion pointed firmly towards the invading cat from No. 6. After all, how could aggravated burglary three times a week *not* be an issue? During the consultation I experienced something that all cat owners should look out for, especially those who haven't considered the potential implications of the cat flap. Smudge and Angel were still occupying sunny spots in the living room but Belle had wandered into the kitchen and Poppy had returned to the warmth of the fleece by the radiator in the bedroom. Suddenly the cat flap rattled with a gust of wind and Smudge and Angel launched themselves high into the air. They landed simultaneously and crouched in readiness for the ensuing invasion. Nothing came, but they continued to be vigilant. I tried to explain to Rachel that the cat flap was no longer the convenient 'open all hours' access to the great outdoors; it was now the portal of Hades to her feline companions.

Belle was spraying urine due to a changed perception of the boundaries of her safe haven. The ground floor had become a no man's land where rights of ownership were being constantly challenged. It represented nothing better than the garden or surrounding properties and was therefore worthy of as much marking activity as the bushes and fences outside. She felt compelled to guard the flap as often as possible (somebody had to) and her constant desire to go in and out was everything to do with patrolling and checking and nothing to do with a pleasant constitutional. Smudge was just too terrified to pee outside with the threat of the beast from No. 6 ever present so she retained urine to bursting point then flooded the shag pile when she could hold no longer. Tensions were high and all four cats started to take it out on each other in desperate acts of redirected aggression.

The solution to this sort of problem is to redefine the boundaries of the house as a zone of safety. Cat flaps don't signal security to cats (it's a little like leaving the front door open when you go away on holiday) so they rarely form part of a therapy programme to restore a sense of safety. Unfortunately the provision of exclusive-entry cat flaps, together with magnetic keys on collars, once a house has been invaded, is rarely enough. It may prevent all but the most determined interloper from gaining access but the concept is a little complicated for the average cat to grasp. Any invasion changes everything and no amount of magnetism will make an ounce of difference.

We had to take more drastic measures to restore harmony and this in itself created other potential problems. If we blocked the cat flap completely, so that it disappeared from view, it left the resident cats in one of two distinct places at any one time: either outside or inside. Few owners would feel happy about suddenly leaving their cats out all day or night, and probably rightly so in this busy world. Entry and exit would only be achieved with the help of either Rachel or her boyfriend and they weren't always at home to be at the beck and call of their charges. The other potential risk is that the enemy is actually within the house when the flap is shut and battle commences as stress levels reach fever pitch. I discussed the options at some length with Rachel but she was extremely concerned that the cats would be largely confined to the house apart from times when she was there. We eventually agreed on a compromise and installed the formulaic number of litter trays indoors to satisfy Smudge and ensure the carpet was no longer seen as the only suitable latrine. Rachel agreed to shut the cat flap at night and keep the cats in to gauge their response to this new regime.

She reported later that week that the first night was fraught with anxiety. All six of them were huddled together listening to the relentless banging of the cat flap as the cat from No. 6 tried as hard as he could to break in. Belle didn't even venture downstairs, such was the ferocity of his endeavours. Squirts of sprayed urine were everywhere in the living room and kitchen when Rachel returned from work the following evening. Things were not going well, but at least Smudge et al thought the new litter facilities were a great idea. Rachel was also greeted that evening by almost everything the four cats could produce, in the urine and faeces department, neatly piled up in the new toilets. The trays were clearly a success for them but this just represented another chore for Rachel, unfortunately. After the first week she was exhausted and she agreed that we had to renegotiate the whole cat-flap thing. She and her boyfriend started to plan their diaries and, after careful consideration of shift patterns and flexitime, it was discovered that their working life could be adjusted to such an extent that the house would only be empty for a couple of hours during the day. This was a breakthrough and steps were taken to board up the cat flap at the front and back of the opening. Soon the wall appeared solid again.

For the next few weeks Rachel and her boyfriend were constantly on the go, letting them all in or out on demand. Nevertheless, there was an increased friction between the cats and a significant rise in active fighting. I was concerned that my worst fear had been realized and the enemy was indeed within the home. Luckily, dutifully reported by Rachel, it was a temporary setback and the cats soon adjusted to their new regime. The cat from No. 6 must have been confused to be faced with a blank wall where a flap and a free meal once stood but he probably got the message and sightings became sporadic. The best news of all was that Belle stopped spraying urine on the pedal bin and the CD rack. The toaster, settee and curtains were untouched and the house stopped smelling of urine and fear.

A few months later Rachel experimented and took the dangerous step of re-establishing the cat flap, at least during the day, so that she could return to her previous working hours. She had discussed this with her boyfriend and they felt the cat from No. 6 had been absent for long enough to give it a go. Six months later she phoned me to report that all was back to normal. The girls were relaxed with each other but happy to remain indoors with the cat flap locked during the night. The litter trays, after the initial novelty had worn off, were being used by Smudge and Angel only, so Rachel had removed two of them to reduce the extra work and expense of servicing so many. Belle had not sprayed for seven and a half months and (touch wood) Rachel felt we had cracked it. I agreed, at least until the next time . . .

Tinker – or Genghis Khan to his friends

If you have read *Cat Confidential* you may remember the case of Hercules, the despotic Burmese. Rarely are cases more frustrating than those that involve third parties and their pets. I cannot complete a chapter on the cat's relationship with its territory and all within it without focusing once again on this unfortunate phenomenon. All cats should be territorial, it is an important survival strategy for a solitary predator, but many domestic cats maintain a measured response when exercising this natural behaviour. They may scrap in their garden if Sooty comes a-calling with evil on his mind but they don't go looking for trouble. Sadly, some cats take the concept of 'natural behaviour' to another level.

Tinker was a beautiful two-year-old snow-leopard-spotted Bengal. He was a masterpiece of creative perfection, all muscle and silky fur, and I could certainly see his appeal. His owners Anita and Simon were captivated by his charm and good looks and he appeared to be the perfect pet. I, of course, knew other-wise; the mere fact that I was there was a bad sign.

Tinker and his owners lived in a residential area in Berkshire. They had a big house and garden surrounded by other large properties and the bottom of the garden backed on to a quiet cul-de-sac of bungalows. It was an obvious haven for cats and, for the first two years of his life, Tinker seemed to enjoy the delights of the outdoors and the comforts of the home in equal measure. He was a perfect, loving pet – prone, in my opinion, to extreme manipulation of Anita, who was absolute putty in his paws, but nothing that would constitute a treatable problem. Most owners would have relished his affectionate, gentle and slightly naughty character. And then, one day, Anita and Simon received the shock of their lives. They discovered that, for some time, Tinker had been leading a double life. Simon had a phone call from an elderly gentleman called John. He lived in one of the bungalows in the cul-de-sac behind their house and he had indulged in quite a bit of detective work to find out their identity, address and telephone number. He had been looking for the owners of 'Genghis Khan'.

Apparently (and this was astounding to Simon) Tinker had quite a reputation locally; hence the pseudonym. John and several of his neighbours had known of his presence for some time. He was, after all, a handsome and distinctive beast, but his looks were no compensation for his recent heinous acts of violence. Simon listened as John related tales of victimization, break-ins and vicious attacks, but he wasn't prepared for the next revelations. John's cat Fluffy had been a regular recipient of a good bashing from 'Genghis'. If this wasn't bad enough, the attacks had all taken place in the supposed safety of Fluffy's home. Tinker had burst through the cat flap and actively sought out his victim, minding his own business on the kitchen chair.

John had only seen the retreating tail disappearing through the cat flap when he had rushed to his pet's rescue before, but last night was different. John managed to get himself between Tinker and the cat flap and he made a grab for him to push him away from defenceless Fluffy. Tinker turned and lunged at John with teeth and claws and the poor man ended up in Casualty. All Simon wanted to say in response to this was 'You are obviously mistaken; this cannot be our Tinkiepoos' but somehow, deep down, he knew John was telling him the truth. Tinker had obviously been playing around with chemicals and potions and managed to effect a Jekyll-and-Hyde-type trans-formation. There could be no other explanation.

Simon, all credit to him, confronted the serious nature of this information immediately. Within forty-eight hours I was sitting in his kitchen, with both owners and a wide-eyed, purring Tinkiepoos. He had been confined to barracks since the call from John to show the couple's determination to stop this nightmare. They were, I think, hoping that I could confirm their suspicions of Tinker's long hours in the laboratory (figuratively speaking) and produce an antidote that would return him to normal. I had to take a deep breath and explain that this wasn't something that could be fixed; this was the nature of the beast. Some years ago stories of this kind almost always included a handsome Burmese. Now that the popularity of the Bengal has reached incredible levels I now feel that they have become the new Burmese (only, with spots or stripes). The situation has to be seen in the right perspective, though; there are a lot of Burmese and Bengals out there and most of them make perfect pets. However, when they go wrong . . .

Anita and Simon had exactly the same dilemma as Ted and Angela had with Hercules. John was being perfectly co-operative but was adamant about his inability to confine his cat. My suggestions, given to Simon prior to my visit, of timeshare arrangements and cat-flap blocking at night were non-starters when he broached the subject with John. We explored cat-proofing the garden; we even went down the dubious route of investigating wireless fencing systems that involved giving Tinker low-current electric shocks when he approached Fluffy's cat flap, but we had become quite desperate by then. Tinker could not be confined so Anita and Simon started ringing John when Tinker was outside to prepare him for attack. John would ring back as soon as Tinker entered his garden, and Anita or Simon would rush round and collect their cat before too much damage was done. This was working after a fashion but all life had stopped to accommodate Tinker's violent streak and the strain was showing.

The following weekend I remember several tearful phone calls with Anita. Tinker had just started to spray urine indoors (and allegedly in several other neighbours' homes) and this really made Anita think that she was keeping a cat in circumstances that were making him deeply unhappy. Was she being selfish? The biggest dilemma when dealing with these cats is twofold: convincing the owners that rehoming is a feasible option and finding a home on a relatively small island that will accommodate a cat with such grand-scale ideas of territory. Anita and Simon were absolutely brilliant and the selfless and painful decision they made that weekend still makes me emotional. Unlike Hercules' owners they didn't have a conveniently placed aunt in the middle of the Outer Hebrides or a friend of a friend on the Yorkshire Moors. Their friends and family were no better placed to give Tinker a home than Simon and Anita themselves. The calls and emails from them were gut-wrenching: 'Can't we just drug him? Do we have to give him up?' When they eventually decided to take him to a rural cat rescue centre (with prior agreement, given his special circumstances) they drove back twice with the sole purpose of bringing him away again. I can only imagine how heartbreaking that must have been and I will always admire their courage.

So, Tinker found himself in an adoption centre with a prominently displayed notice on his cage reading:

Tinker is a highly territorial cat, very much as nature intended for the feline. This is an inherent characteristic and, if presented with a number of cats in close proximity within his territory, he will be proactive in his aggression. He will not tolerate cohabiting with another cat so he needs to find a home as a singleton. It would probably be advisable for the home not to have a cat flap.

Despite his aristocratic good looks he has the needs of a hunting/shooting/fishing feral and a wide open space would be ideal, with plenty of opportunities to forage, explore and hunt. A smallholding or rural environment would be perfect. He will continue to fight if presented with other cats in his home range but this is the nature of the beast. He will, paradoxically, be a wonderful affectionate kitten-cat for his new owners. Tinker is the true 'tiger in your living room'.

The law and your cat

Over the past couple of years I have seen a worrying trend emerge in the type of phone calls I am receiving. There has been an alarming rise in the cases involving disputes between neighbours resulting from disputes between their cats. Tinker's case is a typical example of the despotic cat causing havoc; other cases include injuries to neighbours, damage to property and compensation demanded for vet bills. I am extremely reluctant to get involved in these cases so I hope the next few paragraphs will be helpful to all those poor souls who find themselves in this predicament.

A couple of years ago there was a rather disturbing article in the London *Evening Standard* newspaper about

●

a five-year-old Bengal. The sensational piece of journalism accused him of fighting with every cat in his neighbourhood, killing one and leaving two others so severely traumatized that they had to be put to sleep. The rest of the story had familiar themes that I had experienced many times before. The owners were in complete denial; they insisted that their beloved pet was not vicious but they had agreed to erect an outdoor pen for him and confine him during the day. The neighbours had formed an action group and the police had become involved. The owners of the injured parties insisted on compensation for their extensive vet bills and the language was emotive and confrontational. The Bengal's attack cry was described as 'blood-curdling' and his walk was 'like a leopard on the prowl'. There was even a reference to Bengals' being classified as wild cats rather than domestic pets. Death threats had been made by desperate neighbours; one had allegedly said that he would despatch the Bengal once and for all with the aid of a heavy garden implement.

I was severely traumatized myself by this story, although I have never yet been involved in a case of territorial aggression where a cat was killed or put to sleep as a result of its injuries. As far as I could tell from the article none of the attacks were witnessed and the injuries sustained could well have resulted from other causes. However, the frightening fact is that any cat, especially a large muscular cat like a Bengal, is perfectly capable of killing another cat. The reason why this doesn't happen more often is a result of generations of domestication and a diluting of the territorial instinct that allows cats to cohabit without ripping each other apart. Most cats will defend their territory, either passively through threat and intimidation or actively through violence. I have to admit that Bengals and Burmese are over-represented in cases of extreme territorial aggression, but maybe this is just a trait that has been bred into them by accident?

I have been concerned for some time now that very soon such cases will go to court. It has always been understood that cats are classified in law as 'free spirits', beyond the control of the owner as they roam by nature. However, we cannot get away from the fact that they do cause damage and they do fight, resulting in high veterinary bills. Even given the protection of the term 'free spirit' there seems to be increasing pressure to review cats' culpability. One day very soon a frustrated owner will seek damages from the owner of a warring cat; I'm not sure I would like to be an expert witness but I'll have to be in the public gallery for that one.

I'm no lawyer, but I wonder how relevant the Animals Act 1971 would be when discussing liability for damage or injury caused by a pet cat if the 'free spirit' angle became invalid as an excuse?

The Animals Act 1971

Extracts from Section 2

2   Where damage is caused by an animal which does not belong to a dangerous species, a keeper of the animal is liable for the damage, except as otherwise provided by this Act, if:

- the damage is of a kind which the animal, unless restrained, was likely to cause or which, if caused by the animal, was likely to be severe; and
- the likelihood of the damage or of its being severe was due to characteristics of the animal which are not normally found in animals of the same species or are not normally so found except at particular times or in particular circumstances; and
- those characteristics were known to that keeper or were at any time known to a person who at that time had charge of the animal who is a member of that household and under the age of sixteen.

Extracts from Section 5

1   A person is not liable under sections 2 to 4 of this Act for any damage which is due wholly to the fault of the person suffering it.

2   A person is not liable under section 2 of this Act for

any damage suffered by a person who has voluntarily accepted the risk thereof.

3   A person is not liable under section 2 of this Act for any damage caused by an animal kept on any premises or structure to a person trespassing there, if it is proved either: that the animal was not kept there for the protection of persons or property; or (if the animal was kept there for the protection of persons or property) that keeping it there for that purpose was not unreasonable.

I've read the Animals Act several times and it raises some important questions for cat owners. Could a cat owner be held liable for his or her pet's behaviour? The query I have concerning Section 2 relates to the interpretation of 'normal' behaviour for the species and prior knowledge of 'characteristics'. There will always be a debate about what is normal or abnormal; you could argue that it is abnormal for a cat *not* to fight with another in its territory. In fact a great deal of what the domestic cat gets up to these days arguably isn't normal for the species. If you knew that your cat, like the Bengal in the newspaper article, was particularly aggressive and that it was almost inevitable he would get in a fight every day and cause injury, would this make you liable for the damage he caused? There is no need to be proved negligent to be liable under the Act. However, if I have interpreted Section 5 correctly, you wouldn't be liable if the damage was the fault of the person suffering it, or if they had voluntarily accepted the risk of its happening to them. Could you describe it as 'fault' if an owner intervened between two fighting cats and got injured as a result? Do you 'voluntarily accept' the risk of injury or damage to your property if you fit a cat flap?

I apologize for ending this chapter with questions and no answers. As far as I am aware there is currently no legal precedent for cases of this kind. I may be worrying completely unnecessarily, but the volume of calls I receive on this very subject is increasing daily. My own opinion is that we should all accept that cats are solitary predators, defenders of territory and potentially danger-ous creatures. That is the nature of the beast. We have a moral duty, as good citizens, to listen to neighbours' grievances and take reasonable measures to address their complaints if the alleged 'attacks' take place in their own home. However, we also have a duty to our own cats to take every precaution to ensure that our homes are suitably protected from invasion by other cats. Therefore I honestly believe it is the victim's responsi-bility to maintain the security of the property. Cats will fight; it is a natural behaviour and some cats are more natural than others. There have to be occasions in life when the compensation culture does not apply.

CHAPTER 4

Cats and All Things Furred, Feathered and Finned

Fish, hamsters, gerbils, mice, birds and rats, to name but a few, are all common household pets. Many families also have cats, but this combination is naturally the pairing of a hunter and its prey. There are countless anecdotes told about unusual relationships arising between such mismatched species, but caution is the keyword; you really don't want Sooty running off with your child's hamster in a moment of madness. Many cats, however, if brought up with other species, will develop friendships that defy nature. They will see all living things around them as part of the social group and behave accordingly.

I have a very good friend, Pete, who was persuaded by a local zoo to take on a meerkat. This particular individual had been hand-reared after being rejected by his mother and proved impossible to integrate back into the group. The meerkat is a social creature and the zookeepers felt that my friend's menagerie (including eight cats, two dogs, many ferrets and even more gerbils) would be sufficient company for any such gregarious beastie. To cut a long and fraught story short, the young meerkat settled in extremely well and I have several photographs of him with any one of the eight cats, holding their faces in a vice-like grip with his front paws and washing them like there was no to-morrow. He also has a habit of sitting on their backs and rummaging through their fur for fleas. The cats accept both activities with a good grace and a look of great contentment. These cats had become accustomed to sharing their home with dogs, ferrets, tortoises, seagulls, lambs and any other waifs and strays that needed Pete's attention; another species made little difference to them. They merely embraced the meerkat behaviours that pleased them and left the little fellow in no doubt about those that didn't. It never ceases to amaze me that cats can turn any situation to their advantage.

Probably the most popular companion for our favourite pet is a canine friend. There is occasionally what appears to be a love–hate relationship going on but both partners can surprise us with their loyalty when the chips are down. Bonds can develop between cat and dog, born of adversity, that change their relationship for ever. One such tale involves a rather rotund grey and white cat called Dusty, belonging to another friend of mine. Dusty had been with Gill and her family for twelve years when a bouncy golden Labrador called Holly joined the household. Dusty was slightly appalled but chose the path of least resistance in order to deal with the new situation. She stuck her little nose in the air and just pretended the dog didn't exist. After a short period of curious sniffs Holly figured that the spherical grey furry thing wasn't that interesting after all and their parallel lives began.

This state of affairs continued until four years later when Dusty had a bit of a bad day. She often sunned herself on the cover of the large water butt by the garden shed. She decided that a few hours of soaking up the rays was as good a plan as any that morning so she jumped up to make herself comfortable on the wooden platform. Unfortunately it wasn't sitting quite right just then and the whole thing tilted up and deposited her in three feet of water before returning to its horizontal position as if nothing had happened. Nobody had seen her fall . . . except Holly.

Gill was preparing food in the kitchen when Holly rushed in, barking furiously and bouncing up and down. Gill had absolutely no idea that Dusty was in danger and probably going under for the third time (she wasn't built for swimming) so she was slightly irritated by Holly's insistent behaviour. She told her firmly that she couldn't play with her and to return to the garden. Gill had trained her dog well and she was confused when Holly continued to 'misbehave', rushing in and out of the kitchen, barking and looking behind her. Eventually Gill decided to follow to see what the fuss was all about. Holly led her straight to the water butt and it was then that Gill heard the faint splashing sounds of the sodden Dusty. The poor cat was swiftly removed and rushed to the kitchen for drying, TLC and a good cuddle. Holly had saved her life. Since then the relationship between Labrador and moggy has changed dramatically. They cannot pass in the hallway without a nose-to-nose greeting. Dusty curls up beside Holly in her bed and each stares adoringly into the other's eyes. Holly has become rather parental in her attitude towards the little grey and white cat and she can often be seen guarding Dusty, at a discreet distance, as the latter sleeps peacefully under the bushes in the garden.

I have had occasion a number of times throughout my career to marvel at the symbiotic nature of some inter-species relationships. A little three-legged ginger cat called Stumpy used to come into the surgery when I was working as a veterinary nurse. He came from a household with a very eclectic mix of residents, from Chinese crested dogs to African Grey parrots,

Persians and garter snakes. As an individual he was probably as nonchalant about all things furred and feathered as any of my friend Pete's eight cats. When Stumpy visited the practice for his annual check-up, the staff often remarked on the condition of his teeth. I remember asking on one occasion if he was eating dry food, since it is an accepted fact that this type of diet tends to delay the onset of plaque and tartar. The owner's reply was somewhat unexpected. 'Stumpy does eat some dry food,' she said, 'but I think it's the parrot that helps enormously.' Apparently the parrot, a free-flying member of the family with little regard for his cage, would approach Stumpy when he was resting and gently start to peck at his face. Stumpy would then roll onto his side with his mouth open and the parrot would while away an enjoyable few moments delicately extracting food particles from the teeth of his feline friend. Isn't nature brilliant?

One of my own personal favourites, probably since it represents such a contradiction, is the relationship that can exist between cats and rabbits. Despite the obvious hunter/prey potential it can be a rewarding friendship for both parties. Some years ago I used to own several rabbits. They had all been adopted from the local RSPCA after pressure to 'give them a good home'; rabbits are victims of neglect and cruelty in huge numbers but rarely make the headlines. Over the years I looked after Harvey and Pooka (members of an unwanted litter resulting from the union of two alleged 'females' according to the pet shop assistant), Mr Murphy and Elwood (abandoned in small hutches when their owners moved house) and Barrie (a fluffy Angora with unmanageable fur found matted and covered in maggots). Sadly, after some years, Pooka and Elwood died but Harvey, Mr Murphy and Barrie made the transition from outdoor rabbits (with vast hutches and runs) to part-time house bunnies. They were extraordinary creatures and I cannot tell you what pleasure and amusement they gave Peter and me. House training to a litter tray was a breeze; getting them to use the cat flap was a piece of cake. 'Why don't more people keep house rabbits? They are so user-friendly,' I thought – until I realized they planned to start a large house fire by chewing every electric cable in sight. We rectified this rather serious problem by putting casings over any exposed wires and refraining from leaving the rabbits unsupervised.

The point of this story is that I also shared my home with seven cats at the time. They were (and some of them still are) great hunters and part of their staple diet was young juicy rabbit. It may have appeared some-what foolhardy to introduce food to the living room and expect the cats to resist the temptation of a nibble on an ear or two, but I had already watched the outdoor transition from food to family member as the cats became used to the rabbits' frolicking and general day-to-day activity. All my rabbits were well handled and sociable and I allowed the cats to enter their enclosed garden and get used to them. They seemed to understand perfectly that these rabbits were big, for a start (not quite such easy pickings); they didn't panic or freeze when they saw the cats and they smelt like me, to an extent. After a while I didn't see them as prey and predators at all.

Many an evening would be spent in domestic harmony; two humans, seven cats and three rabbits all cohabiting as some watched the television, some played, two slept and one rearranged sticks (Harvey had a thing about twigs and he spent hours picking them up and sorting them into parallel rows). I remember one evening with great fondness. My cat Bakewell, sadly no longer with us, was sitting on the sofa next to me with Barrie (the Angora rabbit with a harelip, ironically) propped against the cushions on his other side with his legs in the air and his belly exposed. This could so easily have been a recipe for disaster (or rabbit stew) but somehow I knew as Bakewell leant towards him that all would be well. With great determination my lovely black cat started to wash Barrie's impossibly long and scruffy fur; the mess of it all clearly offended him and he was attempting possibly to make order out of chaos. Barrie didn't seem to mind and continued to watch television, but Bakewell soon realized the error of his ways. After a matter of seconds he turned to me with a look of embarrassment and a mouthful of white fluff; if only he hadn't even started his act of kindness. Far too big an undertaking! A daft story, I know, but one that emphasizes how natural enemies can become friends in the right circumstances. It is, however, a tale with a big caveat attached to it. The situation worked for me and my cats but it is entirely possible that, given the appropriate conditions, something could have triggered an innate response in Bakewell and Barrie would have been no more. His size probably saved him; I wouldn't try it with dwarf rabbits. I would certainly not recommend that any cat and rabbit are left together without close supervision. The consequences could be too distressing for words.

However, I remember one occasion in veterinary practice when a certain lady, with the best of intentions, broke all the rules. She too had a house rabbit and a single cat and she introduced them carefully and at a safe distance. All went well, apart from the odd awkward pounce or two, so she considered that cat and rabbit were now the best of friends. The time came for them both to go to the vet's for their annual vaccinations, the cat for her flu and enteritis jab and the rabbit for his myxomatosis. The owner had a dilemma, however, since she only had one small wicker basket. But the problem was soon resolved, as we found out when she entered the surgery's waiting room with a very perplexed rabbit and cat squeezed into the same pet carrier. To this day I still do not know whether the look on their faces was one of embarrassment or horror. I would imagine that the trip was uneventful because both creatures had other things to think about. Please do not try this at home; just get a second basket.

I can only really give you my own experiences with inter-species relationships. Some work and some don't, but the important thing to remember is that different creatures' requirements may not necessarily be compatible. The obvious problem is the potential for damage should your cat become confused and suddenly see a family pet as dinner. I will therefore just pass on a few tips to ensure that the cohabitation is as safe and enjoyable as possible for all parties.

Fish and reptiles

Any creatures kept indoors in a tank could potentially be of interest to your cat, purely for the entertainment value. I would never recommend anyone to purchase a fish tank to entertain their cat, despite the fact that many find them fascinating. A responsible pet owner wants all their charges to be content both physically and emotionally, and contentment is probably rarely achieved by any fish or reptile that is stared at constantly by a slavering cat who repeatedly bashes the side of the glass. Most cats find snakes and lizards quite boring since their movement is usually languid and uninteresting, so there are rarely issues of intimidation. However, the tanks are warm and the allure of a hot spot cannot be underestimated. The most significant risk to any reptile is poor husbandry and, although I cannot categorically state that cats would traumatize them, I would want to discourage my cat from any potentially stressful attention to the tank.

- Cover any outdoor pond with netting.
- Ensure that tank covers are secure and that your cat can't comfortably use it as a warm resting place.
- Position tanks/vivaria in locations where your cat cannot make direct contact with the glass.
- Vivaria should ideally be situated in an area your cat doesn't frequent.
- All cleaning of vivaria should be undertaken in a secure environment *without* the cat present.
- Do not allow your cat access to any fish/reptile food or medicine.

Gerbils, hamsters, mice, rats, chinchillas, etc.

These are potentially the most vulnerable of all potential pets as their size and movement best mimic the cat's natural prey. Many of them *are* your cat's natural prey! It is just too much to ask your cat to respect the fact that this particular mouse is one of the family. Once again I would strongly recommend that any rodent is purchased for the right reasons and not just for entertainment value for the cat. Many small animals of this kind are kept in very poor conditions and half the fun of owning them is learning about their natural habitat and trying to create a simulated version in the domestic home. Any animal that is allowed to live in a near-natural environment will potentially be healthier than its less fortunate relations. Rodents will see the cat as a natural predator so, once again, allowing your cat to get up close and personal with your hamster is unfair. Don't be fooled into thinking that your cat isn't interested, either; many rodents are nocturnal so much of the intimidation may be taking place under cover of darkness, when you are asleep.

- Any exercising of your pet mouse/rat/hamster etc. should take place under strict supervision and in a secure room. Your cat should definitely not be present no matter how trustworthy.
- Cages and pens should have a securely locked opening to prevent small hands or paws gaining entry.
- They should be located in an area your cat doesn't frequent – ideally in a place your cat cannot access directly.

- It is not good for your cat to sit on top of the cage in any circumstances!
- Cages and pens should be cleaned in a secure room away from your cat. Your mouse/rat/hamster etc. should ideally be placed in a holding cage for their own safety.

Parrots and all caged birds

It is important to remember that birds are easily stressed and they can become ill or even die if subjected to a severe shock. Birds that cohabit with cats cope better if they are domestically bred and hand-reared rather than imported and wild. As in most cases, strange friendships can flourish if the creatures are raised together. Parrots are extremely intelligent and stimulating pets but they need as much attention as any cat or dog. They can cope very well with the presence of cats but early experience for both species is essential.

- Position the cage in an elevated location in the corner of the room to give the bird a sense of security; provide a covered section to the cage or vegetation for an added sense of camouflage.
- Ensure there are no clever routes that your cat can navigate to the cage (think Sylvester and Tweety Pie and you won't go far wrong).

- Ensure the door to the cage is secure at all times.
- Any exercise outside the cage should be undertaken in a safe environment without the cat present, no matter how nonchalant he appears about the whole thing. Accidents can happen.
- The bird/s should be kept safe when the cage or aviary is cleaned by being placed in a small secure holding cage. Exercise can be taken at this time in a safe environment *if*, once again, your cat is busy doing other things outside or in another part of the house.

Rabbits and guinea pigs

Guinea pigs can be kept indoors but they are not as popular as the up-and-coming house rabbit. Any advice given probably applies to both species since many owners still keep guinea pigs and rabbits together despite my suspicion that guinea pigs are better off with their own kind.

Cats and house rabbits

- Choose your new pet wisely if you intend to have a harmonious cat/rabbit relationship. The ideal companion would be a large, confident and sociable rabbit rather than a shy dwarf breed.
- Get your rabbit settled in a large indoor cage

environment initially without exposing it to the resident cat.

- Once your rabbit seems settled and happy, your cat can enter the room and explore the new addition in its cage without risk of harm.
- The cage can be moved into other rooms where you intend to allow your rabbit but it's always wise to have established indoor quarters for sleeping (away from your cat) that your rabbit can access easily and quickly.
- Rabbits often approach cats, once they have a sense of their own territory, to establish who is boss. If your cat runs away (let's face it, some rabbits are huge) this is often enough to establish hierarchy in your rabbit's head and all will be well.
- Never leave them together unsupervised; despite the obvious hunter/prey relationship each species can do harm to the other.
- Cats soon acknowledge house rabbits as part of the social group and vice versa.
- Having house rabbits won't stop your cat hunting and bringing in wild rabbits for supper (unfortunately).

Cats and pet rabbits outdoors

- Rabbits need exercise runs in the garden but these should be covered to prevent your cat from getting into them.

- Teaching your cat that outdoor rabbits are part of the household takes longer since you spend less time with them and such rabbits are more likely to show normal responses to the presence of cats, especially if they are not exposed to particular individuals on a regular basis.
- Never leave them together unsupervised.

Dogs

I have thought for some years now that the perfect companion for a cat is a dog! Providing there is careful planning at the outset regarding the breed of dog there is every chance that harmony will reign and the cat will run rings round the dog for ever more. Many owners who completed the questionnaire for the 1995 Elderly Cat Survey spoke of the devotion between their dog and cat and the distress caused by the passing of one or the other.

Choice of dog
Puppies are easier to work with as they are young and malleable and will soon become used to the presence of another species, treating it as just another member of the family. Introducing an adult dog to an adult cat can be difficult since many dogs, confronted with a disappearing cat, will automatically give chase even if they have no intention of doing harm should they catch it. If

your cat has no experience of dogs this can be a distressing experience and many, given the opportunity, will leave home for a period of time before coming to terms with this drastic change in the household. The breed of dog chosen will also influence the future canine/feline relationship in your home. Terriers, greyhounds and other breeds designed to chase small furry objects would ideally be avoided – choosing one of these is probably just asking for trouble. The breeds that are traditionally considered good with children such as the Golden Labrador, Retriever or Cavalier King Charles spaniel are probably sensible choices for multi-species living. Sadly they may well be persecuted mercilessly by the wily cat and have to give up their bed, water bowl and favourite sunny spot at the drop of a hat . . . letters from clients over the years have often revealed this tendency to torment. For example: *One of our neighbours got an Alsatian puppy not long after Tigger and Suki joined us – they terrorized him, stealing his bones from under his nose. They also used to ambush him when he was walked past our front garden, coming out from under different plants hissing and bog-brushed – so much so that from about nine months old the dog would not walk past our house.* And another classic example of the cat's ability to frustrate: *One of his main purposes in life seemed to be tormenting the dog belonging to our next-door neighbours. He would nonchalantly sit and wash for hours, right in front of their glass door, not taking the slightest bit of notice when the dog whipped himself into a frenzy of rage and frustration.* But genuinely good relationships can develop too.

Introducing a kitten to a dog

- Initial introduction is safest with the kitten inside a pen (these can be hired or purchased and measure approximately $3 \times 3 \times 3$ feet).
- Allow the dog to explore the kitten and vice versa without the risk of injury or a chase ensuing if the kitten runs.
- The pen can be moved into each room that the dog has access to.
- This process should continue for several weeks, particularly if your dog is protective over food, for example, and may respond aggressively when the kitten approaches his bowl.
- The kitten can be held near the dog with the dog on a lead to prevent chasing once each seems relaxed in the other's presence.
- Ensure the kitten is able to get away if he feels threatened.
- Treats can be given to the dog if he doesn't attempt to chase.

Introducing a puppy to a cat

- Ensure there are plenty of high resting places in the home where your cat can retreat away from the new arrival.

- Consider placing a baby gate at the bottom of your stairs to give your cat the sanctuary of the first floor.
- Introduce your puppy to his new home by using a puppy pen or crate.
- Plan ahead and start to feed your cat in an area away from the location where you intend to locate the puppy pen; this is to stop your cat going off his food.
- Try to place the pen away from the thoroughfare leading to the cat flap or the normal exit route for your cat.
- If litter trays are provided indoors ensure they are located discreetly and in areas where your new puppy will not be able to go.
- Introduce the new puppy to your cat in a room where the cat can easily escape.
- Hold your puppy and allow your cat to approach, if willing.
- Your cat may hiss or growl but if you are holding the puppy you can protect him from any aggressive advances.
- Allow the cat to be in the room where the puppy's pen is located.
- When your puppy is out of the pen it would be advisable to keep a long lead on his collar to stop him from chasing your cat.
- Do not allow any unsupervised encounters until each party is relaxed in the other's presence and the puppy has been trained not to chase.

Amber and Rascal – a cautionary tale

I don't see many cases where a dog is the root of the problem but it can happen. Amber was a pretty tabby and white cat and she lived with Debbie and her family in a town on the Sussex coast. Ever since she was a kitten she had shared her home with Maggie, the German Shepherd dog. Their relationship had been pretty good; Amber would use Maggie as a huge pillow and Maggie would eat Amber's food. It seemed to work very well. Sadly, Maggie died and the family were desperate to fill the void that she left with a little rescue dog. They eventually chose a medium-sized tan mongrel called Rascal, the decision swayed by the fact that the centre staff said he was very good with the cat that wandered in and out of the exercise yard. After a gentle introduction the relationship between Amber and Rascal seemed to be progressing nicely. Rascal became the perfect family pet and the children loved playing with him in the garden and generally fussing him.

After a couple of months something happened that shocked the family. Amber started to soil in the house, pooing behind the TV and peeing under the bed. She had always had a litter tray because she was kept in at night and Debbie couldn't understand why she was now so dirty when she had been so clean. Was she jealous of the attention Rascal was getting? Did she feel upset and rejected? Was she just using a horrible method to seek attention?

Debbie sought help from her vet, who referred her to me. When I visited it was clear that poor Amber had become a bit of a pariah in the family home. When I arrived she was sitting crouched at the top of the stairs with wide eyes as the children and Debbie played and laughed with Rascal. She was no longer allowed in the sitting room due to the heinous acts of the last few months and she knew her approaches would be rebuffed.

As our discussion progressed Amber quietly came into the hallway and Rascal's head lifted as he watched her progress. He was a good dog, he didn't chase her and the family reported that they seemed to be perfectly at ease with one another. He did tend to follow her around sometimes but Debbie felt this was no particular cause for concern. Amber just spent a little more time on top of the boiler in the kitchen. Nevertheless, poor Amber was depressed; as most cats are when they have to resort to urinating and defecating in places that normally wouldn't be considered appropriate. I had to find out why this was happening and I was starting to suspect that the not-so-innocent Rascal was behind her unacceptable behaviour.

Occasionally I am blessed with a gift piece of information from an unlikely source when I am trying to unravel the mysteries of a particular case. Little Ben

(Debbie's youngest son) had taken rather a shine to me and he had been playing by my feet as I talked to his mother. When Debbie left the room to recharge the coffee pot, Ben tugged at my trouser leg to indicate he was about to say something that required my undivided attention. 'I don't let Rascal lick my face 'cos I saw him eating cat poo.' Good for Ben – not only was this a sound strategy, it was also the piece of the jigsaw that completed my puzzle. When Debbie returned I explained the situation.

Dogs love eating cat faeces. This may not be the most endearing feature of our canine friends but unfortunately it happens. Debbie had reported that Amber had turned her back on the litter tray and her usual flower beds in favour of the tiny spaces under the bed and behind the television. I would imagine that Rascal, in anticipation of a warm and tasty treat (sorry), pestered Amber mercilessly with slavering jowls as she attempted to use her normal facilities. This can have a profoundly aversive effect on a cat, hardly surprisingly, and it has to take steps to find secluded areas where the necessary bodily functions can be performed in peace. Amber did well to find two places where only she could go, but they weren't popular with the family, for obvious reasons.

The answer lay in finding safe and acceptable latrines for Amber that were out of bounds to Rascal. A small area at the bottom of the garden was duly fenced off with discreet bushes to shield Amber from prying eyes. Her litter tray was replaced with a shiny new one located within a cupboard with cat-flap access. The soiled areas were cleaned and made inaccessible for Amber now she had comfortable alternatives.

We had one problem when Rascal nearly got his head shut in the cupboard cat flap but the provision of a magnetic flap and a little firm but fair training did the trick. Amber returned to acceptable toilet habits and was embraced once more into the bosom of her family.

Multi-species households can work; cats are capable of forming bonds with most other species if there is something in it for them. I personally believe that cats are sometimes better off if they live with anything *but* another cat. It is, however, very tempting to presume that everything will be just fine and the cat will be able to suppress its natural instincts and distinguish between another member of the household and prey. If you adopt this attitude it may well end in tears. The answer is to enjoy the variety within your home, become knowledgeable about every species you share it with and think safety at all times – for everyone's sake!

CHAPTER 5

The Eternal Triangle

Many of us are taking longer to find our ideal partner these days. If we do take the plunge we divorce more readily and we are rapidly becoming a nation with a significant proportion of single people living alone. This does mean that we do our own thing and have our cats and everything's fine until, usually for romantic or financial reasons, we decide to embrace the concept of sharing again. By 2010 a staggering forty per cent of us will live alone, according to government forecasts. I personally think that all those single people won't remain that way and that as they need to adjust to considering the thoughts and feelings of another, so do their cats!

Oscar, Tabitha and Suki – more an infernal triangle

It would be far too simplistic to say that all eternal triangles involve 'girl plus cat meets boy'; life is rarely that straightforward. Men really do like cats too, despite what *they* say, and I have been involved in many situations that resulted from the union of girl plus cat and boy plus cat. This can be interesting to say the least; Oscar's story is a typical example.

Oscar and Andrew had lived together for eight years. Andrew worked long hours and Oscar did his own thing but was always delighted when his companion returned to the safety of the home. Oscar was a bit of a worrier (rather than the warrior Andrew hoped he would be) and many altercations in the garden ended in tears, abscesses and a constantly decreasing sense of self-confidence. When Oscar was about four he decided that outdoors was just not for him so he made the choice to become agoraphobic. Andrew was un-usually perceptive and tuned-in to Oscar's moods and feelings (it's rather an indictment of the male gender to say so but this is quite unusual) so he accepted his cat's choice and provided him with a discreet litter tray, toys and a scratching post. Four years of voluntary confinement followed until Andrew and his girlfriend, Sarah, decided to set up home together. They had met two years previously and were both delighted to learn they shared a love of cats. Sarah had two six-year-old sisters called Tabitha and Suki and she took to Oscar immediately. He seemed so quiet and gentle; he wasn't exactly friendly with her but she presumed he was shy. He didn't respond very positively to her usual approach (cuddling, squeezing, stroking and kissing) but she reckoned she would win him round eventually.

Andrew and Sarah did discuss the potential implications of integrating two feline households into one, particularly as they were planning to move into Sarah's existing home initially, but they felt that Oscar was quiet and the girls were friendly enough and they would probably enjoy having a 'man' around the house. So the day arrived and Andrew and Oscar moved in. With the benefit of hindsight this clearly wasn't a perfect set-up. Sarah had been quietly oblivious of a rumbling tension between the two feline sisters. Suki was very much in charge; Tabitha stayed out of her way and attempted to go about her daily business with the minimum of fuss to avoid incurring the wrath of her sister. They both went outside but their chosen activities were very different, with Suki beating up everything in sight and Tabitha apologizing for her very existence to any cat prepared to listen. The last thing either of them really wanted was another cat wedged into the household; that would just complicate things.

The introduction was strained. Oscar retreated immediately to the apparent safety of a small gap behind the kitchen units and remained there, as far as Andrew could tell, for three days. When he did emerge, after much coaxing from his owner, his worst fears were soon realized – he had been transported into an environment that belonged to someone else and she was mean and feisty and would undoubtedly destroy him. Over the next few weeks the tension between the three cats was obvious. Tabitha and Suki started to fight actively and both females picked on Oscar whenever he could be found. He merely lurched from one hiding place to another, trying desperately to avoid his adversaries. The warfare was also psychological as the two sisters realized the significance of the newly acquired indoor toilet. They had both always gone outdoors but poor Oscar certainly wasn't going to explore the garden so his usual facility was installed in his new home. Tabitha started to use it immediately, realizing straight away how extremely safe and convenient an indoor toilet was. Suki saw its other potential and took to washing herself casually in the doorway, blocking all potential use by either her sister or the male interloper.

Oscar developed cystitis; hardly surprising really. Sarah and Andrew were still relatively unaware of the extent of the problem. They heard a bit of scrapping and growling but were things really that bad? Sarah did, however, take an intense interest when two distinct things started to happen. Oscar began peeing all over the house and attacking her in the hallway and on the landing. As if the urine wasn't enough he seriously meant business when he grabbed her ankles and poor Sarah didn't really like Oscar any more. She was frightened to come into her own house, there was a horrible smell and she was still trying to come to terms with sharing her home with another human being, let alone a ferocious and incontinent cat.

Sadly the relationship between Andrew and Sarah was a little ragged by the time I was called in. I spoke exclusively to Andrew since Sarah didn't want to know any more. 'It's your ****ing cat, you can deal with it!' she had said, apparently. I had hoped that both owners would have been there during my visit but quite understood the depth of the emotions that kept Sarah away. After many years of hassle-free pet ownership she had been confronted with a cat who wouldn't let her touch him, peed on the sofa and attacked her at every opportunity. Why would you put up with that? Andrew, on the other hand, was bereft. He loved Oscar dearly and saw a troubled soul rather than a naughty and unpleasant cat. We both agreed that he would concentrate on restoring his relationship with Sarah and I would see what I could do about the terrible trio.

New introductions into multi-cat households are

often difficult. When rumbling tensions already exist it can often exaggerate the problem and turn members of an established group against each other. In this case poor Oscar was clearly no match for Suki but the ease with which she could persecute him just made her do it more. Tray guarding is a common problem and a brilliant form of torture to those with a full bladder and Oscar's cystitis may well have occurred as a result of this (see my previous books *Cat Confidential* and *Cat Detective* for more details about stress and cystitis). Oscar couldn't go outside so peeing on the sofa or the bed where there was a soft surface and a smell of his security blanket, Andrew, was a logical alternative to the guarded tray. The aggression towards Sarah was another matter altogether. It didn't necessarily indicate that he held her totally responsible for his ill fortune but he would undoubtedly have been adrenalin-pumped and ready for action in such a tense atmosphere. Pouncing on her in narrow corridors may have seemed his only defence against an imminent attack; Sarah's response and subsequent fear reaction in his presence may well have prompted him to continue. After all, this was probably the first time he had actually made a successful assault on anything. I felt confident that if we resolved the cat issue then the rest would settle down automatically.

I devised a plan for Andrew that I hoped would alleviate the problem. We had to accept the fact that, confronted with the novelty of an indoor toilet, the girls would feel duty bound to use it or abuse it (Suki's guarding ploy). We therefore utilized the magic formula and introduced a further three trays in discreet locations. Andrew was worried that these additions would be firmly rejected by Sarah but I had to leave him to work on her and get her on our side. All these trays were an essential part of the treatment. Sadly it is rare that, once problems occur, things can ever return to the status quo. There is always a compromise and sometimes the solution to a problem can be a problem in itself. We continued with the programme and included more attention for Oscar from Andrew, play sessions (away from Tabitha and Suki's menacing glances), synthetic pheromones (available from veterinary practices) to give a sense of calm at a very fundamental level and the provision of several new private areas and high vantage points to enable Oscar to observe rather than join in the fracas. Before I left Sarah's house that day I asked Andrew if I could at least speak to her on the phone. I didn't feel comfortable asking her to do all this stuff if she was feeling so negative about the whole thing. I had a chat with her (I think she was pleased to feel she had a say in the matter) and explained the need to be moderately inconvenienced to restore harmony.

Andrew was determined to make it work; he was horribly torn between the two 'people' he loved most in the world, Sarah and Oscar. Immediately I left the house he was off to the local pet shop to bulk purchase trays, litter and toys. The introduction of the three new trays in the bathroom, hallway and spare bedroom had an immediate effect. All four trays were anointed regularly and the tension could be seen dissolving away from Oscar's face. Andrew loved him and played with him and Sarah was persuaded to feed him by hand with his favourite treat of ham. As each week went by Sarah became more upbeat. Oscar hadn't urinated anywhere that he shouldn't since my visit and he actually hadn't ambushed her either. She wasn't sure whether this was witchery or not but the reason behind Oscar's transformation was irrelevant to her. I tried to point out the power of multiple litter trays and a bit of play therapy but she wasn't at all sure I hadn't done something odd during my visit.

I cannot say that perfect harmony ever did reign in that household. Things settled down; Andrew and Sarah appeared to have resolved their differences and Oscar was definitely happier, but it was an enormous compromise for him. Tabitha ignored him and Suki could ban him from a room with one look, but it was a tolerable lifestyle. Should anyone in a similar situation ever ask me what to do, I would say plan ahead and take advice before you even try to combine two cat households into one, especially if one group is entering an established residence. Adjusting to the pleasures and pitfalls of cohabitation with another human being is tough enough without having to deal with the same issues in our pets' relationships.

Sandra meets Gary and Blue gets the hump

Sandra and her four-year-old grey cat, Blue, experienced a similar dilemma but the outcome was not quite so satisfying. Sandra had owned Blue from a tiny kitten and they had lived contentedly together ever since. She went to work and he went out to patrol his territory and visit his tabby friend, George, across the street (yes, occasionally cats do pal up). He would rest there awhile or stroll through the herbaceous borders until he heard the sound of Sandra's car. As she stepped out he would greet her by winding round her legs and pushing his head against her hands. She loved coming home to such a welcome. Blue comforted her when she was sad and de-stressed her when she was tense. Isn't this part of the reason we have cats when we live on our own? Three years into their relationship Sandra met and fell in love with Gary. Within the first twelve months they knew they were meant to be together and Gary moved in.

Blue had been wary of men ever since he was a kitten. Whenever Sandra had male visitors Blue would disappear out of the cat flap and only return once the man had gone. Sadly his reaction to Gary was no exception and on first sight he turned tail and thundered through the flap. The big problem was that, on this occasion, he didn't come back. He had taken an immediate dislike to Gary and Sandra had to trick him into returning home the following day. When Gary moved in, things went from bad to worse. He tried desperately hard to make friends with Blue (after all, the way to a woman's heart is through her cat) but this just made the poor grey cat wet himself in fear. Sandra even tried nailing shut the cat flap to force Blue to face his phobia but his paws became two claw hammers as he pulled out the nails, broke the cover to the flap and escaped in terror. The first few weeks of their time together in the same house consisted of a disconsolate Gary watching television on his own whilst Sandra crouched outside trying to coax Blue from under the conifers. Tears flowed and tension rose and they eventually agreed that the situation was becoming untenable. Blue had virtually moved in with George, his tabby friend, and Sandra felt as if she had gained a partner but lost a cat.

Before I visited Sandra we agreed that Gary would, temporarily, be banished from the house. A signal via Sandra's mobile phone would summon him home but the door would be opened by Sandra so he wouldn't use his key (Blue's signal for departure). I spent a pleasant hour with Sandra and Blue (tempted home with a few prawns) as we discussed their problem. He was a lovely cat, a little wary of me initially, but the lure of my magic bag soon had him rolling around the floor and looking generally chilled. Sandra was deeply distressed since her sense of divided loyalties was tearing her apart. She dreaded coming home and was finding everything very difficult to cope with. Unfortunately her mood was impacting on Blue, making him even more certain that Gary represented a major threat since his owner was apparently uptight about him too. In preparation for Gary's arrival we had barricaded the cat flap fairly comprehensively with a small chest of drawers, a large wicker picnic basket, a shoe rack and a box of vegetables (I wanted to test Blue's motivation to escape). I had spoken to Gary prior to his arrival and asked him to come into the room quietly with his eyes lowered and sit down on the chair. The phone call was made; Gary parked his car round the corner and walked towards the house. Sandra let him in and he entered exactly as instructed and sat down. Simultaneously, Blue jumped up and exited stage right, flinging the items blocking the flap in various directions as if he was frantically seeking bargains at a car-boot sale. Within thirty seconds he was out; that was a motivated cat!

Gary was a very willing participant in our therapy programme. He really wanted it to work since he could see the problem was almost driving a wedge between him and his lovely girlfriend. I asked Gary to enter the house in future as I had instructed during the consultation. He should initially talk in a whisper (he had a loud, deep voice naturally) and keep as still as possible, not making eye contact with Blue. Sandra had to relax so I asked if she could calm down since her anxiety was making Blue worse. A large wooden board was fitted to the back door to block the cat flap in such a way that Blue could not remove it in any circumstances, and this would stay in place for increasing periods of time to expose him to his enemy in a calm and positive atmosphere. Sandra played with him and gave him his favourite treats of cheese and Marmite, but only when Gary was in the room. One of the most important tasks for Sandra was to stop all the reassurance she had been giving Blue. Whenever Gary was at home she had fussed over Blue and comforted him constantly and it wasn't doing any good at all. She had to signal that time spent with Gary was safe and enjoyable.

Sandra and Gary followed the programme carefully over the next few weeks. Sandra did struggle with relaxing and she was a little despondent that Blue would still bolt through the flap as soon as the board was removed. Gary was also frustrated because he couldn't see that his efforts were reaping any benefits. However, after a couple of months they had a breakthrough. Blue started visiting Sandra in her bed whilst Gary was there. This was unheard of previously but, providing Gary remained horizontal and still, Blue seemed to be quite comfortable even if Gary wasn't. Blue had also spent fifteen minutes in the living room in his basket while Gary and Sandra were watching television. This was a triumph and things seemed to improve daily from that time forward. Regular telephone reports from Sandra were extremely positive and I almost put the file away with a big FIXED written on it. Sadly I hadn't predicted the complete mental aberration that poor Gary suffered the following week. He had returned home before Sandra to find Blue curled up in his basket. He was really pleased to see that the cat just got up and stretched lazily rather than disappearing immediately, and he felt an over-whelming surge of something that he was obviously unable to control. He walked towards Blue and tried to pick him up and give him a cuddle. He could have done no worse if he had taken a mallet and a chainsaw to him.

Blue panicked. He screamed and leapt out of Gary's arms, head-butting the wall hard in his frantic attempts to escape through the cat flap. Gary knew he was in trouble so called me first to tell me what he had done. Clearly he couldn't explain it as anything other than a moment of madness but the damage was done. We were at a very sensitive stage in the therapy programme. Blue was just beginning to redefine his opinion of Gary and was becoming more confident by the day. It was *not* the time to attempt physical contact, since the fragile relationship that was being created could shatter irrevocably with one false move. This one action sent Blue back to square one and beyond and his first response was to move in with George and not leave his friend's house for anything. Luckily Sandra and George's owners were good friends and at least he was in a safe place, but that didn't stop Sandra crying herself to sleep at the unfairness of it all.

Time went on and Sandra, bless her heart, persevered. She brought Blue home and Blue left again immediately he saw Gary. She almost reconciled herself to spending the next few years carrying her cat from one house to the other every day. Unfortunately the situation became more complicated when George's owners moved house. Their property had been for sale for some time but a cash buyer came along and suddenly things progressed very quickly. Sandra was concerned about Blue's losing his friend and the obvious confusion that her little grey cat would feel when he couldn't enter his sanctuary any more. She spoke to the new family when they arrived and explained her predicament and they gladly agreed to continue to allow Blue to come in. Their cat, Buttons, though, had other ideas and just wasn't having any of it. Blue subsequently spent most of his time under a hedge in the neighbour's garden or, worst of all, on the window sill looking into the house he used to call home. If Sandra tried to open the window and let him in he would run off. It broke her heart. It was time for the three of us to do some serious decision-making. We had to be sure that we were trying to keep Sandra, Gary and Blue together for the right reasons. All three were currently miserable: Blue missed George, Sandra missed Blue and Gary missed his happy stress-free girlfriend. I had a plan but I wasn't sure how Sandra would feel about it. I knew that all she really wanted now was for Blue to be happy. What if Blue and George could be together again? Sandra had already told me on a previous occasion that George's owners had reported that he was moping around in his new home and they suspected he was missing Blue. A couple of phone calls later George and Blue were reunited. Blue adjusted well to his new environment and was soon wandering round the garden and exploring his territory. Blue and George were often found in the evening washing each other or playing together.

I often think about this case because I don't believe I have ever worked with a cat so determined to hate one individual. I am absolutely convinced that Gary never harmed him in any way; Blue just took an instant dislike to him. It is sad that things were improving initially before the setback but I would guess that his firm resolve afterwards indicated the true nature of his feelings. Sandra visits Blue from time to time (always by herself) and she knows he's happy. She would desperately like to share her home with her boyfriend and a cat but she probably never will now after what happened to Blue. That's a shame, because she and Gary would provide a loving home, but you can see their point really.

Horace – sometimes they are not as upset as we think!

When couples come together, bringing their respective pets, it is always a slightly traumatic time. Will they get on? Will the resident cat leave home in disgust? Marion had recently acquired a lovely British Shorthair kitten. Her old cat, Tom, had died and she had always thought that having a pedigree would be wonderful. Tom was great but he had turned up as a stray and she always felt that he was very much his own cat. Maybe a pedigree would love her more? She called her kitten Horace and he moved in and all was going just fine. She knew she was spoiling him but he was worth it! He was very inquisitive and she spent the first few weeks rushing round after him, gasping when he tried to go up the chimney, panicking when he jumped on high surfaces and generally wrapping him in a thick layer of cotton wool to protect him from all life's dangers. She had already decided that the great outdoors was far too dangerous a place for such a sensitive soul. A couple of years went by and the bond between Horace and

Marion was growing. He waited at the door for her to return from work, followed her everywhere and appeared to hang on her every word. Marion was delighted and felt that purchasing a pedigree had obviously been the right choice; he clearly loved her to bits. She did feel he was a little nervy and highly strung but she presumed that this was a result of his breeding.

Whilst Marion and Horace were getting to know each other there were developments in her romantic life. When Horace was about two years old, Marion's long-term boyfriend, Patrick, suddenly announced that he wanted to take their relationship to a greater level of commitment. He felt it was time for him to move in with Marion (bringing his dog with him, of course). Marion was delighted; it was exactly what she wanted to hear, but she worried about Horace. She wondered how he would cope with a big dog; admittedly Patch was ancient, slow and soft, but he probably looked terribly frightening. Marion spent many nights over the next few weeks lying awake with Horace curled up at her side, contemplating the future with some trepidation. The time came for Patrick to move in and Marion was full of mixed emotions. She was excited about living with her boyfriend but anxious that Horace wouldn't cope. The little cat got extra cuddles that morning.

Patrick arrived with Patch and the first encounter was encouraging. Horace had been brought up with a dog at the breeder's home so his first response was actually one of curiosity rather than fear. Still, Marion couldn't resist grabbing him every time he approached Patch and scooping him into her arms. When she had done this a couple of times Horace rushed off and hid under the bed, and Marion instantly felt that her little cat hated the intrusion. Two weeks later things hadn't really improved. Horace avoided the newcomers and, on the arrival of various items of furniture from Patrick's house, anointed a bed and a pile of books with a flood of urine. Marion was beside herself and I was called in to help Horace come to terms with his new situation.

I listened carefully to Marion's story and watched the young cat playing around his owner's feet. At one point he tentatively approached the fireplace and just as he started to sniff the chimney Marion leapt out of her seat and shouted, 'No, Horace, it's dangerous!' The cat flattened on the floor and looked terrified before being grabbed and squeezed by his owner. Patch came into the room (a dear old dog) and flopped in front of the fireplace. Marion's hold on Horace tightened as she watched him suspiciously.

There are times when we really can be victims of our own paranoia. Ever since Horace first arrived Marion had lavished intense protective care on the little kitten; she had assumed an air of extreme caution round her charge. Every time poor Horace attempted to explore and challenge himself in order to develop and grow emotionally, his efforts were thwarted. Eventually he learnt to be helpless and dependent on his owner to protect him from all these unseen dangers. He became tuned in to Marion and responded to her every twitch and jump. He probably thought Patch looked like great fun initially but when he saw Marion's body language and her desire to protect him he feared the worst. When Patrick brought in the furniture and books with their challenging smells it all became too much for him, hence the breakdown of his previously exemplary toilet habits. Things had got on top of him.

I really didn't feel that Horace was bothered about Patrick *or* Patch. Patrick occasionally worked from home during the day and Horace seemed to enjoy the company. Patrick reported that Horace could often be found curled up beside Patch fast asleep when Marion was at work. The solution to this problem lay with Marion, not Horace. If she could bring herself to accept that Horace was perfectly capable of being in charge of his own life things would be vastly different. The little cat spent many hours gazing wistfully out of the kitchen window; he often rushed out of the back door when his owner wasn't looking only to be whisked back indoors by a panic-stricken Marion. They lived in a quiet cul-de-sac with a long and secure garden. What was the problem about allowing Horace the opportunity to explore the great outdoors? When I put that question to Marion she found it hard to find a suitable reply. I explained that if she backed off and allowed Horace to make his own decisions regarding what was and wasn't safe he would benefit enormously. I gave her details of appropriate products to clean the bed and suggested that she throw away the smelly books. She positioned two discreet litter trays in private areas (just in case Patch was a little too interested in the cat's toilet habits) to ensure that Horace always had a comfortable and safe place to eliminate indoors. And then I asked Marion to relax and let Horace explore his capabilities alone.

Over the next few weeks Marion was very brave. She introduced Horace to the garden; needless to say he took to it like a duck to water. She allowed Patch to sniff Horace and lick his head and didn't intervene when Horace climbed over him to get to the kitchen. Horace didn't have any more accidents and Marion soon realized that he had become less anxious as soon as she stopped fussing. She felt happier and Horace was clearly having a ball. As far as he was concerned the addition of one man and his dog was a bonus! A few months later I had to laugh when I opened a card from Marion and her family. There was a photograph inside showing Patch sitting in front of the fireplace staring intently at the empty hearth. Marion had circled something and on close inspection I could clearly see Horace's tail as the rest of his body disappeared up the chimney.

❀   ❀   ❀

I want to end this chapter with an honest confession. I am currently in the midst of a little turmoil with my own personal eternal triangle. Having resisted cohabitation for seven years (all great fun, I have to say) I have now met a man with whom I am happy to share my home. As I write we have been living together for several months but my dearest Mangus, my little Devon Rex, is not happy. Certain privileges have been curtailed since (how typical is this) Vicky has decided to fall for an ailurophobe who is also allergic to cats. I have spent the last few months following all my own advice: I don't force Mangus upon him nor do I remonstrate with him for his ridiculous and unfounded fear/dislike of cats. I have exercised the utmost patience whilst watching man and cat locked in a psychological battle for my affections. Mangus has learnt that, if she is very quick, she can lie across me in the evening in such a way that it is impossible for a third party to get anywhere near me without the risk of touching her. I sit pinned to the sofa with Mangus's tail in my face and her front legs spread across mine and I watch as they outstare each other. Every now and then, when she catches him unawares, she licks his hand or face. This is guaranteed to endear her to me ('Oh, look at her, she likes you and she's trying to make friends') but send him rushing for hot water and soap. I am not that easily fooled but I think her shenanigans are working on him. Successes thus far include:

- he cleaned out Mangus's litter tray when I had flu
- he sneakily gave her a piece of his steak when he thought I wasn't looking
- he greets her before me when he comes in from work.

What all of us cat lovers have to remember is that not everyone is made the same. You can be a good person and not 'get' cats because you just haven't had the personal experience of the joys of living with one. When an allergy is a problem then you are even less likely to indulge in pet ownership. All these people need is gentle, controlled and positive exposure to cats without someone screaming 'I told you so' when they start to succumb to the feline's obvious charms.

With all this in mind, my situation goes from strength to strength. He hasn't sneezed for some time now and recently he forgot to show complete disgust when Mangus licked him. He has read *Cat Confidential* (my first book) from cover to cover and I honestly think my little Devon Rex is grinding him down. Time will tell.

CHAPTER 6

How To Love Your Nervous Cat

I have received hundreds of calls over the past ten years asking for advice about nervous or timid cats. All the owners are experiencing problems with visits to the vet, medicating and the general day-to-day practicalities of dealing with a cat who will only be touched under very specific conditions. These are the cats who won't be picked up and whose response to approaches from humans is fuelled by adrenalin; they either escape as far away as possible, freeze (and occasionally wet themselves), or fight with teeth and claws with or without prior warning. Even the latter group are not aggressive cats by nature; they are scared and their chosen strategy for dealing with such danger is to remove the obstacle as swiftly and efficiently as possible. If you ever approach a cat who is low to the ground with its ears back and dilated pupils it is probably a very frightened pussy. If you ignore the warning you do so at your peril and merely reinforce the cat's belief that all humans are bad news.

Persistently timid cats are probably born that way to a degree. A cat's personality is a complicated mix of genetics and experience but if you are born scared the best early socialization in the world will probably still leave you hooked on routine as an adult and frightened of anything vaguely challenging. It is safe to say that the ones who hide from you are best avoided when you first go to view a litter of kittens, particularly if you are looking for a laid-back lap cat. The most significant period in a cat's behavioural development is between the ages of two and seven or eight weeks. If they are not exposed to positive contact with humans at this time (as is the case with most feral cats) they will grow to be suspicious of them and often extremely fearful. Given the right contact later, however, it is entirely possible to re-educate them to the delights of human company, providing a great deal of patience and careful handling is employed.

Whilst some are born that way other nervous cats are created over time by over-zealous or over-anxious owners. These are the ones who can be worked with and manipulated by changing the human's signalling and behaviour, which can have very rewarding outcomes for all concerned. However, even if your cat was born timid there are still strategies that can be adopted to make life as easy as possible. My own scaredy-cat Spooky lived with me for ten years after being rescued as a young adult from a local sanctuary. She was still scared of many things when she died but I can honestly say that the list was considerably shorter than when we first met.

Not all nervous cats benefit just from interactive changes. Some bypass the significance of the human/cat relationship totally and focus on the environment to fuel their fears and phobias. A letter I received several years ago from a cat owner perfectly illustrates the importance of the right environment to many individuals: *She was always very nervous and could never be persuaded to go outside. She never stayed in the same room as the family although she was quite affectionate with me. In fact, she has spent most of her life behind the boiler, under beds and in all other sorts of nooks and crannies she can find. The ring of the door bell signalling a visitor would have her dementedly looking for a safe place to hide! Yet ... since moving to our present house, three years ago, Twiggy has undergone major behavioural changes! She now stays in the same room (on the settee), almost tolerates visitors, is reluctant to move even when I vacuum and this summer has spent a great deal of time in the garden – asks to go out in fact.* If all else fails for you and your nervous cat you could always consider moving house!

The next few stories concern several aspects of nervousness; I hope they help by giving a better understanding of the pressure we sometimes put these cats under.

Daisy – a case of unrequited love

Lower urinary tract disease can become a real problem for persistently anxious cats. Some individuals seem to be predisposed to contracting cystitis when stress levels are high. Many progressive vets will now recommend appropriate diets and medication but also focus on behaviour therapy to address the necessary lifestyle changes. These problems usually occur in cycles so if stress triggers are removed it is possible to have a symptom-free life. I visited Daisy and her owner, Mark, for just this reason. Daisy was a little middle-aged black and white cat who had been diagnosed with idiopathic cystitis (this is a term used for a condition that is believed to be stress-related in combination with other factors) and was receiving the necessary treatment. Her major symptom had been blood in her urine but it was because she urinated on her owner's bed or on the carpet that the vet recommended a visit from me to see what was wrong with her world.

Mark was a lovely, enthusiastic and caring, if somewhat untidy, entomologist. He lived in a small two-bedroom flat with two friends, Tony and Brian. This did make things rather crowded but the sofa in the living room doubled up as a bed at the relevant times and they all seemed to rub along together without too much trouble. Daisy had lived in a number of places over the years since Mark left university and he had always felt that she adapted well. She spent most of her time asleep but she did enjoy attention from Mark, providing he waited for her to ask for it. He was very sympathetic to her needs and he had soon worked out that if he went to her he got a scratch; if she came to him the interaction was tender and meaningful. She had been suffering from cystitis, on and off, for a year and Mark knew when she was ill because she started to pee on his bed. During the consultation I asked to see his bedroom since I understood that all her physical needs (food, water, litter tray) were being met within this small room. Two things struck me when I entered his domain: first the smell and second that every available piece of floor space had been filled and I couldn't work out where my feet were supposed to go as I walked in. I asked Mark, as diplomatically as possible, how he coped with the eye-melting stench of ammonia from Daisy's indiscretions. Poor Mark had got to the stage where he couldn't smell it any more. I'm still not quite sure whether that is a good or a bad place to be if you ever have friends round but I accepted that, in the circumstances, Mark was fortunate.

When we left his bedroom, Mark added that there was another issue he would like advice on. Brian completely ignored Daisy and caused her no problems whatsoever but Tony was a big cat lover. Sadly Daisy hated Tony with a passion and attacked him on sight or peed on his bed whenever she got the chance. Could I make her like him more? Tony did actually appear at this point and explained that he constantly tried to talk to her and stroke her but ended up battered by paws and claws every single time. Daisy spent as little time as possible in the communal part of the flat, focusing instead on the crowded sanctuary that was Mark's bedroom.

Idiopathic cystitis is a relatively common problem in the modern cat and one discussed at some length in both my previous books, *Cat Confidential* and *Cat Detective*. The origins of the disease are still poorly understood but stress plays a significant role in triggering episodes of painful urination. Cat behaviour therapists work alongside veterinary surgeons to address the individual's specific hangups in an attempt to ensure that stress factors are kept to a minimum. When I am called upon to investigate these cases I tend to look at several predetermined aspects of the cat's life. Together with diet and lifestyle the most common problems are other cats, access to acceptable toilet facilities (indoors or out) and human/cat relationships. In Daisy's case we could discount the impact of other cats because she was fortunate enough to have a place of her own. The toilet facilities were certainly a problem. Mark had dutifully positioned a small tray in the only available space between the bedside table and the wall. In order to use this comfortably Daisy had to approach in first gear and leave in reverse or vice versa. There was no room to turn round or generally scrape about; yet the fact that it was full to bursting when I visited was testimony to her determination to use this unsuitable latrine as often as possible. The rest of the room was full with the bed, Daisy's food and water, a scratching post, Mark's shoes, CDs, books and dirty clothes. Hardly surprising that floor space was somewhat lacking or that Daisy found urinating on the bed more comfortable when her bladder was playing up. This was an obvious problem and one that needed sorting as soon as possible.

There was, however, another issue that I felt was causing Daisy some grief. I don't think we should ever underestimate the stress caused to cats by unwanted human attention. Many people just have to touch and hug all cats irrespective of whether or not the pleasure is mutual. Not all cats are made the same and some just don't understand the clumsy way we communicate. It can even be perceived as threatening, hence Daisy's defensive aggression whenever Tony approached and her avoidance of him whenever possible. Could this be as troubling for Daisy as her inadequate toilet facilities?

I discussed the problem diplomatically with Mark. It was clear that he had a great rapport with his cat and the relationship had blossomed because he had respected her personal space and her desire for solitude at times. He understood the limitations of his bedroom and acknowledged the fact that he had often seen Daisy backing out of the litter tray. He also mentioned that she cried and sniffed at it for a while and paced round before using it; quite understandable in the circumstances. I hate to come between a man and his bedroom clutter but things had to change. It was an accepted fact that Daisy needed to be catered for within the confines of his one room so drastic measures were required. I suggested the use of plastic storage containers and we devised a plan for some serious de-cluttering; it was not the first time that I have suggested a 'home makeover'. Minimalistic homes can be a nightmare for cats (so little stimulation) but there is a compromise between that and complete chaos. All Mark's stuff was placed in stacking boxes and arranged in a compact, albeit tall, column in the corner. The bedside table was removed and replaced with a shelf unit attached to the wall to house his alarm clock and various bits and pieces. Daisy's food bowl and water were placed on the deep window sill where she enjoyed sitting watching the road outside. This left the carpet exposed at the bottom of the bed for the very first time. We placed one new large open tray against the wall at the end of the bed and one in the original location. A nice fine-grain litter substrate replaced the original granules and the bedroom/Daisy's room was complete.

We then turned our attention to Tony, who was a little miffed that he had read the situation so badly and potentially caused Daisy so much angst. I asked him to ignore her for the agreed period of two weeks as an experiment to judge the impact of this lack of attention. If Daisy seemed to respond positively we would adopt it as a strategy for life. I was asking Tony to go about his business without talking to, touching or making eye contact with Daisy. If she should make a sociable approach (miracles do happen) he was asked to acknowledge her briefly and enjoy the opportunity to cohabit rather than manhandle.

I left the boys' flat with high hopes for Daisy's recovery. Mark, Tony and Brian were enthusiastic young men and they appeared to be taking the responsibility for Daisy's well-being extremely seriously. After two weeks I received a call from Mark to relate a miraculous improvement. Mark's bedroom had been transformed into an oasis of calm with spacious trays for Daisy's ablutions. The bedding, duvet and mattress had been cleaned according to my instructions to remove the offensive odour of past indiscretions. Tony and Brian reported that their eyes no longer watered as they passed Mark's door so I figured this was a good sign. Tony, in the meantime, had taken to his challenge well and had ignored Daisy completely. After a mere four days Daisy started to venture back into the living room and seemed content to sit some distance away from the boys observing their interaction. Since my visit Daisy had used both trays consistently and spent a great deal of time spinning round, digging and manoeuvring just for the hell of it.

It's impossible to judge how significant Tony's role was in Daisy's stress but it was quite clear that a change in behaviour coincided with a chilled and sociable cat. Daisy is still thriving in her tiny world with, as far as I know, no further urinary tract problems.

Saphie and Minnie – the nervous ferals

Andrea was a busy working woman in her early thirties who had always loved cats. When she left her family home she took her beloved Alfred, a tabby moggy of considerable stature, with her. He had been her constant and loyal companion for seven glorious years until, at the age of seventeen, he became ill and was peacefully put to sleep. Andrea was bereft; she had no idea how she would cope with the loss. She felt terribly alone but was completely unable to take in another cat since that would surely be an act of betrayal. Eventually, after two years, she decided that the time was right to look for further feline company. As a tribute to Alfred she wanted to give a home to a cat (or cats) who really needed a chance in life. Maybe a little mite whom nobody wanted and would otherwise be neglected and face an uncertain future. She visited a local London cat charity that specialized in 'rehabilitating' feral cats. Andrea chose two sisters, ten-week-old kittens who had been captured together with a number of others from an area behind a disused building. Andrea was so motivated by her desire to rescue, reform and rehabilitate that she took little notice of the fact that she couldn't touch them. She also disregarded the hissing and spitting and wide-eyed look of fear from both of them as she stared at them through the bars of the cage; such was the nature of her conviction.

She took the kittens (now named Saphie and Minnie) home to her one-bedroom ground-floor flat with its pretty walled courtyard at the back. She had decided that it was best for the kittens to live exclusively indoors; that way she could protect them and nurture them and keep them from harm. Their first few weeks of life had been harsh and she felt that her flat would represent a safe haven of warmth and security. Sadly things did not go quite as expected when she got home. For two months the furry duo holed up behind her cupboard units in the kitchen. Quite how they found the impossibly small hole was a mystery to Andrea but she had to leave the entry point open because they only came out when she was out or fast asleep. She was beginning to feel that the rewards of feral rehabilitation were rather few and far between; she was spending a fortune on food and litter for two cats she never saw. Many of her friends suspected that she had been working too hard and the cats were merely a figment of her imagination.

After the first couple of months there was a break-through. Saphie and Minnie left the apparent sanctuary of the gap behind the kitchen cupboard in the early hours of one morning and moved their lair to the even smaller gap behind Andrea's bed. She was thrilled; this had to be a major step forward and an obvious gesture of trust towards their new custodian. I'm afraid I saw it rather more as the only other small and inaccessible place in the flat but I was happy to bow to Andrea's interpretation of that one. For a further six months they maintained their routine of activity when Andrea was out (the evidence was everywhere that a good time was had by all when she was at work) or asleep in bed. The rest of the time they remained entwined behind the headboard. By the end of the first year both kittens (now well over a year old) were moving about the flat in Andrea's presence. They were, however, still jumping at the slightest sound and continuing to resist her advances. Saphie would just about tolerate a light touch under the chin when Andrea was lying quietly in bed but Minnie was not having any of it.

Andrea had made slow progress but she felt she had reached a plateau and she asked her vet for a referral to me to see if I could shed any light on her apparent failure. The first thing that struck me when I met Andrea was her enormous energy. She spoke extraordinarily rapidly and loudly and moved around her flat as if she was in an incredible hurry. By the end of the first hour in her presence I was feeling distinctly uptight myself. I saw nothing of Saphie and Minnie during my visit apart from a sneaky glimpse as I knelt on her bed and leant over the headboard. I always tell people not to disturb cats in their private hiding places but I made an exception that day; Andrea was keen for me to see how beautiful they were and she wasn't the sort of person to take no for an answer. None of her friends and visitors had ever seen the cats, apart from in photographs, so she really wanted me to be the first of many.

I praised Andrea's patience and tenacity in trying to resolve her dilemma but I felt that a new and different approach was needed to get the two sisters to the next level of their introduction to the delights of domestic life. The two cats had by now become accustomed to Andrea's presence. After a year this was inevitable. However, Andrea oozed anxiety with a slight hint of panic, and this must have created an atmosphere of constant tension and potential danger when she was around. If Andrea was frightened then the cats probably felt their best strategy was to remain behind the headboard until things quietened down. That is undoubtedly why she made the most positive progress when she was relaxed and lying in bed. Saphie and Minnie needed to experience more; they needed more input into their lives to challenge them and encourage them to do all the things cats should be doing. They were certainly entertaining themselves in the hours of darkness and when the house was empty but we needed to introduce some sort of activity that was so enjoyable they were even prepared to do it when Andrea was in the room.

I persuaded Andrea to invest in a system to secure her little walled courtyard. It was full of exciting plants and insects and would undoubtedly provide enormous stimulation for the two cats. Andrea had always been worried about the danger of the cats getting out and disappearing for good so this seemed like a compromise she could actually live with. We also talked about making them forage and explore for their biscuits rather than receiving them in a boring bowl. With the aid of forty-two cardboard toilet-roll tubes, donated by friends, family and colleagues, Andrea constructed two pyramid-shaped feeding units (the design is described in my previous book, *Cat Detective*). These would contain a random scattering of biscuits and each cat would then have to use their paws to extract the biscuits once discovered. This would entertain whilst promoting self-confidence when a meal was acquired as a result of their initiative and skill. We talked about a number of other sources of stimulation such as modular climbing centres, water features and toys but I was yet to discuss the most important element of the whole programme: Andrea herself. She really wasn't giving off the right vibes and if she wanted to communicate with them physically she needed to change her methodology. The insistent voice and staring eyes would have to go, together with the outstretched hands and the tendency to crawl towards them across the floor. We had to make her look so attractive that they would decide for themselves that she was completely irresistible and worthy of exploration.

I asked Andrea to take time out every evening to relax and meditate. It would not only be good for her as a stress-buster at the end of the day but the cats would find her demeanour much more endearing at these times. I told her to avoid direct eye contact or approaches and to speak in a softer and gentler voice. I suggested she call them 'beautiful' by accentuating all the syllables in a calm voice whilst slowly blinking her eyes. This word, for some reason, can have a hypnotic effect on some cats and I thought it might be a good discipline for Andrea to avoid her usual rapid-fire speech that the cats found so threatening. Special highly palatable titbits of ham or prawns would be used as a bribe to encourage approaches; Andrea was to introduce the concept of exciting and novel foods by placing small amounts in a bowl once a day. Once they appeared to relish the new experience, Andrea would sit or lie on the floor (or bed) with an outstretched open hand (containing a goody) and then stare into space in anticipation of a little furry mouth approaching and gobbling up the tasty treat. We would then build on this until they were brave enough to take the titbit directly from her hand in close proximity to her body. Play was another important part of the bonding process and I encouraged her to use fishing-rod toys to enable the game to be enjoyed at a safe distance.

Andrea was extremely encouraged that at last she had a plan that sounded hopeful. I went away and suggested she take a while to get all the new routines established and then call me for a chat. What a wonderful woman! She called me ten days later, having put into action all my recommendations, and her first report showed some early improvement. The courtyard had been secured and that very day she had allowed both cats out to explore in the evening. The previous owner of the flat had already installed a cat flap so I encouraged Andrea not to worry if she couldn't get them in. Propping the cat flap slightly open for a couple of days would be sufficient to teach them the entry point. All the play and feeding regimes had been adopted and Saphie had already taken a prawn from her flattened and outstretched hand (poor Andrea had lain there for a whole hour before she did).

By the fifth week Andrea had become fairly interesting at last. She had taken to the 'ignoring' stuff very well and she was delighted to report that both Saphie and Minnie had started sleeping on her bed. This was wonderful news and Andrea was overjoyed. I continued to support Andrea beyond the usual eight weeks because progress was being made on a weekly basis and I wasn't going to miss any of it! By the time we had got to the fifth month the two were going in and out of the courtyard constantly, being stroked by Andrea daily and continuing to sleep on her bed as a nightly ritual. As we agreed to part company since Andrea was happy to go it alone, the final report came through. Both Saphie and Minnie had come into the room when Andrea had a visitor as if they had been doing it all their lives.

I always feel that the task of taking on a feral cat is fraught with danger and complications. I'm not sure there is much in it for either party since a domestic life can be stressful for those not accustomed to the ways of humans or the sense of restriction. However, if the cats in question are young kittens, then, with a great deal of patience and gentle determination, they can make reasonable pets.

Sophocles and Demetrius – learning fear the Burmese way

Fear is contagious and few cases illustrate this point better than that of Sophocles and Demetrius. They were eighteen-month-old brothers: handsome, glossy chocolate Burmese. They lived with Jennifer and I visited them after she called me one afternoon to say she had the most dreadful problem. Sophocles and Demetrius had become shuddering wrecks, frightened of their own shadows. Jennifer didn't know what to do for the best; she couldn't understand why such confident youngsters should have become so nervous. Within a week of our conversation I was sitting in her living room being watched by the Burmese equivalent of CCTV as both boys sat hunched on the top of a tall bookcase surveying the mystery stranger in their midst. I tried to ignore them, since this would obviously be kinder than drawing attention to their safe observation point, and listened to Jennifer as she relayed the story of their gradual decline into fearfulness.

She lived in a large ground-floor apartment in a rambling Victorian building in a country village. The road leading to her home was relatively busy but a long sweeping drive approached the house and the rear of the building was surrounded by extensive grounds full of areas of lawn interspersed with thick mature shrubbery. Cat paradise, really, and Demetrius and

Sophocles had enjoyed the first few months after their vaccinations frolicking in the undergrowth. Jennifer, however, was not happy. One of her neighbours had acquired a dog and she was most concerned that one day her boys would meet this beast with terrible consequences (and whilst cocker spaniels are not renowned for killing cats this was clearly a genuine concern for her). She began supervising their excursions outdoors and shepherding them around the garden with an eye constantly on her neighbour's doorway for signs of canine approach. After a while the cats started to pick up on their owner's vibes and became hesitant and twitchy; what was it exactly that she was so frightened of? After a couple of months Jennifer could stand it no more. She made the decision to keep her boys as indoor cats; after all, many breeders recommended this for their safety and well-being and the road outside was very busy and dogs are dangerous creatures . . .

Demetrius and Sophocles remained indoors for the next six months. They destroyed a bit of furniture, they became rather clingy towards Jennifer, but most of all they were vigilant and tense. Jennifer's new worry was how to stimulate them sufficiently to prevent boredom and she devoted a great deal of time and energy to entertaining them. Her demeanour within the flat became rather unusual to say the least. She didn't seem to relax; every day there was a need to ensure she was doing right by her beloved cats. A noisy neighbour coming downstairs, mail coming through the letterbox or a telephone call would send all three of them into orbit. Jennifer was no fool and she realized something was very wrong. She decided to take a huge step and reintroduce the cats to the garden they had previously loved so much. She had actually met her neighbour's cocker spaniel on several occasions since the Burmeses' incarceration and she had been greatly reassured that he was completely harmless. She started to take the boys out on harnesses but the process wasn't particularly successful. She would step out of her door clutching both leads tightly in her hand, and walk slowly and carefully whilst constantly reassuring the cats that all was well and each noise or movement was nothing to worry about. Demetrius and Sophocles, restrained and unable to escape any potential danger, dissolved into two heaps of frozen panic; Jennifer's reassurances merely confirming that danger lurked round every corner. This was not fun and Jennifer understood at this point that she needed help.

I was quick to confirm her suspicions, in the nicest way possible, that Sophocles and Demetrius's fear was a product of her behaviour. The Burmese had become dependent on her for stimulation, entertainment and security, as so often happens when cats are deprived of the ability to behave naturally. Her signals of tension meant danger to them and they were quite happy to hide behind her skirts until the big bad monster was gone.

The solution to this problem was very simple. Jennifer had to let go, relax and accept that the cats were perfectly capable of surviving without her intervention. They would probably, in the circumstances, cope more effectively if they didn't have one eye on their owner to gauge her response to any challenges. I suggested that Sophocles and Demetrius should be allowed outside (without the harnesses) for increasing periods of time every day. Jennifer could go with them but only if she could remain relaxed about the whole thing. She should avoid the temptation to comfort them if they rushed back indoors at the sight of something terrifyingly innocuous; they had to learn that Jennifer was no longer bothered. Cats are not stupid. Many times I have given the advice to 'relax' or 'appear confident' to owners, depending on the problem they are trying to manage. What I should really say is, 'Don't even bother unless you are truly relaxed or confident because you will be sussed immediately.' Owners don't realize that if they fake it they just look ridiculous to their pets (and to the trained eye of a cat behaviour counsellor!), appearing to walk and talk like a dodgy automaton. It has to be genuine and that can sometimes be extraordinarily tough.

Jennifer was made of strong stuff and she counselled herself quietly over the next few days to ensure she was *truly* relaxed before the boys ventured outdoors. She let them out first when teatime was approaching, always a good ploy to ensure they had half a mind on food rather than lengthy exploration of the great outdoors. She opened the door in an absent-minded fashion and casually deadheaded a few roses before sauntering in and awaiting the results of this first experiment. I'm sure I would have been proud of her had I been there. She spied on the cats discreetly through the kitchen window and watched as they crept from bush to bush with their bellies on the ground. Not exactly bold and brassy but it was a start. She shook the biscuit box shortly afterwards (she wasn't sure how long she would remain '*truly* relaxed') and the boys galloped in. They looked a little chunkier and more masculine that evening; Jennifer even described them as strutting around the flat for a change. It's amazing what a little bit of 'owner manipulation' will do to a cat's psyche! Sophocles and Demetrius (and Jennifer) went from strength to strength and all three are now happily and casually spending time outdoors at will. Jennifer has continued to encourage her cats to be self-reliant and they are blossoming into the cocky Burmese that they were always meant to be.

Flower – the cat who was scared of thunderstorms

There are several ways that we can get it wrong as owners of anxious cats; here is another example. Kathy and Andrew had a little cat called Flower; she was three years old when I met her. She had lived with the couple from a kitten but she had always been timid and jumpy. She had taken to Kathy immediately and often spent her waking time in her company. Andrew had fitted a cat flap to the back door so that she could go outside during the day when the couple were at work. Instead, she mainly chose to sleep during the day and get Kathy to open the back door in the evening so that she could have her constitutional. Kathy and Andrew began by shutting Flower into the spacious kitchen/diner at night but she started to scratch at the door and pick at the carpet. Kathy felt it was probably cruel to shut her in if she was unhappy so she got up one morning at 2 a.m. to let her out and never confined her again.

Flower had never liked storms or sudden noises and Kathy would always comfort her if she heard a loud bang. During storms she would rock Flower in her arms or cover her with a blanket to make her feel safe. A couple of months before my visit there had been a violent storm and Kathy had decided to take Flower into the bedroom with her and Andrew to comfort her. Since then Flower had gone to Kathy every night to tread up and down on her, miaow and purr and generally disrupt any sleep that was going on at the time. Kathy was worried about Andrew (he needed his sleep to function) and she ended up spending her nights on the sofa with Flower curled up on her chest to ensure that Andrew wasn't disturbed. Needless to say this was not a good strategy as Flower had started to get Kathy up several times in the night for entertainment, food or whatever took her fancy. It soon became clear why poor Kathy looked so tired. She would get up in the morning feeling terrible just as Flower settled down for a good day's sleep after a night of frenzied activity.

There were two problems here. First, Flower had a 'topsy-turvy' sleep/wake cycle that needed to change. Second (and most important), all that reassurance and comfort had turned Flower into a dependent creature totally reliant on Kathy for everything. Not content with being totally reliant on her owner she had also developed incredibly effective attention-seeking behaviour that turned Kathy into one enormous toy and source of entertainment. You can't blame Flower for being clever and working this out as a good strategy. We had to argue 'more fool Kathy' for giving in to it.

Kathy could see the error of her ways but she had the age-old notion that if she didn't do what Flower said then her little cat wouldn't love her any more. *This is a myth!* I bargained with Kathy and said that we would try it my way for a month and if it didn't work I would admit I was wrong. I did diplomatically point out that something had to change and we were actually stuck for any better ideas. The principle behind ignoring this type of attention-seeking behaviour is that succumbing to it isn't in the best interests of the cat. The more they get, the more they want, and it becomes quite stressful to keep pushing for extra (this is covered in more detail in Chapter 8). If Kathy withdrew from the relationship and encouraged Flower to be independent, things would definitely improve for everyone.

I asked Kathy to shut her bedroom door at night. We attached a spare piece of carpet to the area near the door so that any inevitable scratching could be ignored. Kathy and Andrew had to remain steadfast; any screaming for attention at night should be completely ignored. Relenting after several days because they couldn't stand it any more would be the worst thing that could happen. I suggested earplugs as an appropriate measure during the initial period of adjustment. The guest bedroom was made alluring with a radiator hammock and a small bowl of dry food to encourage Flower to rest in there for a change. Kathy would stop opening the back door for Flower and once again go through the cat-flap training to ensure she got the message. Any storms in future would be completely ignored and Kathy and Andrew would go about their business as if nothing was happening. This is always a far more effective approach than reassurance; that merely shows the cat that she is perfectly right to be afraid.

A letter received eight weeks later read . . . *just to let you know that Flower is fine. She's used to the cat flap and has not bothered us at night. She also seems more confident. She spends a great deal of time outside and has lost some weight and is much more active.* It's amazing what a little healthy neglect can do.

❊   ❊   ❊

I will probably continue to receive countless calls about nervous cats. Things can be done, as you have seen, to make life as comfortable as possible but there will always be problems. Whenever I speak to owners I caution them about expecting too much from their charges. These leopards rarely change their spots completely.

Tackling anxiety by changing the relationship

- Do not make direct eye contact; view your cat out of the corner of your eye or under half-closed lids. Blinking slowly signals sociability and lack of aggressive intent.

- Avoid outstretched hands since, like a raised paw, this can appear threatening.
- Talk normally in the presence of your cat since hushed voices can signal your own tension and anxiety and these emotions are contagious.
- Speak to your cat in a gentle voice with a slightly higher pitch than normal.
- Use your voice in this way when producing food and interacting in a positive way.
- Avoid direct approaches since this signals a challenge and potential danger; even if you are just intending to walk past your cat, try to take a less direct route.
- Discover what motivates your cat (play, toys, food, titbits) and use these to create positive associations with you.
- Provide safe hiding places where your cat can seek sanctuary and don't disturb him whilst he is resting there.
- Do not reassure a nervous cat since this can reinforce the fear and make your cat too dependent on you as a minder.
- Touch your cat gently, initially for short periods during feeding or play. Avoid vulnerable areas such as the belly and legs at all costs and focus round the cheeks and chin initially.

The sad tale of Billy

Despite the fact that we are focusing on the benefits of changing our relationship with our cats when tackling nervousness I have to remind everyone of an important point. There is still no substitute for veterinary involvement since behaviour is all too often influenced by pain or disease. I want to tell you the sad story of Billy. Billy's owner, Angie, called me one evening last year, having been given my name and contact details by her vet. She was exceedingly upset because, subsequent to a visit to the local cattery, Billy's personality had changed dramatically. He was a seven-year-old moggy and he had previously been the model pet. He was confident and affectionate, playful and passive with the neighbour's cats, home-loving and talkative. He had a companion at home, Ted, a young neutered male, with whom he had a reasonable relationship. He hadn't been thrilled when the kitten arrived and had become a little quieter generally, but on the whole they played together, groomed each other and could often be found resting in close proximity to each other.

In January of that year the two cats had visited the cattery for one week whilst Angie and her husband went on holiday. When they collected the cats Angie noticed that Billy looked distinctly cross: his pupils were dilated and he was growling quietly. The couple just thought he was angry about being left, but when they got him home he was ravenously hungry yet too weak to jump onto the work surface in the kitchen. He seemed very nervous, so Angie took him to the veterinary clinic where they gave him antibiotics and a painkiller despite being rather nonplussed about the nature of his complaint. A blood test showed nothing diagnostic and by the end of the week Billy seemed to be more like his old self. Then, approximately a week later, he woke in the night in a very agitated state; he alerted Angie and her husband with his loud stressful cries and he appeared to be terrified, running round looking for places to hide in his frantic attempts to escape whatever was frightening him.

The veterinary practice recommended that they separate Ted from Billy as they felt that there must have been some social problems during their stay in the cattery. During the next two weeks Billy had good days and bad days; he would fluctuate between normal behaviour and apparent terror at the sight of Angie or her husband. He seemed to have lost all confidence in jumping up or down and he seemed clumsy. He even wet himself one morning when Angie approached him. Further blood tests for feline leukaemia virus (FeLV), feline immuno-deficiency virus (FIV) and feline infectious peritonitis (FIP) all proved negative. Billy continued to miaow mournfully at the windows and his restless pacing was interspersed with moments of complete panic.

By the fourth week the finger of suspicion was still pointed at Billy's companion so Ted was placed in the cattery for a week to see if his removal impacted on Billy's state of mind. There was no significant change and his return a week later was met with curiosity rather than anything particularly negative. Week five saw a further deterioration as Billy urinated and defecated at the sight of his owners. The vet had prescribed amitriptyline (a potent tricyclic antidepressant) and Billy had seemed a little more alert and receptive to contact and affection. This was when I stepped in and, after careful examination of the facts, I was reluctant to accept that this was a behavioural problem. I informed Angie that I was on the case but wanted to discuss things with colleagues before committing her time and money to a behavioural consultation.

The man I always go to when confronted with this sort of case is a retired veterinary surgeon and practising pet behaviour counsellor called Robin Walker. The man is truly a genius and there is little he doesn't know, in my opinion. Having seen the history so far he set off down the road of a physiological rather than psychological diagnosis and mentioned a possible differential of Key-Gaskell syndrome (dysautonomia). This is a comparatively rare condition but I could certainly see where he was coming from. He also suggested trauma to the head causing a brain injury and I was of a similar opinion at that stage.

I persuaded Angie to see a specialist; I didn't want to delay any diagnosis by visiting and looking for behavioural motivation without checking all the medical options first. Billy continued to behave very strangely, waking her in the night and seeming to want her to follow him and then stopping at the top of the stairs and howling. The specialist did tests for liver function and blood parasites. He informed Angie that the next stage was an MRI scan. He had been worried about Billy's crouched movement; Angie had interpreted this as fear but it can also indicate a problem with the brain.

By week seven the vets were fluctuating between a neurological and a behavioural diagnosis. Angie was still convinced that the kitten and the cattery stay were instrumental in Billy's current problem but as his condition deteriorated she was persuaded by one of the vets to sanction the MRI scan. Four days later Billy had the scan and, hey presto, a tumour approximately two inches in diameter was found behind his eye socket. The specialist felt sure that the condition was operable since the tumour was benign and very accessible. He had performed many such operations before so Angie took Billy to the surgery with high hopes for a complete recovery. Sadly, Billy didn't survive the surgery; the removal of the tumour went well but Billy never regained consciousness. I didn't meet Billy during the three weeks that I was involved in his case but his passing distressed me greatly. Sometimes it seems so logical that behavioural changes occur as a direct result of a bad experience. Fear in cats is always considered to be a valid response to danger, even if the threat is perceived rather than actual. However, in Billy's case the fear was mechanical, resulting from abnormal brain responses due to the pressure of the tumour. And the only really apparent symptom of his condition was the fear.

CHAPTER 7

How To Love Your Aggressive Cat

Anyone who has never experienced cat aggression at first hand would be dismissive. They would marvel that anyone could be frightened or intimidated by such a small creature. There speaks the voice of ignorance; I have a healthy respect for all felines because I know they are capable of great things, regardless of their size. Nature has equipped the cat with a formidable arsenal of weapons. They have razor-sharp teeth in powerful jaws and claws that can disembowel a rabbit (nasty thought, but true). I have seen injuries inflicted on grown men that look more like the result of an argument with a lawnmower.

Aggression is very much part of the cat's survival strategy. It is required for feeding, defence of territory and sex. How naive of us to believe that we can wipe out such a fundamental drive just by inviting cats into our homes. To a certain extent we are acceptant of predatory behaviour and fighting with the neighbour's cat, and we usually neuter our pets so the sex thing ceases to be an issue. Why then are we surprised when they occasionally turn on us? The reason lies in our misunderstanding of the relationship.

Not all cats have had the benefit of a domestic upbringing where socialization has taken place at the earliest opportunity to enable the individual to form positive associations with humans. This learning process shows the kitten how humans express non-threatening sociability; we gaze longingly into its eyes, we embrace it and stroke it. To the uninitiated these acts of love appear to be nothing more than acts of aggression. They feel they have no alternative but to escape, freeze in abject terror or fight. Combine that basic misinterpretation of signals with a restrictive and boring lifestyle and you have the recipe for disaster.

All is not lost since certain expressions of aggression from our cats are easily defused by changing our role in the owner/cat relationship. Following the simplest of rules and developing an understanding of feline etiquette will get the most amazing results. Here are three tales of owners and cats who, sadly, got it wrong.

Wickham – the wicked dictator in a leopard-skin coat

My first contact with Charlotte was a tearful and desperate telephone call. I should point out that she was the one who was crying but, with hindsight, given my knowledge of the case now, it ought to have been me. All was not well in her house and she fretfully told me her sorry tale. She lived with her parents, John and Margaret, and an elderly Labrador called Fred. She had recently returned to the family home to live and she felt the need to have her very own pet that she could love and nurture. She had always been crazy about cats but she didn't want just 'any old thing'. She researched her breeds carefully and eventually decided on the Bengal as being the most suitable for her needs. She understood the breed to be sociable, outgoing, intelligent and dog-like. They are also blessed with the most extraordinary good looks so it wasn't difficult to fall in love with a young male kitten at a local breeder's home. She called him Wickham (she felt something 'Austen-esque' would be appropriate for someone so handsome) and brought him home. All went well and Charlotte, John, Margaret and Fred soon found themselves living with a rumbustious leopard-spotted bundle of energy and fun. He would leap on Fred's back, rugby-tackle human feet and survey his domain from the comfort of the top of the sitting room's velvet curtains. He had great entertainment value and friends and family would visit from far and wide to see him perform.

As he grew he started to venture outdoors and experience all the thrills and spills of neighbourly disputes and territorial spats. Charlotte and her family were vaguely amused to discover that, for all his energy and tough-guy behaviour indoors, he was the local wimp when it came to fighting. He would often burst through the cat flap at colossal speed to seek solace in Charlotte's arms as an angry tabby moggy pressed his face against the flap, only stopping short at the sight of the menacing large black Labrador within.

Charlotte couldn't really say when things started to go wrong. However it happened, the household relationships had taken a sinister twist. Wickham's boisterous assertiveness indoors had changed into something far more menacing. The bouncing on Fred and the foot-chewing had developed into genuine aggression, accompanied by a 'devil-cat' countenance that sent shivers down the spines of all who saw it. Fred had been threatened and intimidated to such an extent that he had been held against his will in the kitchen, afraid to venture anywhere for fear of injury from Wickham's teeth and claws. Every member of the family had at some stage been a victim of his controlling and malevolent behaviour. John and Margaret were unable to enter the kitchen without repeatedly feeding Wickham tasty snacks to avoid assault. The dog bed, best chair in the house, computer keyboard and anything else remotely significant in his eyes were now under his control. Wickham had achieved a *coup d'état* and Charlotte's household was now governed by a small spotted mammal.

I had visited many homes in my career which were being ruled with a rod of iron by the family cat. I had a healthy respect for such creatures (they really are scary) but an even healthier respect for my reputation as a fearless pioneer in the face of any feline dilemma. Whilst travelling to Charlotte's home I determined to let Wickham know that I wasn't taking any nonsense from him. Armed with only my trusty briefcase and a pair of stout ankle boots for protection, I entered the house.

My first sight of Wickham (purely from the corner of my eye; I wouldn't give him the satisfaction of an acknowledgement) was of a beautiful leopard-spotted creature lying curled up on an oversized bed by the radiator in the living room. I knew immediately that this used to be Fred's favourite spot. My heart melted as a sad black face peered through the glass door from the kitchen, almost pleading with me to return him to his rightful place in his soft, warm basket. Patience,

Fred, patience. I sat down on a chair adjacent to the dog's old bed and explained to the family that, during the consultation and for a very good reason, I would not be acknowledging Wickham. I always feel it's important to point this out because nobody likes a stranger to appear dismissive of their pet.

As I took notes I watched Charlotte, John and Margaret as their eyes constantly flicked towards Wickham lying nonchalantly on his new throne. Then something happened. Wickham rose and stretched and looked across the room at John sitting in his favourite armchair. John immediately got up and walked slowly towards the fireplace, where he stood rather awkwardly with his hands thrust deep in his pockets. Wickham walked purposefully towards John's chair and jumped up. He circled a few times before flopping into the delightful embrace of a newly vacated warm cushion. I had to say something, so queried, 'John, what happened just then?' John replied that he knew Wickham wanted his seat since it had become his favourite chair and that if he hadn't relinquished ownership he would undoubtedly have been attacked. I was outraged. I walked confidently towards Wickham and gently but firmly pushed him off the chair. Wickham looked completely dumbfounded and was obviously too shocked to retaliate (fortunately). John, however, looked petrified and in the true tradition of any victim of cat bullying was extremely reluctant to re-establish himself in the chair for fear of future reprisals. I promised that I would protect him whilst I was there and that it was important he reclaimed his chair. Wickham returned to the dog bed and washed himself in a rather distracted fashion.

After much discussion I explained to Charlotte and her family why their cat had become such a monster. Wickham had a very particular kind of personality; he was acutely aware of territory and the need to patrol and defend it outdoors. Sadly his attempts (unusually for a Bengal) were failing miserably and he often retreated to the comparative safety of the home for solace. However, another element of his character didn't really get the whole 'human-loves-cat-loves-human' thing. Everywhere he went within the house he was the focus of their attention. In cat parlance this spells trouble, and he found it quite distressing, particularly once he matured socially and started to understand his role in life. In frustration he started to lash out and soon learnt that this actually enabled him to control the actions and movements of these annoying people. At least he could be boss at home even if he couldn't cut it outside. Contrary to his owners' opinion, though, Wickham wasn't that happy with this new regime and he constantly paced or sat with his tail swishing furiously. If only they would just leave him alone!

All the members of the family were listening

carefully. I was delighted to have such an attentive audience so launched into a plan of action straight away. We had to return control to the mortgage payers and demote Wickham to the lowly position of family pet. Whilst this sounded great in theory there was the slight practical complication that all members of the household, including Fred, were terrified of said family pet. I explained that the key was attitude – positive mental attitude is the phrase, I believe. They had to sit, walk and talk with confidence and ignore Wickham's posturing and aggressive threats. If the confidence was there he wouldn't strike; cats only attack in these circumstances if they can safely predict the outcome. I had proved this time and time again when visiting aggressive cats but it is the hardest thing in the world to convince the owners that such defiance is in their best interests. We needed a secret weapon, something that would automatically make them feel brave. Margaret and Charlotte were horsey ladies with serious no-nonsense, nothing-scares-me attitudes when it came to all matters equine, so I encouraged them to adopt a similar approach to their relationship with Wickham. I emphasized the point that he wouldn't strike if they moved around the house as if he didn't exist and they seemed satisfied that I could be trusted. They promised to walk around with their heads high and a generally dismissive air of slight contempt for everything. It made them look a bit daft but it would work wonders.

John was a different matter. He had unfortunately adopted the persona of a particularly submissive Uriah Heep and his whole body language screamed apology and humility. He may have been a retired high court judge but his demeanour now certainly didn't reflect such eminence. John was an intelligent and forceful character who had been completely deflated by a small spotted creature only twelve inches tall. I wouldn't dream of deriding him for it, since there but for the grace of God goes any one of us. He had been attacked and intimidated so many times that he couldn't even enter a room if Wickham didn't want him to. Advising him to be 'dismissive' just wouldn't work. I therefore suggested various techniques that might help him to feel more confident and less vulnerable to Wickham's inevitable attacks. We eventually agreed on shin pads, stout shoes and motorcycle gloves (anyone who has read *Cat Confidential* will probably remember my obsession with dressing my clients up in biker gear). This would prevent injury to the main target areas of John's legs and hands. I also suggested a regular feeding regime to avoid the need to give titbits, and various other symbolical gestures to ensure that Wickham got the message.

John was sitting quietly during the latter part of this discussion and I realized that something was worrying him. He felt he needed something a little more substantial than a shin pad or two to deal with the frightening scenario when Wickham came to the door of his study and blocked his exit. We settled on a devious plan. There was one thing within the house that Wickham feared: the vacuum cleaner. It was agreed that the appliance would be stored in John's study in future and any attempts by Wickham to block his exit would result in a sudden desire to do a bit of cleaning. This would undoubtedly take the wind out of Wickham's sails and send him running.

Four days went by and I received another tearful phone call from Charlotte. Things were not going well. I must admit I was shocked until I heard the reason. Her father had blatantly refused to do anything. He would not accept that shin pads and a more positive walk could have any impact on a cat who was clearly vicious. I was obviously mad or just plain stupid to believe that such simple and 'airy-fairy' actions would transform his wicked pet. And I thought he liked me! Charlotte was trying very hard and getting some results but Margaret, taking her lead from John, was continuing to behave exactly as before and bickering with her daughter every time the subject was broached. Even Fred was trying harder than his owners! I was stumped. How could I get them to at least try it my way? If it didn't work, *then* they could call me a fool! I asked Charlotte to have another gentle go at talking it through with her mother and suggested that Margaret give me a call.

I heard nothing for several days and made a note on

the file that this was probably not going to work out particularly well without my terrier-like persistence and refusal to let go. I was going to have to be far more persuasive and make sure that they knew I wasn't giving up even if they were. I resolved to leave it a week before becoming proactive and making the phone call myself, but I didn't have to wait that long. On the sixth day I had a phone call from Margaret; John had been attacked again. Margaret and I had a long chat (John wouldn't come to the phone and I didn't press it) and we decided that enough was enough. Margaret finally relented and agreed that my methods were worth a try since everything they had done up to that point had been a resounding failure. I asked the six-million-dollar question – what about John? Margaret promised that she would persuade him by fair means or foul to follow the programme for at least a couple of weeks to see what happened. I was delighted; at last Wickham would be off the hook and able to relax in the know-ledge that he was no longer the focus of everyone's attention. The initial frustration would be difficult for him because violent manipulation had been his modus operandi for some time. I was convinced, however, that he would soon learn to relax once he realized that the need for aggression had passed.

I held my breath and waited for the next report. It came a week later and included an interesting twist with an attempted Plan B from Wickham. Suddenly everyone was behaving differently and he was slightly wrong-pawed. Nobody seemed to notice his death stares any more and he was a little confused about his next course of action. A stroke of genius suddenly occurred and he directed his attention to the delicate porcelain and glass ornaments on the shelves in the living room. Surely walking clumsily amongst the Royal Doulton would get a response. It certainly did, and Margaret hurried across the room to rescue her cherished breakables. However (good old Margaret), his further attempt to get her into the kitchen now he had her attention failed. I was thrilled and explained to the family that the only reason he was targeting china and glass was his inability to get their attention any other way. So Wickham's Plan B simply showed that the family had regained the driving seat. The ornaments were immediately removed to the safety of a cupboard and the programme continued with renewed enthusiasm.

During the eighth week I received a phone call to say that a miracle had happened. (There was me thinking it was just an effective behaviour therapy programme!) Wickham had transformed into a quiet and relaxed Bengal. Once the initial frustration resulting from the shift of power had passed, he was able to breathe a sigh of relief and concentrate on being a cat doing his own thing. Fred now strutted his stuff and had regained control of the dog bed in the living room (dogs know when cats lose their edge). All the members of the family had become used to walking confidently and ignoring Wickham, who was now approaching them rather submissively from time to time for a rewarding stroke. John and Margaret admitted they had been wrong but, as I told them, it's hard to embrace the principle that something so dramatic can result from such small changes in behaviour. As we parted company at the end of our programme together I warned the family that they must not get complacent. Cats like Wickham are very beautiful and it's hard to resist the urge to touch, squeeze and stroke. If they reverted to their old 'look at the cute pussycat' ways then Wickham might well revert too. As far as I know he continues to behave impeccably. I wonder if John is still wearing those shin pads?

Whisper – the cat who was squeezed once too often

Monica called me about her cat Whisper. She was extremely distressed after a visit to her vet with her beloved moggy. She was convinced that he had a brain tumour or was extremely sick because he had done the unthinkable twice in one week. He had attacked Monica so viciously, on the first occasion, that she had been a prisoner in her own bathroom until her husband returned to rescue her that evening. She gave me a blow-by-blow account of the incident although, typically after such a frightening and shocking experience, I couldn't really get to grips with the actual facts. I wasn't entirely clear about what led up to the attack or indeed what happened afterwards; it was all a bit garbled. However, it was clear that he 'looked like the devil', 'went all bushed up' and 'screamed' before he lunged at her and bit her leg repeatedly. Nasty. The description of the second attack was equally confusing. He had rushed downstairs on sight of her and she had managed to escape back out of the front door as he slammed against it with his head in his attempts to get to her. More 'screaming' and 'devil eyes' accompanied this incident and he took a while to calm down sufficiently for her to feel safe to enter. The vet had given him a clean bill of health and, observing his apparently normal demeanour in between attacks, felt the problem was behavioural and a matter for me.

I visited Monica as soon as I possibly could, which was four days later. No further attacks had taken place since her phone call but she was staying vigilant. As I approached her driveway she greeted me cheerfully at the door and showed me into her tiny house. It had a small narrow lounge/diner and a separate and compact kitchen. Stairs in the hallway led to a bathroom and two small bedrooms. This may seem a deviation from the case in point but Whisper was an indoor cat and his world really was very small when I actually got to see it. Monica started to repeat her stories about the events but I carefully steered her away from this to go right back to the beginning. Almost all cat owners experiencing problems want to launch straight into the nitty gritty but I need to approach the case far more systematically. I need some background on the cat, the family and the lifestyle before I even start to talk about the reason for my visit.

In this particular instance I felt the clues to Whisper's terrifying behaviour would be revealed in the history-taking. I had my trusty consulting bag with me, full of exciting textures and smells and interesting toys. Whisper plunged in with relish and hooked out a small battered mouse that he proceeded to fling about the room with great gusto. Well, the gusto was as great as it could be in such a confined space; he did bump into a lot of furniture and stuff on the way. As we were talking I was making notes but it was all still a bit garbled, I'm afraid. The chronology didn't stack up and there were a host of contradictions. Monica and I just weren't talking the same language. Anyway, I persevered, but I started to get far more interested in what was going on in the room than in what I was writing. Every time Whisper swept past Monica she would attempt to grab hold of him and squeeze him. 'Look, he loves it when I do this.' I begged to differ, but only secretly. Whisper's efforts to complete his game were eventually thwarted and he ended up sitting on the back of Monica's chair with a lashing tail as she cooed lovingly and generally pulled him about.

I asked carefully why Monica didn't let Whisper outside and I was greeted with a fairly abrupt and irate response. Wasn't it obvious? She was a cat lover and, as such, she couldn't possibly expose him to the dangers of the great outdoors. There were other cats, cars going up and down her cul-de-sac, people, dogs and all sorts of other potential dangers. Honestly, what was I thinking? She did, however, take him outside on a harness into the garden to sniff the flowers. And it actually got worse. Monica had a lot of breakable ornaments in her living room and, during the day when she was at work, Whisper was shut into the hallway and upstairs.

We went through the details of the attacks again and I started to understand where Whisper was coming from. For the entire two and a half years of his life Whisper had been restricted in his activity. He had spent his time being loved to distraction by his owner. She hand fed him from her plate, she squeezed him, she slept with him and she carried him around upside down to prove how compliant he was and how relaxed in her company. When I asked her how often she played games with him she replied, 'Every day for at least half an hour.' I would never dream of calling a client a liar but I was totally convinced that this wasn't true. There was no evidence of fishing-rod toys or proper cat things and her body language told me she was merely telling me what I wanted to hear. Poor little Whisper had one toy, a knitted doll that he used to carry around in his mouth and repeatedly attack. He also used to 'make love' to this toy and I realized that Monica was using a euphemism for masturbation. Many neutered male cats indulge in this activity, using toys, bedding or items of their owner's clothing. Whilst somewhat unsavoury for many to consider, this hedonic behaviour often indicates a generally unsatisfying and frustrating existence. Thank God for the knitted doll, I say.

Monica pressed me once again for answers. Why did her lovely cat turn on her? I explained as carefully as I could that it was probably a symptom of a cat in crisis. Aggression is an essential tool for cats living a normal life. When cats are deprived of a natural outlet for this part of their nature it is almost inevitable that it will be redirected at some stage. All Whisper was allowed to do was exist within the confines of the relationship that Monica was having with him. This just wasn't enough. Many cats cope remarkably well when their natural behaviour is suppressed in an unsuitable and un-stimulating environment. Others, like Whisper, become frustrated and chronic frustration can lead to explosive displays of intense emotion or 'rage'. Whatever caused Whisper to crack on that particular day will probably remain a mystery but his body whipped up a storm of adrenalin, his pupils dilated ('devil eyes'), his fur stood erect ('all bushed up') and he attacked as if under the influence of a 'red mist'. The second attack was probably provoked by an association between the intense emotion and the sight, sound or smell of Monica.

Once again I approached my discussion of the programme and hopeful solution with some trepidation. How could I tell Monica that her behaviour was squashing Whisper emotionally and that the aggressive attacks were an indication that things had to change dramatically? I started to explain to Monica how important it is for cats to be allowed to behave naturally and the dreaded glazed expression appeared on her face. If I know I am telling owners what they don't want to hear I immediately try another tack. I discussed the use of distraction and entertainment for Whisper outside the owner/cat relationship. I told Monica that this would allow him to 'let off steam' and stop targeting her in the future. We talked, negotiated and bartered about letting him outside but I was never going to win that particular battle. We eventually agreed on an outside enclosure attached to the house that would be accessed via a window in the kitchen. Whisper would then at least be able to feel the wind in his fur and take in the sights, sounds and smells of the ever-changing and exciting environment outside.

We continued to plan further interesting and challenging games for Whisper to play indoors. We introduced food foraging, cardboard-box towers and various other entertaining bits and pieces. I persuaded Monica to move her ornaments to the safety of a glass cabinet and allow Whisper into the whole of the house when she was out. At least that gave him a little more to do. I was now approaching the most crucial of the changes that needed to be made and that was to the relationship between Monica and Whisper. I explained that, despite the fact that he clearly loved her, Whisper needed time out from the relationship to be a cat. I encouraged her to play fishing-rod games with him every time she felt the urge to pick him up and dangle him upside down whilst kissing his belly. I wanted her to understand that love for a cat can be shown in many different ways and play was a very important 'I love you' message.

I left Whisper and Monica that afternoon with a little apprehension. I wasn't convinced that she had fully grasped the implications of *not* following the therapy programme, but I hoped that, after reading the written report I was planning to send her, she might finally agree that this really was the way forward for her.

Monica never reported freely after our consultation but I kept in touch with her. I couldn't abandon Whisper knowing that he was so unhappy. The outside enclosure was built and in use within three weeks and represented great progress. I am not convinced that Monica wasn't still squeezing Whisper and dangling him upside down but, luckily, he was so delighted with his outside enclosure that he was rarely indoors. A cat flap was fitted into a pane of glass in the kitchen window and Whisper often chose to spend nights on his wooden perch surveying his new nocturnal paradise. I asked Monica to keep in touch, but she didn't. Sometimes clients are happy just to get the results they want and don't feel the need to give the counsellor feedback. After my first call and with the knowledge that at least Whisper had his outdoor pen, I privately wished him well and filed the case notes.

Jeffrey – the cat who was loved too much

Every now and then you meet a patient and just know that that particular cat will be part of your caseload for ever. Jeffrey was such a cat. He belonged to a truly delightful lady called Paula and I first met him when he was just five months old. He was a magnificent example of the blue Burmese and as soon as I met him I knew he would be trouble. Paula had called me to her home to discuss various issues about her newly acquired kitten. Her long-term companion, a black and white moggy called Sparky, had recently passed away and she felt that he was going to be a hard act to follow. She couldn't imagine life without the company of a cat but she didn't feel that the average crossbreed would have half the character of her dear departed Sparky. She therefore did some careful research and came up with the perfect solution to her dilemma: a Burmese, described as 'dog-like', 'sociable', and 'highly intelligent'. What more could she want? So she found her nearest breeder and fell in love with Jeffrey at first sight.

She brought him home and fully expected a period of shyness as he became accustomed to his new environment. Surprisingly he exited the cat basket like a rocket and proceeded to charge round her cosy little flat bouncing off walls, climbing up curtains and generally behaving like a hooligan. Paula was initially a little dismayed as she chased him to retrieve the ornaments that fell in his wake. However, she felt that he clearly had a huge personality and might just be the one to replace her Sparky. Over the next couple of months she tried to instil some discipline into his life; after all, she couldn't let him trash the place every day. She said 'NO' when he walked across the kitchen table and 'NO' when he scratched the furniture and 'NO' when he climbed the curtains, but her reprimands fell on deaf ears. She felt a little out of her depth so she contacted her vet for my telephone number to see if I would assist her in a rather preventative type of behaviour therapy.

Paula greeted me like a long-lost friend when I arrived on the appointed day and I immediately warmed to her. She sat me down with a pot of tea and a selection of mouth-watering biscuits and produced four sheets of A4 paper containing all the questions and points she wished to discuss during our meeting. I was thankful I had had the foresight to put four hours' worth of money into the parking meter that day. The list seemed endless: 'How do I stop him being destructive, how do I get him to like opera, how often should I feed him, where is the optimum location for his litter tray, should I let him outside and if so should I get him a harness, how do I stop him biting my friend . . .?' I was writing copious notes as she talked but I had to challenge that last query. I asked about the biting and Paula told me that when her friend visited and they became involved in a hearty debate on politics or current affairs, Jeffrey would jump up and bite him. Another interesting point about our initial conversation was Paula's tendency to credit Jeffrey with incredible language skills. Words like V-E-T, C-H-I-C-K-E-N and M-O-U-S-E were all spelt out to me to ensure that Jeffrey didn't get the gist of the conversation. I had to concentrate to get the gist myself. We conversed for an hour or so and it became clear that Jeffrey was a lively, smart kitten with plenty of ways up his sleeve to run rings round Paula. He probably *could* understand each word and associate it with the appropriate experience; sadly his vocabulary didn't extend to the word NO. Shouting loudly merely entertained Jeffrey and the instruction behind the noise was lost in the sheer excitement.

I was keen to make things work for Paula but I remember quite clearly saying that day, 'Paula, I have to tell you, I think you will need my services again in the future for this little fellow.' At the time, I felt that the biting and generally boisterous behaviour was resulting from Jeffrey's intense need for 'input'. He needed to find out about his environment and understand his place in the world. Jeffrey was a bright cat and, given the undivided attention of the human in his life, he was making the most of an unnatural lot. He couldn't get out of the flat to experience all the excitement of outdoor pursuits so he worked the indoor environment as best he could. Every demand was met, even if the response was often not quite what he had in mind, except when Paula had visitors. When her attention was drawn towards others it wasn't long before Jeffrey realized that a strategically placed nip was not only fun but also a perfect tool for bringing the focus back to him.

We trawled through all her questions and requests for advice and we agreed to a little strategically placed double-sided sticky tape for the furniture and a plethora of scratching posts, Pavarotti at a slightly lower volume, dry food supplied via cardboard tubes and boxes, and a litter tray in a discreet corner of the bathroom. The issue of the great outdoors was a little more difficult to address. Paula and Sparky had enjoyed a beautiful relationship based on many years of mutual understanding. Sparky would go out hunting during the day and curl up on Paula's bed at night. Sometimes he would choose to do it the other way round when a certain delicious prey was only available in the nocturnal hours. Paula didn't inflict her opinions and wishes on him and vice versa. She trusted him to return safely whenever he wished and had a comfortable understanding that he would come back unharmed because that was what he had always done. Suddenly, presented with a new little life ready to explore the hidden mysteries of the garden, Paula was nervous. What if he was eaten by a fox? What if next-door's terrier chased him? What if he got trapped in a vacant flat along the road? What if he found his way to the front of the property and the busy road? Paula panicked and, confronted with the enormous decision whether or not to expose Jeffrey to all this danger, chose not to. She had decided that a little harness-walking round the garden was quite enough to stimulate even the most inquisitive kitten. She had convinced herself that he was a hopeless creature with no strategies for survival whatsoever and much better off in the sanctuary of her tiny flat with the person who loved him more than anything. I did try to persuade her otherwise but she was becoming a little resistant to my coaxing so I decided to leave it to another day. I gave her some advice about protecting her visitor whilst ignoring Jeffrey's attention-seeking behaviour and promised to keep in touch regularly over the next few months to monitor his progress. During that time I spoke to Paula frequently and used to look forward to our weekly chats. Jeffrey was making progress of sorts but my hidden agenda was to convince Paula that access to outdoors was very much the way forward for him. She must have raised every objection in the book and I must have come up with the most elaborate and persuasive reasons why her objections were unfounded. Eventually she relented and agreed that, between the hours of noon and four in the afternoon, Jeffrey would be allowed into the garden. She even very kindly sent me a photograph of him knee-deep in rough grass at the bottom of her garden to prove she was a lady of her word. It wasn't ideal to set a limit to his activity, and the time of day coincided with his usual afternoon nap. However, he soon realized that it was then or never and he changed his sleeping habits accordingly. He really was a very smart cat. By the end of our eight-week therapy programme Jeffrey had activity indoors and four hours of fun and frolics amongst the bedding plants. Paula wasn't brilliant about dealing with the attention-seeking behaviour – 'Are you sure it's right to ignore him, dear?' – but we came to a sort of compromise by arranging for her visitors to come between the hours of noon and four o'clock in the afternoon. If alternative plans were made Jeffrey was confined to the bedroom with a few tasty morsels, water, a litter tray and a host of soft toys. It was a compromise.

The following Christmas I received a card from Paula and Jeffrey with a new photograph showing me how helpful he had been to his owner that summer when she was gardening. I don't think, looking back, I was fooled for one minute.

The following year I received the call I had been dreading. Jeffrey had attacked Paula savagely and she had received injuries to her right arm from teeth and claws. She wasn't in robust health at the best of times and I was concerned about her ability to cope with an assault from nasty bacteria lodged firmly under her skin. She was receiving antibiotics and said that she was okay, all things being equal. She also admitted that Jeffrey had done the same sort of thing two or three times before but not with such devastating results. Somehow she had managed to avoid injury up till now by pushing him away, but this time he caught her unawares. Typically, Paula was full of guilt, believing that Jeffrey's behaviour was purely her fault. She must have done something wrong for him to hate her so much. I agreed to visit her for a second time as a matter of urgency.

It was really good to see Paula again, such a lovely lady, but I was angry that it was under such circumstances. Had I let her down? Should I have been more forceful about my warnings for the future and her need to tone down the relationship? We spoke at some length and I watched Jeffrey, now a muscle-bound two-year-old, out of the corner of my eye. Paula was very concerned that I should remain safe and not be harmed by him; apparently she was not the only victim of his aggression. Both her cleaner and the vicar had been attacked on a number of occasions as they approached him to say hello. I assured her that I wasn't about to approach him to say anything, and the consultation continued.

The outdoor access had declined a little over the last year since Jeffrey started to bring in baby birds. Paula was a real bird lover and this distressed her so much she felt it would be best if he stayed indoors unless strictly supervised to prevent further nest-raiding. She did, however, compensate, or so she thought, by providing some intriguing and elaborate indoor games. I asked her to show me how she played with Jeffrey and she dutifully went to the 'T-O-Y-B-O-X' in the bedroom to get out the first example. This, apparently, was called 'Twizzlebonk' and consisted of a string with a ball made of wool attached to the end (the sort that used to be made with leftovers wound around cardboard rings). Paula proceeded to rotate this around Jeffrey's head in a wide circle (illustrating the 'twizzle' part) and he flattened himself on her bed with his head jerking frantically from side to side as he tried to focus on the whirling ball. Paula was stirring the string with great energy until finally Jeffrey launched himself (the 'bonk' bit, presumably) and brought it down. Truly exhausting even to watch; I was hesitant to ask what game would follow that. 'Rattytattat' was a multicoloured cylindrical piece of heavy card wrapped in dyed rabbit fur in unpleasant fluorescent colours (completely irrelevant to Jeffrey but nauseating all the same). Paula proceeded to scream 'Rattyrattyratty' in a high-pitched squeak whilst leaning towards Jeffrey and waggling the weasel thing from side to side very rapidly. Her voice was achieving a banshee-like quality and I seriously contemplated grabbing 'Rattytattat' myself just to make it stop. Fortunately Jeffrey was on the case and, with a wiggle of his bottom and pupils as round and black as they could possibly become, pounced on the toy and proceeded to chew it and rake at it with his powerful back claws. Paula, with a nimble withdrawal, just managed to remove her hand in time to avoid laceration. I thanked Paula for demonstrating these favourite games so enthusiastically and asked if we could return to the quiet of the living room for a serious talk.

Jeffrey had turned into a little monster, not unassisted by the vigorous games involving a waving human arm. It was no coincidence that Jeffrey's 'attacks' targeted hands and arms. During our discussion it was also clear that he was becoming bored, destructive, frustrated and plain nasty when things weren't going his way. Paula, ever the dutiful owner, was falling over backwards trying to please him and failing dismally. We talked at some length and I was starting to feel the knot in the pit of my stomach that has become familiar to me over the years.

It heralds that stressful moment when you realize no matter what you do, a particular cat is not right for the owner. I suggested letting him out again; Paula refused. Every trick I could think of to resolve this problem was going to be fraught with complications. Paula wanted a cat to love and squeeze. She wanted a companion to talk to and to keep her company in her little flat. Paula was lonely and all she wanted was a friend. Jeffrey wanted to hunt, to fight and to play with the leaves in the wind. This was not a union made in heaven. I had to tell her so I took a deep breath and said something like, 'You know, Paula, I'm not sure Jeffrey is the right cat for you. If you keep him permanently indoors I don't think I can ensure your safety.' She wasn't outraged by my comments but she used the one sentence that was guaranteed to get me right back on track: 'I don't think I could carry on living without him.' So we devised a plan.

This was not open to negotiation; Paula knew it was absolutely essential to get the programme right. One false move or a weakening resolve could potentially result in another attack. Paula *had* to stop focusing on Jeffrey, there could be no compromise. Since at least one of the previous attacks occurred in the bedroom I was concerned about the proximity of her face and vulnerable eyes when he grabbed her arm in bed, so he was banished from the bedroom at night. This was a major step for Paula but, bless her, she wanted to please me, since she understood how serious the situation was and how determined I had become to keep her safe. She finally agreed to allow him out again with fewer restrictions on his hours. He now had access to the garden during daylight and all her nesting boxes were given to a friend living nearby. I felt it was a good compromise to at least ensure he didn't have any more easy pickings. Twizzle and Rat were out of the picture and replaced with alternative toys on string attached to long sticks. We agreed on bamboo canes so long that Paula didn't even need to be in the same room whilst Jeffrey was charging after his twitching prey. Surely this would prevent his seeing arms and hands as fair game any longer? I promised Paula I would be on her case, because she *had* to change the relationship – for everyone's sake.

We spoke the following week and great progress was already being made. Paula was trying extremely hard but finding it very difficult to change her relationship with Jeffrey. She was absolutely strict about the new night-time ruling and, surprisingly, Jeffrey wasn't that bothered when the alternative facility was a brand-new heated cat bed in the living room. The bit that wasn't going right was the whole 'Jeffrey says jump, Paula says how high' arrangement that the couple had had for the past two years. Paula really felt that, since he was already deprived of his nocturnal cuddles, any further rejection was tantamount to cruelty. She had always kept up a continual dialogue throughout the day with

Jeffrey, commenting on the weather, the news and the latest dramas on the soaps. I actually didn't mind that so much; I was more concerned about when this chatter was interrupted in response to a 'request' or an approach from Jeffrey. I just felt that if she was working on her computer and Jeffrey chose to sit on it at the same time she should move him off and finish what she was doing. That's not too unreasonable, is it? We needed to establish who was in control. Actually, what we needed to establish was something slightly different again. Jeffrey needed to understand that Paula was in control of her life and he was in control of his. This programme had to work; after all, if he attacked her again I would have to be *really* firm. Paula resolved to pull out all the stops.

The following week her routine report didn't come. I wasn't unduly worried because I felt sure that she would have contacted me had the worst happened. I hoped it was good news and this was confirmed the following week when she reported a real breakthrough. The previous evening she had been sending some emails, surfing the internet and working for some time on her computer. Normally, Jeffrey would have been outraged by her apparent lack of interest and interfered within minutes. She suddenly realized that she hadn't seen him for a while, and on investigation she found him idling away his time watching the world go by from the bedroom window sill. This may not sound like much but in fact it was progress indeed. At that moment Paula was in control of her life and Jeffrey was in control of his. There was a glimmer of hope.

From that point Jeffrey and Paula never looked back. I wouldn't say they drifted apart but they started to find interests and activities outside the confines of their relationship. Jeffrey would go out for the day and, despite initial trepidation, Paula accepted it was necessary for him to do his own thing. He always returned safely, just like Sparky. Jeffrey became more placid and calm indoors and the apparently unprovoked attacks ceased. In a way it's ironic that Paula resisted the notion of letting him out so much, seeing it as rejection and lack of care. Once persuaded, she was able to see that they both benefited emotionally and physically from the new regime.

Jeffrey and Paula are still together; their relationship has changed but they are much happier together than they have ever been before.

Bonzo – the guard cat

I have to relate Bonzo's story because it moved me greatly. Incidentally, he also ruined a perfectly decent pair of leather ankle boots, making the whole case less than cost-effective, but what the heck!

Bonzo was seven years old when I met him and a

handsome, broad and masculine cat if ever I saw one. He also weighed 8 kg so he really wasn't the sort of cat you would want to have an argument with. His size was even more evident when you saw him in his own environment: a small one-bedroom apartment in central London. His owner, Judith, had adopted him as an eight-week-old kitten. Unfortunately, during the first year of Bonzo's life, Judith had become seriously ill and she spent long periods in bed, with friends and carers visiting to look after her. Bonzo was hugely supportive at this time as he rarely left her side and they formed a strong bond with each other. Judith gradually returned to good health and by the time Bonzo was two years old she was able to go out and start her life again. Whenever she came home Bonzo was delighted to see her and the relationship went from strength to strength. He had developed some interesting idiosyncrasies, mainly due to rather boisterous play conducted by several of Judith's male friends when he was young. As he grew to adult-hood he believed it was incredibly good sport to swipe feet as they passed or hands that waved round on the arms of the sofa. Guests soon became aware of this habit and trained themselves to remain as still as possible to look less tempting.

Judith couldn't quite remember when things changed but malevolence had seeped into his interaction with strangers, and this had become a real problem over the years. He had started to challenge people as they entered the tiny flat. Initially this would be nothing more than a blocking of the narrow hallway and a hard determined stare. If the recipient of the warning did not heed it and continued to enter the flat Bonzo's next ploy involved laceration of feet and legs using a rotating, scything motion with both front paws. I had avoided this experience when I first entered the flat as Judith had wisely shut him into the bedroom, a confinement that he found deeply frustrating. After hearing the details of his attacks I couldn't resist seeing him in action myself. How frightening could a cat be, for goodness' sake? Unfortunately I knew the answer to that question all too well. I had often been the victim of feline attacks and I can say that my resolve is wobbly on occasions, particularly when the cat in question looks like a grumpy bull terrier. Judith let Bonzo out of the bedroom at my request and her cooing, lovey-dovey noises seemed somewhat incongruous when you saw the object of her affection. Yes, he was a handsome cat, but the expression on his face made it hard for anyone to instantly warm to him. He walked slowly towards me, staring intently, with his hindquarters slightly raised, his tail lowered and his neck stiffened. I continued to talk to Judith, at which point she became agitated. She informed me quickly that I really shouldn't ignore Bonzo because he didn't like that. I didn't actually like being stalked either but I explained to Judith that there was method in my madness. Over the next three or four minutes (it felt like an eternity) I was mauled several times by Bonzo with increasing intensity. I moved my consulting bag and he attacked my hand. I walked to the bathroom and he attacked my feet and legs. I was extremely tempted to stay in the bathroom indefinitely but I knew I had to come out eventually. My exit prompted the worst of all the attacks. He launched himself at me with great gusto, obviously believing that he had the advantage of surprise. He punched my feet and ankles so hard with his paws that I felt every blow. He howled like a banshee but still I walked back to my seat. I had seriously upset him but now I wanted him to calm down; I had discovered what I needed to know. I also only had half a boot left on each foot and I wasn't sure how much more punishment the leather could actually take.

Judith was shocked, since she had never witnessed such a severe attack before. She herded Bonzo back into the bedroom and sat down with me to discuss the problem.

Bonzo had become extremely attached to Judith over the years. He inhabited an incredibly small world in that tiny flat and everything within it had assumed huge significance, especially Judith. He relied on her totally for food, comfort, entertainment and companionship. In return he took on the role of defender of the realm. Cats have various ways of dealing with danger; Bonzo had adopted the fight-to-the-death strategy and was prepared to use violence to protect himself and Judith. The initial 'attacks' had been misplaced predatory behaviour but they may well have taught him an important lesson. Humans scream, flail their arms and eventually leave if you run at them and swipe them with your paws. It was also an exciting thing to do, representing probably the biggest adrenalin rush Bonzo had ever experienced.

The solution to this problem was a tricky one. Bonzo was locked into a cycle of behaviour that was closely associated with his current environment. The aim of behaviour therapy in this case would be to prevent further triggers for the attacks whilst promoting acceptable alternative activity that would be equally rewarding for him. This was my dilemma: what could I possibly do in such a small space? I also had another complicating issue. Judith was deeply emotionally attached to Bonzo and in order to modify his behaviour she would need to withdraw from the relationship and encourage self-reliance. She would also have to take some level of authority back from her cat. She used phrases such as 'he'd rather not be picked up', 'he doesn't like me doing that' and 'he wants me to do that at four in the morning, so I do!' Maybe this was why Bonzo felt such a burden of responsibility for his owner; she certainly didn't seem to be taking control. I suppose it's debatable whether or not cats are capable of such complex feelings. One thing I do know is that cats are control freaks, as I have said many times before. They are at their most content when they feel a sense of predictability and command over their surroundings and social situations. If Judith didn't appear to be in control then Bonzo may well have adopted this responsibility. However, rather than meet and greet friends and relatives as Judith would have done, Bonzo merely wanted to repel them.

We had many emotional discussions over the next few weeks. Judith was finding it very difficult to withdraw from Bonzo. I had suggested that she shut him into the bedroom when visitors came. I was seriously worried that she might adopt the strategy of never asking people round and I didn't feel this would address the underlying problem at all. For a short while she adopted my plan but lapsed soon after because she couldn't stand the plaintive crying from the bedroom as Bonzo objected to his confinement. Judith was unhappy and so was her cat and we just weren't making any headway. I had asked her to create some activity in the flat so that Bonzo could entertain himself foraging for food, climbing and exploring novel items. This was exciting for a while but Bonzo kept trying to return everything to the status quo. Why couldn't he just stick himself to Judith like he used to and get her to do all the stuff for him?

It is very hard to discuss these things with people. I really liked Judith and I understood everything she had been through in recent years with her illness and other difficult emotional upheavals and trauma. Bonzo gave her consistent and non-judgemental love whatever was happening in her life and however she was feeling. She didn't have to try to be loved, he did it unreservedly. If only he didn't attack everyone she wouldn't care how clingy he was. Unfortunately it is unfair to place this amount of emotional responsibility on a member of another species, particularly a cat. However much they seem to reciprocate love and affection in a human world it is hard for them to cope if they are not, to some extent at least, allowed to maintain a certain degree of 'cat-ness'. Yet Judith might feel that I was criticizing her or implying she was a bad owner if I explained this. I didn't want to make a depressed individual more so by remov-ing the one thing that represented a degree of continuity in her disarranged life. We spoke at great length and after some time Judith said to me, 'Do you think Bonzo would be happier elsewhere?' This was a breakthrough and I was then able to talk to Judith about the possible implications of moving Bonzo to an environment with access to the great outdoors. I did explain that she didn't need to be out of the equation if Bonzo had a lot more to do. Wouldn't it be great if Judith could move house?

Our conversations over the next few weeks centred round this one theme. Could Judith pack up and walk away from London and make a new start in a rural idyll? It was a complicated situation since social isolation was the last thing that she wanted or needed at the time. If she were pushed into too rural a location she ran the risk of seriously compromising her quality of life, even if Bonzo was having a party. But Judith was becoming acutely aware, now she understood the situation better, that Bonzo was crying out for something (anything) outside their relationship. He would love to feel a breeze on his fur or damp grass underfoot; even a scrap with next-door's cat might have an exciting allure. Judith was racked with the conflicting emotions of love, guilt, resentment and frustration. It was a difficult time for her and there was very little I could do at that stage apart from listen and understand something of what she was going through.

Fortunately, as so often happens in life, fate intervened and along came Judith's cousin Lucy. Lucy had a smallholding in Suffolk and a no-nonsense attitude to animals. She had never met Bonzo but she had listened to his story with some interest. She had once remarked that what he needed was a 'jolly good hunting session in my hay barn'; an entirely accurate assessment in my view. Lucy suggested giving Bonzo a holiday. If he liked it there he could stay and Judith could visit frequently. Lucy figured it was probably the best solution for everyone.

So Bonzo and Judith went to Suffolk for a holiday. Judith returned and Bonzo stayed and is still there to this day. He has a few battle scars and he tends to go off for days at a time but he just looks right (all 8 kg of him) stalking along the hedgerows; he's even been nicknamed the Beast of Bury St Edmunds due to his rather larger than normal physique. The transition wasn't completely without problems; it was hard for him to totally redefine his concepts of space and activity but I always find that cats cope well once adjusted if they are returning to the lifestyle that nature intended. Judith visits regularly and Bonzo hasn't attacked anyone since. He loves to see Judith but he fits her into his busy schedule now rather than devoting huge amounts of time to her – which makes it much easier for her to leave Bonzo behind when she goes home.

Wickham, Whisper, Jeffrey and Bonzo were all exhibiting aggression with differing motivations. The common theme, however, was relationships with their owners that needed to change. There is no question that their owners' emotional demands were of primary importance in the development of their aggression. It might have been born of frustration in Wickham's case due to the constant focus, putting him very much in the spotlight. Whisper and Jeffrey may have suffered from boredom and lack of stimulation resulting from their owners' inappropriate concern for their safety. Whatever the root cause it is perfectly clear that they were loved and cared for to the highest standards. The mistake many of us make is to view our furry friends as small people and see them as vulnerable childlike individuals who need us to provide emotional security. Sometimes we have to accept that cats always have and always will survive perfectly well without us.

Tackling aggression by changing the relationship

There is no substitute for professional pet behaviour counselling if your cat is being aggressive towards you or other humans. There are many motivations for this problem, including pain and disease, and it is essential to seek veterinary advice before trying any self-help approaches. There are, however, non-invasive changes that you can make to your behaviour around the cat that will minimize the risk of injury whilst professional help is sought.

- Avoid direct eye contact with your cat.
- Walk with confidence around your home whilst avoiding, whenever possible, a direct approach.
- Protect your vulnerable arms and legs if necessary by wearing stout clothing or gloves and boots; this will enable you to move around freely without being apprehensive.
- Avoid, whenever possible, passing your cat in narrow passageways or corridors.
- Ignore your cat and adopt the attitude that you are merely cohabiting.

- Don't put your cat 'in the spotlight'.
- Feed a dry formulation so that your cat can eat little and often throughout the day; this will prevent any frustration or aggressive episodes at mealtimes.
- Try to give your cat as natural a lifestyle as possible; access outdoors is always a benefit.
- Do not stretch out your hand to show affection.
- Acknowledge your cat only when he or she makes a friendly approach; even then only give brief physical contact.
- For safety reasons keep your cat out of the bedroom at night.

*　　*　　*

I cannot end this chapter without providing an important let-out clause. Nowhere is it written that you should persevere with a pet cat who shows constant aggression towards you, your family or your friends. You can be the most conscientious and devoted cat owner and still make no impact on a cat that lives firmly by tooth and claw. Sometimes the relationship and the environment are just not right for that particular cat. Take professional advice and listen to it and don't feel remotely guilty for something that is not your fault. Human/cat relationships should be mutually pleasant and if you are being attacked and your cat feels the need to be the assailant then neither of you is happy.

CHAPTER 8

How To Love Your Dependent Cat

This chapter tackles one of the most complex and fascinating elements of my work as a cat behaviour counsellor. What happens when a relationship between human and cat oversteps the boundary of what is considered 'normal'? What actually constitutes a dysfunctional relationship and why is one so undesirable? I have therefore decided to group together a number of issues that relate to this topic. I want to look not only at dependent cats but dependent humans: people who have intensely emotional attachments to their cats. These attachments are wonderful on a certain level but they can become extremely distressing when the cat dies or becomes ill. They can also be experienced to the exclusion of other humans and whilst some people would argue 'Who needs a human when you have a loving cat?' I feel slightly uneasy about this. I have always suggested as diplomatically as possible that cats are ill-equipped to reciprocate in these intense relationships; maybe some of the problems illustrated in the next few stories will back up my reservations.

I also want to discuss attention-seeking behaviour. This manifests itself in (what appears to be) wilful manipulation of the owner by a cynical little cat with nothing better to do with his time than get the owner up at three o'clock in the morning to heat up some prawns, *just because he can!* I will admit this can be extremely amusing and entertaining until it happens to you. It can also be detrimental to the emotional health of the cat, who becomes too dependent on the owner for inter- action and very uptight because the more he demands, the more he wants.

Rob and Flossie

Over-attached relationships are not always the domain of the female. Men also often live alone and work long hours and coming home to a warm welcome from a cat is as important to them as it is to us women. There are many books available that tell us that men come from a different planet and their brains just don't work the same way as ours. It is certainly true that in my experience a cat could enter a room and do a complicated song-and-dance routine complete with cane and top hat, and most men would be oblivious if watching the television. Attention-seeking behaviour rarely works in those circumstances. However, this is not to say that some men do not have the ability to multitask or to understand the nuances of their cats' behaviour. Some men are also keen to please their cats and provide everything they need to make them happy. Rob was such a man and a nicer client you couldn't wish to meet.

Rob had left university and set up home alone with a good job in a strange town. He had muddled along relatively well for a couple of years but realized there was something missing in his life. His family had always had cats when he was growing up and he remembered with fondness how each individual had helped him through difficult times with exams, girlfriends and all the tribulations of growing up. He felt his life would be greatly enhanced if he took the plunge and acquired a cat from the local rescue centre.

Rob was a bit of a softie and taking a softie into a rescue cattery virtually guarantees that at least seven will leave with him or her. However, he was after all a man and the rational part of his brain took over and chose one small black cat. She had belonged to an elderly lady who had died and she sat in her cage looking dishevelled and unloved. Rob reached in to pick her up and her purr in anticipation melted his heart. Her subsequent scratch to his arm when he held her for just a little too long sealed it for him and he signed the adoption paperwork and took her home. This was for life!

Rob wanted to do everything to guarantee Flossie's comfort and safety. After all, she'd lost her previous owner and was probably mourning; she needed cheering up. He fitted a cat flap to the back door to give access to the garden and he provided her with the best food that money could buy. All was going really well until they suffered their first invasion. Rob had just said goodnight to Flossie in the living room and retired to bed. When he found himself saying goodnight to Flossie again under his bedside table he realized something was wrong. He chased the interloper out of the house and thought nothing more of it until a big black and white cat started the same trick. This had to stop since it was obviously distressing Flossie. She had developed the unfortunate habit of regurgitating her food if she saw this cat through the window or heard him banging at the cat flap. Rob thought she might be ill but veterinary examination could not find a definitive cause for her parting company with her breakfast so consistently. He was determined to restore Flossie's sanctuary so he shut the cat flap and provided her with a litter tray. If she wasn't safe outside then she would have to stay in.

Rob spent unhappy evenings watching Flossie wince every time the black and white cat bashed at the cat flap trying to break in. He was really worried, because he could see that she was deteriorating. Her coat became unkempt and she seemed to rely heavily on him. If he passed her sitting on the sofa she would squeal at him and only settle if he sat down and provided her with the warmth and security of his lap. He was almost getting to the stage where he couldn't do anything at home apart from provide comfort to his cat. His chores were left unfinished and he gave every moment to Flossie when he was at home. It seemed to help for a while, particularly when he took a week off work, but as soon as he went back Flossie panicked. That very evening Rob returned to find a wet patch of urine on his sofa and a little black cat desperate for a fuss.

Poor Rob had very mixed emotions because he started to blame himself. He felt that this 'dirty protest' was a direct result of his depriving her of his company. He should never have given her all of him and then taken it away. It was cruel in the extreme and he should have predicted the response. What was the answer? Try to get the bosses to allow him to work more from home? Employ a cat-sitter? Give up work completely and become a permanent carer for Flossie? Whilst none of these options was seriously considered a thousand things were going through Rob's head when he rang me to arrange a visit. Flossie had continued to soil on the sofa and regurgitate her food and her overall condition was suffering. She looked older than her years and all she wanted to do was sleep (preferably on Rob's lap) or cling to him and howl when awake. He felt wretched every time he went to work and he even felt his own health was suffering as a result. He couldn't wait to get home but secretly dreaded the immense responsibility of being everything to Flossie.

I spent a couple of hours with Rob and Flossie going through the events that had led to the current situation. Flossie truly was a dear little thing and she watched Rob's every move like a devoted hawk. Her dreamy gaze was withdrawn every now and then as her glance flickered between the door to the kitchen and the living-room window. What was she hearing? What was she afraid of? Rob had reported that she seemed keen to go outside but merely sat on the step and cried when she did so. After an hour the sight of a big black and white face at the living-room window confirmed my suspicions. Flossie's main concern was out there. It was certainly true that her owner had tied himself in knots and ended up with a dependent cat, but the primary cause of her dependency was a lack of security brought on by other cats, not Rob's behaviour. I think it was an enormous relief to Rob to know that it wasn't he who had screwed her up.

We talked about the three main problems at some length, namely the regurgitation, the soiling and the apparent dependency. We also discussed the main cause – the black and white cat and all his pals outside who were keen to take over the domain of the new little black cat on the block. A pattern started to emerge when we discussed the regurgitation of her food. It didn't happen after every meal but it would definitely occur if she had seen the cat outside the window, heard a bash at the cat flap whilst eating or been deprived of Rob's company after a period when he had been at home. Could it be stress-related? Her urination on the sofa seemed to follow a similar trend. We had to create a situation that would increase Flossie's sense of security in the home without Rob's having to leave his job and take permanent responsibility. In the long run dependencies are never in anyone's interest since twenty-four-hour preoccupation with our pets is rarely an option (and even if it were I truly wouldn't recommend it). If we become indispensable to our furry friends then every time we try to leave them it is incredibly distressing for all concerned. It would be a far better strategy to prevent it from happening in the first place.

I asked Rob to block up the cat flap on both sides. Locking a flap just doesn't deter potential invaders; they just bang on it and keep returning until it breaks or some fool unlocks it. If the cat flap suddenly disappears one day (a big sheet of plywood will do it) then it no longer represents a weak point in the defences of the home. Cue for big black and white cat to move on to another target elsewhere in the street. Flossie still had a strong urge to go outside, which seems to be relatively common in such cases – these poor persecuted individuals don't particularly want to bump into their enemy but they feel compelled to check the territory daily to see what they have been up to. Flossie clearly couldn't do this alone but she might like to take a constitutional if Rob was in the garden. I wasn't condoning Rob's role as her minder but his presence in the garden, occupied with other things, might give her the confidence she needed to make her mark in the garden and check for the whereabouts of you-know-who.

Flossie was not a young cat (despite the rescue centre's referring to her as 'adult, probably about five years old'). I felt she was at least double that and with her advancing years came all the insecurities that go hand in hand with old age. She needed somewhere warm to sleep that was a suitable alternative to Rob's lap. If he wasn't responding to her plaintive cry for him to sit down and provide a bed maybe she would take to something else? We decided on a piece of synthetic sheepskin that would be spread over the sofa (on the as yet unblemished part of the seat) to tempt her. Rob was instructed to purchase various toys that I felt Flossie would find irresistible. Their interaction would in future focus on predatory play rather than cuddles and strokes. Whilst cuddling was great it didn't do anything but confirm Rob's status as nurturer and comforter. That wasn't really what we were after at that moment.

Rob agreed to groom Flossie more often to keep her coat as well maintained as possible. She had given up grooming since all this started and she was looking a little moth-eaten. That would enable Rob and Flossie to have bouts of the physical contact that they both clearly enjoyed with the more positive end result of a glossy coat. Various other recommendations were made such as an additional litter tray away from any windows and a change to a fine sand-like litter material. I also suggested that Rob follow a 'little and often' approach to feeding so that Flossie couldn't take too much food down at once on a stressed stomach. With the aid of a couple of automatic feeders, Flossie would have four meals a day instead of two from then on.

Over the next eight weeks we saw a great improvement in Flossie. She seemed to have more life in her and a definite spring in her step. She took to her thermal sheepskin bed immediately and she was found curled up and toasty every evening when Rob came home. The blocking of the cat flap seemed to provide her with a symbolic gesture of security. Rob's lap wasn't as essential as before for deep relaxed sleep now that the risk of invasion had seriously diminished. Play sessions were fun exercise and a valuable distraction for Flossie from all the worries of defending her home. If the weather was pleasant excursions into the garden took place during the evening and at weekends and Rob discovered the stress-busting delights of pottering in his garden.

Unfortunately there were continuing spates of peeing on the sofa and vomiting her food but these were still directly attributable to the rather sinister black and white cat (called, we believe, Cuthbert) who had taken to pulling faces at her through the living-room window when he found he couldn't penetrate the defences at the back of the house. The problem was soon resolved relatively easily by securing various objects to the front window sill which made it impossible for Cuthbert to land comfortably and maintain his balance whilst eyeballing. Nothing looks less threatening than a cat about to fall off something backwards.

Time went by and Flossie went from strength to strength. The incidents of urination on the sofa became a thing of the past and Rob felt she was showing him the true cat who had been lying underneath the clingy one all along. He used to keep in touch regularly via emails and one message spoke volumes. *So all in all, we're a much happier household. I'm having those wonderful moments again where I walk into the room or look up and see Flossie and say to myself: look, a cat! And it's in my house!*

As Rob stopped worrying about Flossie so much he

relaxed and learnt to enjoy her. She in turn became less distressed by the ever-diminishing attentions of Cuthbert and the sofa became an area for sleeping rather than peeing. She continued to gain weight and her coat became glossy as she started to groom herself once more. Excursions outside were no longer such an urgent necessity (Cuthbert soon lost interest) but, if the weather was nice, she could always be found watching Rob as he did a little pruning.

Snuggles – the case of acquired dependency

Dependency can come in many guises and develop in different ways. Snuggles was about ten years old when I met her. She had lived previously with her companion, Bossy, a large elderly black cat, and their relationship had appeared blissfully content. Sadly he had died several months before and his demise had seemed to herald a dramatic change in Snuggles, hence my visit.

Snuggles and Bossy had never been 'in your face' cats; they delighted in each other's company and socialized pleasantly with their owners when the mood took them. They had been perfect pets really, no trouble at all and ideal companions for a busy couple working from home. When Bossy died poor Snuggles seemed to lose the plot. She wandered aimlessly around the house wailing and searching for her misplaced friend.

Catherine and Michael, her owners, felt terribly sorry for her and they found themselves comforting her constantly and going about their business with her cradled in their arms like a baby. As soon as they put her down she would start wailing again so they attempted a shift system of attention-providing to reassure their bereaved pet.

A couple of months later they had to go away on business and they arranged for a friend to visit and feed Snuggles whilst they were gone. When they returned they couldn't believe their eyes; their beautiful Snuggles looked moth-eaten and unkempt. She had systematically removed her fur in patches from various locations on her belly, sides and legs. As Michael and Catherine walked round the house they found clumps of fur in little piles as if Snuggles had tugged on her coat and pulled it out in pawfuls. They took her to the vet's the following morning and they did a complicated series of tests to establish a reason for this sudden hair loss. After an exhaustive investigation the vet found nothing tangible and referred Snuggles to me as potentially suffering from stress.

When I visited Catherine and Michael it was obvious that Snuggles had started to rule their lives. She was on either his lap or hers throughout our discussions and when she wasn't she sat and licked her coat and pulled chunks out with her teeth. Every time this happened there was a chorus of 'No, Snuggles, darling!' and either Michael or Catherine would scoop her up and rock her gently whilst speaking words of comfort. They reported that sleep was a thing of the past for them both as all they could hear all night was 'lick, lick, pluck, lick, lick, pluck' and it was driving them to distraction. They tried to shut her out but the lick, lick, pluck just continued outside their door accompanied by howls of protest. Every morning they were greeted with piles of hair on the carpet and a cat who had so much loose fur sticking out of her mouth she looked like a cannibal. They decided that allowing her access to the bed was the lesser of two evils. At least she wasn't screaming. Planned holidays were abandoned and their lives were redefined as carers for Snuggles. Unfortunately, despite their best efforts, all the attention they were lavishing upon her failed to stop the constant lick, lick, pluck and incessant whining.

Snuggles was a sweet little creature and her pathetic appearance and countenance provided the perfect excuse for anyone to pick her up and comfort her. Ironically this was not having the intended effect and Snuggles was becoming totally reliant on reassurance and attention from her owners. Theirs had truly become a dysfunctional relationship, with the added complication that her stress was causing her to pull her fur out. Cats have limited ways of dealing with stress; they can't turn to drink or drugs and they can't talk things through with counsellors (which would make my job easier). Instead they have to rely on predictable, safe patterns of behaviour such as eating, grooming and sleeping to fill those times when they need to pacify a worried mind. It isn't a coincidence that the country is full of cats overeating, over-grooming and sleeping their lives away when faced with difficult situations.

I explained this concept to Catherine and Michael and suggested that a gradual withdrawal of their attention would be a positive step towards her recovery. However, this should never be attempted without first finding an alternative pursuit to distract the cat. Failure to provide other things to do when the owners aren't giving attention can send an already stressed cat into orbit.

Catherine and Michael were blessed with a wonderful garden with a sunny rockery, a pond and shady trees. Snuggles used to go outdoors when Bossy was around but only to follow him and generally bask in his shadow. She had seemed to give up the great outdoors on Bossy's demise and her life now revolved around the Aga, her little wicker bed and her owners. Nothing works better than the smells, sights and sounds of a beautiful garden to revive a depressed cat so I suggested that Snuggles be encouraged to spend more time outside. A new regime began that confined Snuggles to the spacious kitchen at bedtime. Michael and Catherine wouldn't be able to hear the complaints and could (hopefully) avoid the temptation to comfort her in the night. Snuggles was provided with a late supper of her favourite food and her wicker bed was placed next to the Aga. In the morning she would be greeted by her owners and taken outside for her morning constitutional. I suggested that this should initially be an escorted ramble to give her the confidence to soak up the sights, but she would hopefully start to go it alone at some stage.

We were blessed with some good weather over the next two weeks and the arrival of a pair of ducks on the garden pond. Snuggles was captivated by the ducks and would sit crouched at a safe distance just watching them for hours. Catherine put her wicker basket just outside the kitchen door in the sun and Snuggles seemed to be in heaven. Michael and Catherine had been instructed to ignore Snuggles's plucking and screaming. That, as always, was tough but they kept reassuring themselves that giving attention hadn't worked in the past so anything was worth a try. Snuggles continued to approach her owners for the usual attention but their averted eyes and turned backs made her realize all was not right. She tried even harder to get their attention but her swishing tail gave a hint that she was really in two minds about persevering. After all, those ducks were back and the sun was out and the breeze felt good on her bald bits . . .

Several weeks went by and each morning Michael and Catherine were greeted with ever-decreasing piles of fur when they opened the door to the kitchen. For the first two weeks they found Snuggles pressed up against the door (I did try to convince them that she had merely responded to their footsteps on the stairs and had not been at the door howling all night) but after that she was found in a variety of different poses and locations in the large room. When they started to find her pressed up against the back door instead, ready to go out, they thought that things were turning the corner. Over-grooming of this kind doesn't disappear overnight and many cats need a little help with the transition to more normal cleaning regimes. Vets often prescribe a type of antidepressant in these situations but that really wasn't an option for Snuggles as it was felt she was a little old for such aggressive medication. Whilst these drugs are comparatively safe at the appropriate dose a cat's liver isn't really designed to deal with such toxic substances. We knew, therefore, that the old habit of lick, lick, pluck would take some time to disappear.

Eight weeks later Snuggles was transformed. She didn't whinge or whine and she sat outside in her little wicker basket as if she truly owned the place. She had her morning routine of patrolling the boundaries of the walled garden followed by a quick sniff round to see where her duck friends were hanging out. She still popped into the kitchen to see her owners but if they were intent on the morning papers or working on their computers she would turn tail and disappear back outside. She still plucked her coat in a couple of places but Michael and Catherine were delighted to see that her beautiful tabby and white fur was returning in others. They eventually booked a holiday and, despite a little extra fur loss down one front leg, she survived the ordeal of being home alone with a couple of cat-sitters visiting daily.

As cats get older they tend to become more prone to dependency and over-attachment but it isn't inevitable that it will lead to stress-related illness and sleepless nights. Most owners relish the increased attention afforded to them by their elderly felines and nobody suffers. Occasionally other things, such as the death of a cat companion, will tip the balance and cats will develop dependencies (like Snuggles) that don't do anyone any favours. With careful handling and sensitive withdrawal, coupled with alternative activities, a sense of self-reliance can be reinstated and life can go on as before.

Betty, her daughter et al.

Betty and her daughter presented quite a dilemma to me some years ago and I have never forgotten my utter frustration and complete inability to make an ounce of difference. Whilst not exactly an illustration of a dependent cat, it certainly shows how complicated some relationships can be between women and their cats. I'm rather reluctant in a way to describe the details of this particular story since I never really had the answer; guidelines to address similar situations are beyond me. However, we tackled the whole issue with good humour (even if mine was more akin to hysteria) and Betty and Hilary seemed happy enough with the outcome.

The two ladies in question lived together in a small cottage in a quiet village in Sussex. They both initially had full-time jobs and always had a cat in the house. Over the years, and they couldn't say exactly how, they had managed to acquire a total of six feline residents. They had come as strays or from local rescue centres but they all had one thing in common. I found this quite surprising since I can honestly say I had never seen a household with so many cats with similar personalities. They were all scaredy-cats; they were frightened of their own shadow, each other, noises, movement and humans. Just about everything, really, that any cat would encounter in normal domestic life. When I visited Betty and Hilary I caught glimpses, but the cats were mainly nowhere to be seen. I asked them whether the similarity was a coincidence or did they gravitate towards the cowardly, and they didn't really seem to know. They said things like 'we felt sorry for them' and 'nobody else would want them' and 'we thought we could make a difference'.

Sadly, they hadn't quite made the difference they had hoped for. The cats had firmly resisted attempted handling and expressions of love and they had each adopted an area in the house they called their own. Every day they would retreat to these private places or disappear outdoors and only visit or have contact with their owners when it was time to eat. This is where the problem lay, and poor Betty and Hilary had got themselves in a bit of a pickle trying to compensate for the lack of affection they could show to their beloved cats. They wanted their charges to feel loved and they decided the best way to achieve this would be to express their devotion through food. So they devised a feeding plan and daily regime that went something like this:

6.00 a.m.   Cook fish for Stripey and Elmo.

6.15 a.m.   Feed the fish to Stripey and Elmo, give rabbit chunks to Monty (in the back bedroom), give tuna in brine to Elsie (under Hilary's bed, otherwise she won't eat), give hypoallergenic biscuits to Sandy and lamb in gravy to TC on top of the kitchen cupboard.

11.00 a.m.   Call all the cats in for elevenses – cooked chicken or tinned ham.

2.00 p.m.   Put lunch down in four different places and hope they all get some whilst calling their names repeatedly.

6.00 p.m.	Cook more fish.
6.15 p.m.	Feed it to Stripey and Elmo, rabbit chunks to Monty, tuna in brine to Elsie, etc.
10.00 p.m.	Fish-flavoured biscuits and prawns for supper (all the cats would usually come in from the garden for such a tasty morsel).
10.15 p.m.	Shut all the cats indoors for the night. Alternatively, stay up until four in the morning trying to get some of them in.

I was scribbling this down as they spoke, thinking all the while that this seemed to be an impossible regime and that one week of it would have sent me mad. I was not surprised to hear that poor Betty had given up her job six months earlier because she just didn't have time to work. She had also become increasingly reluctant to go outside or carry out any errands that required leaving the house for any length of time since she was concerned the cats would panic if she wasn't around. She even did most of her cleaning with a dustpan and brush since she was concerned that the vacuum cleaner would distress them.

Hilary had managed to keep a degree of perspective and she constantly scolded her mother for her obsessive behaviour. This just created friction between mother and daughter and made matters worse. Betty knew it was wrong, but there didn't seem to be any alternative now that she had started living her life that way. After all, some of the cats were coming to her now and nagging her for food. Surely that meant that she was loved and needed?

I shall never forget that visit to Betty and Hilary. I spent four hours there and we talked and talked. We looked at options and consequences and eventually it was unanimously agreed that none of the cats would suffer if we changed the regime and gave Betty back a little of her life. Betty sat forward in her seat and nodded with great enthusiasm as I detailed a new feeding regime and way of life for her and her cats. Gone were the days when she would follow them round, look at them and speak to them all the time. Gone were the days when she stayed up all night to make sure they came in; it had never been an effective ploy anyway because they still came in when they wanted to and not before. We were also going to radically change the hugely expensive and wasteful feeding regime to well-balanced nutritional meals that would suit all palates. I felt quite proud of myself when I left that house because I was convinced that four hours of persuasion and coercion had shown Betty the light and things would be different from then on. Fat chance!

I had a call from Hilary several days later. Nothing had changed except that Betty had become even more stressed because she couldn't adhere to the new regime. She still stayed up all night, she still fed fish and tuna under the bed and she still swept her floors rather than use a noisy cleaner. I asked Hilary to put Betty on the phone; I wanted to hear her side of the story and why she thought she was failing so dismally. It was quite simple, really: she couldn't resist the cats. To deprive them of their food and their routines would be cruel. She was the one who had to change and she would just have to get used to the sleep deprivation, the loss of earnings and the constant struggle from one meal to the next. Logic had clearly gone up in smoke but I found myself almost understanding where she was coming from. These cats were her life now and their perceived feelings and wishes actually outweighed her own. She couldn't possibly attempt to change anything for her own sake since that would undoubtedly have been totally selfish. What a dilemma. I tried very hard over the telephone to emphasize that the changes needed to be made for the cats' benefit but she wasn't convinced. I even made her a plastic-coated poster to put up in the kitchen with all the rules of the new regime but it failed to impress.

Some weeks later we had reached a stalemate. Betty was very unhappy as she couldn't follow the pro-gramme at all. Hilary was unhappy because Betty couldn't follow the programme and there were constant arguments. I returned to their house, determined to have a last go at improving things for everyone. I suppose I succeeded on one level; both Hilary and Betty fully accepted I was right. However, Betty was suffering from emotional inertia. She couldn't change just in case the alterations were disapproved of by the cats. She was helpless.

There are occasions when I just have to walk away. This really had become Betty's problem, and my field of expertise is with the cats not the owners. I knew the cats would benefit from my suggestions but I was powerless to help. I was honest with Betty and explained my frustration. I wanted to make her life and that of her cats better. I wanted to make a difference, but I couldn't. I often feel that that particular case taught me as much about myself and my motivation for doing this job as it did about Betty!

Chunky – dependency works both ways

I once had a client called Terri; I remember her with some affection because she was such a nice person. I also remember her because she illustrated so well how complicated (and self-destructive) love for a cat can be. Many times when I have lost one of my wonderful cats I have sobbed 'I'm never having cats again; it's too painful when they die!' and I know I'm not the only cat lover to have said that. A great deal of the emotion we feel for these creatures is painful and occasionally, as Terri found, the pleasure of ownership becomes a distant memory but the love remains with a vengeance.

Terri called me in tears to ask if I could help her dear old Chunky. It was hard to accurately ascertain over the telephone what was grieving her about her fourteen-year-old cat; she talked of depression, anxiety, not adjusting to his new home, illness . . . I spoke to her veterinary surgeon, a personal friend of mine, and it was agreed that I would visit Terri to see what could be done to make Chunky happier.

Terri and her husband, Joe, lived in a newly built house that they had moved into only two months prior to my visit. They were surrounded by JCB diggers, noise and mud and their pristine home sat with three or four other occupied properties on a massive building site. I was shown into her lovely new sitting room and I sat down next to the curled-up figure of a little black and white cat (not so chunky now), breathing deeply and fast asleep. Terri sat on the other side of him on the sofa and, as she fiddled, caressed and poked him, she told me his story.

Chunky had lived with Terri from a tiny kitten. He had been every young girl's ideal pet, a real tomcat outdoors and a gentle creature full of affection for his young owner indoors after a busy day's hunting in the fields surrounding her family home. Chunky was with Terri when she met Joe and, when they decided to marry, he moved with them to their first new home. He accepted Joe and even started to show him great affection once he had registered his initial protest through cool indifference. Life carried on and all three were perfectly happy going about their normal day-to-day business for the next ten years. Sadly, since then, things had not been so good for Terri; she had been made redundant and found it difficult to get another job, there had been money worries, her father had become seriously ill, her best friend had died and Chunky had had a series of worrying illnesses. He had developed a cancerous growth on his face (that had subsequently been removed) and then suffered a mysterious problem with bald patches that had appeared virtually overnight. Terri had found it all too much and, combined with the recent house move, she had become seriously depressed and anxious and was now on antidepressants in order to cope.

Chunky had not adjusted well to the move. He seemed to hate all the noise and a young cat next door insisted on sitting on the fence and staring through the patio doors at him. He had lost his appetite and suffered from intermittent explosive diarrhoea. The vet had suggested he might be suffering from inflammatory bowel disease and had prescribed an easily digestible prescription diet. Chunky hated the new food; Terri was panicking and Chunky just looked downright depressed. He was no longer the sleek, muscle-bound hunter of old. He didn't want to go outdoors any more and, when he wasn't emitting diarrhoea, he just slept for hours on end. He looked frail and

Terri was petrified that she was going to lose him.

Terri and Chunky had become very close over the years. He had always spent a lot of his time outdoors but every moment spent inside was devoted to Terri. She loved him with a passion and focused totally on him. He loved the attention and the relationship was described by Terri as being 'completely tuned in to one another'. Chunky would never leave her side when she was sad or ill. He seemed to understand those moments when she needed him most.

Terri had very eloquently described how she felt about her cat. She also fully understood that she was at a low ebb and everything seemed worrying and out of control. There are many occasions in my work when the owners' emotional state has an enormous impact on their cats. It is a constant challenge to understand the implications of this and work to address it whilst ensuring that the owner doesn't feel that I am trying to help them emotionally too. I am not a psychologist and there are many times when I have said to my clients, 'I wish I could help but I'm not qualified; you should see someone.' However, I have to understand what motivates the client because, as in this case, their behaviour can be at the very least influential, and at the worst the primary cause of the cat's problem.

I spent the next half an hour explaining to Terri, as gently as possible, what the past few years had been like from Chunky's perspective. He had suffered from a tumour and had undergone several stressful visits to the veterinary practice culminating in uncomfortable surgery. His owner had changed her behaviour dramatically and been obviously persistently worried by the events in her personal life. Her anxiety would have been viewed by Chunky as a response to danger so he would have felt an element of her distress. As time progressed he was getting older and therefore less secure and Terri's behaviour (and the obvious changes in the household routines that would have been evident) would have heightened that insecurity. This may have been the motivation for his over-grooming. A house move followed and he found himself living on a noisy building site in a completely new territory. As an old insecure cat with an insecure and nervous owner, would he really have felt robust enough to take on the challenge of exploring?

There was also another twist to the tale that Terri hadn't mentioned but I had observed throughout our discussions. She just couldn't leave him alone. She was poking him and fiddling with him and waking him up from his restful sleep. She admitted that, when he went off his food, she was frantic and would spend hours chasing round after him with various bowls of tempting food. She even recalled crying and beseeching him to eat something whilst trying to thrust a prawn into his face. Trust me, this is not the most effective way to promote a healthy appetite. It almost always has the opposite effect and can give cats serious psychological hangups about food and eating. I soon discovered that many of Chunky's bouts of diarrhoea were more than likely to have been caused by eating a huge variety of rich foods provided by an anxious owner. It is certainly true that stress can cause intestinal disturbances but Terri's overzealous attempts to feed were probably making things worse. Both Terri and Chunky were locked into a cycle of stress, anxiety and depression. Something had to change and undoubtedly that something was Terri.

She was a smart lady and as I discussed the position with her it was clear that she suddenly realized the implications of her actions. I always try to be amusing in my consultations no matter how distressing the facts of the case may be. This doesn't mean I appear heartless; I make sure the owner understands why I joke on occasion. Terri, like practically all my clients, had a keen sense of humour and after shedding many tears during our meeting was soon laughing at the image of her crawling round after Chunky, trying to push food into a cat who clearly thought she had gone mad.

We devised a plan for the future. Chunky's bowel had obviously become sensitive so it was agreed that she would feed the prescribed diet exclusively. A small bowl of slightly warmed food would be placed in Chunky's normal feeding area and Terri would walk away. She would not look at him or encourage him, and if he hadn't eaten it within half an hour the food would be removed and another helping would be put down a few hours later. Chunky wasn't active at all so it was entirely likely that his appetite would be smaller than usual and non-existent some days. Terri also agreed that she would stop touching Chunky all the time and waking him up. Older cats normally sleep for 75 per cent of the day and it's never pleasant to be woken from a deep sleep.

During the consultation I had played with Chunky using a piece of string. He thoroughly enjoyed it and even went outside shortly afterwards for the first time in weeks. Sometimes it pays to stop treating old cats like invalids! Terri was certainly impressed by his sudden youthful response and she promised to play with him regularly rather than hold his paw and gaze dolefully into his eyes. She vowed to stop all over-concerned behaviour around him and I agreed that it would be more beneficial to voice any worries to me over the telephone than to let Chunky see her anxiety. I couldn't take away Terri's depression or her stress after everything that had happened recently in her life but I could hopefully help her to understand the potential impact on Chunky. I left that afternoon full of hope that things would soon change for the better.

Three days later I had the first phone call from her to say that she had noticed an incredible improvement. Chunky seemed much happier and he had started to eat the prescription food; not much, but enough to reassure her that he wouldn't starve to death. He was spending more time sitting in the garden and even Joe had noticed that Chunky was more alert and like his old self. We had taken away the stressful impact of Terri's insistent behaviour, and when she relaxed, Chunky relaxed too. To his brain, the crisis she was expressing was obviously over. I cannot say that Terri was never concerned about Chunky's health again or that she didn't occasionally wake him up to squeeze him or hold his paw. It did, however, become a less tense relationship for the rest of Chunky's days. He died two years later, peacefully at home, with Terri at his side.

BF – the obsessed cat

It is interesting to see that the last two cases have illustrated the dependent element of a human/cat relationship as very much the owner's problem. Dependent cats are often created by a dependent human but every now and then, in a cat behaviour counsellor's lifetime, we get to see a truly bizarre case that illustrates how complicated the domestic cat can be. I was contacted by a lady in Scotland, Jane, who worked for one of the large animal rescue charities. She wanted support with a distressing case and asked if I would be willing to help her via the telephone and relevant videos. I agreed to assist if I could and asked her to tell me the story of BF. He had arrived in the charity's cattery as a ten-week-old kitten and at the age of five months he was transferred into a foster home. He remained there with a number of other young cats for four months and during this time he went missing. He had left the foster home as an affectionate and loving kitten but he returned with a problem. He started to defecate randomly in front of the foster carers on carpets or hard floors; it didn't seem to matter. The common denominator was that he emptied his bowel as near to the humans as possible. They found this intolerable after a time and returned him to Jane's cattery. Jane already had several cats of her own and didn't feel she could cope with another full time in her house. She had a dilemma, though, because the alternative was to return BF to an outdoor pen and chalet. She compromised by allowing him restricted access to her home during the day for a couple of hours, access to the garden and the pen at night.

He settled well, and seemed to be perfectly happy with her other cats, but there was something very strange about BF. He wouldn't keep still; he latched on to Jane immediately and didn't want to leave her side for a second. His toilet habits were not the best. He always urinated in the various litter trays provided or in appropriate areas of Jane's garden, but he defecated wherever he felt like it, preferably on or near Jane's feet. If he was away from her he would content himself with eliminating right in the middle of his pen or on the lawn. It's really nice when cats seem to want our company twenty-four hours a day but it soon loses its appeal when you cannot sit down or stand for any length of time without a cat climbing up your legs and trying to put its head in your mouth. That was BF's other party piece. Whenever he saw Jane he would become so excited that he would start to hyperventilate (breathing rapidly through his mouth). He would then climb up her body and attempt to push his head into her mouth. This cat didn't sleep since his whole purpose in life seemed to be to get to Jane. Once there, his response was to defecate and get thoroughly over-excited.

Jane sent me a video and I studied it in detail. I have to admit I found it quite distressing. The video showed BF pacing backwards and forwards in his pen, crawling up Jane and defecating on a shelf when he saw her. Jane's veterinary surgeon had been puzzled by his behaviour and prescribed a tricyclic antidepressant to try to calm him. The drug he chose had once been used to treat humans with obsessive-compulsive disorder. BF was given a relatively high dose but rather than make him calm or even a little dozy it seemed to have the opposite effect. I was completely perplexed. I contacted colleagues in the Association of Pet Behaviour Counsellors and we discussed all sorts of possibilities.

Some suggested it was a rather dog-like bonding disorder, a mixture of frustration and fearful insecurity. Others thought it might be an unusual attention-seeking behaviour that had been inadvertently reinforced by Jane and the previous owners. I even remember some talk of ADHD (attention deficit hyperactivity disorder) in cats.

We tried increased stimulation, challenging feeding regimes, the introduction of other carers and various other ideas to focus him elsewhere. Robin Walker, my wonderful colleague and friend and a real expert on such things, suggested that the paradoxical effect of the antidepressant could have been due to a deficiency of a certain chemical in BF's brain called serotonin (a mood-stabilizing hormone). He gave advice on a home-made diet to provide nutrients that converted to serotonin but we were just too late. I received a letter from Jane saying: *BF put to sleep 9.20 a.m. today. A very sad day for all who knew him. I will miss him very much. Thanks for all you have done.* Several years later I still don't understand what happened to BF to make him behave in this way. I am still searching for the answers.

Damson and Cherry and the delights of ylang-ylang soap

I see a lot of undesirable attention-seeking behaviour,

but there is little that competes with this case. Damson and Cherry were two delightful (if somewhat 'in your face') lilac Burmese sisters. They lived with their stylish and equally delightful owner called Arabella. I visited them because the two cats were causing havoc in the home and Arabella felt powerless to control their wilful behaviour. Over the telephone I had heard stories of launched attacks and bizarre eating habits including recent surgery to remove a foreign body from Damson's intestines. Apparently she had been shut into the bedroom one day and, in sheer frustration, had eaten the carpet. I was somewhat apprehensive when I arrived at the apartment.

I was greeted enthusiastically by Arabella and directed into one of the most exquisite rooms I have ever seen. It was a fairytale land of cream, gold and white with embroidered cushions, fur throws, thick carpet and huge lumps of quartz crystal everywhere. The lighting was soft and the whole impression was one of tranquillity and calm until the two Burmese skidded into the room. My first impression when I saw them was 'Gosh, what skinny Burmese!' They were five years old when we met so there was no question they were juveniles waiting to fill out. Whilst attractive, they certainly looked as if they needed a good meal. As I sat taking notes and listening to Arabella's story I watched in fascination as Damson and Cherry worked as a team around the room, intent on achieving centre stage and their owner's full attention. Damson jumped on a shelf and pushed a crystal candlestick slowly and purposefully towards the edge. As Arabella leapt to the aid of the fragile ornament it was Cherry's turn to take a silk cushion in her mouth and chew it, staring directly at her owner. Arabella turned quickly, still talking, and whisked the cushion away before too much damage had been done. Every movement and response to their continuous taunts was swift and obviously well rehearsed; Arabella had definitely done this before.

It's quite wrong of me to use such subjective language when talking about cats but it was impossible to see any of their behaviour as anything but a well-planned attention-seeking game. Their every destructive action was being met by Arabella's immediate response, the most fascinating element being the way they seemed to take it in turns to display each new and devious plot to keep their owner on the go.

Arabella told me that she had acquired them as kittens to keep her company during her long working days at home. She was a designer and she worked in a small studio attached to the living room. She bought two, thinking they would be company for each other, but she had had no idea they would eventually work as a team to send her completely mad. Her biggest worry was the 'kitchen fiasco' as she referred to it; she suggested that I sit down in the comfort of the living room and witness the carnage as she went to make some coffee. As she got up to walk in that direction both Burmese rushed in front of her and swiftly jumped to the top of the kitchen cabinets, one on either side of the door. She entered the room (slightly hunched and obviously bracing herself for something) and both cats leapt towards her. Damson bounced off her left shoulder and landed on the work surface. Cherry clutched on to her back and hair and remained there as she tried to switch the kettle on. The whole thing looked hideously uncomfortable and very stressful as every cupboard that was opened was immediately filled by two lilac cats. Arabella explained that they raided the bin and the cupboards constantly and had even tried a four-pawed attempt to open the fridge. Cooking for herself was now impossible unless she nipped into the kitchen when they weren't looking and shut the door just long enough to prevent them eating the carpet on the other side. How could she live like this?

I asked Arabella about their unusual eating habits (behaviour referred to as 'pica') and she listed a whole catalogue of tasty treats including fabric, plastic, card-board and their absolute favourite, ylang-ylang soap. When I asked what more conventional food they ate I wasn't surprised to hear the answer. She divided half a tin of Whiskas between the two cats; this she gave to them in four small meals throughout the day. Herself a strict vegetarian, she also gave them rice, potatoes, vegetables and fruit in small quantities. She was extremely anxious about their becoming overweight so she was very precise in the amounts she fed. The only thing she couldn't control was their consumption of her furniture and possessions.

We chatted for a while longer and I commented how svelte Damson and Cherry were (a euphemism in my book for 'far too thin'). Her reply alarmed me. She thanked me for the compliment, and said, 'I really do believe you can never be too rich or too thin and that goes for my cats too!'

There is a tremendous temptation for some people to inflict their particular views, habits and lifestyle choices on their pets. I suppose I should have been grateful that Arabella hadn't imposed her strict vegetarianism on her cats; they would of course be dead now if she had – meat protein is essential for their survival. She was, however, imposing her views on weight on them and this was leaving the poor things permanently starving. This is the only case I have ever seen where the consumption of non-nutritional substances was actually about hunger.

I had to be careful since I didn't want to contradict Arabella or appear to judge her for what she was doing. After all, she loved these cats and wanted desperately to do the right thing. I explained to her that Damson and Cherry were actually underweight and this left them with a huge appetite and an owner they saw as the only source of proper food. Their lives had therefore started to focus round Arabella and gaining her attention at all times, especially when she was in the room that housed all the edible stuff. We needed to feed the cats more and take away the perception of Arabella as the provider. Increasing their dietary intake would have to be done extremely gradually since too much too soon would probably only result in regurgitation or vomiting. I calculated an accurate daily increase of the cat food and an introduction of a cat biscuit to enable Arabella to abandon the vegetable and carbohydrate titbits. I explained to Arabella that my main aim was to get both the cats on dry complete cat food only. This would enable her to feed throughout the day by secreting the biscuits in various places. The cats (let's face it – they were bright) would search round the apartment and find all the food without Arabella's being involved. For the period of the programme we put away cushions, soap, cardboard and all things seen as 'edible' by Damson and Cherry. We introduced more cat toys, water fountains, scratching posts and paraphernalia to increase their general level of entertainment. I felt it was also important to have a few more house rules; Arabella had really lost control of her life. I asked her to ignore their attention-seeking with clear signals – no speaking and no eye or physical contact. Any response, even shouting, would be seen by the cats as a victory. The kitchen door was shut when Arabella was in it and her studio door was shut when she was working. Fixing the handles so that they worked only when they were pulled upwards solved the dilemma of both cats' being able to open doors by swinging on the handles. At last Arabella felt she had the chance to get one step ahead of the dastardly duo!

I received a phone call a couple of weeks later from Arabella and the news was encouraging. She had followed the gradual increase in food to the letter and the cats were now receiving the appropriate daily allowance of complete cat biscuits. Damson and Cherry were highly delighted to find these pellets of food hidden in small empty plant pots in various parts of their home and they spent hours running from one room to the next to see what treasures they could discover. Arabella reported that they seemed calmer and less active; she couldn't remember the last time she had seen them sleeping for long periods during the day. I cautioned her about getting complacent. Her strategy of ignoring their attention-seeking behaviour was working at this early stage but cats like Damson and Cherry have a habit of regrouping and coming back with a blistering counter-attack that is difficult to overlook. She had to maintain her resolve and continue to ignore their unreasonable demands.

As predicted, the counter-attack came as Damson started to stand on the back of the sofa or the mantel-piece and bang the paintings on the wall with her paw. This caused them to rock precariously and, sure enough, Arabella dashed to their rescue, thinking of injured cats and damaged artwork. Immediately, she could have kicked herself, but her instincts had taken over. She knew what had to be done and all pictures that were remotely accessible to either cat were removed and placed with everything else in the now bulging-at-the-seams cupboard.

As the weeks went by the cats became a little bored with the flower pots so Arabella and I agreed we needed the versatility of cardboard to make the acquisition of their biscuits even more challenging. I love building pyramids from toilet-roll tubes (so that cats can use their paws to pull out individual biscuits) but had resisted the temptation in this case, given the cats' previous eating habits. However, now was the time to put their progress to the test and Arabella set out cardboard boxes, loo-roll pyramids and paper bags to make things a little tougher. Miraculously the cardboard remained intact – well, almost – and we felt a little chewing was a small price to pay and a perfectly normal response to material of this kind.

Damson and Cherry never became fat cats. Any vet would have been proud of their optimum weight and healthy physique. Arabella continued to have the occasional problem with them. It was so tempting for her to let her guard down and allow them to sit in the kitchen while she cooked, or distract her from her work. As soon as she did so they started bullying her again and she realized that she would never be able to be anything but a strict disciplinarian. The phrase 'give them an inch and they'll take a mile' could have been coined with these two characters in mind.

❖   ❖   ❖

Whether your cat's dependency is manifesting itself as attention-seeking, helplessness, manipulation or anxiety there is one essential thing to remember: dependencies are not in the best interests of either party. Many owners call me for advice because their cats are keeping them up at night, vocalizing excessively or demanding food, and every one without exception feels guilty if they ignore their furry friend. Many of these cats live exclusively indoors and the owners believe that they have to give in to their every whim to keep them happy. Often the reverse is true. Dependencies don't make the cats happy at all. I have had my own personal battle with my lovely little Devon Rex, Mangus. She has tried every trick in the book with me and I will admit I have succumbed during moments of weakness. I am then rewarded with the most insistent and ridiculous behaviour for about a week until she eventually goes back to normal. I increase the activities provided for her in my flat and decrease my availability. The result is always a more content Mangus so I can honestly say I know what owners are going through when they live with a dependent cat – and I know what gets results!

Tackling dependency by changing the relationship

Dependency is a downward spiral; for example, the more you reassure your cat the more helpless he or she will become. Whilst it's great to feel loved it's important to understand that you can only maintain this relationship if you are there for your cat twenty-four hours a day. If you dare to sleep or go shopping you may have a problem. Dysfunctional dependencies can be avoided by following these suggestions:

- Do a quick 'activity budget' on your cat's typical day. If it only includes sleeping and following you around like a bad smell, then you may have a problem!
- Encourage your cat to be a cat as much as possible. If he or she has access to a garden then make sure it is a safe and attractive environment. The more time your cat spends doing cat things the less likely he or she will be to need your constant attention.
- If you live on a busy road it may be possible to build an outside enclosure or secure your garden to keep your cat safe.

- Bullying from other cats can be a problem too and it can prevent insecure types from exploring. Securing your garden will keep them out.
- If you are busy, relaxing or otherwise occupied it is perfectly acceptable to deny your cat attention. This will not make them love you less; it may actually make you more attractive!
- Consider feeding your cat 'ad lib' with a dry complete cat food. This will encourage grazing little and often (a very natural way for a cat to take in food) and take away the emphasis on you as the sole provider of sustenance.
- Feel free to visit friends, work for a living or go on holiday. You are perfectly entitled to a life too and your cat will be delighted to see you when you return rather than pining away to nothing when you leave. Start as you mean to go on; even servants get time off.
- It isn't essential to share your bed with your cat. They often cope extremely well if they are given a quiet, warm area to snooze the night away, without your snoring and constant thrashing about. This can teach them an important lesson: that life can be good without you.
- Some cats benefit from four-legged companions and this can take the heat off you. Dogs and cats can work well (see Chapter 5) and even other cats can be a blessing for those likely to form close attachments.

- If you feel your cat is exhibiting problem behaviour resulting from a dependency, call in an expert with a referral from your vet. Sometimes we are just too close to the relationship to change it for the better without professional help.

CHAPTER 9

Why Do We Love Cats So Much?

My job is the sort of career that requires all kinds of objective analysis from time to time. In my darker moments I have even asked 'What's in it for the cat?' and questioned the whole concept of pet ownership. Is it really as good for them as it is for us? Luckily, I have come to the conclusion (all things being equal) that the relationship between human and cat is positive for both parties and here to stay. I think this is a fascinating subject and worthy of further exploration. In order to get the best out of the relationship for both parties we have to at least attempt to understand our cats better.

This is not about judging ourselves (I include myself in every comment and theory I have); it's far more constructive than that. I just want to know why we love them so much!

In my quest for a better understanding of the human/cat relationship I felt it necessary to start from a more familiar viewpoint: human/human relationships. There are literally thousands of self-help books available that offer advice on and analysis of every conceivable relationship we may possibly encounter during a lifetime. As far as I can tell (and I've read many of them) they mostly fall into the following categories:

1 How to be a good parent and not mess up your children.
2 How to survive childhood (if your parents didn't read Book 1).
3 How to get the best out of work relationships to guarantee promotion.
4 How to attract a possible partner and start a relationship.
5 How to make the most of your relationship and ensure it lasts.
6 How to understand your partner who apparently comes from another planet.
7 How to spot the tell-tale signs if your partner is having an affair.

8   How to avoid displaying the tell-tale signs if *you* are having an affair.

9   How to survive a relationship break-up after you read Book 7 and he *didn't* read Book 8.

This is not an exhaustive list, but you get the picture that this is a very overworked genre. I read five or six books on this topic in quick succession and my main concern was that they encourage over-analysis and rather too much soul-searching. I can't help feeling that you will find a problem if you look hard enough. My other suspicion is that I am inadvertently adding to the list by writing a book specifically about our relationships with our cats. Maybe they don't merit analysis? Maybe delving too deeply will merely open a Pandora's box of issues we would rather not address? If, however, it produces one tiny piece of enlightenment that enriches our cats' lives it has to be worth it. These relationships must *never* be about our specific needs alone and maybe appreciating those needs honestly will enable us to accept that cats have needs too and they are probably not the same as ours.

The female/feline attraction

In this chapter I want to look first at the extraordinary nature of the female/feline attraction. I am still not entirely satisfied that describing cats as feminine and sensual is enough to explain the obsession we women have with them. There has been a great deal written over the years about why women seem to gravitate towards cats and become so besotted with them. It is quite clear that, given the history of the cat's domestication, this is not a modern-day phenomenon. Whilst we may make more extreme emotional demands on our cats these days it seems that they have been demigods in the eyes of humans for many thousands of years. We may not bow in front of them any more or worship them in the religious sense, but we do rather surround ourselves with symbols and effigies (how many cat ornaments have you got?). We also love them to distraction and give them just about anything their hearts desire. Most of us do fall apart when we lose them and show immense grief, falling short only when it comes to shaving our eyebrows off as the Egyptians did. Have things really changed all that much?

There is no doubt that women have incredibly complex emotional needs. We turn to our partners, children, friends and family to fulfil those needs but, sometimes, it just isn't enough. Many women cat lovers I have spoken to over the years talk about their human relationships. Their stories are full of perceptions of disappointment and lack of loyalty; somehow humans never quite get it right. Men are often described as distant and uncommunicative, leaving a woman's emotional needs largely unfulfilled. Then, just when we need them most, along come the nation's cats: small humans, we think, in zip-up furry coats. We may deny we see them like that, but on some level, it is true. We stare longingly at them, we talk to them constantly, we touch them, we caress them and we kiss them. If your cat was a small child in a zip-up furry coat it is possible that he or she might flourish under such conditions of intense love and adoration, but I must admit I'm not convinced. Children surely would be smothered by a love as intensely demonstrated as that? And if you tried to love a partner in the same way as you love your cat, he or she would definitely not find it so attractive: you would look intensely needy. Cats cannot question our unreasonable demands for attention and affection; they can either put up or shut up. They may respond by becoming dependent and needy themselves or capitalize on our incredible compliance and run rings around us. Whatever they choose to do in response to our intense devotion it will never be disloyal and they will never betray us. The beauty of the ambiguity of their communication is that they 'say' whatever we want them to say. They can act their part in any complicated emotional scenario and be word-perfect because we give them the lines. No matter what we need from a relationship at any given time, we have it right there in a curled-up furry ball at the bottom of our bed. I am convinced that a cat provides the sort of relationship that we need, but cannot have with our children, friends or partners.

Do women and cats have something in common?

In defence of those who believe I am merely over-complicating the situation, I should say that it is entirely possible we just like cats because they are beautiful, entertaining, soft and cute. An alternative theory could even be that the relationship between cat and woman works so well because we can relate to so many of their unique traits. Whilst promoting *Cat Detective*, my previous book, I was interviewed by a number of radio presenters for regional BBC stations. One I remember with some interest. I won't mention names but he started the interview by saying, perfectly politely, that he didn't like cats because they were so like women. My immediate response was to ask what he was actually telling me: did he dislike women (and cats merely reminded him of them) or were cats the real enemy and women appeared feline and therefore unpleasant? He said that cats were manipulative, devious and con-fusing, thus mirroring the worst traits of the average woman. Are cats like women? Do we gravitate towards them because we feel empathy? I would like to think cats *are* like women, because they are graceful and tactile; most of us would love to believe we are elegant and almost all of us are touchy-feely. However, cats are indeed great exponents of psychological warfare; maybe this is the equivalent of the games some women play to get their own way. Women often resort to verbal manipulation and gestures of appeasement and other passive techniques but this is where the similarity ends. Cats prefer not to resort to violence because they themselves are too dangerous; women prefer not to because they are not physically dangerous enough. Correct me if I'm wrong; this does look like a similar survival strategy but I don't think it means we are one and the same.

Are cats just bad boys?

Just to put the cat amongst the pigeons, I have my own personal theory. I have offered it up for general consumption during many late-night discussions with various people, both cat lovers and (dare I say it) cat non-lovers. Most if not all have nodded sagely whilst saying it's an interesting way of looking at the root of the cat's appeal to women. Very few have flatly refuted it as rubbish; admittedly one or two have patted me gently on the head and filled up my wine glass but I remain undeterred. I'll discuss it with you and leave you to reach your own conclusions. I dearly want to deny that this is a plausible theory on *any* level but I just can't.

There is a book called *He's just not that into you: the no-excuses truth to understanding guys*. It gives advice to women who hang on the every word of men who don't return their calls, don't turn up and generally treat them badly. As far as I can remember it was a bestseller and prompted a great deal of discussion in newspapers and women's magazines. There is also a saying 'Treat them mean, keep them keen', implying that the best way to win fair maiden is to feign complete disinterest. Neither the book nor the saying would exist if the phenomenon of women loving 'bad boys' wasn't real and alive in the twenty-first century. I find it quite appalling that women can be attracted to dismissive people and it's hard to rationalize the motivation. I would like to think that most of us would see the obvious error in falling for such a man since it would inevitably end in tears or frustration at the very least. However, we still do it, even though we are now fortunate enough to live in a society where we are perfectly capable, both financially and practically, of caring for ourselves. This made me question whether or not this attraction was desirable from an evolutionary perspective. There has to be an innate attraction to virile men with high testosterone levels and a high sex drive. Such men represent healthy specimens who would be excellent providers and defenders, thereby increasing the odds of the offspring's survival. The more 'male' an individual is (according to all the current gender studies) the more likely they are to be competitive, aggressive, non-communicative and seriously not in tune with the desires of women to be loved and cosseted. These men are the sort of guys who don't praise you, never give a word of encouragement and certainly don't know the meaning of the word compliment. However, if they happen by some miracle to say 'nice dress' we are overwhelmed with gratitude and continue with our attempts to solicit the next loving gesture.

The whole 'treat 'em mean, keep 'em keen' philosophy represents a type of reward referred to in learning theory as partial reinforcement. If behaviour is reinforced occasionally, but certainly not always, it becomes more strongly learnt. For example, the nature of gamblers is such that they thrive on partial reinforcement. They keep going because, every now and then, they are rewarded big time. I don't think it's that great a leap to suggest that women are, to some extent, emotional gamblers – hooked on achieving the odd gesture or sentiment expressed by an otherwise dour individual with much more important things on his mind. We twenty-first-century women have a veneer of sophistication that allows us to override this primitive urge but, if we are honest with ourselves, are we not addicted on some level to dismissive and aloof men?

This is where I make another theoretical leap to the

nature of the woman/cat relationship. Are not cats capable of being dismissive and aloof? If you look at the results of the relationship survey in the next chapter, you will see that 50 per cent of owners had been ignored by their dismissive cats and 38 per cent, responding to a different set of questions, referred to their cats as 'aloof' on occasion. How many times do owners use the sentence 'He/she is very loving but very much on his/her own terms'? Yet still we pursue them in this feline version of an addictive partial reinforcement programme. I accept that not all cats are made the same and neither are all women; I just keep thinking there is something in this. I have found myself recently being very self-aware when I am around Mangus and I am guilty of the most fickle behaviour sometimes. She has moments when she wants to be alone and independent and I call and call to get her into the bedroom with me at night to no avail. I go looking for her just to give her a cuddle and feel delighted when she brushes past only to become frustrated when she walks casually away. However, when she is in a 'clingy/in your face' mood she drives me nuts and I can't wait to get into my bedroom to shut the door for a bit of peace from her neediness. Is it just me who sees the parallels between this sort of behaviour and a typical male/female courtship? I'm not saying all female owners behave in this way towards their cats; I just feel that to say women like them because they show unconditional love is a bit simplistic and not really the whole picture.

Men love cats too!

I do have a tendency to focus completely, when discussing this topic, on women. This is totally appropriate since most of my clients are women, most of the people who read my books are women and 96 per cent of all the helpful cat owners who completed the relationship survey discussed in the next chapter were women. However, every now and then, I come into contact with the other 4 per cent. Whilst loving their cats, in my experience, seems to come quite naturally to gay men, every now and again I am privileged enough to be there when heterosexual men open up about their love for their feline companions. I always listen intently because you never know when you are going to receive the piece of information that represents the missing bit of the puzzle.

I have been sent many letters over the years and occasionally I receive them from men. Those that show the true nature of the human/cat relationship best are those written when the cat dies. This particular gentleman was indeed speaking about the loss of his cat. He wrote: *There is an aching void here, quite impossible to describe. Since his friend Hughie cat left us some five years ago,*

Lenny and I have been very dependent on each other. So much love and understanding. He was eighteen years old and understood my pattern of life in great detail – gentle, loving, constant and so faithful. I miss him enormously and nothing can fill his place in my life. And I will always think of him and miss him terribly – my dear dead lovely Lenny. Bless you, my friend. I could almost feel the pain when I read this and it was quite clear that Lenny had been his dear companion, particularly since the death of the other member of the household, Hughie cat. Here was a constant in this man's life and it was gone and he was obviously struggling to come to terms with life alone.

I was in my office one day writing this book when I received a phone call from a gentleman who had lost his cat about a year previously. He was obviously an extraordinarily intelligent and eloquent man, a senior lecturer at a university, but he wanted answers about the last few moments of his cat's life. We spoke for some time about the subject but we mainly focused on a more philosophical approach to the subject of loving and losing a pet. He asked me about the nature of the cat's mind and its sentience. I could discuss some of my own thoughts and feelings on the subject but there was definitely a point beyond which I couldn't go because I just didn't have the answers. He told me that he had kept a notebook and he wanted me to read it. I asked his permission to reproduce some of it here because I think it is extremely relevant. I have, however, changed the name of his cat and omitted to mention his to respect his privacy.

He wrote:

I have kept a notebook since my cat was put to sleep. The book is now filled and though I have another one of the same size I set out to complete my reconciliation with the facts by the time I reached the end of this one. I have not used the other one and I don't think I have anything more to say that would be useful to me.

I kept the diary because I did not think I could talk to anyone about what happened. Because there were medical details I wanted to understand there was no point in talking to anyone who did not know anything about them. In addition there were questions about Harry's own physical experience and mental life that I could never discuss with another person who had not arrived at the same understanding as me. People, even vets, might be sympathetic; but I did not need sympathy. I needed knowledge.

If I had not expressed or articulated my thoughts and feelings about the death of my cat I would still be going around in circles or getting sunk in some kind of emotional swamp. I know some people 'steel' themselves and 'not talk about it'. But these are just defences against hurt. Unless this pain is properly explored there can be no understanding and no release. Defences against emotional pain erect an artificial wall between emotion and thought and prevent understanding. Being 'macho' about these things is just so much stupidity. I suspect those who adopt this attitude (it can hardly be called thought) towards animals have not allowed themselves time to think what they are doing. Perhaps they have been swept up in that community of people with 'practical common sense' whose commercial values crowd out less practical forms of thought. This includes assumptions about 'animals' that places them in some order of worth rather than the developing complexity of evolution.

If I was to understand what happened to Harry I would have to get answers to the questions still troubling me. Just when I was supposed to 'let go' and 'move on' I felt I had to ask questions, the answers to which often went right over my head. The questions I asked were not dissimilar from those I asked about relatives. When my aunt was dying she was able to tell me how she felt. She told me she was tired of life and that she really wanted to die. Being able to approach one's death in this way is a consolation for everyone. Without making any judgements about how proper is the comparison, animals are unable to share accounts of their mental or physical experience of illness and dying. If I have grasped the fact of my cat's sentience and awareness and I have shared this in some way yet to be explained, then I want to understand what mental or physical experience my cat underwent. To try to understand this I asked different people, the local vet, the animal hospital vet, the manager at the RSPCA, the nurse. I asked them the same questions and this helped me get a comprehensive grasp of what happened to Harry. It also helped me test the veracity of the answers I was given and I *needed to do this so that I could finally live with them. At some stage I had all or most of my questions answered and by that stage I found I was already letting go of the past. There will always be doubts and these pull me in that backwards direction. But those doubts have become like all those day-to-day doubts that can be put aside without really understanding.*

In my opinion this is a perfect example, beautifully and painfully expressed, of a man coming to terms with a loss. Where he differs from many men (and women) is in his ability to communicate his feelings so well in writing. I also feel it shows a tremendous need to gain control of something he couldn't control. He couldn't tell his cat how he felt; therefore it was imperative that the gentleman found out, to the best of his ability, what Harry was experiencing just prior to his death. He felt he could only move on if he accepted that he had done everything to prevent unnecessary suffering (according to the experts) and provided the best possible emotional and physical support at the end. I wrote about grief and pet bereavement in *Cat Confidential* and I wish I had had the opportunity to discuss Harry then. This man truly loved his cat; his personality was such that he had to face the tough questions we all ask ourselves at such a time. Where others may have skirted round them or dwelled for a while without being able to be proactive, he tackled difficult subjects head-on. This man saw the incredible nature of the cat as companion and friend and he wasn't afraid to express his feelings when he lost him. I can relate personally to his approach because I feel that I have tackled bereavement on several occasions in an equally 'aggressive' way. We all face this most difficult of times in the way that best suits our life experiences and our personalities. Whether it is entirely healthy to look for answers and be so hard on ourselves about our potential failings at the end is debatable. I hope that I was able in some small way to help this gentleman on his journey; I so want him to forgive himself for something that wasn't his fault.

Men are perfectly capable of loving cats too; I am absolutely convinced of that. It just happens in smaller numbers and, like most matters of the heart, they rarely speak of it. Most men, in my experience, are also more likely to view problems within the human/cat relationship with a much more black and white attitude than women. They will love the cat until it soils the duvet or attacks a visitor. Their partner will become upset and the man will do what he does best: offer a solution. This solution usually is something like 'the cat's gone wrong so it has to go'. Whilst this looks great on paper it hardly represents a workable compromise. Many partnerships are at breaking point by the time I get involved for just this reason. They want their loved ones to stop hurting but the best answer they can find is to remove the problem, i.e. the cat. Behaviour therapy is usually perceived as complete mumbo-jumbo ('You can't possibly train cats; they're not dogs') and I consider myself very fortunate if the husbands are even present when I arrive for the consultation. If they are, I know it's going to be OK because, with very few exceptions, they catch on quickly. They soon realize that the combination of a solution that means the cat can stay and Brownie points for showing willing is a complete win/win situation!

Just to add credence to my male cat lover argument, research conducted in 2004 by Dr June McNicholas for Cats' Protection showed an even more positive picture of the modern cat/man relationship. In the UK today apparently there are 1.28 million male cat owners. I really do feel this is a product of the pressures on men to be something else – they had become 'indoctrinated' by society to be 'in touch with their feminine side' and more sensitive – but maybe this is a simplistic reasoning behind a very modern phenomenon. Dr McNicholas's research showed that single men are almost as likely as single women to consider choosing their cat over a partner or friendship. Since most of the men I come into contact with in my work are part of the man/woman/cat triangle it is difficult to comment on these statistics. I would, however, say that the single men I have met really are capable of loving their cat as intensely as any woman is. The research also showed that women are more attracted to men who like animals and male cat lovers are perceived to be nicer and more caring than the rest, so I would suggest that acquiring a cat is a good strategic move for any single man!

It is what it is

I love the expression 'it is what it is'. It perfectly describes how we should all ultimately feel about the relationships we have with our cats. Trying to understand the finer psychological elements of an inter-species partnership like ours is probably doomed to failure (but fascinating all the same). The best thing we can all do is accept the unique nature of every relationship between human and cat. I also believe that it is essential to the success of the partnership that we ensure we take time out to love our cats *their* way. Then everyone's happy.

CHAPTER 10

The Relationship Survey

I always intended this book to offer a voice to the cat-owning public. This isn't just about how *I* feel; *Cat Counsellor* should reflect the human/cat relationship from a much broader perspective. It is perfectly valid for me to form my own opinions through my work and my own experiences (this is a very subjective topic) but I needed to open up a forum for the debate. The easiest way to achieve this was to conduct a survey to find out how cat lovers really feel about their pets. I compiled a questionnaire and placed it on my website (www.vickyhalls.net) and in the back of my last book,

Cat Detective, hoping that owners would allow me a little insight into their relationships with their cats. The bulk of the questionnaire included statements against which the owners had to tick either AGREE, DISAGREE or NOT SURE to show their response. Many of the questions I asked were about emotions and feelings and sometimes it is difficult to be objective about ourselves and how we behave. I was not surprised to find a number of owners who completed the survey seeming to show incredible ambivalence as they agreed with two statements about their relationship with the cat that were the exact opposite of each other. Some owners ticked the NOT SURE box on just about everything. I actually think this is an extremely honest approach since a great deal of our relationship is taken for granted and rarely analysed. I personally found that the more I thought about a question, the more likely the answer was to change. The 'knee jerk' response to the statement was often not the true one. There are always going to be limitations to this sort of survey but I was still delighted with the response and I have included here the initial results from the first 150 completed questionnaires to help us all better understand this relationship phenomenon.

About you:

Age: 18–30 31%, 31–40 27%, 41–50 21%, 51–60 13%, 61+ = 8%

Sex: male 4%, female 96%

Marital status: married/cohabiting 58%, single (never married) 34%, divorced/separated 7%, widowed 1%

No. of children living at home: 0 88%, 1 7%, 2 5%, 3+0%

Working: full-time 72%, part-time 15%, retired 5%, not working 5%, unable to work 3%

No. of cats in household: 1 41%, 2 37%, 3 14%, 4 5%, 5 0%, 6 0%, 7+3%

Any other pets?: Yes 24%, No 76%

The first set of questions was to establish the demographics of the survey. I wasn't surprised to see that the majority of those completing the questionnaire were women. I target women specifically, sometimes subconsciously, in my writing, lecturing and during my consultations and I feel these results have validated that approach. I will not dismiss the male as an unworthy cat lover, however, and I hope I have allowed men to have their say throughout this book.

It would be a perfect stereotype to show the typical cat lover as a single female who has never married but this clearly isn't the case. I have actually known this for some years, since the majority of my clients are married or living with a partner. Certainly a third of those surveyed were single but a greater percentage of owners were not living alone. The majority of the owners had no children living at home; is this significant? I have certainly worked with many women whose cats have been their 'children' until the real thing comes along; more of the 'child substitute' debate later.

Nearly three-quarters of those surveyed were working full-time, adding weight to the theory that people own cats because they work and therefore cannot have a high-maintenance dog. I am not convinced because I still subscribe to the view that there are defined cat lovers and dog lovers and a bunch of people who fall between the two extremes. A quarter of the cat owners had other species of pet too and I would probably describe them as part of that 'bunch'. However, it has to be said that I have other pets (a horse and a donkey) but I would consider myself to be a dyed-in-the-wool cat person!

I was gratified to see that 41 per cent of the owners had one cat. My views on multi-cat living are not a secret and I think you are fortunate if all the variables work in your favour and your cats get along. However, having just one cat does make it more likely that an intense bond can develop if the relationship is a true one-to-one sort of thing. I often think that my dear Puddy (my favourite cat, who passed away in 2002) and I would have been even closer if the other cats hadn't been around. (For those who haven't read *Cat Confidential*, I admit I was at one time the proud owner of seven cats. As a multi-cat household it worked fairly well because I benefited from a large home surrounded by fields and marshland and very little else. All individuals had plenty of opportunities to respect each other's personal space and things were largely peaceful. However, as I have said, variables such as environment and cat population density often conspire against the multi-cat household.)

About your cat:

Age of cat: < 2 yrs 28%, 3–5 yrs 27%, 6–8 yrs 29%, 9–11 yrs 7%, 12+ yrs 9%
Sex: M(n) 55%, F(s) 41%, M(e) 0%, F(e) 4%
Pedigree/breed: domestic 74%, pedigree 26%

There was a nice cross-section of ages for the cats included in the survey. The ratio of 3:1 for moggies to pedigree does not reflect the total cat population but in this case it's probably appropriate. Pedigree owners have spent a great deal more money on the acquisition of their cats in the first place (that isn't necessarily a sign of the ultimate cat lover) and they tend to be enthusiastic and proactive owners since they have a certain expectation of their pet to behave as befits the breed. It was good to have a great mix: everything from Sphynx to Ragdoll and all variations in between.

Indoor/outdoor:

My cat has unlimited access outdoors: 31%

My cat has access outdoors but I shut him/her in at night: 36%

My cat has restricted access outside under supervision: 12%

My cat is taken out for a walk on a harness and lead: 5%

My cat is kept indoors but has an outdoor pen: 6%

My cat has access outdoors but doesn't go out: 2%

My cat is kept exclusively indoors: 8%

Forty-eight per cent of those surveyed restricted their cats' access outside and 19 per cent kept them exclusively indoors, took them for walks on a lead or contained them within an outdoor pen. Interestingly only 2 per cent had access outside but chose not to go out. The density of the cat population in certain urban areas is increasing daily and I am amazed that the less emotionally robust cats are not becoming agoraphobic in huge numbers.

What kind of relationship do you have with your cat?

My cat is a pet: 18%
My cat is a family member: 64%
My cat is like a child: 25%
My cat is a companion: 28%
I find it hard to explain my relationship with my cat: 1%

This was the first section that asked the owners to explore their feelings about their cats. Many of us will cohabit for years with various felines and never stop to question the type of kinship that has developed. Many owners specified more than one type of relationship, for example a child *and* a family member. This is perfectly valid and I admit that I would probably have ticked several of these boxes. Ironically, I would have ticked the box that said *I find it hard to explain my relationship with my cat* since, as such a deep thinker on the subject, I feel there are unique qualities within the cat/woman relationship that defy analysis and pigeon-holing. Only 1 per cent of those surveyed agreed with me!

The survey did confirm, however, the modern think-ing that cats are gradually upgrading their status from pet to family member. This implies that the cat's perceived wishes are considered when making decisions, including those about holidays and moving house. I know of many owners who don't go away because the cat would be lonely, don't sit on the sofa because the cat's comfortable, get up in the middle of the night because the cat's bored and generally put themselves way down the list of priorities. That's some family member!

Over a quarter referred to their cat as a companion (but not a pet). If we consider our cats to be companions, without the proviso of also being pets, this surely implies equality by definition and describes a relationship with a degree of exclusivity? This is probably the modern definition of the human/cat relationship. By bestowing on them the title of 'pet' we are somehow denigrating their actual status as something much more than that. It is interesting to look at the dictionary definitions for both pet and companion: *Pet: 1. a tame animal kept in a household for companionship, amusement, etc. Companion: 1. a person who is an associate of another or others; comrade. 2. (esp. formerly) an employee, usually a woman, who provides company for an employer, esp. an elderly woman. 3. one of a pair; match.*

I often get castigated for using the terms 'own' and 'pet'; surely I should use more favourable phrases such as 'custodian', 'servant' or 'cohabiter'? I don't actually believe that stating 'I own a pet' is remotely derogatory. If you look at the dictionary definition above for 'pet' it is quite clear that that is *exactly* why most of us keep them (given that the et cetera will refer to all the other complex reasons why, known only to ourselves). Just because they are referred to as pets doesn't mean we do not care for them as well as anyone calling them something more serious on the scale of meaningful relationships. I'm probably labouring a point that is nothing more than confused or irrelevant terminology but defining the relationship has got to go some way towards understanding it and therefore ensuring it works for both parties.

A quarter of those surveyed referred to their cat exclusively as a 'child'. I am not convinced that all those who see their relationship in this way are merely biding time until they have a real baby with slightly less fur. Many women I have spoken to personally have chosen not to have children but still refer to their cats in a maternal way. I think this has a great deal to do with our innate programming as nurturers. Whether we make the decision to pursue careers instead of families or remain childless for another reason we still need to perform the role of mother for which we were designed. Just as cats will hunt shoelaces or rolled-up pieces of newspaper when they cannot be predacious, maybe we, as female humans, need to simulate natural maternal behaviour? It is also infinitely easier to practise parenthood on cats since the need for consistency and leading by example are mainly irrelevant and therefore you can perform all the enjoyable and simplistic elements of being a mother without the serious responsibility of helping to mould a brand-new person. Admittedly breeders do have more of a responsibility in that respect than most of us but it really isn't on quite such a grand scale.

Safety

I worry that my cat will come to harm when he/she is outside: AGREE 79%, DISAGREE 13%, NOT SURE 8%

I worry about the dangers of traffic: AGREE 82%, DISAGREE 13%, NOT SURE 5%

I worry that my cat may go missing: AGREE 76%, DISAGREE 15%, NOT SURE 9%

I worry about my cat fighting with others and getting injured: AGREE 67%, DISAGREE 25%, NOT SURE 8%

I worry that someone may steal him/her: AGREE 46%, disagree 43%, NOT SURE 11%

I like to know where he/she is at any given time: AGREE 61%, DISAGREE 29%, NOT SURE 10%

One thing that parenthood prepares us beautifully for is worrying. However, this emotion isn't the exclusive domain of those who think of their cats as children. Nearly 80 per cent of those surveyed worry about their cat coming to harm when outside the safety of the home. Many of these have actually confronted this fear and decided to restrict their pets' access outdoors. Roughly the same percentage were concerned about the dangers of traffic and their cats going missing but less than half believed that getting stolen was an issue for concern. Fighting or injuries worried two-thirds of the owners and almost the same number were only happy when they knew exactly where their pet was at any given time. This is something that is apparent in almost every case I have seen over the years. The owner's love for the cat is so intense that the fear of loss is equally great. It is why my age-old plea 'if you love them enough, then let them go' will always fall on deaf ears. Love is very difficult to view from an altruistic standpoint; I am not entirely sure if true altruism is even possible. We perceive our love in such a way that it revolves around our own pleasure. We do something that we think gives our cats pleasure therefore we are happy. These things rarely give us pain because, coincidentally, we believe that their pleasure, is our pleasure. It is possible to argue that the person who cooks fish at 3 a.m. because that's when the cat wants it can hardly be having fun. The interesting point here is that it is the owner who has decided that this has to be done otherwise the cat will suffer in some way. The reality is quite the opposite but if we decide for ourselves what constitutes pleasure and happiness for our cats it can, due to the obvious 'lost in translation' element to the communication, only be judged by our own interpretation and beliefs. I think what I am trying to ask in a very roundabout way is 'If we restrict our pets' access to the great outdoors because *we* are worried, are we considering *their* feelings and needs?' I don't dispute that they may well live longer, but will they be happy?

Interaction

I approach my cat for interaction more than he/she approaches me: AGREE 20%, DISAGREE 65%, NOT SURE 15%

My cat approaches me for interaction more than I approach him/her: AGREE 20%, DISAGREE 60%, NOT SURE 20%

My cat and I approach each other an equal number of times throughout the day: AGREE 65%, DISAGREE 24%, NOT SURE 11%

Sometimes my cat will ignore me or seem uninterested when I approach: AGREE 50%, DISAGREE 44%, NOT SURE 6%

I will respond to my cat at any time of the day or night: AGREE 60%, DISAGREE 35%, NOT SURE 5%

I always respond to my cat's approaches: AGREE 65%, DISAGREE 31%, NOT SURE 4%

I will check to see where my cat is if I haven't seen him/her for a while: AGREE 93%, DISAGREE 5%, NOT SURE 2%

I will occasionally wake my cat up to stroke him/her:

AGREE 46%, DISAGREE 48%, NOT SURE 6%

I will seek my cat out if he/she is hiding: AGREE 52%, DISAGREE 39%, NOT SURE 9%

My cat will seek me out if I go into another room: AGREE 71%, DISAGREE 22%, NOT SURE 7%

My cat is by my side most of the time I am home: AGREE 41%, DISAGREE 53%, NOT SURE 6%

I can't sit down without my cat jumping on my lap: AGREE 26%, DISAGREE 65%, NOT SURE 9%

I talk to my cat occasionally at feeding times: AGREE 61%, DISAGREE 32%, NOT SURE 7%

I talk to my cat all the time: AGREE 80%, DISAGREE 15%, NOT SURE 5%

I hardly ever talk to my cat: AGREE 1%, DISAGREE 91%, NOT SURE 8%

My cat is very vocal and 'talks' back: AGREE 66%, DISAGREE 25%, NOT SURE 9%

In this particular section I was trying to ascertain how the owner and cat interacted on a day-to-day basis. Were the owners chasing harassed cats round the house or were the cats really hanging on their every word and not leaving them alone? It appears that the general consensus of opinion showed that contact was initiated equally between cat and owner in at least two-thirds of the households.

I was particularly interested in the results of the next few questions because they went a small way towards reinforcing my theory about why cats *really* turn women on (see the previous chapter). Half the people surveyed agreed that their cats occasionally ignore them or seem uninterested when they approach. Sixty per cent responded to their cats' wishes any time of the day or night, 65 per cent always responded to their cats no matter what they were doing and practically everyone went wandering round the house looking for their cats if they hadn't seen them for a while! Nearly half of the owners even woke their cats up to give them a stroke and a similar number will drag them out from cupboards or under the bed if they are hiding. I honestly believe if a cat is hiding it is doing it for a reason and whilst ill health is a possible cause it is just as likely to be having a private moment that should be respected as such. These last few questions relate to a lot of extra owner-to-cat approaches. I wonder whether the true picture of who initiates contact really shows the equal fascination that the majority of the owners describe? Just a thought!

The next three questions give a better insight into the cat's behaviour round its owner. Nearly three-quarters of the owners agreed that their cats would actually seek them out if they went into another room. Forty-one per cent were constantly by their owner's side and over a quarter couldn't wait for their owner to sit down to plonk themselves on their laps.

The vast majority of the owners were clearly talking a

great deal to their cats and a significant majority of cats (although not quite so many) talked back. I received one letter from a talkative owner who wrote: *Most people think I am totally nuts about Jasper, talking to him like a human being, but as the saying goes, 'The more people I meet the more I like my cat.' That couldn't be more true.* I hear this sentence so often from cat lovers; sad really, because I don't think the love of humans and cats should be mutually exclusive. Only 1 per cent of the owners rarely spoke to their cats; I find it extraordinary that anyone would remain mute in the presence of a cat. Whilst most of us believe that their ability to understand English is minimal, we as humans communicate verbally and it would be impossible to form a relationship with another creature without doing so (unless we physically cannot). I say some crazy things to my cat Mangus; I am completely aware that she doesn't understand but she does appreciate the emotion behind the words and she enjoys the attention. She, like most other cats, will 'talk' back because it reinforces the attention and guarantees more of the same. Cats are not daft; talking means attention and attention means food or something equally pleasant.

Bedtime

My cat sleeps with me on the bed: AGREE 58%, DISAGREE 34%, NOT SURE 8%

I shut my cat out of the bedroom at night: AGREE 18%, DISAGREE 75%, NOT SURE 7%

My cat is given the choice but chooses to sleep elsewhere at night: AGREE 32%, DISAGREE 55%, NOT SURE 13%

My partner doesn't like my cat sleeping with us: AGREE 14%, DISAGREE 70%, NOT SURE 16%

I don't want my cat sleeping with me: AGREE 11%, DISAGREE 75%, NOT SURE 14%

Part of the whole relationship thing takes place at night. Many cats love to sleep with their owners, but don't be fooled. Their motivation is often warmth, security and familiarity of odour representing safety. Occasionally your company is useful at night when they get bored and start poking your nostril with their claws to see what happens. Just have a look at how much bed you are actually left with to see if there is any consideration for *your* needs at night-time!

Over half of the owners slept with their cat at night. A third of the owners gave their cat the choice but they chose to sleep elsewhere. Now I think I've seen a flaw in these statistics. If 18 per cent of owners shut their cats out of the bedroom at night and a total of 25 per cent either don't want their cat sleeping with them or have partners that think that way, simple maths tells me that there are some cats somewhere who are really getting their own way.

Personality

My cat is loving and attentive: AGREE 90%, DISAGREE 5%, NOT SURE 5%

My cat is sociable with everyone: AGREE 36%, DISAGREE 57%, NOT SURE 7%

I am the only person my cat wants to be with: AGREE 15%, DISAGREE 82%, NOT SURE 3%

My cat is very confident: AGREE 42%, DISAGREE 37%, NOT SURE 21%

My cat is self-reliant: AGREE 55%, DISAGREE 28%, NOT SURE 17%

My cat is needy: AGREE 30%, DISAGREE 50%, NOT SURE 20%

My cat can be aloof: AGREE 38%, DISAGREE 51%, NOT SURE 11%

My cat is very timid: AGREE 23%, DISAGREE 71%, NOT SURE 6%

This was always going to be a difficult section to complete because assessment of character and personality is incredibly subjective. I left the owners with a dilemma: for example, their cats may love one moment and be aloof the next. These traits are not mutually exclusive and I would hope that, from the results, most of the owners could see that these elements of their cats' personality are rarely exhibited all the time.

Ninety per cent of owners agreed that their cats were

loving and attentive. A third of the cats were sociable with everyone but 15 per cent only wanted one specific person, their owner. One owner wrote: *Kim has never played and does not like people very much, but with me he is completely happy and I think I am blessed with a companion who is as near human as any animal could be*. She obviously feels immensely flattered that she has been singled out as the one person worthy of attention and this must feel good. It is also interesting to note that she refers to her companion as nearly human; this seems like the perfect compromise. A pseudo-human with all the positive traits, none of the negative and loads of soft fur! I've seen many cats who only want one person; this is often the result of poor early socialization or a complete lack of it. Some hand-reared cats bond exclusively with their carers and timid cats never get used to strangers if their owners have infrequent visitors.

Forty-two per cent of owners said their cats were confident and over half those surveyed agreed that their cats were self-reliant. This is encouraging since these are probably the two best qualities to prepare a cat for a life as a domestic pet. Thirty per cent agreed that their cats were needy. In our quest for the ultimately dog-like cat we try to breed selectively for sociability. As I have said before, this sometimes creates a dependent personality rather than a sociable one. It looks the same (lots of attention etc.) but nearly a third of the owners appeared to see it for what it really is.

Neediness is not a positive trait in cats; it puts an enormous strain on the owner and, if left unchecked, can be the cause of much anxiety for the cat (see Chapter 8 for further details).

Twenty-three per cent of the cats were described as timid. Whilst a healthy suspicion of all novel things is a good survival strategy it is not in the animal's best interests to spook at every sudden noise or movement. These are tough cats to live with (see Chapter 6) and often, dare I say it, fairly unrewarding pets. The amount of love and attention given by the owners is never in proportion to the stuff they get in return. If you are looking for the whole 'unconditional love' thing these are probably not the cats for you.

Relationship

My cat knows what I am thinking: AGREE 25%, DISAGREE 49%, NOT SURE 26%

My cat understands when I am ill: AGREE 61%, DISAGREE 25%, NOT SURE 14%

My cat understands when I am depressed: AGREE 58%, DISAGREE 25%, NOT SURE 17%

My cat responds adversely when I am stressed: AGREE 35%, DISAGREE 45%, NOT SURE 20%

My cat would miss me terribly if I went away: AGREE 49%, DISAGREE 25%, NOT SURE 26%

My cat prefers my company to anyone else's: AGREE 46%, DISAGREE 40%, NOT SURE 14%

My cat understands what I am saying: AGREE 41%, DISAGREE 27%, NOT SURE 32%

My cat has a sense of humour: AGREE 48%, DISAGREE 30%, NOT SURE 22%

My cat would struggle to cope without me: AGREE 18%, DISAGREE 63%, NOT SURE 19%

I would struggle to cope without my cat: AGREE 63%, DISAGREE 24%, NOT SURE 13%

I wouldn't rehome my cat even if I knew he/she would be happier somewhere else: AGREE 15%, DISAGREE 49%, NOT SURE 36%

Nobody would care for my cat like I do: AGREE 43%, DISAGREE 35%, NOT SURE 22%

At this point in the survey I felt that the owners were sufficiently absorbed to be prepared to look at the deeper elements of their relationship. Twenty-five per cent of the owners truly believed that their cats knew what they were thinking. Interestingly, 26 per cent more were not sure whether they did or didn't. This is a tricky one since it is quite obvious that cats don't read minds. However, they are capable of the most incredibly accurate interpretation of the most subtle body language or changes in our tone of voice and this will often give them a very good impression of what we are thinking. If the question was asked on that basis – *Is your cat so tuned into your behaviour that it appears he can read your mind?* I would probably have ticked AGREE. Later in this section the owners were asked if they thought their cats understood what they were saying. This is another example of their accurate interpretation of non-verbal cues rather than their ability to speak English. Forty-one per cent agreed that they did understand and a hefty third of the total number sat on the fence again, prepared to keep an open mind about the whole thing because sometimes it certainly seemed that they did.

Many people I have spoken to refer to instances when their cats have shown tremendous consideration for their feelings. One owner sent me a letter about the importance of her cat to the family when nobody else could help. She wrote: *His undemanding, uncritical affection has been a lifeline for depressed members of the family, for whom human communication has been impossible.* Over half of those surveyed agreed that their cats understood when they were ill or depressed and gave them comfort. One lady wrote: *If Gem had been human she would have been a hospital matron. Whenever my father was ill she stayed with him, stroking his face with the back of her paw. Since Father's death, over which she grieved for about six months, she has watched over me.* It is hard to imagine how another human could get this so right at such a difficult time.

Over a third of the owners felt that their stress impacted on their cats. I have seen many cases in my career where the owners' stresses have made life even tougher for their cats, who are already dealing with something else much more on a cat level. If the cat has a strong bond with the owner, any perceived stress will be seen as imposing on the human the same level of threat that the cat is feeling. They don't see it being caused by a problem at the office; it's always going to be about them.

Nearly half of the owners agreed that their cats would miss them terribly if they went away. This is another factor that influences the owners' perception of their relationship with their cats. Loving someone means missing them if they are not around, therefore the cats must miss them because they love them. Many cats do miss the presence of their owners since it represents a significant change in the social dynamics of the household if the neighbour pops in to feed them and the familiar routines are absent. It can also mean a visit to the local cattery, which represents a twofold change, both social and environmental. I genuinely do believe, having said all that, that cats can form strong bonds and miss their owners terribly. I always feel more comfortable, however, if they stop short of actually fretting and becoming seriously anxious.

Just for fun I asked if the owners felt their cats had a sense of humour. Without exception I have found cat people to possess a sharp wit and many of the things cats do can be extraordinarily funny. Nearly half said they agreed that their cats had a sense of humour and another 22 per cent weren't sure. I just think they appeal to the incredible sense of humour that we cat lovers seem to have.

I then went back to the concept of loving and losing and suggested that their cats would struggle to cope without them. Sixty-three per cent realistically disagreed with this statement, understanding that they really weren't the centre of their cats' universe. This is exactly how it should be since if our cats want us rather than need us it makes it so much easier for them to function normally. Sadly, and rather disturbingly, exactly the same percentage of owners felt differently when asked if they would struggle to cope without their cats. Sixty-three per cent agreed they would. This is an example of the sort of letter I receive from people finding it difficult to come to terms with the death of their cat: *These companions, like no others, give us unquestioning love, devotion and the privilege of sharing their lives, so long as they are treated with the respect due to them. The loss of these precious friends leaves a hole in one's heart that can never be replaced. Indeed it is as if a part of us passes away with them. And yet, if we really search, our dear friends can still be seen, in the home and garden. They are young again, free, well and happy to be with us – for ever, if we want. First we must look and listen. They will always be there, patiently waiting for us. It is all we can ask and hope for.* This distresses me deeply because you can almost feel the writer desperately trying to create scenarios in her mind that make the absence of her pet more bearable. It is by far the easiest thing to believe they are still there, and a perfectly normal stage of the grieving process.

The next question goes back to the age-old challenge: do you love your cat enough to let him go? Fifteen per cent of the owners agreed that they wouldn't rehome their cat even if they knew he would be happier else-where. Nearly half, however, disagreed, implying they would. The rest honestly admitted that they weren't sure how they would react, given that situation. I would love to think that we are all capable of such selfless love that we would rehome our cat if it was unhappy. The reality, however, is very different. I think the key to this is the word 'know'. I honestly believe that if we could know beyond doubt that our cats would benefit from rehoming we would do it, albeit reluctantly. On the rare occasion that I have to recommend this to a client, the 'know' part is purely my advice. I hope that nobody finds themselves in this situation but it takes a very strong person indeed to sacrifice their own needs for those of the cat. Ironically, owners who give up their cats are often judged as poor owners or so unattached to their pets that they are making a decision based solely on convenience. In my experience this is almost always not the case and the individuals who have been forced to make this decision are punished twofold, by losing a loved pet and being castigated for it by all and sundry.

Forty-three per cent of the owners felt that nobody else would care for their cats as well as they did. A third of the owners disagreed and 22 per cent were not sure. Going too far down the line of believing that we have the exclusive rights to perfect cat care is dangerous. Many of those people who are referred to as 'collectors' suffer from this delusion. The RSPCA, the police and the council all become involved in removing large numbers of animals from tiny dwellings, many suffering from appalling neglect. These owners have created their own private 'rescue' centre and misguidedly believe that they are the only people who can save and protect their charges. The truth is quite the opposite and these poor souls are suffering from a recognized mental illness. I am not saying for one moment that those owners taking part in the survey who agreed with the statement *Nobody would care for my cat like I do* are certifiable! I just believe that there are numerous ways to express love for your pet and it is possible to get it right in more than one situation; it is also possible to take the 'nobody would care for my cat like I do' thought to an unhealthy extreme.

Love and support

My cat has given me comfort at a particularly difficult time in my life: AGREE 71%, DISAGREE 21%, NOT SURE 8%

My cat has supported me through bereavement: AGREE 34%, DISAGREE 53%, NOT SURE 13%

My cat has supported me through a relationship breakdown: AGREE 19%, DISAGREE 70%, NOT SURE 11%

My cat has supported me through illness: AGREE 45%, DISAGREE 48%, NOT SURE 7%

My cat feels unconditional love for me: AGREE 49%, DISAGREE 25%, NOT SURE 26%

My cat feels cupboard love for me: AGREE 22%, DISAGREE 40%, NOT SURE 38%

My cat's love is conditional on the way I treat him/her: AGREE 32%, DISAGREE 54%, NOT SURE 14%

My cat doesn't love me: AGREE 3%, DISAGREE 86%, NOT SURE 11%

My cat's love is very different from the expression of human love: AGREE 84%, DISAGREE 7%, NOT SURE 9%

My cat seems to love me sometimes but not others: AGREE 26%, DISAGREE 58%, NOT SURE 16%

If I don't do what my cat wants he/she won't love me any more: AGREE 1%, DISAGREE 93%, NOT SURE 6%

My cat would still love me even if I rejected him/her occasionally: AGREE 88%, DISAGREE 5%, NOT SURE 7%

This set of questions referred to the most complex of emotions: love. I asked first whether their cats had helped them through a difficult time in their lives.

Seventy-one per cent agreed that their cats had been a great comfort to them. Thirty-four per cent had been supported through bereavement, 20 per cent through a relationship breakdown and 45 per cent through illness. This is an extract from a typical letter showing how important a cat's support is at a traumatic time: *My cat has been such a friend and stayed close to me ten years ago when my husband left us. He shadowed me for weeks, months, only leaving me when I had visitors to keep me company. He is a real gentleman.*

I then made the classic statement *My cat feels unconditional love for me* and asked for the owners' reactions. Nearly half agreed that their cats did indeed show unconditional love but the rest disagreed with the statement or were unsure about its validity. Many people refer to the love of a pet as unconditional but I think you will have seen by now that I think it is far more complicated than that. I personally wouldn't feel comfortable in a relationship where the other party showed 'unconditional love'. This suggests in my mind that the love is somehow undervalued because my behaviour within the relationship is irrelevant. I understand the appeal of being loved 'warts an' all', but surely we still have to make *some* effort?

I then made the rather more cynical statement that cats show 'cupboard' love; we are merely large tin openers, chicken cookers and packet rippers. Only 22 per cent agreed with me and I'm rather glad about that because this may be a strong motivation for cats but it certainly isn't the whole story. The next statement, *My cat's love is conditional on the way I treat him*, seemed to me to be a far healthier perception of our role in the relationship. Only a third agreed and 54 per cent disagreed. It is not surprising to see that this is a similar percentage to those who believed in cats' unconditional love so I obviously wasn't making any headway with them!

When I suggested that a cat's love is very different from the expression of human love a resounding 84 per cent agreed. I think this is an incredibly important point since it could show the general disillusionment that many people feel about human relationships. As I have said before, the human/cat equivalent is capable of mimicking many of the best bits without the constant disappointments that loving another human seems to create. Cats are very compliant in this respect; it is clear from all the anecdotal evidence that cats are delighted to perform this role and be whatever we want them to be in our heads. As long as there is a friendly face, a warm bed and a good meal they are fairly laid back about the complexities of the emotional undertones.

Once again working on the theme of partial re-inforcement, I suggested that some cats seemed to love their owners sometimes and not others. Over a quarter of the owners agreed with me but most were convinced the love was consistent despite their responses to similar statements earlier in the questionnaire.

Only 1 per cent agreed that their cats wouldn't love them any more if they didn't do what they wanted. A huge 93 per cent disagreed – that love really *is* unconditional! Joking apart, it is also quite healthy because it is entirely right that we shouldn't always do what our cats want. Eighty-eight per cent thought their cats would still love them if they rejected them occasionally and this also is absolutely the right attitude. Attention-seeking problems are rarely present in households where the owners understand this principle.

Behavioural problems

My cat has shown aggression towards another cat in the household: AGREE 34%, DISAGREE 56%, NOT SURE 10%

My cat has shown aggression towards me or another person: AGREE 28%, DISAGREE 68%, NOT SURE 4%

My cat has soiled in the house: AGREE 23%, DISAGREE 77%, NOT SURE 0%

My cat has sprayed urine in the house: AGREE 13%, DISAGREE 86%, NOT SURE 1%

My cat has been treated for a behaviour problem: AGREE 5%, DISAGREE 93%, NOT SURE 2%

Since I am a cat behaviour counsellor I had to take this opportunity to check that all was well at home from a behavioural perspective. The majority of the owners disagreed with statements concerning aggression and soiling but regrettably (but not surprisingly) a third of the cats had been aggressive to others in the household, nearly a third had been aggressive towards humans, 23 per cent had soiled indoors and 13 per cent had sprayed urine. In yet another example of our incredible power to tolerate and forgive, only 5 per cent of those surveyed, despite the significant number of problems, had sought professional help.

I shall leave the last word in this chapter to you. I asked at the end of the questionnaire how the person would summarize their feelings for their cat in fifty words or less. Here are a few examples of your replies.

Rosie is the joy of my life. Having no children I feel she is my child. Rosie is a cat amongst cats – I cannot think of a single thing she does that makes me angry. Life without her will be very difficult for me. I have had other Siamese, great cats, but Rosie is and always will be very, very special.

I feel unconditional love for her – however I don't like her outside too long and feel I am a 'mean Mum' BUT when I have to go out for 1–2 hours she appears to dislike it and will play me up, refusing to come in or acknowledge my calling her! So, I don't go out a great deal any more, as her reaction distresses me!

She is like a little child. Sometimes I can love and hate her at the same time. She is constantly on my mind when I am away. I sometimes feel frustrated for not understanding what she wants. I love this little menace to bits.

I love him. He makes me laugh. He cheers me up. He has helped me through a difficult time and he is like a mobile comforter. But I don't smother him so I think we have the balance about right. Best friend, clown, comforter, toe-warmer but still a cat!

And my own personal favourite . . .

He's like my husband: lazy, eats constantly and getting more rotund by the years. I would not change a thing.

Epilogue

Cat Counsellor has been rather an emotional journey for me. Coincidentally, I have had the opportunity to personally evaluate a number of cat relationships in my own life. During the writing of this book I have lost another of my beloved cats in Cornwall (Bakewell) and started my very first one-to-one relationship with a cat (Mangus). I have embarked on a 'textbook' eternal triangle with Mangus and an allergic ailurophobe man and marvelled at the challenge it represents. The impact these relationships have on all three parties is profound.

If I had to sum up the unique flexibility of the cat and

what it means to me, it would be thus. Cats are chameleons. They change themselves to suit the situation, with the overall objective to remain safe and get the most out of the environment and everything in it, and that includes the owners. The enigmatic nature of their responses and behaviour allows the owners to make of the relationship what they will. Whatever the cat is 'saying' with its body language and vocalization can be interpreted to suit the owner's perception of the relationship. For example, a cat with poor coping strategies for life can easily form a dependency on an owner that is unhealthy and not in his best interests. The owner sees a really friendly cat and remarks, 'He loves me so much he won't leave me alone, bless him,' all the while thinking, 'I must be a very special person for my cat to love me so much.' It is just as easy to mis-interpret sedentary behaviour in the chronically anxious cat – an individual so distressed and unsure that he rarely moves but whom his owner describes as 'laid-back and chilled'. How easy it is to be misled by the companion we feel we know so well.

In my quest to spread a better understanding of our relationships with these special creatures I make no apologies for the serious nature of some of my comments in the last couple of chapters. I realize I have always preached that human/cat relationships should be fun but I don't believe this should be at the expense of the knowledge of what we are taking on. We are making ourselves responsible for the well-being of another creature and, therefore, we have a duty to appreciate the relationship for what it truly is and behave accordingly. These relationships should not merely be a reflection of what we long for or need; they should always be mutually beneficial. If you honestly believe that you respect your cat's need to be feline then I am delighted. You are doing your very best for your cat, and if I have contributed in any way to that understanding, I am deeply gratified.

I spend the greater part of my life thinking about cats and our relationships with them. All opinions expressed in *Cat Counsellor* are nothing more than my own thoughts and musings. There is no perfect way to love a cat and I would tie myself up in knots if I tried to define it. I hope that, if nothing else, this book has made you think and re-evaluate your own opinions, particularly if you have been experiencing problems.

There are always going to be those who marvel at the fact that I have devoted a whole book to the relationship aspect of cat ownership. There are many people who consider the whole concept of human/cat relationships to be frivolous and self-indulgent and I respect their right to have this opinion. Ironically, even some owners with a low level of attachment to their pets have cats that are perfectly content. This is one fact that keeps coming back to me when I advise clients with unhappy or unruly cats to merely 'ignore them'. Loving your cat your way doesn't necessarily bring it happiness. Cats tend to work with what they are given and if an owner considers them to be nothing more than an impulse buy and a bit of a nuisance, cats can still make it work for them and go about their business unhindered. Those cats that remain true to their nature can easily survive in an atmosphere devoid of the sort of love that many humans consider essential. The whole thing goes wrong, however, when it comes to veterinary care, as low-attached owners are rarely prepared to pay the huge bills that many serious conditions merit. So maybe being 'cared for' by them does have its disadvantages.

This leads me to a depressing aspect of the human/cat relationship where the debate becomes even more complicated. Veterinary medicine has progressed incredibly over the past few years and procedures such as complicated heart surgery and kidney transplants are now being carried out. This creates a dilemma in my mind: is it right to elect for this sort of treatment for our cats just because we can? Is it worse for a cat to be humanely put to sleep as a result of severe injury or disease, rather than be treated painfully and stressfully for many months? We might be prolonging life but we are changing the cat's perception of the trustworthiness of humans for ever. Some cats cope well with lengthy veterinary treatment but many don't.

This really is a tough one; I personally would do anything for my cats but I am adamant that it must be *for* my cats and not for me. I believe that when and if we are ever faced with this sort of decision we should throw out the largely human drive to avoid death at all costs. Cats have no concept of their mortality; they do not fear death or have religious beliefs about the sanctity of life. They understand fear, pain and suffering and face death with resignation. This is a depressing debate but a fascinating one none the less. Making these sorts of decisions is all part of the relationship. Should our own sensitivities be uppermost when we find it hard to let go?

I promise that is my very last sombre note! Cats are fun and fascinating and so are cat owners and I say a big 'thank you' to everyone who has taken the trouble to write to me about their amazing companions. Every letter is read carefully and thoroughly enjoyed and each one illustrates the enormous variety that exists in cat personalities and cat/human relationships. Some owners are struggling with nervous cats and some feel terribly rejected when their cats resort to violence to get their own way. Most feel the failure is their own if something goes wrong and I doubt whether I will ever convince people that it is rarely that straightforward.

If you have tried loving your cat your way and feel you are failing maybe it would be worth taking a few moments to reflect on the true nature of your relationship with your cat. If in doubt, get to grips with what your cat actually wants and needs and try to show your love the feline way instead. Do let me know what happens!

Index

Able Seaman Simon 28
  adoption of adult cat 81
  aggression 192–233, 325
  multi-cat households and re-
      directed 55–68
  and owners' emotional demands
      232
  as part of cat's survival strategy
      192
  tackling by changing the
      relationship 232–3
Animal Magic 35
Animals Act (1971) 113–4
Annie 21
art
  cats in 29–30
attention-seeking behaviour 183–4,
    216, 235, 266–74

Bastet (goddess) 24–7
behavioural development 161

behavioural problems
    medical reason for 187–91
    relationship survey 324–5
Bengals 82, 105,107, 111–2, 194
bereavement 288–93, 318–9
Bink 21
birds
    and cats 127–8
black cats 37–8
Bln 69
Buddhists 29
Burma 26
Burmese 82,105, 107
Bygul 25

cartoons, cat 35
cat fights 43–7, 62–3
cat flaps 240–1
    invasion of by other cats 94–104,
        106–7, 237–8, 240–1
cat lovers and haters, famous 37

cat shows 33–4
Catholic Church
    demonization of cats 30
cats
    encounter with cats outside 87
    persecution of 17, 30–2
    relationship with other cats *see*
        multi-cat households
    relationship with other species *see*
        multi-species households
    revival of 32–6
    spreading of throughout the world
        27–8
Cats' Protection League 33
'child substitute' debate 299, 304–5
China 26
Christian Church 26
companions
    cats as 303
Copts 25–6
core area 85
couples
    bringing respective cats together
        138–59
cystitis
    idiopathic 83, 163–4
    and stress 41, 64, 143, 163–5

death of cat
    coping with 318–9
    men's feelings over 288–92
    in multi-cat households 68–72
defecation 264–5, 325
dependant humans 234–5
    dependency 94, 183. 234–77,
        313
    tackling by changing the
        relationship 275–7
Diana (cat goddess) 27
dismissive cats 287
dogs
    and cats 117–8, 130–3, 153–7,
        276
    introducing kittens to 132
    introducing a puppy to a cat
        132–3
domestication of cats 22
dry food 83, 276

Egypt, ancient 22–5
Elderly Cat Survey (1995) 71, 130
eternal triangle 138–59
eye contact 185, 232

family members
    cats as 302
fearful cats 177–81
Feliway (synthetic feline pheromones)
    89
Felix the Cat 35
female/feline attraction *see* women
feral cats 170–60
fish
    and cats 124–5
France, medieval 30
Freya (goddess) 25, 30

gardens, securing of 275
Garfield 35
genetics 161
gerbils
    and cats 125–6
Greek art 29
'grieving' cats 68–72, 91–3, 244
guinea-pigs
    and cats 128

hamsters
    and cats 125–7
high resting places 46–7, 82, 132, 144
home range 86
human/human relationships 281

idiopathic cystitis 163–5
ignoring of cat's behaviour 46–7,
    183–4, 198–9, 202, 232, 272, 329
indoor cats 64, 81, 301 *see also*
    outdoors: restricting of access to
interaction
    and relationship survey 307–10
Islam 26

Japan 26
Jewish Gospel of the Holy Twelve 26

Key-Gaskell syndrome
    (dysautonomia) 189

kittens 161
    choosing 81, 161
    introducing to a dog 132

law
    and your cat 110–5
Leonardo da Vinci 25
Li Shou (cat god) 26
litter trays, multiple 67, 143–4
lower urinary tract disease 163 *see also*
    cystitis
Lucy 21

McNicholas, Dr June 294
man/woman/cat triangle 138–59
Mangus 21, 158–9, 274, 287, 310, 327
meerkat 117
men
    and cats 235–6, 288–95, 298
mice
    and cats 125–7
Morris, Johnny 35
Muhammad 26
multi-cat households 40–83, 139–45,
    299–300
    breakdown of relationship due to
        sudden trauma 55–61
    and death of one member 68–72,
        91–7, 244
    introducing number two cat to
        number one 41–55
    new introductions into 139–45
    and perception of core area 85
    secrets of a harmonious 80–3
multi-species households 116–37
    dogs and cats 117–9, 130–7, 153–7,
        276
    fish and cats 124–5
    hamsters/mice and cats 125–6
    parrots and cats 119, 127
    rabbits and cats 120–3, 128–9
    reptiles and cats 124–5

Nelson 28
nervous cats 160–88, 312
    fearful cats 177–81
    feral cats 169–76
    and genetics 161

importance of environment 162
and lower urinary tract disease 162
tacking anxiety by changing the
    relationship 185–6
Nichols, Beverley
    Cats' ABC 34
nine lives of a cat 25

'one per cat plus one in different loca-
    tions' 66, 82
outdoors 301
    benefit of access to 179–81, 233,
        247–8
    restricting of access to 178, 207–9,
        214–5, 305–7
over-attachment *see* dependency
over-grooming 245–7, 259–60
over-protection 204–10
owners
    effect of emotional state on cats 66,
        231, 260, 262, 316–9
    ignoring of cat's behaviour 46–7,
        183–4, 198–9, 202, 232, 272, 329
    inflicting of lifestyle choices on pets
        270
    influence of on cat's behaviour 16
owners (*cont.*)
    missing of by cats 317
    need for relaxing 47, 66–7, 174,
        180–1
    pedigree 300–1
    survey on relationship with cats
        298–300, 314–20
    understanding of feelings of by cats
        315–7

parrots
    and cats 119, 127
partial reinforcement theory 285–6,
    323
pedigree owners 300–1
pedigrees 82
personality
    and relationship survey 312–4
pet term 303
plague 30–1
previous homes, returning to 88–9
private places 46–7, 83

proverbs 38
Puddy 69, 299

rabbits
 and cats 120–3, 128–9
redirected aggression
 and multi-cat households 55–68
rehoming 319
relationship survey 296–326
 behavioural problems 324
 indoor/outdoor 301
 and interaction 307–10
 kind of relationship 302–5
 love and support 320–4
 owner–cat relationship 314–20
 and owners 298–300
 and personality 312–4
 safety 305–7
 and sleep 310–11
relaxation
 and owners 46–7, 66–7, 174, 180–1
religion
 and cats 24–7
reptiles
 and cats 124–5
rodent control 22, 27–9
rodents
 and cats 125–7
Roman Empire 29
Ru 24

safe den *see* core area
safety
 worries about in relationship
  survey 305–7
scent marking 87
scratching posts 82
serotonin 266
Siam 26
Siamese 82
Simpson, Frances
 Cats and All About Them 34
Singapore strays 72–7
sleep 262, 310–11
 putting cats to 330
Society for the Prevention of Cruelty
 to Animals 33

soiling 238, 263–6, 325 *see also*
 urination
speaking to cats 186, 309–10
Spooky 162
stress 64–5, 246–7
 cause of intestinal disturbances 261
 caused by unwanted human
  attention 166
 and cystitis 64, 141–2, 163–5
 impact of owners' stress on cats
  316–7
superstitions 37–8
Sylvester and Tweety Pie 35, 127
synthetic pheromones 89, 144

Tabor, Roger 84, 86
talking to your cat 186, 309–10
television
 changing perception of nature of
  the cat 35
territory 85–6, 97–110
 defending of 91–7, 111–2, 198
 invasion through cat flap 94–107,
  236–8
timid cats *see* nervous cats
Tom and Jerry 35
Top Cat 35
'treat them mean, keep them keen'
 philosophy 286–7
Trygul 25

'unconditional love' 322–3
urination 79–80, 83, 95–6, 101, 142–3,
 238

veterinary medicine 330
Virgin Mary 25

Walker, Robin 43, 189, 266
wandering cats 89–91
Weir, Harrison 33
witches 30–2
women
 relationship with cats 25–7, 31,
  281–4, 287, 309

Zulu 69

Secretele Chinei

ASCENSIUNEA UNEI NOI SUPERPUTERI MONDIALE

JOHN FARNDON
Secretele Chinei

ASCENSIUNEA UNEI NOI SUPERPUTERI MONDIALE

LITERA
INTERNATIONAL

Editura „Litera Internaţional"
O. P. 53; C.P. 212, sector 4, Bucureşti, România
tel./fax (021) 3196390; e-mail: comenzi@litera.ro

Traducere şi adaptare: Gabriela Grigore

First published in Great Britain
in 2007 by Virgin Books Ltd

Ne puteţi vizita pe

 www.litera.ro

Editor: *Vidraşcu şi fiii*
Redactor: *Alexandru Macovei*
Copertă: *S.C. Faber Studio SRL*
Tehnoredactare: *Elena Dandara*
Prepress: *Marin Popa*

Tipărit în Germania

. . . .

Descrierea CIP a Bibliotecii Naţionale a Cărţii
FARNDON, JOHN
    Secretele Chinei: Ascensiunea unei noi superputeri mondiale/
John Farndon; trad.: Gabriela Grigore. – Bucureşti:
Litera Internaţional, 2008
    ISBN 978-973-675-457-9
    I. Grigore, Gabriela (trad.)

94(510)
. . . .

SUMAR

Introducere: Noua China..7

1. Economia în plin avânt a Chinei......................................15

2. Politica Chinei...45

3. Urban şi rural...67

4. China murdară?...91

5. China şi restul lumii...103

6. China şi Taiwanul...117

7. Recital de Hong Kong...127

8. China şi Japonia...139

9. China olimpică...149

10. Tânăra Chină..159

11. China – încotro?..177

Cadru istoric..183

Secretele Chinei

5

Introducere:
NOUA CHINĂ

„Nu contează dacă o pisică este albă sau neagră, atâta timp cât prinde şoareci este o pisică bună" – Deng Xiaoping.

Pe data de 18 iunie 2007, Centrul Financiar Shanghai World, încă neterminat, a depăşit în înălţime Turnul Jinmao din vecinătatea sa pentru a deveni cea mai înaltă clădire de pe teritoriul Chinei, având 423,8 m, în comparaţie cu cei 420,5 m ai Turnului Jinmao. Când va fi terminat, în martie 2008, acest turn de 101 etaje va fi a treia clădire din lume, având uimitoarea înălţime de 492 de metri, şi va fi eclipsat doar de clădirea Burj, din Dubai, care va fi gata în cea de-a doua parte a anului 2008 şi care va atinge o înălţime de 531,3 metri, şi de turnul Taipei, din Taiwan, care atinge 508 metri, însă numai cu ajutorul unei turle de 60 de metri.

Centrul Financiar Shanghai World este doar unul dintre zgârie-norii care se ridică în districtul financiar Pudong din Shanghai, parte a ceea ce se dovedeşte a fi cel mai mare program de construcţii urbane văzut vreodată. Cu populaţia sa uriaşă, China a fost întotdeauna capabilă să construiască pe scară monumentală, după cum o dovedesc Marele Zid şi Marele Canal, însă, vreme îndelungată, această abilitate s-a aflat în stare latentă. Acum s-a dezlănţuit din nou, în Shanghai. Cu doar cincisprezece ani în urmă Pudong-ul nu era altceva decât un teren mlăştinos cu aspect rural. Astăzi este un oraş cu 1,4 milioane de locuitori care creşte pe zi ce trece. Pudong-ul este deja de opt ori mai mare decât Canary Wharf, districtul financiar al Londrei, având, aproape, dimensiunea oraşului Chicago. Priveliştea zgârie-norilor săi ultra moderni, opera celor mai vestiţi arhitecţi din lume, face deja ca multora dintre vizitatorii sosiţi cu avionul pe noul aeroport din Shanghai şi purtaţi către inima oraşului „pe aripile" trenului cu levitaţie magnetică, cel mai rapid din lume, Manhattan-ul să le pară mic şi învechit.

. . . .

Construind **China**

Shanghai nu e singurul oraş care asistă la o explozie în construcţii. Zeci de alte oraşe sunt în plină transformare, de la Beijing până la

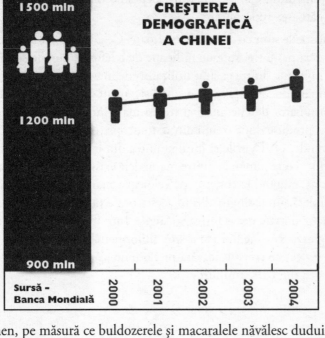

CREŞTEREA DEMOGRAFICĂ A CHINEI

1 500 mln

1 200 mln

900 mln

Sursă –
Banca Mondială

2000　2001　2002　2003　2004

Shenzhen, pe măsură ce buldozerele şi macaralele năvălesc duduind înăuntrul lor, demolând vechile „hutong"[1] şi cartierele de cocioabe pentru a face loc autostrăzilor, mall-urilor cu magazine elegante şi zgârie-norilor scânteietori, deveniţi simbolul noii Chine. Până acum, nici o altă ţară în curs de dezvoltare nu a avut parte de volumul de investiţii străine de care a beneficiat China în ultimii douăzeci de ani, nici o alta nedispunând de o forţă de muncă de asemenea pro-porţii, pe care s-o folosească în scopuri atât de grandioase.

În prezent, în China trăieşte un sfert din populaţia globului, iar în timpurile când Europa era încă în Evul Mediu, era de departe cea mai avansată civilizaţie a lumii. Totuşi, timp de cinci sute de ani, dezvoltarea sa a stagnat, rămânând mult în urma restului lumii. Acum însă toate acestea se schimbă. China se transformă într-un ritm uimitor. După cum proclamă entuziasmaţi numeroşi comen-tatori, China nu mai este „un colţ uitat de lume", fiind pregătită să

---

[1] Hutong = alei înguste printre căsuţele din Beijing

domine lumea în secolul XXI, depășind Statele Unite și devenind următoarea superputere.

Statisticile sunt cu siguranță uluitoare. Cele 1,3 miliarde de locuitori au deja peste trei sute de milioane de telefoane mobile și două sute de milioane dintre ei sunt utilizatori de internet. China este cel mai mare producător de cărbune, oțel și ciment din lume, al doilea mare consumator de energie și al treilea mare importator de petrol. Aici sunt produse două treimi dintre fotocopiatoarele, cuptoarele cu microunde, DVD-urile și încălțămintea din lume și aproape toate jucăriile. Peste jumătate dintre macaralele existente pe glob lucrează în China, ajutând la construcția celor mai mari magalopolisuri văzute vreodată, unul singur dintre aceste orașe putând adăposti o populație mai mare decât întreaga Anglie. Într-adevăr, populația chineză migrează din mediul rural spre înfloritoarele orașe de coastă, într-un proces ce constituie, fără nici o îndoială, cea mai mare migrație umană din toate timpurile.

. . . .

Un consumator gigant sau un **colos totalitar**?

Într-un fel, China pare să se avânte pe calea spre o societate de consum într-un ritm și la o scară nemaiîntâlnite. Unii văd acest lucru ca pe un triumf oarecum înspăimântător al valorilor occidentale. China continuă, însă, să se afle în frâiele aceluiași partid comunist ce conduce cu o mână de fier încă din 1949. În China sunt mai mulți oameni care trăiesc fără un guvern ales decât în tot restul lumii la un loc. În vreme ce majoritatea țărilor lumii s-au îndreptat șovăitor către democrație, China rămâne una dintre puținele care nu are un guvern național ales și nici o garanție a libertăților de bază, iar amintirea masacrului din 1989, din Piața Tiananmen, este încă nevindecată.

Nu există nici o îndoială că tot ceea ce ține de China și de locul ei în lume este urmărit cu sufletul la gură de observatorii occidentali.

Documentare, articole şi editoriale speciale despre noua Chină apar din ce în ce mai des în mass media, alături de nenumărate cărţi noi, cu titluri de success precum: *China cutremură lumea, China: prieten sau duşman?, Faţa în schimbare a Chinei* şi *Scrisul de pe Zid.*

....

Visul oriental

De-o parte a baricadei se află cei entuziasmaţi de ceea ce se întâmplă. Imensele oportunităţi oferite de piaţa chineză par să le dea aripi în special analiştilor economici. Uimitoarea creştere a numărului posesorilor de telefoane mobile, spre exemplu, este amintită ca un semn al imenselor câştiguri ce vor veni odată ce clasa mijlocie din China va avea suficienţi bani de cheltuit. Cu o creştere economică de aproape 10% pe an şi un *boom* fără precedent în domeniul construcţiilor urbane, oportunităţile de investiţii par a fi uriaşe şi de viitor. În acelaşi timp, analiştii politici remarcă cât de mult a deschis ţara guvernul comunist spre economia de piaţă şi spre satisfacerea aspiraţiilor individuale. Pe măsură ce poporul chinez câştigă din ce în ce mai multă libertate economică, consideră aceştia, presiunile în vederea obţinerii libertăţilor politice şi a democraţiei nu vor mai putea fi ignorate. Unii experţi prezic că ţara ar putea deveni, cel puţin parţial democratică, chiar în următorul deceniu.

....

„Pericolul galben"

De cealaltă parte se află cei ce consideră înfricoşătoare ascensiunea Chinei. Unii sunt îngrijoraţi că lumea occidentală va fi în curând copleşită de puterea economică chineză. Proporţiile impresionante şi costurile reduse ale mâinii de lucru chinezeşti fac deja să existe foarte puţine domenii industriale *low-cost* în care companiile occidentale să poată concura cu cele din China. Cu produse simple, precum textilele, China domină deja piaţa mondială. În curând, chiar şi produsele sofisticate cum sunt computerele, se vor fabrica în China. Atunci când China va intra pe piaţa serviciilor, după cum tot ameninţă că va face, economia occidentală va fi în real pericol.

Alte voci nemulţumite susţin că *boom*-ul economiei chineze este, pur şi simplu, imposibil de susţinut. Este un balon de săpun bazat pe credite uriaşe, investiţii masive şi previziuni – ale căror promisiuni vor trebui, mai devreme sau mai târziu, aduse la îndeplinire. Iar atunci, balonul se va sparge, întrucât China nu este decât o ţară cu 800 de milioane de locuitori săraci, nicidecum o uriaşă piaţă profitabilă. Şi când o va face, aşa cum trebuie până la urmă să se întâmple, va arunca lumea într-o recesiune globală mai gravă decât cea din anii '30.

Privind dintr-o perspectivă strategică şi politică, există unii „alarmişti", în special printre neoconservatorii americani şi eminenţele cenuşii de la Pentagon, ce argumentează că această ţară poate deveni o mai mare ameninţare la adresa păcii mondiale decât a fost Rusia în timpul Războiului Rece. Ei amintesc că aceasta este, de multă vreme, o putere nucleară, că are cea mai mare armată permanentă şi că bugetul său de apărare creşte cu cel puţin 10% pe an. În ciuda reformelor, susţin ei, China a rămas o putere totalitară. Prosperitatea sa recent descoperită nu face altceva decât să-i permită să devină şi mai ameninţătoare.

La fel de pesimişti sunt şi cei care atrag atenţia asupra „realizărilor" Chinei în domeniul drepturilor omului, asupra nivelului ridicat de represiune din această ţară, a prăpastiei din ce în ce mai mari existente între păturile înstărite şi cele sărace şi a efectelor potenţial catastrofale ale dezvoltării economice accelerate asupra mediului înconjurător. Tot ei evidenţiază faptul că în China sunt executaţi mai mulţi oameni decât în oricare altă ţară din lume şi că milioane de case ale oamenilor săraci au fost culcate la pământ în iureşul construcţiilor, milioane de oameni ajungând să cerşească, sau să intre în şomaj din cauza lipsei de interes a autorităţilor pentru sistemul de asigurări sociale şi a închiderii întreprinderilor de stat.

. . . .

Enigma Chinei

China a atras întotdeauna exagerările, încă din vremurile în care călători muți de admirație, precum Marco Polo, se întorceau acasă cu povești despre bogățiile fabuloase și rafinamentul său, însă nu și-a dezmințit niciodată faima de țară de nepătruns. Probabil, însă, că adevărul, la fel ca toate celelalte lucruri în viață, este undeva la mijloc, între extreme.

Pentru cei din afară, China a reprezentat întotdeauna o enigmă. Observatorii occidentali sunt atât de obișnuiți cu imaginea unei societăți cu o traiectorie științifică și tehnologică în continuă ascensiune, cu o perpetuă sporire a libertăților politice și a bogăției, încât nu pot înțelege o societate care nu funcționează astfel. Ideea înaintării continue este atât de înrădăcinată, încât realizările și aptitudinile civilizațiilor anterioare sunt adesea subestimate, chiar și în Occident. China nu s-a potrivit niciodată acestui model. Cu o mie de ani în urmă, sub eficienta guvernare confucianistă, cu remarcabilele sale realizări științifice și tehnologice, China atinsese un nivel de rafinament ce-l depășea cu mult pe cel al Europei. Apoi a fost ca și cum, în China, timpul ar fi rămas pe loc, în vreme ce Europa trecea în trombă pe lângă ea, lăsând în urmă o societate înapoiată și predominant rurală, descrisă de Karl Marx ca o „semicivilizație putredă, ce vegetează înțepenită în fălcile timpului."

Așadar, ce a determinat China să intre înapoi în cursă și să capete o asemenea viteză încât să poată depăși Occidentul din punct de vedere economic și poate chiar și tehnologic? În Occident, consensul actual este că libertatea politică și mecanismele capitaliste reprezintă singura rețetă pentru un real progres economic și o societate prosperă, aceasta permițând apariția nestingherită a oportunităților comerciale și exprimarea individuală plenară. Acest punct de vedere a fost confirmat de colapsul Uniunii Sovietice și de succesul din ce în ce mai mare al multora dintre fostele sale state-satelit. Și totuși, prosperitatea crescândă a Chinei pare să fi fost indusă de un guvern ce nu este doar autoritar, ci de-a dreptul comunist, în principiile sale fundamentale. Această situație este atât de paradoxală, încât mulți dintre observatorii occidentali sunt convinși că viitorul Chinei trebuie neapărat să devină unul capitalist și democratic, dacă țara își dorește ca motorul său economic să continue să meargă mai departe. În lipsa acestor libertăți fundamentale, convingerea observatorilor este că izvorul de creștere va seca în curând. Mulți consideră, de asemenea, că pe măsură ce poporul chinez va căpăta din ce în ce mai mult gustul prosperității și al fructelor pe care aceasta le produce, tendința spre capitalismul democratic va fi de nestăvilit. Însă, acest punct de vedere este departe de viziunea conducătorilor chinezi care sunt convinși că înaintează ferm pe calea socialismului; doar că acesta este unul de sorginte chinezească, descris ca fiind „un socialism cu caracteristici chinezești.“

Dacă veți merge în vestul Chinei, pe dealurile din Sichuan sau prin ținuturile în care șerpuiește Fluviul Galben[1], veți descoperi o Chină rurală antică și neschimbată, cu țărani săraci care muncesc în câmpurile de orez la fel cum făceau cu mii de ani în urmă. Însă, dacă vă veți duce în orașele din est, veți descoperi un peisaj urban care se schimbă în fiecare zi, pe măsură ce vechile construcții sunt dărâmate și sunt înlocuite de zgârie-nori, un loc în care stilul de viață al tinerilor este într-o continuă transformare, atât din pricina apariției tehnologiei de consum occidentale, cât și ca rezultat al euforiei produse de propriile lor idei. Care va fi viitorul Chinei, fie ea cea veche sau cea nouă? Va fi el comunist sau capitalist, autoritar sau democratic? Asta rămâne încă de văzut.

. . . .

---

[1] Huang He, fluviu în estul Chinei, cu o lungime de 4 845 km, cunoscut și sub denumirea de Fluviul Galben (n.red.)

Capitolul 1:
ECONOMIA ÎN PLIN AVÂNT A **CHINEI**

„Socialismul înseamnă eliminarea sărăciei. Pauperitatea nu înseamnă socialism, cu atât mai puțin comunism.... A fi bogat este minunat. "

Deng Xiaoping (1904-1997), liderul suprem al Republicii Populare Chineze.

În martie 2007, cei 3 000 de delegați ai Congresului Național al Poporului Chinez (CNP) au votat o lege care poate părea uimitoare într-o țară care, în general, este descrisă ca fiind comunistă. Această nouă lege, consfințită acum și de constituția chineză, garantează proprietăților deținute de persoanele particulare aceeași protecție legală ca și pentru cele de stat. Bineînțeles, legea va conta extrem de puțin pentru țăranii chinezi, ale căror terenuri sunt închiriate pentru foarte scurte perioade de timp de la stat, iar pentru cohortele de proprietari de locuințe din clasa mijlocie, ce iau spațiul locativ în arendă de la stat pe 70 de ani, s-ar putea să aibă o importanță practică și mai redusă. Însă implicațiile acestei noi legislații a proprietății sunt clare – proprietatea privată este un element pozitiv și trebuie protejată prin lege.

Majoritatea economiștilor occidentali sunt de acord că protecția dreptului de proprietate este vitală dacă se dorește susținerea avântului economic al Chinei. Dacă nu ești sigur că vei putea păstra roadele eforturilor tale, nu prea există stimulente pentru a munci sau a investi. Însă, desigur, proprietatea particulară este un lucru tabu pentru comuniștii tradiționaliști. Nu este de mirare atunci, că în momentul în care a fost propusă pentru prima oară în partid, în 2006, legea a fost primită cu proteste și huiduieli din partea conservatorilor de stânga, care o considerau a fi doar ultima dintre numeroasele trădări ale idealurilor comuniste venite din partea liderilor reformatori. Faptul că guvernul a ieșit învingător, sau că cineva s-a gândit, pur și simplu, să propună o astfel de lege, este o mărturie nu doar a nivelului de influență pe care-l dețin în prezent reformatorii economici din conducerea Chinei, dar și a uluitoarei forțe a *boom*-ului economic, ce pare să spulbere totul din cale, făcând ca argumentele opozanților să devină ineficiente.

Ritmul progresului economic chinez a fost într-adevăr amețitor. La sfârșitul anului 2006 China însuma 28 de ani de creștere economică rapidă și constantă, cu o medie de aproape 10% pe an. Această dezvoltare rapidă şi susţinută este impresionantă, însă proporţiile sale o fac şi mai uimitoare. Între 1962 şi 1989, Taiwanul s-a dezvoltat aproape la fel de repede, iar între 1967 şi 1993, acelaşi lucru s-a întâmplat şi în Singapore. Însă aceste două economii sunt minuscule în comparaţie cu cea a Chinei. China este un gigant. În 2006, China a depăşit Marea Britanie, devenind cea de-a patra cea mai mare economie a lumii, surclasată doar de Statele Unite, Japonia şi Germania. Într-adevăr, între 2001 şi 2005, China a fost responsabilă de o treime din întreaga creştere economică mondială. Din 2000, contribuţia Chinei la creşterea economică mondială a fost de două ori mai mare decât a celor trei mari economii emergente – India, Brazilia şi Rusia, împreună. Mai mult de atât, spre deosebire de tigrii asiatici ai anilor '60 şi '80, expansiunea economică chineză nu dă semne de încetinire. Mulţi prezic, plini de încredere, că în următoarele câteva decenii, ar putea depăşi chiar şi Statele Unite, devenind cea mai mare economie de pe glob.

Cât este de **mare**?

Există unele îndoieli în legătură cu proporţiile avântului economic chinez. Atunci când China a depăşit Marea Britanie, în 2006, acest lucru s-a întâmplat, în parte, deoarece China şi-a schimbat maniera de calculare a produsului său intern brut (PIB). În 2005, chinezii au descoperit un surplus de 17% al productivităţii economice în telecomunicaţii, vânzări cu amănuntul şi în afacerile imobiliare, pe care, iniţial, nu-l luaseră în calcul. Efectul a fost ridicarea cifrei produsului intern brut peste cel al Italiei (al şaselea ca mărime la ora respectivă), iar în următorul an peste cel al Franţei şi apoi al Marii Britanii.

În unele domenii, câştigurile raportate de China sunt în mod cert fantasmagorice. În trecut, probabil că oficialităţile le-au supradimensionat pentru a demonstra ce treabă bună făceau. Însă acum, când guvernarea redirecţionează fonduri dinspre estul aflat în plin avânt, către regiunile mai sărace din vestul ţării, tendinţa prevalentă este de a le a subestima. Regiunile prospere din est inventează

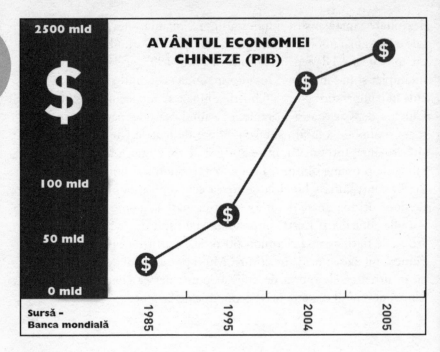

niște cifre mai mici, astfel încât să nu piardă prea mult din fonduri. Regiunile stagnante din vest raportează la rândul lor sume mai mici, pentru a demonstra cât de mare nevoie au de fonduri. Nivelul de frustrare al guvernului în fața acestor manipulări ne este revelat de faptul că, în 2003, a intentat procese de fraudă pentru peste 20 000 dintre funcționarii ce se făceau vinovați de astfel de măsluiri ale registrelor.

Și chiar dacă funcționarii sunt de o probitate exemplară, ei nu dispun decât de cifrele comunicate lor de firme, faimoase pentru dubla contabilitate și alte modalități de alterare a registrelor. În afara acestor aspecte, există și o uriașă economie subterană ce presupune afaceri neautorizate, sau chiar ilegale. Astfel încât, este foarte probabil ca, până la urmă, estimările oficiale ale proporțiilor economiei chineze să fie cu mult mai mici decât în realitate.

Mai există și o altă modalitate prin care economia chineză poate fi subevaluată. Iar aceasta se referă la ceea ce pot cumpăra banii chinezești. De multă vreme deja, China și-a fixat moneda, yuan-ul (cu-

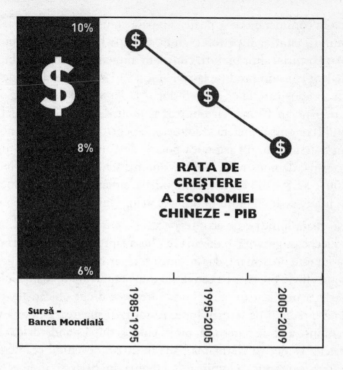

10%

8%

**RATA DE
CREŞTERE
A ECONOMIEI
CHINEZE – PIB**

6%

Sursă –
Banca Mondială

1985-1995

1995-2005

2005-2009

noscut şi ca yen sau Renminbi[1]) la o cotă fixă în raport cu dolarul american, în loc să-i permită o fluctuaţie, aşa cum se întâmplă şi cu alte monede. China este atât de hotărâtă să menţină stabil acest nivel, încât este pregătită să cheltuiască o mare parte din uriaşele sale rezerve de valută pentru a păstra raportul dintre dolar şi yuan. E posibil ca, dacă yuanul nu ar fi scăzut în comparaţie cu alte valute, odată cu dolarul, economia chineză să fi părut cu mult mai puternică.

. . . .

Ce poate cumpăra **yuan**-ul?

În 2001, Jim Neill, de la banca de investiţii Goldman Sachs, a arătat că economia Chinei s-ar putea dovedi şi mai dezvoltată dacă am

[1] Renminbi, unitate bănească în China, a cărui unitate principală este yuan-ul (yen-ul), în traducere înseamnă „valuta poporului" (n.red.)

lua în considerare ce se poate cumpăra cu un dolar în China. Unele bunuri, cum ar fi petrolul, costă aproape la fel peste tot în lume. Dar costurile altor bunuri, cum sunt alimentele, chiriile şi bunurile de larg consum produse la nivel local variază extraordinar de mult. Un produs care te-ar costa 5 dolari la New York, se poate deseori cumpăra, în China, cu puţin mai mult de un dolar. Astfel încât unii economişti preferă să folosească, pentru a compara economiile, un sistem denumit paritatea puterii de cumpărare (PPC). În baza acestuia, demonstrează Neill, economia Chinei reprezenta încă din 2001, 12,5% din economia mondială, situându-se deja pe locul doi în lume, doar cu puţin în urma Statelor Unite.

Nu toată lumea e de acord că acest sistem este unul valid, însă el aduce, cu siguranţă, o dovadă în plus a faptului că economia chineză nu este doar mare, dar ar putea fi chiar mai mare decât o înfăţişează cifrele oficiale. La câţiva ani după raportul lui Neill, Goldman Sachs a publicat un alt raport, care avea drept obiect, de această dată, predicţii pe termen lung. Autorii săi sugerează că ţara va deveni într-atât de puternică, încât, chiar şi după standardele cele mai stricte, va depăşi Germania până în 2010, devenind cea de-a treia putere economică a lumii, apoi Japonia, în 2016, şi, în fine, Statele Unite, în 2041, moment în care procentul său de creştere economică anuală va fi de numai 3,5%.

· ·

Secretul Chinei

Dar care este secretul reuşitei în China? Cum a fost posibil ca una dintre cele mai sărace şi înapoiate ţări din lume să devină o atât de mare putere economică, într-un timp atât de scurt?

O primă şi cât se poate de simplă raţiune a acestui succes este mâna de lucru. China are cea mai mare populaţie de pe glob şi cea mai mare forţă de muncă la nivel mondial. În numeroase privinţe, vasta forţă de muncă chineză ar putea fi descrisă ca cea mai valoroasă resursă mondială. Poate că ţara nu este bogată în resurse naturale, însă are miliarde de mâini capabile să trudească, iar cheia ascensiunii sale a fost şi va fi şi în viitor această vastă forţă de muncă. Însă, chestiunea nu ţine doar de cantitate, oricât de impresionantă ar fi aceasta. Esenţial este numărul imens de muncitori „migranţi" – cele aproximativ două sute de milioane de muncitori ce au invadat zonele urbane, venind din mediul rural ori de câte ori a fost nevoie de mână de lucru necalificată, menţinând fabricile în funcţiune şi construind totul, de la blocuri de locuinţe şi până la stadioane olimpice. Fără aceşti muncitori dornici, adesea neglijaţi şi subestimaţi, însă tot timpul disponibili, miracolul economic chinez nu s-ar fi produs nicicând. În sud, în Shenzhen, acolo unde a început totul, muncitorii migranţi alcătuiesc 85% din populaţia de 10 milioane a oraşului.

O a doua cauză o reprezintă investiţiile. Sumele investite de guvernul chinez pentru a stimula avansul ţării sunt uriaşe şi, cu atâţia plătitori de taxe, nici nu-i de mirare. Există, însă, şi numeroase investiţii străine. Atraşi atât de vasta forţă de muncă, cât şi de uriaşul potenţial al pieţei, investitorii străini au pompat peste 50 de miliarde de dolari pe an aici, de 10 ori mai mult decât în India. Şi într-adevăr, în 2002, China a depăşit Statele Unite, devenind cel mai mare destinatar de valută străină din lume. De atunci, Statele Unite şi-au recâştigat poziţia, însă nu au decât slabe şanse să o păstreze pentru multă vreme. Sume uriaşe au venit din Hong Kong şi Taiwan, nefiind practic vorba de bani străini în adevăratul sens al cuvântului, însă impactul lor este acelaşi. Aceşti bani au fost folosiţi la înălţarea unor noi fabrici, la reconstrucţia oraşelor şi la impulsionarea afacerilor. Iar forţa de muncă a fost întotdeauna acolo, contribuind la transformarea banilor în progres economic real şi în profit.

. . . .

Perioada lui **Mao**

Totuşi, nimic din toate acestea nu s-ar fi întâmplat în absenţa revoluţiei produse în politica economică a guvernării chineze. Totul a început cu dezastrul reprezentat de „marele salt înainte", politica lui Mao Zedong dintre anii 1958–1961, ce promitea Chinei un salt rapid într-un viitor prosper. În realitate însă, în clipa în care agricultura a fost colectivizată în totalitate, aceasta s-a transformat într-o adevărată catastrofă, productivitatea scăzută la hectar aducând cu sine o foamete de pe urma căreia au murit între 30 şi 40 de milioane de chinezi. Industria nu a mers nici ea mai bine, peste 98% dintre proiectele industriale iniţiate fiind un dezastru total. Chiar şi Mao a trebuit să admită că planul său a eşuat şi a demisionat din funcţia de conducător al Republicii Chineze. Deng Xiaoping era unul dintre liderii Partidului Comunist, care promova o abordare mai mult pragmatică decât dogmatică, oferind o mai mare libertate întreprinzătorilor individuali. Cu ajutorul economistului Chen Yun, Liu Shaoqi, el care l-a înlocuit pe Mao în funcţia de preşedinte al republicii, a modificat strategia economică a partidului, astfel încât micii fermieri să aibă puţin mai multă libertate, iar întreprinderile să fie conduse de manageri şi nu de birocraţi.

Cum producţia agricolă şi-a revenit, iar industria părea să ia din nou avânt, pe parcursul anilor '60 economia chineză începuse să arate ceva mai bine. Totuşi, Mao nu-şi jucase toate cărţile, revenind în prim plan alături de marea sa Revoluţie Culturală Proletară, concepută literalmente ca o răzbunare. Liu a fost exclus din partid şi arestat, murind în puşcărie. Deng a fost plimbat pe străzile Beijingului purtând o bonetă de nătâng. Iar Garda Roşie, formată din tineri, a devastat la îndemnul lui Mao toate satele şi oraşele, în nişte atacuri menite a distruge tot ceea ce putea fi numit „cultură". Sute de mii dintre cele mai luminate minţi ale Chinei au fost ucise sau exilate. Economia stagna încă o dată.

Revenirea lui Deng

În 1976, la moartea lui Mao, în ciuda eforturilor de a-l opri ale puţin popularei Bande a celor Patru, Deng Xiaoping şi-a făcut treptat drum înapoi spre putere şi, alături de Chen Yun, a conceput o nouă strategie. Unul dintre aspectele esențiale ale noii abordări a celor doi a fost să permită fermelor colective să se dividă începând cu 1978. Fermele au fost date înapoi în folosință micilor fermieri, care puteau cultiva ce doreau şi puteau vinde mai departe surplusul. Rezultatele au fost mai bune decât s-ar fi aşteptat cineva. Odată ce fermierii chinezi au căpătat în sfârşit controlul asupra propriei lor munci, producția de grâne a crescut cu o treime între 1978 şi 1984, iar cantitatea şi varietatea produselor fermelor chineze a crescut simțitor. Cu banii pe care îi obțineau din vânzarea surplusului de produse, fermierii au putut chiar să pună bazele unor mici afaceri proprii. În numai 7 ani, venitul mediu al gospodăriilor din mediul rural s-a triplat.

Deşi, mai târziu, avântul prosperității rurale a stagnat, intensificarea activității agricole a oferit pentru întâia oară Chinei nu doar stocuri nesperate de alimente şi nişte țărani ceva mai înstăriți, dar şi un imens număr de oameni, înainte legați fără nici un rost de glie, care acum erau liberi să muncească unde doreau. Acesta a fost adevăratul punct de cotitură.

. . . .

Deschiderea **uşii**

Celălalt element-cheie al strategiei lui Deng a fost promovarea unei strategii a „porților deschise". Sub conducerea lui Mao, comerțul Chinei cu restul lumii a fost aproape inexistent. Deng a susținut că, în măsura în care China doreşte să prospere, va trebui să înceapă să interacționeze cu alte țări străine. „Dacă ne izolăm şi închidem iarăşi toate uşile" a spus acesta în 1978, „ne va fi absolut imposibil să atingem acelaşi nivel cu al țărilor dezvoltate în următorii cincizeci de ani." Noua sa strategie a „porților deschise" se va concretiza în nişte Zone Economice Speciale (ZES), în care nivelul impozitelor urma să fie redus la jumătate, iar taxele de import urmau să fie anulate.

Trei dintre primele patru oraşe care urmau să facă parte din aceste zone favorizate (ZES) – Shenzhen, Zhuhai şi Shantou – se aflau în

Guangdong, foarte aproape de Hong Hong, iar oamenii de afaceri din Hong Kong s-au şi grăbit să profite de oportunităţile ce le fuseseră oferite pe tavă. Pentru producătorii din Hong Kong a intra pe piaţa chineză era cel mai normal lucru cu putinţă. În 1990, salariile medii în fabricile din Hong Kong erau de 4 dolari pe oră; în Guangdong abia dacă ajungeau la 50 de cenţi. Deloc surprinzător, fabricile s-au mutat în Guangdong. În 1991, douăzeci şi cinci de mii de afacerişti din Hong Kong deţineau deja fabrici în Guangdong, în care lucrau trei milioane de localnici.

Aceste schimbări au determinat o adevărată explozie în comerţul exterior. În 1985, exporturile din Guangdong erau de 2,9 miliarde de dolari; până în 1994, ajunseseră la 50 de miliarde de dolari. Pe la mijlocul anilor '80, Guangdong a depăşit Shanghai-ul, devenind cel mai mare exportator chinez, iar la începutul anilor '90 ajunsese să deţină 40% din exporturile chineze. Efectele au fost de-a dreptul uimitoare, în special asupra oraşului Shenzhen. În doar câţiva ani, Shenzhen s-a transformat dintr-un mic port pescăresc cu o populaţie de doar şaptezeci de mii de locuitori, într-un înfloritor oraş industrial.

Deloc surprinzător, şi alte regiuni au vrut să intre în afacere. În 1982, altor 14 oraşe de coastă le-a fost conferit un statut asemănător cu cel al zonelor economice speciale, iar un an mai târziu, o serie de alte regiuni, printre care şi delta Râului Perlelor (Zhu Jiang), au fost transformate în „regiuni economice deschise".

Împotmolirea

Cu toate acestea, situaţia nu era nici pe departe atât de senină pe cât ar fi putut părea din exterior. Schimbarea modului de administrare al întreprinderilor a făcut ca acestea să verse un procent din ce în ce mai mic din venitul lor în visteria statului. În acelaşi timp, statul a început să cheltuiască masiv în investiţii directe şi să transfere întreprinderilor sume uriaşe, sub forma împrumuturilor bancare de stat. O situaţie ce nu putea să dureze. În acelaşi timp, după ce, în 1984, producția fermelor a atins o cotă record, spre sfârșitul deceniului, aceasta a intrat în declin, astfel încât statul a fost nevoit să pompeze din ce în ce mai mulți bani pentru a ține prețurile sub control, așa cum cerea planul. Același lucru s-a petrecut și în industrie, fapt ce a pus bazele unui sistem corupt. Întreprinderile de stat și particularii își cumpărau bunurile la prețurile planificate de stat, numai pentru a le vinde apoi, de două ori mai scump, pe piața neagră.

Deng și-a dat seama că primul pas pentru soluționarea acestei probleme este ca prețurile planificate să dispară, liberalizarea lor permițându-le o fluctuație mai apropiată de cea a prețurilor reale ale pieței. Din nefericire, a anunțat această idee înainte de a o pune în practică. Rezultatul a fost un adevărat haos, toată lumea grăbindu-se să prindă prețurile controlate, fapt care a dus la un val de febră a cumpărăturilor care a pus stăpânire pe țară. Deng a continuat politica de liberalizare a prețurilor, însă, între timp, stocurile scăzuseră deja foarte mult, iar tendința de acumulare excesivă a bunurilor crescuse atât de tare, încât inflația a devenit foarte agresivă. La sfârșitul lui 1988, situația scăpase cu totul de sub control. Prețurile controlate de stat au fost reintroduse, iar Deng a asistat neputincios în timp ce un grup de conservatori a impus o serie de măsuri de austeritate.

În acest context al stagnării progresului economic și al anulării reformelor de piață ale lui Deng, China a atras asupra sa atenția întregii lumi, în cel mai rău mod cu putință, prin masacrul din Piața Tienanmen. În mod ironic, acesta a speriat atât de tare poporul chinez, încât guvernul și-a putut continua programul de austeritate fără niciun murmur de protest, împrumuturile de stat scăzând cu aproape două treimi, iar salariile fiind ținute la un nivel minim. Între timp, producția agricolă începuse, încet-încet, să crească. Combinația dintre fluxul monetar restricționat și producția excedentară a readus inflația sub control. Controlul prețurilor devenise și el, în mod discret, mai puțin strict. Cu toate că gradul de încredere în China al unora dintre investitorii străini scăzuse în urma evenimentelor de la Tiananmen, producătorii din Hong Kong erau deja mult prea implicați pentru a se ține la distanță, iar comerțul din provincia Guangdong continua să prospere.

Deng călătoreşte în Sud

În timp ce conservatorii şi reformiştii se luptau pentru direcţia în care trebuia să meargă economia chineză, de cealaltă parte a globului, Uniunea Sovietică se prăbuşea, iar conducătorii chinezi nu puteau să nu remarce manifestările de bucurie ale locuitorilor Europei de Est în faţa eşecului marelui aliat comunist al Chinei. Deng era convins că singura cale pentru ca viitorul socialist al Chinei să supravieţuiască era să continue reformele. Astfel încât, la începutul anului 1992, Deng a plecat spre sudul ţării într-un tren special, într-o călătorie ce a ajuns apoi să fie cunoscută ca *Nan Xun* sau „turneul din sud". Pe 19 ianuarie a ajuns în recent construita gară a oraşului Shenzhen, începând imediat să-şi expună strategia. Turneul lui Deng nu a fost susţinut de conducerea Partidului Comunist, aceasta nici măcar neavând cunoştinţă de el. Mişcarea pe care a făcut-o Deng, aflat atunci la incredibila vârstă de 87 de ani, de a lua iniţiativa şi a stabili agenda partidului, a fost una extrem de riscantă, însă a funcţionat.

Scopul lui Deng a fost să reimpulsioneze procesul de reformă economică exact în clipa în care se acesta se afla la pământ. Mesajul repetat la nesfârşit pe parcursul turneului său de patru zile a fost: „dacă economia nu poate fi relansată, acest lucru va duce la colapsul şi dezintegrarea partidului comunist." Acelor critici ce l-au acuzat de abandonarea spiritulului comunismului, Deng le răspundea convingător că a face bani nu contravine în nici un fel modului de viaţă socialist. El a îndemnat oficialii locali să fie hotărâţi în continuarea reformelor şi să nu acţioneze „precum o femeie cu picioare legate."

Alegând ca tribună pentru programul său oraşul Shenzhen, Deng nu a ales doar un loc unde ochii lumii să fie aţintiţi asupra sa, dar şi unul ce simboliza mai bine decât oricare altul, extraordinarele rezultate ale politicii uşilor deschise. Pe parcursul precedentului deceniu, economia oraşului Shenzhen crescuse cu 50% în fiecare an, iar în 1991, valoarea sa se ridica la uriaşa sumă de 3,5 miliarde de dolari. Zgârie-norii se înălţau la fiecare colţ de stradă şi, în cursa lor către ceruri, constructorii din Shenzen demonstrau că sunt cu adevărat la înălţimea reputaţiei pe care şi-o făcuseră, de muncitori capabili să realizeze trei etaje complet finsate pe zi. În timp ce Deng vorbea, mesajul imaginilor transmise de televiziune era inconfundabil: reformele din China dau rezultate.

. . . .

Deschideţi larg, vă rugăm

Fireşte că strategia lui Deng a funcţionat, iar în octombrie, Congresul Naţional al Partidului a declarat că în China funcţionează o „economie de piaţă socialistă". În curând, fiecare oraş din China îşi dorea măcar o parte din succesul Shenzhenului. În ianuarie 1992, când Deng a pornit în excursia sa spre Shenzhen, existau doar o sută de zone deschise investiţiilor străine. Până la sfârşitul anului, apăruseră 8 700 de astfel de zone. Biroul pentru Zonele Economice Speciale (ZES) dorea să le organizeze pe baza celor „trei alinieri" – de-a lungul coastei, de-a lungul fluviului Yangtze şi de-a lungul graniţei de nord-est. Însă intenţiile acestui birou s-au dovedit a nu avea o foarte mare importanţă, administraţiile locale luându-i-o înainte şi instituindu-şi propriile zone. Această febră a zonelor de dezvoltare a dat naştere unui uriaş val de investiţii pe piaţa de capital şi pe cea imobiliară.

În decembrie 1992, revista *The Economist* a publicat un grupaj special, de 16 pagini, despre China, intitulat „Uriaşul se trezeşte la viaţă", atrăgând atenţia asupra progresului economic al Chinei. Anul următor, David Roche şi Barton Biggs, de la Banca de Investiţii Morgan Stanley, ambii figuri importante pe pieţele de capital, au decis să meargă în China pentru a vedea în legătură cu ce se făcea atâta tevatură şi au rămas uimiţi. Într-un articol ce purta incitantul titlu, *China!*, Biggs scria: „După opt zile în China m-am acomodat foarte bine, am mâncat pe săturate şi sunt cât se poate de optimist în legătură cu ce se petrece aici." „China", se entuziasma el, „va fi piaţa cu cea mai uimitoare ascensiune." În perioada imediat următoare, frenezia investiţiilor de pe piaţa din Hong Kong a fost botezată *chao gupiao*, sau „investiţii la foc deschis", atât de „fierbinte" a fost. Biggs a fost atât de şocat de această febră stârnită de China, încât a început să se îngrijoreze că „toată această agitaţie în legătură cu magia Chinei începe să arate ca un balon de săpun." Când alţi analişti şi-au expus la rândul lor dubiile, banca Morgan Stanley şi-a redus cu o treime pachetul de acţiuni pe care-l deţinea la Hong Kong. În urma acestei decizii, piaţa din Hong Kong a căzut imediat şi mulţi investitori şi-au pierdut banii.

. . . .

TEHNOLOGIA CHINEZĂ

Se presupune adesea că produsele chinezeşti sunt articole ieftine şi vesele precum jucăriile şi hainele. Este foarte adevărat că ei fac aceste lucruri foarte bine, însă recentul **boom** economic chinez a fost determinat de produse mult mai sofisticate. De fapt, o treime din exporturile chinezeşti sunt clasificate ca produse de înaltă tehnologie. Într-adevăr, în 2004, exporturile de tehnologii informaţionale şi de comunicare, cum ar fi telefoane mobile, laptopuri, camere digitale, etc., le-au depăşit substanţial pe cele ale Statelor Unite, ajungând la 180 de miliarde de dolari, în comparaţie cu cele 149 de miliarde ale SUA. În acelaşi an, firma chineză Lenovo a preluat divizia de PC-rui a firmei IBM. Toate indiciile sugerează că piaţa high-tech din China va continua să crească. Cu toate că a fost întotdeauna privită ca un loc în care ideile şi modelele occidentale pot fi puse în practică extrem de ieftin, aceastã viziune pare să se schimbe. China nu are încă un nume de marcă care să poată concura cu cele ale firmelor occidentale sau ale japonezilor, ea are, însă, o nouă generaţie de absolvenţi de informatică ce de-abia aşteaptă să-şi pună ideile în practică. Majoritatea vor ajunge, probabil, să lucreze în firme occidentale, unde vor avea un acces direct la tehnologia şi ideile occidentale, însă este la fel de probabil ca, foarte curând, să se reîntoarcă, punându-şi talentul la lucru în firme autohtone.

. . . .

Deschiderea **Chinei**

Cu toate acestea, criza a fost doar una temporară, şi nu a trecut mult până când toată lumea se grăbea din nou să ajungă în China chiar mai tare decât la reducerile de Crăciun, pentru a vedea pe ce poate pune mâna. În noiembrie 1993, cancelarul german Helmut Kohl se îndrepta spre Beijing, însoțit de un select anturaj alcătuit din reprezentanți ai celor mai mari companii germane, printre care și președinții firmelor Siemens, Volswagen, Audi și BMW. Atunci când Kohl s-a întors bucuros fluturând contracte în valoare de 1,4 miliarde de dolari, inclusiv 6 avioane Airbus și un nou sistem de metrou pentru Guangzhou, scena era pregătită pentru ca în China să sosească un val de delegații comerciale, din țările cele mai bogate din lume. Secretarul de stat american pentru comerț, Ron Brown, ministrul britanic al comerțului, Michael Heseltine și primul ministru francez, Edouard Balladur, și-au făcut cu toții apariția, precum și președinți ai aproape tuturor multinaționalelor importante, de la General Motors la Coca Cola. În mai puțin de doi ani, de la sfârșitul lui 1993 și până la începutul lui 1996, astfel de „vizite" au adus contracte de peste 40 miliarde de dolari.

A durat ceva vreme până ce promisiunile făcute să fie fructifica-te, însă încrederea inspirată de dimensiunea și costurile reduse ale forței de muncă chineze, și de oportunitățile pieței chineze, au determinat numeroși investitori să rămână aici, chiar și în timpul recesiunii economice asiatice din 1997. Atât de ademenitoare era perspectiva viitoarelor profituri, încât mari multinaționale, pre-cum General Motors, erau pregătite să înfrunte orice obstacole și să investească sume enorme de bani, doar pentru a obține licența de operare în China de la guvernul chinez, a cărui amabilitate era extrem de costisitoare. „Experți" în problemele chineze, precum Henry Kissinger și George Bush senior, au făcut mici averi din turneele de relații publice întreprinse în numele unor companii ce încercau să-și asigure locuri profitabile pe piață. Până de cu-rând, multinaționalelor străine nu le era permis să facă afaceri pe cont propriu în China, fiind nevoite să intre în parteneriat cu fir-me chinezești. În ciuda dificultăților reprezentate de găsirea unui partener potrivit și a unei maniere adecvate de lucru cu acesta,

SCHIMBAREA BAZEI ECONOMICE A CHINEI PE SECTOARE (% DIN PIB)

Din care producţie 34,9%

1985   1995   2004

A – agricultură I - industrie S - servicii

**Sursă –
Banca Mondială**

nenumărate companii străine au considerat că merită să-şi asume
aceste eforturi.

. . . .

Comerţul

Nu e nici o îndoială că uşa comerţului Chinei s-a deschis spre lume
mai larg decât şi-ar fi imaginat cineva acum treizeci de ani. La începutul politicii uşilor deschise iniţiate de Deng, China era o economie practic închisă, care nu importa aproape nimic din afară şi
care nu vindea nimic în exterior. Exporturile şi importurile luate
laolaltă, reprezentau mai puţin de 10% din PIB-ul ţării. În zece ani
ajunseseră la 30%, iar în 2002, reprezentau mai mult de jumătate
din produsul intern brut al ţării. Cum, pe parcursul acestei perioade, economia chineză a continuat să crească cu aproape zece la sută

pe an, acest lucru a însemnat un pas uriaş în economia mondială. În 1978, China reprezenta doar 0,6% din comerţul mondial. În 2001, când a fost admisă în Organizaţia Mondială a Comerţului, ajunsese să reprezinte peste 5%. În 2004 depăşise Japonia, miracolul economic postbelic, ca al treilea mare exportator, cu exporturi de aproximativ 593 de miliarde de dolari, în comparaţie cu ale Japoniei de 565 de miliarde de dolari. Doar Statele Unite (819 miliarde de dolari) şi Germania (915 miliarde de dolari) exportau mai mult.

. . . .

Preţuri chinezeşti

Fără îndoială că apariţia dramatică şi neaşteptată a Chinei pe scena economică mondială a avut un impact uriaş asupra întregii lumi. În cartea sa, *China Inc.* (2006), Ted Fishmann explică cum un raport din 2003 al Băncii de Rezerve Federale din Chicago descria că producătorii de piese de maşini americani se plângeau că producătorii de automobile le cereau „preţuri chinezeşti" pentru achiziţiile lor. Prin asta ei înţelegeau cel mai mic preţ posibil, fiindcă indiferent la ce preţ ofereai produsele, chinezii puteau să le ofere la un preţ mai scăzut. Potrivit caracterizării revistei *Business Week*: „În general, preţurile chinezeşti înseamnă cu 30 – 50% mai puţin decât cele la care se pot fabrica produsele în Statele Unite. În cel mai rău caz, ele pot ajunge chiar sub costul materiilor prime. Producătorii de echipamente, încălţăminte, aparatură electrică şi mase plastice, care de zeci de ani erau nevoiţi să-şi închidă fabricile din SUA din pricina concurenţei străine, ştiau foarte bine că este inutil să încerce să facă faţă preţurilor chinezeşti (citat din cartea din 2007 a lui David Smith *Dragonul şi Elefantul*). Acest mod de gândire a alimentat ideea că, pentru unele companii, singurul mod de supravieţuire era de a-şi muta, cel puţin o parte din afaceri, în China.

Dacă preţurile chinezeşti constituiau un motiv de îngrijorare pentru producători, ele sunt cu-atât mai ameninţătoare pentru angajaţii acestora. Chiar şi în cel mai bun caz, cel în care firma ta îşi păstrează fabrica din lumea occidentală pe linia de plutire, prețurile chinezești îți vor submina serios puterea de negociere salarială. Cei aflați în vârful ierarhiei sociale și economice o duc bine datorită expansiunii dramatice a comerțului mondial, însă cei aflați mai jos descoperă că salariile lor bat pasul pe loc. În cel mai rău caz, compania ta se închide și își mută operațiunile în China, sau pur și simplu dă faliment. Un sondaj efectuat în rândurile muncitorilor americani a dezvăluit faptul că o treime dintre ei se tem că își vor pierde slujbele din cauza competiției externe. Și au toate motivele să se teamă. De la începutul secolului XXI, sectorul producției americane a pierdut mai multe locuri de muncă ca niciodată. Între 2000 și 2003, Statele Unite au rămas fără aproape trei milioane de locuri de muncă numai în industrie.

Pentru cei care-au fost îndeajuns de norocoși încât să-și păstreze locurile de muncă și salariile, prețurile chinezești au reprezentat o adevărată mină de aur. Prețurile la articole vestimentare, încălțăminte sau dispozitive electronice au scăzut brusc. Produse precum DVD-urile, rezervate odinioară doar marilor ocazii, pot fi acum achiziționate dintr-un impuls de moment, de aproape orice locuitor al țărilor bogate (și nu numai). Chiar și prețul computerelor personale a scăzut simțitor.

. . . .

Momeli chinezești

Dacă impactul vastei forțe de muncă chinezești a fost remarcabil, cel al pieței sale de dimensiuni legendare a fost mult mai mic. Unul dintre motive este faptul că, în ciuda uriașei sale economii, populația sa este atât de numeroasă, încât venitul mediu al acesteia este încă destul de scăzut. Venitul național brut al Chinei (VNB) este de 1 740 dolari pe cap de locuitor, sau mai puțin de 5 dolari pe zi. Este de două ori mai mare decât cel al Indiei, însă pălește în comparație cu cei 37 600 dolari pe cap de locuitor în Marea Britanie, sau cu cei 44 000 dolari pe cap de locuitor în Statele Unite. Chiar dacă luăm în considerare faptul că dolarul poate cumpăra de patru-cinci ori mai multe produse în China, decât în Statele Unite, o persoană cu un venit mediu din China, tot are foarte puțini bani de cheltuit. Și, desigur, puțini cum sunt, oricum nu prea vor să-i cheltuiască.

Chinezii, în special cei mai în vârstă, sunt cei mai mari economi din lume, deținând, potrivit celor mai moderate estimări, economii de peste 1,25 trilioane de dolari. Spre deosebire de populația din economiile occidentale, care este gata să se împrumute și să cheltuiască cu lejeritate, contribuind, astfel, la mersul înainte al pieței, chinezii pun deoparte fiecare bănuț în plus pentru zile negre și nu împrumută bani pentru nevoi personale decât extrem de rar, sau chiar niciodată. Chinezii au fost întotdeauna un popor prudent, iar cu amintirea sărăciei generale și a vremurilor grele încă proaspete în memorie, nu e deloc surprinzător că acum sunt chiar mai prudenți decât înainte. Odată cu recenta dispariție a plasei de siguranță reprezentată de sistemul asigurărilor sociale de stat, majoritatea sunt conștienți că trebuie să economisească pentru toate cele, de la urgențele medicale până la educația copiilor, pe care trebuie să le plătească acum, integral, din buzunarul propriu.

Mai mult, deși populația din Occident este îngrijorată de o eventuală pierdere a locului de muncă, trebuie să fim conștienți și de faptul că, în primii ani ai acestui secol, 40 de milioane de chinezi și-au pierdut slujbele – de două ori numărul de slujbe din industrie în Statele Unite – mai ales că, în China, nu există ajutor de șomaj. Schimbările din economia chineză înseamnă și că mulți oameni își pierd locurile de muncă pe măsură ce înaintează în vârstă, iar mai bătrân poate adeseori însemna, trecut de 40 de ani. Cum pensia a dispărut la rândul ei, e normal să ții banii „la ciorap" și să nu faci datorii.

. . . .

CE ESTE MAI BUN ÎN CHINA

În iulie 2007, între China și Statele Unite era pe punctul să izbucnească un scandal în legătură cu siguranța și calitatea produselor. În ultimile câteva luni, o serie de produse stricate, sau de proastă calitate din China, cum ar fi pasta de dinți, anvelopele, jucăriile, sau peștele, au ajuns să fie atent examinate de autoritățile americane. Unii politicieni au început să ceară exercitarea de presiuni asupra acelor companii americane care, în goana lor după produse din ce în ce mai ieftine şi profituri din ce în ce mai mari, nu controlează corespunzător produsele importate din China. Alţii, însă, au argumentat că vina aparţine Chinei şi absenţei reglementărilor mai stricte din fabricile sale. Chinezii au răspuns prompt, interzicând acele produse alimentare americane considerate responsabile de răspândirea anumitor boli. Oricare ar fi rezultatul acestei dispute, semnele de întrebare ce planează asupra standardelor de calitate respectate de fabricile chineze nu vor dispărea prea curând. Nu doar calitatea produselor stârneşte îngrijorare, în special cea a jucăriilor pe care China le produce în cantităţi foarte mari, ci şi siguranţa muncitorilor. Nu există nici o îndoială că proprietarii de fabrici chinezi fac rabat la calitate şi la siguranţă pentru a depăşi concurenţa şi a respecta termenele, însă este dificil de spus care este adevărata extindere a problemei. Uneori ies la iveală adevărate poveşti de groază despre condiţiile inumane de lucru ale muncitorilor şi sumele mici de bani cu care sunt plătiţi. Alteori, e vorba de munca la negru a copiilor. Însă, este greu de spus dacă acestea sunt întâmplări la ordinea zilei, sau cazuri excepţionale. Activiştii pentru drepturile omului susţin că vina pentru proliferarea acestor abuzuri trebuie repartizată, în mod egal, între companiile străine ce-şi fac achiziţiile din China şi firmele chinezeşti producătoare. Aceste întreprinderi pot foarte bine închide ochii la ceea ce se întâmplă, însă presiunea lor de reducere din ce în ce mai drastică a costurilor şi a termenelor limită este cea care întreţine astfel de abuzuri.

Cheltuieli în Beijing

Liderii Chinei sunt totuşi conştienţi de efectul de frână pe care tezaurizarea banilor îl are asupra economiei naţionale. În martie 2006, Prim-ministrul Wen Jiabao a transmis Congresului Naţional al Poporului că va găsi o modalitate de a elibera banii blocaţi ai Chinei. Recunoscând că temerile legate de viitor ale populaţiei sunt întemeiate, el a afirmat: „Vom face tot ce ne stă în putinţă pentru a învinge spaima cetăţenilor noştri că o creştere a consumului i-ar putea lipsi de mijloacele necesare traiului."

Cu toate acestea, deşi domnul Wen va avea mult de furcă în a-i convinge pe chinezi să renunţe la lichidităţile lor, unii nu mai au nevoie de nici un stimulent. Tinerii locuitori din oraşe, cu venituri peste medie, au încurajat deja o explozie consumeristă în zonele urbane. Probabil că aceştia reprezintă doar o mică parte din populaţia Chinei, dar sunt destui pentru a crea o piaţă substanţială. În raportul său asupra Chinei din 2005, Organizaţia pentru Cooperare Economică şi Dezvoltare (OCED) citează statistici ce demonstrează că la 100 de gospodării chineze există 46 de frigidere, 94 de televizoare color, 12 calculatoare, 28 de aparate de aer condiţionat şi 59 de maşini de spălat. Cum în China există sute de milioane de gospodării, piaţa pentru astfel de articole este una destul de mare.

În oraşe există, de asemenea, o piaţă în creştere a articolelor de lux. Asociaţia Chineză pentru Strategii de Brand informează că, în 2005, 175 de milioane de chinezi au înregistrat venituri de peste 30 000 dolari pe an, putându-şi astfel permite un număr mai mare de astfel de plăceri extravagante. Un raport din acelaşi an al firmei Ernst & Young, prognoza că vânzările de bunuri de lux în China vor creşte cu 20% în fiecare an, între 2005 şi 2008, apoi cu 10% pe an până în 2015. Dacă cei de la Ernst & Young au dreptate, atunci, în mai puţin de zece ani, China va deveni cea mai mare piaţă mondială a bunurilor de lux şi va reprezenta o treime din cererea mondială. Când vine vorba de lucrurile pe care doreşti să le cumperi, în China mărcile străine continuă să se bucure de un consum ascendent în faţa celor autohtone. Tinerii locuitori din mediul urban tind să cumpere maşini germane, electronice japoneze, îmbrăcăminte modernă şi cosmetice europene, cum ar fi Chanel, Prada şi Gucci. Astfel încât, toate aceste mărci vor pătrunde cu siguranţă puternic pe piaţa chineză, pentru a profita din plin de aceste oportunităţi.

. . . .

Săracii Chinei

Tinerii din mediul urban cu venituri de 30 000 dolari, oricât ar fi de numeroşi, reprezintă totuşi excepţia. Majoritatea chinezilor câştigă cu mult mai puţin. Într-adevăr, salariul mediu în China abia ajunge la 1 500 de dolari şi mulţi dintre ei duc acasă şi mai puţin. Sărăcia este acută, în special în mediul rural, unde 800 de milioane de locuitori câştigă, în medie, o treime din cât câştigă cei de la oraş. Iar 26 de milioane de locuitori din China rurală trăiesc într-o stare de „sărăcie pură", ceea ce înseamnă un venit mai mic de un dolar pe zi. De fapt, condiţia lor este atât de nevoiaşă, încât nici măcar nu au un pat în care să doarmă, sau suficientă mâncare cât să-şi potolească foamea.

Totuşi, deşi populaţia Chinei este departe de a trăi îndestulat, foarte puţini mai suferă acum de acel tip de sărăcie inumană, atât de frecvent întâlnită în India şi în Africa. După dezastrul din anii în care China s-a aflat sub conducerea lui Mao, ţara a reuşit să depăşească sărăcia mai bine decât în oricare altă parte a lumii. Într-adevăr, din 1978, de la iniţierea reformelor, 400 de milioane de locuitori au fost scoşi din sărăcie. Şi mai mult, numărul celor care trăiesc într-o sărăcie absolută s-a redus cu 90%, de la 250 de milioane în 1980, la 26 de milioane în prezent. În anii '90, numărul de oameni din lume ce trăiau într-o sărăcie absolută a scăzut de la 1,29 până la 1,17 miliarde, însă fără acea reducere drastică din China, numărul acestora probabil ar fi crescut. Iar China nu a îmbunătăţit doar veniturile săracilor săi. Indicele dezvoltării umane al Naţiunilor Unite a plasat China pe locul 85 din 177. Deşi, din perspectiva veniturilor pe cap de locuitor, China încă era o ţară săracă, ea avea, totuşi, un nivel de alfabetizare şi o speranţă de viaţă asemănătoare celor din ţările cu venituri medii precum cele din Europa de Est.

Aceasta este una dintre marile sale realizări. Cu toate că numele lui Paul Wolfowitz, fostul director al Băncii Mondiale, a apărut în ziare mai mult cu prilejul demisiei sale forţate din funcţie pentru comportament necorespunzător, el a fost un observator atent al economiilor internaţionale. Când Wolfowitz a vizitat China în 2005, el a remarcat: „Asia de Est a cunoscut cea mai mare creştere în bogăţie, pentru cea mai mare populaţie, în cel mai scurt timp din istoria omenirii."

Nu există nici cea mai mică îndoială că această scădere a sărăciei se datorează, în mare parte, mişcării Chinei spre piaţa mondială, mişcare ce a adus un mare flux de monedă în ţară. Totuşi, această reducere treptată a sărăciei a început să încetinească, în special în mediul rural, iar în vreme ce unii rămân din ce în ce mai mult în urmă, în cursa în care, potrivit faimoaselor cuvinte ale lui Deng, „înainte de toate, trebuie să se îmbogăţească", prăpastia dintre bogaţi şi săraci devine din ce în ce mai profundă. În anii '90, guvernul a sistat ajutoarele acordate firmelor de stat falimentare, construirii de locuinţe, educaţiei şi sănătăţii. Măsura a dus la deblocarea unor fonduri ce puteau fi astfel investite în viitorul ţării, a redus ineficienţa şi a permis expansiunea întreprinderilor particulare, însă a redus, în acelaşi timp, şi susţinerea acordată multor categorii vulnerabile, în special cea a persoanelor în etate. Rezultatul a fost că, în prezent, China este o societate mai profund divizată în ceea ce priveşte nivelul de venit, chiar şi decât Statele Unite.

. . . .

PORTRET: DENG XIAOPING

În 1997, când Deng Xiaoping s-a stins din viaţă, la vârsta de 92 de ani, revista **TIME**, care în trecut îi acordase de două ori titlul de Om al Anului, l-a descris ca „Ultimul Împărat." Titulatura era potrivit aleasă prin natura sa contradictorie. Lui Deng i se recunoaşte pe drept meritul de a fi iniţiat reformele care au făcut din China o economie de piaţă şi care au ajutat la scoaterea a sute de milioane de oameni din sărăcie. La înmormântarea sa, preşedintele Jiang Zemin a declarat: „Decizia de a situa construcţia economică în inima politicii de stat reprezintă realizarea fundamentală înfăptuită sub conducerea tovarăşului Deng Xiaoping, în efortul său de a face ordine în haos." Jiang avea dreptate, pentru că guvernarea lui Deng a fost cea care a scos China din dezastrul ce a urmat Revoluţiei Culturale, conducând-o pe drumul său către progresul economic. Însă, tot Deng a fost cel care l-a susţinut pe Mao în planurile sale economice catastrofale pentru „marele salt înainte" şi cel care a refuzat constant să slăbească controlul partidului comunist asupra vieţii oamenilor obişnuiţi. Faptul cel mai cunoscut este însă, că Deng s-a aflat în spatele brutalei reprimări a manifestărilor studenţeşti din Piaţa Tianamen.

Deng a făcut parte din vechea gardă a comuniştilor chinezi, iar longevitatea este cea care i-a permis să-şi câştige faima nepieritoare, pentru că realizările sale cele mai remarcabile nu s-au produs decât după ce împlinise 80 de ani. S-a născut în 1904, într-un sat din apropierea localităţii Chongqing, sub numele de Deng Xiansheng, dar a plecat la studii în Franţa înainte de a se întoarce în China pentru a se alătura tinerilor comuniști ai lui Zhou Enlai în 1920. Pentru a marca ocazia, și-a schimbat numele în Xiaoping, care înseamnă „mica pace". Deși mic de statură, era puternic din punct de vedere fizic, având o contribuție importantă în Lungul Marș și în războiul civil, care i-a adus, într-un final, pe comuniști la putere în 1949. În scurt timp, Deng a ajuns să joace un rol important în conducerea partidului, în special în planificarea economică, dar a avut numeroase confruntări cu Mao. Deng considera că Mao are o mentalitate învechită, iar Mao considera că Deng este arogant. Cât timp a trăit Mao, Deng a fost continuu marginalizat, dar apoi a revenit pe poziții. De-abia după ce Mao a murit, în 1976, a putut Deng să-și consolideze poziția de lider al Chinei, dar, chiar și atunci, a trebuit să lupte pentru a-și recâștiga statutul, după o epurare la nivel înalt, inițiată de Banda celor Patru și condusă de văduva lui Mao.

Începând de la sfârșitul anilor '70, când puterea lui nu mai era pusă în discuție, a introdus o serie de reforme, printre care și cea care le permitea țăranilor să cultive parcelele pe care le aveau în proprietate și cea care legaliza înființarea de societăți comerciale mixte, în care statul era doar partener. El a inițiat, de asemenea, mișcarea de deschidere a Chinei spre comerțul exterior și investițiile străine, creând Zonele Economice Speciale din sud, care au devenit în scurt timp motoarele dezvoltării economice chineze. În momentul retragerii sale de pe scena politică, la jumătatea anilor '90, înaintarea Chinei către economia de piață era în plin avânt, însă Deng avusese grijă să facă astfel încât stăpânirea Partidului Comunist asupra populației sale să fie la fel de fermă ca întotdeauna.

. . . .

„Afaceri cu pălărie **roșie**"

Unul dintre motivele agravării discrepanțelor dintre păturile avute și cele sărace este puțin cunoscuta, dar dramatica schimbare a modului în care se desfășoară afacerile în China. Schimbările le-au permis întreprinzătorilor chinezi să se dezvolte, aducând Chinei o nouă prosperitate, dar, în același timp, au făcut și ca bogăția să fie concentrată în mai puține mâini.

Totul a început în orașul Wenzhou, de pe coasta de est, cu aproape un secol în urmă. În acele zile, Wenzhou era destul de izolat de restul Chinei, fără cale ferată și fiind înconjurat de lanțuri muntoase ce nu se puteau traversa decât pe drumuri nepavate. O zicală locală spune: „Când mașina ta începe să se zdruncine, ești pe drumul spre Wenzhou." Însă, tocmai această izolare este cea care a făcut ca revoluția afacerilor din China să înceapă aici, departe de ochii iscoditori ai Beijingului, o necesitate vitală, dat fiind că totul era cât se poate de ilegal.

După 1978, imediat ce cooperativele lui Mao au început să se desființeze și gospodăriilor particulare li s-a permis să intre în afaceri cu primăriile și cu micile întreprinderi locale, populația din Wenzhou s-a grăbit să profite de ocazie. În fiecare sat din Wenzhou familiile și-au înființat propriile mici afaceri. În unele sate, nouă din zece gospodării intraseră în afaceri. În doar șase ani, apăruseră o sută de mii de mici întreprinderi; în nouă ani, erau o sută nouăzeci de mii. Toate au pornit ca întreprinderi foarte mici, ceea ce chinezii denumesc *gian dian hou chang* (în traducere – magazinul în față, fabrica în spate) – fiecare dintre ele, o mini-fabrică ce producea bunuri de larg consum, precum stilouri, brichete, pantofi și îmbrăcăminte.

Problema era că nu aveau dreptul legal să se extindă. Legea le interzicea să „exploateze" mai mult de cinci muncitori și, totodată, să împrumute fonduri pentru extindere. Astfel încât, extrem de descurcăreții locuitori din Wenzhou au găsit tot felul de căi ingenioase de a ocoli aceste reglementări. Au înființat „cooperative pe acțiuni", o denumire cu o rezonanță cât se poate de socialistă, asemănătoare celei a cooperativelor de stat, în care puteau angaja oricâți lucrători ar fi avut nevoie. În realitate, acestea nu erau decât niște întreprinderi particulare, care-și păstrau aparența socialistă cedând un sfert din profiturile lor angajaților. Un alt truc era înființarea unor societăți gospodărești parazit, în care afacerea de familie pretindea a fi o sucursală a unei societăți de stat, reușind astfel, nu numai să obțină împrumuturi, dar și să fie scutită de taxe. Majoritatea acelor șiretlicuri funcționau fără probleme, iar fabricile-pirat din Wenzhou au făcut ca venitul orașului să crească de șase ori în doar doisprezece ani. Cu toate acestea, oficialitățile din Wenzhou erau atât de neliniștite de viitoarea reacție a Beijingului în fața acestor activități la limita legalității, încât atunci când au înregistrat producția în creștere au trecut-o la rubrica „activități colective", întreaga expansiune economică a orașului părând a fi o minunată „realizare" a ingeniozității socialiste. În Wenzhou, această mistificare a fost botezată *dai hong maozi* (în traducere – punerea pălăriei roșii), acest tip de afaceri hibride începând să fie cunoscut ca „afaceri cu pălărie roșie."

. . . .

Traversând râul

Treptat, ideea afacerilor „cu pălărie roșie" s-a răspândit în întreaga țară, iar guvernul a închis ochii. La fel cum lui Deng îi venise ideea de a le permite fermierilor să-și cultive propriul pământ, aflând de activitățile ilegale asemănătoare ale unui grup de 18 renegați, „pălăriile roșii" și întreprinderile locale au arătat conducerii că o afacere privată poate funcționa și într-o țară socialistă. După cum a recunoscut și Deng, a fost un adevărat șoc. „Era ca și cum o armată străină ar fi apărut dintr-o dată la țară, începând să producă și să vândă o sumedenie de lucruri," a spus el în 1987. „Aceasta nu a fost o realizare a guvernului nostru central... la așa ceva nici nu m-am gândit... a fost o adevărată surpriză." Cu faimoasele cuvinte ale lui Deng, „China a fost nevoită să traverseze râul, pipăindu-și drumul cu tălpile."

Problema este că, adeseori, statutul legal al acestor afaceri-hibrid este departe de a fi unul sigur. Acestea au o mare varietate de forme și, chiar și astăzi, dezbaterile continuă asupra modului în care ele se pot integra în structurile industriale de tip socialist. Funcționând în interstițiile legii, astfel de afaceri au conferit mediului economic chinez particularități neîntâlnite în alte țări. Pentru a obține performanțe, oamenii de afaceri chinezi trebuie să fie la fel de abili în a înșela sistemul, pe cât sunt în afaceri, știind să ocolească, sau să încalce regulile în caz de nevoie, folosindu-se de mită, învoieli secrete și de o formă specific chinezească de influență socială, denumită *guanxi*. Adeseori, străinilor care fac afaceri în China, sau care concurează cu firmele chinezeşti, li se pare că paravanul de secrete, reţelele de influenţă şi lipsa de respect pentru formele legale sunt profund frustrante, dar acesta este modul în care chinezii au fost nevoiţi să lucreze pentru a-şi pune afacerile pe picioare, în ceea ce continuă să fie o ţară socialistă.

. . . .

Afacerile statului

Succesul afacerilor „cu pălărie roşie" şi al micilor întreprinderi locale a creat o adevărată problemă pentru conducerea centrală pentru că scotea în evidenţă ineficienţa marilor întreprinderi de stat.

Până la mijlocul anilor '90, aproape jumătate din forţa de muncă de la oraş – peste o sută de milioane de oameni – lucra în întreprinderi de stat, care produceau totul, de la biciclete până la beţigaşe de mâncat. Multe dintre acestea, în special în Shanghai, erau foste fabrici particulare, naţionalizate după revoluţie. Altele, în special cele din nord, erau uzine înfiinţate în timpul primului val comunist, din anii '50, concentrând o mare parte din industria grea a Chinei – rafinăriile de petrol, oţelăriile şi minele de cărbuni. Aceste întreprinderi de stat erau foarte diferite de cele din Marea Britanie, unde naţionalizarea a păstrat caracteristicile industriei, schimbând doar proprietarul. În China, întreprinderile „poporului" sunt aproape un stat al bunăstării în sine, asigurându-le muncitorilor asistenţă medicală, educaţie pentru copii, cazare şi chiar şi pensii. Şi într-adevăr, oamenii puteau să-şi petreacă o viaţă întreagă în aceste întreprinderi, din fragedă pruncie, până la moarte. Adesea, muncitorii erau înlocuiţi în funcţie chiar de copiii lor.

Sprijinul şi siguranţa pe care acestea le ofereau, făceau ca posturile la stat să fie extrem de râvnite. De-a lungul celei de-a doua jumătăţi a secolului XX, întreprinderile de stat au asigurat stabilitatea socială în mediul urban şi, într-o anumită măsură, acesta a şi fost rolul lor cel mai important. Însă, aşa cum o demonstrau cu supramăsură afacerile hibride, marea lor problemă o constituia faptul că erau îngrozitor de ineficiente. Producția era tot timpul extrem de mică, iar materiile prime, energia și munca erau irosite în cantități impresionante.

În urmă succesului societăților mixte, guvernul chinez și-a dat seama că trebuia să transforme mamuții industriali de stat în întreprinderi profitabile. S-au încercat diferite măsuri pentru a le repune pe picioare. În Shanghai și Shenzhen s-au înființat noi burse de mărfuri în încercarea de a atrage investiții. Mișcarea a funcționat pentru întreprinderile mai mari, însă numărul celor care doreau să-și investească banii în niște afaceri prost administrate, împovărate de imense responsabilități sociale, era extrem de mic. O altă măsură le-a permis managerilor să păstreze o cotă-parte din profiturile uzinei, sperându-se că astfel vor fi mai motivați în a obține o mai mare productivitate, însă, din moment ce întreprinderile de stat cumpărau materia primă la prețuri scăzute, controlate de stat, singurul rezultat a fost că directorii s-au umplut de bani de pe urma statului. O a treia inițiativă a dus la fuziunea întreprinderilor prost conduse cu unele a căror administrare era mai eficientă, pentru a vedea dacă nu se descurcă mai bine laolaltă.

. . . .

Un „thatcherism" cu
caracteristici chinezești

Nici una dintre aceste măsuri nu a funcționat, guvernul realizând, într-un final, că va trebui să trateze întreprinderile de stat ca pe niște firme private. Omul din spatele reformelor a fost Zhu Rhongji, viceprim-ministru al Chinei între anii 1993-1998 și prim-ministru între 1998 și 2003. Domnul Zhu era un mare admirator al doamnei Margaret Thatcher, premierul Marii Britanii, și studiase cu mare interes privatizările pe care aceasta le făcuse în anii '80. El era convins că la fel cum doamna Thatcher inițiase și finalizase o „raționalizare" a forțelor de muncă din industria britanică a mineritului și din cea siderurgică, și el va trebui să reducă drastic numărul de salariați din întreprinderile de stat. În viitor, China va trebui să se bazeze pe forțele pieței și pe întreprinderile particulare pentru a crea noi locuri de muncă. Numeroase voci susțin că eforturile depuse de Zhu Rhongji pentru a determina China să adere la Organizația Mondială a Comerțului au fost motivate, cel puțin în parte, de conștientizarea faptului că s-ar putea să aibă nevoie de ajutor din afară pentru a duce reformele la îndeplinire.

Lumea a acordat atât de multă atenție miracolului economic chinez, încât, adeseori, impresionantele proporții ale devastatoarelor reforme inițiate de Zhu, par să fie trecute cu vederea. În doar câțiva ani, aproape patruzeci de mii de întreprinderi de stat au fost închise, iar între 1996 și 2001 cincizeci și trei de milioane de oameni și-au pierdut locurile de muncă. În multe orașe din nord, jumătate dintre lucrători au devenit de prisos aproape peste noapte. În cartea sa, *China Inc.*, Ted Fishmann face o comparație elocventă – pierderea acestor locuri de muncă a fost mult mai gravă decât ar fi fost cea provocată de închiderea simultană a cinci sute dintre cele mai mari companii mondiale, de la Wal-Mart, până la Exxon. Unele întreprinderi au dat oamenii afară, dar au continuat să le ofere ajutor social – deci plăteau, dar nu primeau muncă în schimb. La alte întreprinderi, muncitorii disponibilizați nu și-a pierdut doar locul de muncă, ci și casele, alocațiile pentru educația copiilor, ajutorul de sănătate și pensiile.

. . . .

XIA GANG, SAU „DISPONIBILIZAȚII"

Guvernul a informat că intenționa ca surplusul de forță de muncă reprezentat de muncitorii **xia gang** – cei „disponibilizați" de la întreprinderile de stat – să fie canalizat înapoi înspre societate, urmând să fie creat un nou sistem de asistență socială, separat de locul de muncă. Desigur, va mai dura ceva până când bazele acestui viitor sistem vor fi suficient de solide. Între timp, zeci de milioane de chinezi se luptă să supraviețuiască. Lovitura a fost deosebit de grea pentru cei trecuți de prima tinerețe, mai ales pentru femeile de peste 40 de ani, cărora le era imposibil să găsească de lucru în fabrici sau în domeniul serviciilor, unde angajatorii nu se sfiesc să ofere posturi doar femeilor tinere, atrăgătoare şi necăsătorite. Problema este că oamenii între 40 şi 50 de ani au rareori alte competențe decât cele minime, deprinse în fabricile de stat şi, pentru că provin dintr-o generație care a crescut în timpul Revoluției Culturale, au şi foarte puțină educație. În Shanghai, au fost înființate 4 050 de centre care să ofere soluțiile necesare pentru ca această generație să se poată reîntoarce „în câmpul muncii" – însă, pe listele de angajări, predominante sunt posturile de menajeră în casele tinerilor înstăriți de la oraş, astfel încât, la jumătate de secol de la revoluția comunistă, în China renaşte clasa servitorilor.

. . . .

Astăzi, sectorul privat chinez reprezintă peste jumătate din producția industrială a Chinei. Societățile cu capital străin şi firmele mixte reprezintă cealaltă jumătate. Abia o cincime provine din întreprinderile de stat. În mod asemănător, doar o cincime din forța de muncă neangajată în mediul rural lucrează în industria de stat. În consecință, majoritatea companiilor chinezeşti şi angajații acestora trebuie să îşi croiască destinul, oricare va fi acesta, pe piață. Unii au numit acest fenomen „socialism de piață", alții i-au spus „socialism cu caracteristici chinezeşti" – alții spun că nu este altceva decât un capitalism cu mască chinezească. Însă, orice ar fi, el schimbă cu siguranță China, şi o face uimitor de rapid.

. . . .

Capitolul 2:
POLITICA **CHINEI**

„Mergem pe un drum greşit. Ţara întreagă este în primejdie. "

Scrisoare deschisă din partea a şaptesprezece foşti înalţi oficiali ai Partidului Comunist şi academicieni conservatori, 16 iulie 2007

Scrisoarea din care a fost extras citatul de mai sus a apărut pe internet în iulie 2007. Pe internet mai apar, uneori, scrisori critice la adresa conducerii chineze, însă sunt imediat blocate, majoritatea acestora provenind din partea activiştilor pentru drepturile omului, ce protestează în legătură cu lipsa de libertăţi din China. Scrisoarea de faţă, însă, nu este una obişnuită. Ea nu a venit din partea unor liberali din afara partidului, ci din cealaltă tabără, cea a conservatorilor din cadrul partidului, printre semnatari aflându-se un număr de foşti membri ai guvernului.

Critica lor nu se referea la faptul că partidul era insuficient de receptiv în faţa reformelor, ci dimpotrivă, că devenise mult prea permisiv. Semnatarii acestei scrisori erau extrem de nemulţumiţi, considerând că partidul a înaintat prea mult pe calea liberalizării economice. În martie 2007, ei au condamnat adoptarea legii ce reglementa proprietatea privată, resimţind-o ca pe o trădare a principiilor socialiste, o măsură ce nu va face altceva decât să protejeze averile funcţionarilor corupţi şi câştigurile necuvenite ale oamenilor de afaceri necinstiţi. Ei doreau să anuleze decizia din 2002, care le permitea oamenilor de afaceri să adere la partidul comunist, şi să impună un număr de restricţii investiţiilor străine. O altă cerinţă era stoparea privatizării proprietăţilor statului. Partidul înainta pe drumul periculos către capitalism, susţineau ei, iar prăpastia dintre bogaţi şi săraci se adâncea. Dacă nu va fi suficient de precaută, China va avea, în curând, propriul său Borin Elţin, şi atunci, „pieirea partidului, dar şi a ţării, va fi iminentă. "

. . . .

PARTIDUL COMUNIST CHINEZ

Având peste 70 de milioane de membri, Partidul Comunist Chinez este cel mai mare partid politic din lume. Spre deosebire de alte partide occidentale, PCC-ul este puternic implicat în viaţa cotidiană, controlând totul, de la programa şcolară şi emisiunile TV, până la tipul de slujbe, de locuințe, și chiar și dimensiunile familiilor chineze. În fiecare sat există un reprezentant al partidului care supraveghează lucrurile. Spre exemplu, dacă o femeie dintr-un sat rămâne însărcinată, oficialii locali ai partidului vor ști imediat ce află și ea. În ultimii ani, după ce țăranilor li s-a permis să-și cultive pământul așa cum doresc, influența partidului în zonele rurale a scăzut. Același fenomen poate fi observat și în zonele urbane, odată cu dispariția marilor întreprinderi de stat. Ca atare, oamenii nu mai sunt chiar atât de dornici să intre în partid ca înainte, această opțiune nemaifiind sinonimă cu o poziție socială asigurată, putând constitui unul dintre motivele pentru controversata deschidere din urmă cu câțiva ani a partidului, ce a permis chiar și întreprinzătorilor particulari intrarea în rândurile acestuia.

Cu toate acestea, calitatea de membru de partid continuă să fie însoțită de importante privilegii, acesta fiind și motivul pentru care numărul membrilor nu încetează să crească. Membrii sunt ținuți la curent cu ceea ce se întâmplă în țară, ajung să-și facă relații personale importante, pot aplica pentru slujbe la care au acces doar cei din partid (inclusiv posturi guvernamentale importante), iar copiii lor urmează școli mai bune. A intra în partid nu este deloc un lucru ușor, fiind necesară susținerea mai multor membri de partid, o verificare atentă, apoi un an de probă și școlarizare. În aceste condiții, nu e deloc surprinzător că PCC-ul este departe de a fi un partid reprezentativ pentru China, procentul membrilor de sex feminin fiind sub 20%, iar cel al persoanelor de peste 35 de ani, aproape 80%.

. . . .

Partidul comunist preferă să păstreze aparențele unui front unitar, rezolvându-și disensiunile interne în spatele ușilor închise. Aceasta a fost, probabil, prima oară, când o dispută internă a patidului a fost dezvăluită atât de vizibil în public – cu toate că site-ul a fost blocat în ziua imediat următoare. Scrisoarea în sine, nu este, de fapt, atât de relevantă. Demonstrând, mai degrabă, frustrarea semnatarilor în fața lipsei de interes cu care le sunt întâmpinate revendicările, decât puterea lor. Demn de atenție este faptul că, puțin înainte de apariția scrisorii, cea mai fierbinte știre ce-și făcuse loc în paginile cotidianului *China Daily* anunța că, începând din 2002, trei milioane de oameni de afaceri se înscriseseră în partid. E posibil ca această informație să fi dat semnatarilor senzația că paharul e deja mult prea plin.

Însă, alegerea momentului protestului lor este semnificativă. La doar câteva luni de la data publicării scrisorii, două mii de lideri de partid urmau să se întâlnească la Congresul Național al Partidului.

. . . .

PARTIDELE DIN CHINA

În afară de Partidul Comunist Chinez, în China există alte opt partide „democratice" recunoscute oficial: Partidul Naționalist Chinez, Liga Democratică Chineză, Asociația pentru Construcția Națională Democratică, Asociația Chineză pentru Promovarea Democrației, Partidul Democratic al Muncitorilor și Țăranilor din China, Partidul Zhi Gong Dang, Societatea Trei Septembrie și Liga de Autoguvernare Democratică a Taiwanului. Însă, nici unul dintre aceste partide nu constituie o opoziție reală în fața Partidului Comunist. Sunt partide de dimensiuni mici, care supraviețuiesc doar pentru că PCC-ul le-o permite. Singurul lor merit este că au acceptat invitația oferită de P.C.C. la congresul de înființare al Republicii Populare Chineze, din 1948, fiind de acord să nu se abată de la linia de conduită stabilită de comuniști. Dacă, vreodată, s-ar opune în mod serios partidului comunist, ar fi desființate imediat. Cu toate acestea, unii dintre membrii partidelor democratice reușesc uneori să ajungă în posturi importante, cum s-a întâmplat și cu Duanmu Zheng, care a devenit vicepreședinte al Curții Supreme în 1990.

. . . .

Marele **Partid**

Congresul Național al Partidului este un eveniment al partidului și nu trebuie confundat cu Congresul Național al Poporului, care este versiunea chineză a parlamentului. Congresul Partidului are loc odată la cinci ani și este cel mai important eveniment din viața politică a Chinei. Atunci se decide direcția generală a politicii partidului pentru următorii cinci ani. Tot atunci se stabilește componența Comitetului Central al Partidului, care îi alege, apoi, pe cei 24 de membri ai Biroului Politic, dintre care 9 vor alcătui Comitetul Biroului Politic Permanent – acel cerc al inițiaților care ia toate deciziile importante și care conduce, de fapt, China. Cum toate aceste alegeri au loc simultan, Congresul Partidului este, în principal, un moment în care partidul decide cine rămâne și cine pleacă. Deși câștigătorii și perdanții nu sunt niciodată anunțați public, îți poți da seama care sunt favoriții după poziția fotografiilor lor din ziarul oficial al partidului, *Cotidianul Poporului*.

La Congresul din 2002 schimbarea s-a produs chiar la vârf, președintele Jiang Zemin demisionând din funcția de Secretar General al partidului. Secretarul General este atât conducătorul oficial al partidului (înainte de 1980, președintele era conducătorul), cât și președinte, fiind, astfel, cel mai puternic om din China. În primele zile ale Republicii Populare, puterea izvora mai degrabă din influența personală, decât din poziția ocupată în ierarhia formală, astfel încât Mao a continuat să aibă un cuvânt greu de spus, chiar și după ce a demisionat din funcția de conducător al partidului, în 1962, iar Deng Xiaoping a condus practic China, pe parcursul anilor '80 și la începutul anilor '90, chiar dacă nu deținea funcții oficiale în partid. Cu toate acestea, poziția oficială a devenit, treptat, esențială. Astfel încât, atunci când, la Congresul din 2002, Jiang Zemin a demisionat, cedându-i locul lui Hu Jintao, care a devenit, în 2003, atât Secretar General, cât și Președinte, schimbarea produsă în conducerea partidului a fost una majoră – probabil prima transmitere formală și clară a puterii din istoria Republicii Populare Chineze, în ciuda faptului că Jiang încă mai are o oarecare influență. Acel moment a fost fatal și pentru prim-ministrul lui Jiang, Zhu Rongji, deoarece doar unul dintre susținătorii săi, vicepremierul Wen Jiabao, reușise să acceadă în Comitetul Permanent al Biroului Politic, în anul următor Zhu fiind și el nevoit să demisioneze.

. . . .

PROFIL: HU JINTAO

Deși Hu Jintao este, încă din 2003, președintele unei Chine aflate în cea mai activă perioadă a sa de expansiune internațională din ultimele decenii, el rămâne o figură puțin cunoscută pe plan mondial. Când a venit la putere, jurnaliștii străini l-au descris ca pe un om misterios. Revista **Newsweek** scria: „Cel mai remarcabil lucru la el este cât de puține se cunosc despre el." **Chicago Tribune** sugera, sub forma unui compliment insidios, că anonimatul său ar putea fi rezultatul unei decizii deliberate: „Îți trebuie o măiestrie extraordinară pentru a rămâne o persoană atât de neînsemnată." Acum el este mai bine cunoscut, dar continuă să fie un personaj misterios, cineva care crede în reținere și precauție, în lipsa nevoii de a te grăbi. Mandatul său prezidențial a fost caracterizat de eforturi de conciliere și de construcție a consensului politic, caracteristici ce pot explica poziția mediană a lui Hu, aflată între forțele liberale, adepte ale unei economii în care piața să aibă cuvântul precumpănitor, și cele conservatoare, ce-și doresc anularea reformelor economice și întoarcerea la un socialism cât mai pur. Viziunea declarată a lui Hu era de a construi „o societate armonioasă" prin grija acordată săracilor și celor dezavantajați și, totodată, prin crearea bogăției. Provocările pe care le întâmpină în atingerea acestui țel sunt uriașe, acesta fiind, probabil, și motivul pentru care a fost atât de dornic să dezvolte relații de cooperare pașnică cu exteriorul. S-a luptat pentru creearea a ceea ce unii au numit „diplomația zâmbetului" față de vecinii Chinei și a jucat un rol esențial în reducerea unora dintre tensiunile cu Japonia.

Născut în Jiangsu, în 1942, Hu era absolvent de inginerie hidraulică și a intrat în partid prin intermediul Ligii Tineretului Comunist, cea care l-a și susținut în avansarea sa ulterioară. Deng a fost cel care l-a ales, în 1992, pentru a fi liderul celei de-a patra generații și care s-a asigurat că va deveni cel de-al doilea cel mai tânăr membru din istoria Comitetului Permanent al Biroului Politic. În curând, a devenit clar că Hu îi va urma lui Jiang Zemin la conducere, reușind, prin modul său extrem de politicos și curtenitor de comportament, să nu-l irite niciodată. În 2003, ascensiunea sa la putere a fost, după standardele chineze, destul de lină, în ciuda numeroaselor ezitări ale lui Jiang de a părăsi scena politică. Într-un profil din ziarul **New York Times**, Robert Zoellick remarcă: „Cea mai mare moștenire a lui Hu s-ar putea dovedi a fi selectarea acelor lideri care să-i continue strategia pe plan intern și care să acționeze neîntârziat pentru a conferi Chinei un rol cât mai constructiv pe plan internațional."

. . . .

Societatea armonioasă **a lui Hu**

Predarea puterii de către Jiang Zemin și Zhu Rongji, către Hu Jintao și Wen Jiabao, care a devenit premier după Zhu, a marcat o schimbare de direcție în politica chineză. Jiang și Zhu erau adepți convinși ai politicii „ușilor deschise" și înavuțirii a lui Deng, mergând chiar mai departe decât acesta în încurajarea liberului schimb, a investițiilor străine și a dezvoltării întreprinderilor particulare. Jiang a fost cel care a susținut deschiderea porților partidului pentru oamenii de afaceri particulari, iar Zhu a fost cel ale cărui eforturi au făcut ca, în 2001, China să fie admisă în Organizația Mondială a Comerțului.

Hu și Wen au fost, însă, mult mai prudenți în abordarea pieței. Hu și-a îndreptat atenția spre prăpastia care s-a deschis între bogați și săraci ca rezultat al liberalizării și al desființării ajutoarelor de stat. Această discrepanță a dus la creșterea tensiunilor sociale, declanșând o intensificare alarmantă a protestelor asupra unor probleme precum acapararea abuzivă a terenurilor. Scopul lui mărturisit era de a reduce tensiunile prin rezolvarea tuturor acestor probleme, pentru a crea, în cele din urmă, „o societate armonioasă." În practică, acest lucru însemna mutarea accentului de la creșterea economică înspre ajutorul social, în special în zonele rurale, și redirecționarea fondurilor pentru dezvoltare dinspre zonele de coastă către interiorul țării, care de-abia reușea să supraviețuiască.

Este puțin probabil ca schimbările ce se vor produce la nivel înalt cu ocazia Congresului din 2007 să fie la fel de dramatice precum cele din 2002, deoarece se așteaptă ca Hu Jintao să fie președinte până la următorul Congres, din 2012, Wen rămânând, cu siguranță, în funcție, alături de el. Cu toate acestea, vor exista o serie întreagă de promovări importante.

. . . .

DIVIZIUNILE ADMINISTRATIVE

În China există patru diviziuni administrative majore: națională, provincială, a prefecturilor și rurală. Țara este împărțită în 23 de provincii, printre care și Taiwanul, plus 4 municipalități aflate sub conducerea directă a Consiliului de Stat (Beijing, Shanghai, Chongqing și Xi'an) și 5 regiuni autonome (Tibet, Xingjiang, Mongolia Interioară, Guangxi și Ningsia), cu o formă de organizare oarecum diferită pentru minorități. La nivelul imediat următor provinciilor se află 300 de prefecturi și municipalități mai mici, formate din aproximativ 2 500 de județe.

. . . .

Relaţii şi **facţiuni**

În lipsa dezbaterilor publice şi a partidelor, politicile Chinei depind în întregime de alegerile făcute de guvernanţii săi. Astfel încât, pentru aceştia este esenţial să se înconjoare de oameni cu aceeaşi mentalitate, dobândirea sprijinului fiind un element-cheie în politica chineză. Ascensiunea în viaţa politică se face prin bunăvoinţa personajelor suspuse, iar sprijinul vine din partea propriilor protejaţi. Înaintea Congresului, Preşedintele Hu trebuie să fi fost extrem de ocupat în culise, evaluând oamenii şi asigurându-se că persoanele alese de el primesc slujbele potrivite pentru a-i consolida puterea.

Cu toate acestea, în cadrul Partidului există 2 facţiuni, situaţie ce a dat naştere uneia dintre acele expresii concise, atât de iubite de chinezi – „un partid, două facţiuni." De-o parte se află coaliţia Shanghai-ului, formată, predominant, din oficiali care provin din înfloritoarele oraşe ale provinciilor de coastă. De cealaltă parte se află *tuan pai*, facţiunea Ligii Tineretului Comunist, ai cărei membri provin din ligile de tineret din mediul rural mai sărac din interiorul ţării. Unii descriu coaliţia Shanghai ca fiind de dreapta, elitistă şi favorabilă continuării liberalizării pieţei, în timp ce Liga Tineretului li se pare a fi mai populistă, tinzând să pună un mai mare accent pe sporirea ajutorului social pentru districtele rurale mai sărace. Însă ar fi greşit să le considerăm doar nişte grupuri politice obişnuite, în sensul occidental al cuvântului. Ele se bazează mai mult pe interacţiune personală decât pe unitatea ideilor politice.

Baza puterii lui Hu Jintao stă în Liga Tineretului Comunist, tocmai de aceea, este foarte probabil ca el să-i favorizeze pe cei intraţi în partid pe această cale. Spre sfârşitul lui 2006, Hu a făcut o mişcare îndrăzneaţă pentru a reduce influenţa facţiunii Shanghai înainte de anul în care avea loc Congresul Partidului. Figura tutelară a grupului Shanghai este Jiang Zemin, care, deşi nu mai este la putere, îşi menţine din culise o influenţă considerabilă. Hu nu îl putea ataca direct pe Jiang, astfel încât l-a supus atacului pe Chen Liangyu, preşedintele filialei din Shanghai a Partidului Comunist. În timp ce Hu îi oferea lui Jiang o lansare generoasă pentru noua sa carte, poliţiştii din Beijing au descins la sediul de partid al lui Chen, din Shanghai, demascând o afacere coruptă, ce implica deturnarea fondurilor de pensii ale cetăţenilor înspre nişte afaceri imobiliare riscante. Ca rezultat, Chen a fost dat afară din toate posturile de partid, iar puterea facţiunii Shanghai a scăzut considerabil.

Pe val

Din moment ce Hu deţine acum mâna câştigătoare, este foarte probabil ca la Congresul Partidului, şi chiar şi după acesta, să promoveze interesele „tinerelor speranţe" ale grupării *tuan pai,* cum ar fi Li Keqiang, pe care unii îl văd deja în postura de viitor preşedinte al Chinei, sau Li Yuanchao. În China, într-o manieră ce aminteşte foarte mult de respectul confucianist pentru bătrâni, eşaloanele de putere îşi urmează unul altuia în ordinea vârstei, astfel încât cei care ţin frâiele au tendinţa să fie de vârste apropiate. Jiang şi Zhu au fost descrişi ca a treia generaţie de lideri ai Chinei, Hu şi Wen, ambii în jurul vârstei de 60 de ani, sunt consideraţi a fi cea de-a patra generaţie, iar liderii în ascensiune, precum Li Keqiang şi Li Yuanchao, având între 40 şi 50 de ani, sunt cea de-a cincea generaţie.

PROFIL: LI KEQIANG

Născut în 1955, la Dingyuan, în provincia săracă Anhui, Li Keqiang face parte din mai tânăra generaţie „a cincea" de politicieni, ce aspiră la conducerea Chinei. A intrat în partid prin intermediul Ligii Tineretului, ceea ce explică atât strânsele sale legături cu Hu Jintao, cât şi faptul că, în 1999, când a preluat conducerea celei mai populate provincii a Chinei, Henan, a devenit cel mai tânăr guvernator statal din istoria ţării. În 2004 i s-a oferit cea mai înaltă funcţie de partid în provincia Liaoning, cea de Secretar al Comitetului Partidului Comunist al acelei provincii. Unii îl descriu ca un personaj direct şi caustic, alţii, cum ar fi revista **Newsweek** l-au considerat „prudent şi cu relaţii" şi atât de minuţios în pregătire, încât se pare „că îşi memorează discursurile şi nu face nici o greşeală." Probabil că tocmai caracterul său demn de încredere este cel care, potrivit unor voci, l-ar fi determinat pe Hu Jintao să-l ia sub aripa sa.

. . . .

Dat fiind că o atât de mare parte a luptelor pentru putere din China se desfăşoară în spatele uşilor închise, este greu de spus cum arată ele exact. Cert este că trebuie să fie mult diferite de cele din interiorul guvernelor democratice occidentale. În China, există trei baze esenţiale ale puterii – Partidul Comunist, guvernul şi Armata de Eliberare a Poporului. În ultimii ani, deşi bugetul armatei a crescut, puterea sa nu mai este aceeaşi, mai ales datorită faptului că nu i se mai permite să-şi înfiinţeze propriile întreprinderi de producere a echipamentelor militare. Aşadar, Partidul şi guvernul conduc de fapt China.

. . . .

Situaţia **partidului**

Fără nici o îndoială, Partidul Comunist este principala putere, însă relaţia sa cu guvernul este în acelaşi timp subtilă şi complexă. Ambele sunt organizate ca structuri piramidale, ce-şi corespund perfect în oglindă, de la miile de diviziuni locale aflate la bază, trecând prin diversele paliere ale grupurilor regionale şi provinciale, până la nivelul naţional aflat la vârf. La bază, partidul şi guvernul sunt clar separate, reprezentanţii locali ai guvernului fiind rareori şi oficiali ai partidului. Însă, pe măsură ce înaintezi în ierarhie, partidul şi guvernul se întrepătrund din ce în ce mai tare, astfel încât, la vârf, ele fuzionează complet, toate poziţiile cheie ale guvernului fiind ocupate de membri marcanţi ai partidului. Acesta este motivul pentru care Hu Jintao este atât Secretar General al partidului, cât şi Preşedintele Republicii Chineze.

În fruntea partidului şi a guvernului se află Congresele Naţionale – pentru partid, este vorba de Congresul Naţional al Partidului, ce are loc odată la cinci ani, iar pentru guvernul chinez, de anualul Congres Naţional al Poporului, care durează două săptămâni. Însă, nici una dintre aceste adunări nu are vreo putere reală, rolul lor fiind doar acela de a oficializa alegerea candidaților din cadrul propriilor structuri de conducere. Pentru Congresul Partidului, structura de conducere este Comitetul Central; pentru Congresul Național al Poporului este Comitetul Permanent. Ambele structuri au propriul lor organ director. Pentru Comitetul Central al partidului este vorba de Biroul Politic; pentru Comitetul Permanent al Congresului Poporului este Consiliul de Stat, organismul cel mai asemănător unui guvern occidental, fiind condus de către premier și alcătuit din miniștri. Biroul Politic, format din 24 de persoane și Consiliul de Stat, format din 50 și ceva de persoane, sunt adevăratele centre de putere ale guvernării chineze, dar chiar și acestea se întrunesc rar, controlul real aparținând unor cercuri extrem de restrânse, cel alcătuit din cei 9 membri permanenți ai Biroului Politic, în frunte cu Secretarul General Hu Jintao, și cel format din cei 11 membri ai Comitetului Permanent al Consiliului de Stat, condus de Wen Jiabao.

. . . .

Inima **puterii**

Într-o anumită măsură, Congresul Național al Partidului, cu cei 3000 de membri ai săi, este un fel de parlament al Chinei, fiecare lege trebuind să primească acceptul acestora înainte de a fi promulgată. La rândul său, Consiliul de Stat este ca un guvern al Chinei, elaborând proiectele de lege ce urmează să fie supuse votului Congresului Poporului și administrând țara. Însă, faptul că Congresul Poporului nu se întrunește decât două săptămâni pe an, nu este deloc unul întâmplător. Existența negocierilor de culise face ca asupra tuturor legilor propuse spre aprobare Congresului, conducerea partidului să se fi pus deja de acord, astfel încât acestea sunt întotdeauna aprobate în unanimitate. Se întâmplă foarte rar ca un proiect să fie respins sau ca dezbaterea să fie una reală. La Congresul Poporului din 2006 a existat o dezbatere foarte aprinsă privind propunerea de lege ce viza protecția proprietății private, dar asta numai pentru că subiectul acesteia acutiza diferenţele de viziune dintre tabăra celor de dreapta, ce-şi dorea extinderea reformelor de piaţă, şi stângiştii ce o considerau un pas prea mare în direcţia capitalismului. Astfel de dezbateri par să marcheze un nou început, unii analişti considerând că, în viitor, ar putea deveni mai frecvente.

Biroul Politic şi Consiliul de Stat

Comitetul Permanent al Biroului Politic şi Consiliul de Stat sunt centrul puterii chineze. Întrucât Consiliul de Stat este format din membri marcanţi ai partidului, între cele două organisme există o considerabilă suprapunere. În anii '80, Zhao Zhiang, un oficial de rang înalt al guvernului, a încercat să instituie o separare clară a puterilor între acestea, Biroul Politic formulând politicile, iar Consiliul de Stat trebuind să le pună în aplicare, însă instituţiile erau atât de strâns întrepătrunse, încât sarcina s-a dovedit irealizabilă. Cu toate acestea, dacă în China există un pol central al puterii, acesta nu este altul decât Comitetul Permanent al Biroului Politic.

Totuşi, în ciuda acestor ambiguităţi, fiecare lider politic din partid ocupă un loc bine stabilit în ierarhia acestuia. Aceasta din urmă nu este niciodată făcută publică oficial, însă protocolul ierarhic este atât de solid încetăţenit, încât presa de stat îl respectă întotdeauna cu stricteţe – ceea ce înseamnă că articolele sunt întotdeauna ordonate în funcţie de rangul liderului de partid despre care se vorbeşte, şi nu în funcţie de interesul, sau importanţa ştirilor. Şi la întâlnirile oficiale liderii trebuie să se aşeze tot conform rangului lor – ca să nu apară, mai târziu, diverse probleme. Pe la mijlocul anului 2007, poziţia în topul celor 6 lideri era: 1 – Hu Jintao; 2 – Jiang Zemin; 3 – Wu Bannguo (preşedintele Comitetului Permanent al Congresului Poporului); 4 – Wen Jiabao; 5 – Jia Qinglin; 6 – Zen Qinghong (vicepreşedinte).

CORUPȚIA CHINEI

Pe data de 10 iulie 2007, unul dintre liderii chinezi, Zheng Xiaoyu, a fost executat pentru corupție. El a fost unul dintre cei mai importanți oficiali chinezi condamnați vreodată la moarte, iar execuția sa a demonstrat cât de serios tratează guvernul chinez combaterea corupției, dar și cât de gravă și răspândită este această problemă. Zheng era șeful Administrației Chineze pentru Alimentație și Medicamente și a ajuns la putere în postura unui reformator preocupat să facă ceva pentru aprovizionarea Chinei cu medicamente sigure. Până la urmă, tentația mitei oferite de jucătorii de pe piața farmaceuticelor s-a dovedit a fi prea mare, paznicul transformându-se în braconier. În mărturisirea lui, acesta a scris: „Oare de ce toți acei prieteni ai mei care mi-au dat bani sunt șefii unor companii de produse farmaceutice? În mod evident, pentru că eu eram cel aflat în fruntea acestei ramuri a administrației."

Deși Zheng a fost unul dintre vinovații cu cea mai înaltă funcție, politica chineză este bântuită de corupție de câteva mii de ani. Inițial, PCC-ul a reușit să o țină sub control, dar recentele reforme economice au adus atâtea tentații, încât ultimul sfert de secol a cunoscut un nou val de practici necinstite. Numai în 1987, 109 000 membri de partid au fost dați afară pentru corupție, iar de atunci, alte câteva sute de membri sunt executați în fiecare an, asemenea lui Zheng, pentru delapidare. Din când în când, conducerea partidului lansează campanii împotriva corupției. În 1993, spre exemplu, după ce Jiang Zemin a fost alarmat de excesiva atracție pentru bani, mită, extravaganțe personale și sex ilegal a membrilor partidului, Comitetul Central a lansat o acțiune de curățenie. Însă aceasta a avut un efect limitat, iar în 1997, noul apel la reformă internă al lui Jiang Zemin a dus la înființarea Comitetului de Îndrumare pentru Construcția Civilizației Spirituale. Totuși uriașele cantități de bani care intră în China și numărul enorm de contracte oficiale au alimentat probabil și mai mult corupția. Zheng n-a fost altceva decât vârful unui iceberg extrem de mare și de murdar.

Republică **populară**?

În afara granițelor Chinei au loc numeroase dezbateri în legătură cu viitorul democrației în această țară. La un moment dat, mulți comentatori erau convinși că deschiderea economiei chineze către restul lumii și influența crescândă a mecanismelor pieței și a proprietății private vor conduce, în mod necesar, la o creștere a presiunii populare, cetățenii dorind să aibă și ei un cuvânt de spus în propria guvernare. Se pare, însă, că recenta prosperitate a Chinei a dat din nou încredere populației în înțelepciunea guvernului, atenuând imboldul către democrație. Observatorii occidentali au început să se întrebe dacă optimismul lor nu a fost cumva deplasat. Într-un articol din *Foreign Affairs*, din numărul pe iulie–august 2007, Azar Gat sugerează că China și Rusia „ar putea reprezenta o cale alternativă viabilă către modernitate, fapt care sugerează, la rândul său, că victoria finală a democrației liberale și viitoarea dominație totală a acesteia nu sunt inevitabile."

În acest moment, China este, într-adevăr, extrem de puțin democratică. Începând din 1988, celor 930 000 de sate chineze li s-a permis să-și aleagă liderii locali, iar de la mijlocul anilor '90, li s-a permis să ia parte la numirea oficialilor locali ai Partidului Comunist. Dar acestea nu sunt decât gesturi simbolice, din moment ce partidul hotărăște cine poate candida, iar preferințele populare nu sunt luate în seamă decât în alegerea celor mai mărunți funcționari din administrație. Unii comentatori susțin că astfel de măsuri pot chiar întârzia adevărata democrație, făcând-o să fie mai puțin dezirabilă.

PIAȚA TIENANMEN

Figura studentului singuratic, care s-a așezat în fața tancului, în iunie 1989, în Piața Tiananmen, este puternic gravată în conștiința lumii occidentale ca una dintre imaginile definitorii ale secolului XX, iar masacrarea sutelor de studenți protestatari din piață de către armata chineză rămâne o pată de neșters în istoria Republicii Populare Chineze.

Motivele din spatele protestului au rămas încă nedezvăluite de către istorici, iar versiunea occidentală a celor întâmplate continuă să fie contestată de către oficialitățile chineze. Orice căutare pe internet, referitoare la evenimentele din Piața Tienanmen, este blocată de autoritățile chineze, acestea rămânând inflexibile în susținerea versiunii oficiale, potrivit căreia „înăbușirea revoltei a fost o măsură justificată, menită a menține stabilitatea socială."

În 1989, reformele economice abia începuseră să-și facă simțite efectele. Pentru unii, acestea au însemnat o viață prosperă, însă, pentru cei afectați de închiderea întreprinderilor de stat, ele nu au adus decât greutăți. Conducerea era încleștată într-o luptă amară asupra direcției în care trebuia să se îndrepte țara. De-o parte a baricadei, membrii mai vârstnici din partid, inclusiv Deng Xiaoping și Chen Yun, considerau că deschiderea economică nu trebuie să fie și una politică. De cealaltă, Biroul Politic, condus de Zhao Ziyang, susținea că partidul ar trebui să accepte „necesitatea construirii unei democrații socialiste." Cum nici una dintre părți nu părea să cedeze, profesorii și studenții din Beijing, temându-se că „vechea gardă" a partidului ar putea câștiga confruntarea, reinstaurând regimul de represiune, au început să pledeze în favoarea unei mai mari libertăți și a nevoii de democrație.

În aprilie 1989, decesul liderului de partid Hu Yaobang, personaj pe care promotorii democrației îl considerasă a le fi favorabil, a determinat 500 de studenți să meargă să demonstreze în Piața Tiananmen. Cinci zile mai târziu, o jumătate de milion de oameni s-au adunat în piață pentru funeraliile lui Hu. Deși studenții din Beijing au intrat în grevă, mare parte a pieței s-a golit, până când, o săptămână mai târziu, un editorial provocator din **Cotidianul Poporului**, scris la îndemnul lui Deng, i-a acuzat pe studenți de inițierea unei conspirații și a unor „tulburări" menite a îndepărta conducerea partidului de la putere. Imediat, jumătate de milion de potestatari au umplut piața, mulți continuând să rămână acolo, unii chiar intrând în greva foamei. Zhao Ziyang, plecat într-o călătorie în Coreea de Nord, s-a întors și și-a cerut scuze pentru editorial, iar mai târziu, chiar a vizitat studenții în piață.

În timp ce piața devenea din ce în ce mai plină și autoritățile păreau să dea înapoi, în aer începuse să plutească o senzație de optimism, studenții ridicându-și corturi și cântând, unii dintre ei închipuindu-și că și China ar putea avea propria sa „revoluție de catifea." Conducerea chineză s-a simțit, însă, umilită, atunci când planurile pentru vizita oficială a lui Mihail Gorbaciov, din 15-22 mai, au fost eclipsate de proteste. Deng și alți membri ai „vechii gărzi" au intervenit, dându-l afară pe Zhao și proclamând legea marțială. Armata a înaintat până în suburbii, oprindu-se acolo, și, pentru două săptămâni, protestatarii au crezut că aceasta nu va merge mai departe. La acea dată, muncitorii din Beijing, îngrijorați de pierderea locurilor de muncă, se alăturaseră deja studenților, cerând o participare sporită în administrarea întreprinderilor. Atunci, în acea teribilă noapte de 3 spre 4 iunie, armata a intrat cu tancurile. Nimeni nu știe exact câți morți au fost, dar au existat mai multe sute, poate chiar o mie. Deși cea mai cunoscută imagine este cea a studentului așezat în fața tancului, acei locuitori obișnuiți ai Beijingului care au căutat să împiedice intrarea armatei în piață au suferit pierderi mult mai grele. După masacru, a fost pornită o uriașă campanie de arestări, sute de oameni fiind trimiși în lagărele de muncă și mulți chiar executați. China părea să treacă prin niște clipe de coșmar, care i-au întunecat pe bună dreptate imaginea în lume. Mai ales locuitorii Beijingului au fost extrem de șocați și întristați. Și cu toate acestea, uluitor este faptul că, doar trei ani mai târziu, Deng, acum un bătrânel blajin și zâmbitor, cu tolba doldora de aforisme confucianiste, își făcea din nou apariția în Turneul din Sud, pledând pentru continuarea reformelor. Iar asta, în timp ce Zhao Ziyang se afla în arest la domiciliu, situație în care va rămâne pentru tot restul vieții.

. . . .

. . . .

GUANXI

În fiecare lună, sute de săraci din toată China vin la Beijing, la biroul de petiții al guvernului, și așteaptă răbdători la coadă, zile întregi, pentru a-și depune plângerile. Majoritatea sunt victime ale unor triste nedreptăți. Unul dintre fiii lor a fost bătut, sau vreo bucată de teren le-a fost luată de vreun antreprenor. Ei sunt convinși că este suficient ca guvernul central să le audă plângerea, pentru ca răul să fie imediat îndreptat. Eforturile aproape tuturor acestor petiționari sunt zadarnice, pentru că ei nu au guanxi**-ul potrivit; pur și simplu nu cunosc acele persoane capabile să tragă sfori pentru ei.**

Guanxi este un cuvânt chinez intraductibil, o combinație între **guan**, care înseamnă ,,aproape'', și **xi**, care înseamnă ,,a fi''. Cea mai bună aproximare a lui ar fi ,,**relație specială**''. Guanxi este un concept străvechi, cu rădăcini în idealurile confucianiste de creare a unor legături bazate pe încredere și pe obligații reciproce, care a ajuns să joace un rol central în viața chinezilor, în special, în politică și afaceri. Pentru a se descurca cât mai bine în viață, chinezii își creează o adevărată rețea de relații personale în afara familiei, care le va fi de foarte mare ajutor în caz de nevoie.

Am putea-o considera un ansamblu de relaționări interpersonale, dar, de fapt, este mult mai personală și profundă decât simpla terminologie sociologică folosită pentru a o descrie. Nu este vorba doar de a intra în contact cu oamenii potriviți; **guanxi** înseamnă, mai degrabă, dezvoltarea unor legături personale solide, pe care să te poți baza. Este vorba despre crearea unor legături pe care nu le mai poți rupe, nici măcar în perioadele cele mai vitrege. Politicienii îi vor răsplăti pe cei care le stau aproape la nevoie, fiindcă și-au dovedit puterea **guanxi**-ului lor. Firmele care rămân alături de cei aflați la putere într-o perioadă de mari încercări își dovedesc, la rândul lor, forța **guanxi**-lui. Cei care fac afaceri în China sunt, adeseori, iritați de răspândirea universală a **guanxi**-ului, plângându-se că acesta miroase de la o poștă a nepotism și a favoritism – sau, chiar mai rău, a ineficiență, din moment ce contractele sunt acordate în baza legăturilor personale și nu a competitivității ofertelor. Cu toate acestea, chinezii îl privesc mai mult ca pe o rețea de întrajutorare care menține stabilitatea și buna rânduială în societate, oferind talentului imboldul necesar pentru a reuși. Oamenii de afaceri chinezi pun un mai mare preț decât cei occidentali pe crearea unor legături personale cu clienții lor. A vizita clienții acasă, a le oferi cadouri, sau ajutor, poate părea cu totul deplasat în Occident, dar în China, nu este decât o încercare de atragere a **guanxi**-ului. Doar atunci când rețeaua ta de **guanxi** este foarte bine dezvoltată, poți începe să te bucuri, cu-adevărat, de viață.

Proteste și petiții

Nu există nici o îndoială că locuitorii Chinei nu mai sunt atât de docili cum păreau odinioară – sau poate că au devenit doar mai îndrăzneți în a-și manifesta sentimentele. De-a lungul ultimilor zece, cincisprezece ani de zile, diferitele forme de protest social, cum ar fi revoltele, demonstrațiile și petițiile, au crescut la număr, alimentate mai ales de acutizarea discrepanțelor de avere dintre pătura înstărită de la oraș și săracii din mediul rural. Statisticile oficiale arată că, în 2005, au existat aproape 85000 de astfel de acțiuni protestatare, în comparație cu cele 10000 înregistrate în 1994. Cu toate acestea, protestele nu reprezintă un apel la democrație, ci o formă de atragere a atenției asupra diferitelor nedreptăți locale. Oamenii se ridică la luptă atunci când vine vorba de deversările unor substanțe toxice de la întreprinderi, de repercursiunile construirii unor baraje asupra mediului și a localnicilor și, mai presus de orice, de exproprierile făcute în numele dezvoltării economice. Aceste proteste au foarte rar motivații politice. Într-adevăr, majoritatea protestatarilor par să creadă că nedreptățile sunt provocate de oficialii locali și că dacă ar reuși să se facă auziți de liderii de la Beijing, toate relele ar fi îndreptate. O credință îndreptățită, într-o oarecare măsură. Date fiind dimensiunile uriașe ale Chinei și faptul că funcționarii locali acționează la o asemenea distanță de centru – și sunt extrem de dornici să suprime orice știre despre proteste – Beijingul nu află de aceste abuzuri decât atunci când nemulțumiții ajung în capitală.

Demn de remarcat este faptul că cetățenii chinezi par să-și facă cunoscute plângerile într-o manieră ce amintește surpinzător de mult de epoca imperială, când țăranii mergeau cu jalba pentru a li se face dreptate chiar de către împărat. Între 1994 și 2004, numărul petițiilor adresate Beijingului a crescut uimitor, în 2004, acesta fiind de 13,7 milioane. Guvernul a decis să reducă acest val de petiții, instituind diferite reglementări care să-l țină sub control. Cu toate că, în 2005, numărul petițiilor a scăzut cu un milion, cel al solicitărilor care primesc răspuns a rămas în continuare același. Cercetătorii angajați de guvernul chinez pentru a studia problema au descoperit că procentul celor care primiseră un răspuns la memoriul lor era mai mic de 0,2%.

. . . .

FALUN GONG

În anii '90, în vreme ce puterea eticii socialiste începuse să scadă sub influența forțelor de piață, unele persoane, mai ales cele vârstnice, s-au îndreptat către religie și misticism, căutând liniștea și pacea pe care le ofereau acestea. În ciuda presiunii exercitate de autoritățile atee, o sumedenie de secte budiste, creștine și daoiste au început să se răspândească în zonele rurale, iar în orașe, mulți au început să exploreze străvechile principii ale **Qigong**-ului chinez (arta dezvoltării armonioase a **qi**-ului, energia vitală a corpului).

Qigong era o combinație de misticism și arte marțiale, „febra" stârnită de acesta cuprinzând chiar și unele personaje de rang înalt din rândurile armatei. Unul dintre generali chiar a sperat că maestrul de **qigong** Zhang Baosheng ar putea să „fure secrete nucleare de la ruși sau americani". Cea mai mare parte a acestor activități s-a desfășurat cu acordul autorităților, care le și finanțau, prin intermediul Asociației Qigong. Însă apoi, o nouă sectă, denumită **Falun Gong**, a fost înființată în nord-estul Chinei de către Li Hongzhi, un fost funcționar și gornist în armată, ce pretindea că fusese inițiat, încă de la o vârstă fragedă, de un maestru budist.

Potrivit literaturii grupului, **Falun Gong** datează din timpuri preistorice, dar a ajuns în atenția publică doar atunci când Li a înființat un centru de studiu la Beijing, în 1992. Mișcarea combină credințele budiste și pe cele daoiste, cu exercițiile **qigong**. **Falun Gong** înseamnă „legea roții", iar exercițiile sunt concepute astfel încât fiecare practicant să-și poată dezvolta „roata" proprie, centrul energetic situat în partea inferioară a abdomenului, prin care energia universului intră în individ.

La început, a părut a fi doar un regim de exerciții și sute de oameni, mai ales bătrâni, se adunau în piețe pentru a face mișcările specifice. Dar maestrul Li a retras **Falun Gong** din Asociația **Qigong**, probabil din cauza unor neînțelegeri financiare. Decizia a făcut ca **Falun Gong** să devină ilegal, iar autoritățile i-au interzis publicațiile. Reacția **Falun Gong** a fost una surprinzător de combativă. În aprilie 1999, mii de membri au pichetat în tăcere sediul central al Partidului Comunist din Beijing. După trei luni de deliberări, mișcarea a fost interzisă și etichetată ca „un cult al răului", iar autoritățile au început să-i persecute membrii de pe tot cuprinsul Chinei, trimițându-i pe cei care refuzau să se dezică de convingerile lor eretice în lagăre de muncă forțată. Aflat în siguranță, în exil la New York, Li și-a îndemnat discipolii să reziste. Aceștia au organizat un protest în Piața Tiananmen, în urma căruia sute de manifestanți trecuți de prima tinerețe au fost târâți pe jos și înghesuiți în dubele poliției, provocând furia occidentului.

Afacerea **Falun Gong** continuă să agite spiritele, nu doar în China, ci în întreaga lume. În februarie 2006, spre exemplu, excluderea **Falun Gong** de la Parada Chineză de Anul Nou, din San Francisco, a stârnit un adevărat scandal, grupul pretinzând că aceasta a fost motivată politic.

Grupuri de inițiativă

Asemenea petițiilor, numărul grupurilor de inițiativă a crescut dramatic în ultimele decenii. În 1988, în China erau doar 4500 de organizații nonguvernamentale. În 2005, erau deja 317000. Dacă luăm în considerare faptul că trebuie să fie înregistrate oficial și susținute financiar de organizații guvernamentale, numărul lor este uriaș. Mai mult, în afara ONG-urilor înregistrate, agenția oficială de presă, Xinhua, estimează că există peste 2,6 milioane de organizații neînregistrate. Majoritatea acestora, chiar dacă au ca scop protestul, sunt orientate, în special, asupra unor probleme locale care țin de mediul înconjurător, sau de chestiuni sociale, fiind rareori politice. Iar acele organizații care chiar au o agendă politică trebuie să fie, mai mult ca sigur, extrem de puțin bătătoare la ochi. Potrivit unui articol semnat de Carin Zissis, apărut în *New York Times* (18.06.2007): „În ultimii doi ani, autoritățile și-au intensificat investigațiile în legătură cu grupurile străine și autohtone ce activează pe teritoriul Chinei. Mai mult, autoritățile au făcut presiuni asupra voluntarilor, încercând să-i determine să nu mai lucreze pentru diverse organizații din care făceau parte, sub amenințarea sistării finanțării de stat, sau a retragerii autorizației de funcționare.“

Conducerea chineză este, cu siguranță, conștientă de existența unui curent democratic, pe care a trebuit deja să-l ia în seamă în relațiile sale cu Hong Kong-ul, dar nu pare deloc grăbită să o apuce pe această cale. Acum, când investitorilor străini le este din ce în ce mai ușor să facă afaceri profitabile cu guvernul comunist, presiunile externe în această direcție par mai degrabă să scadă. Într-un articol din februarie 2007, Wen Jiabao (Premierul Consiliului de Stat al Chinei) scria că liderii partidului considerau că prima fază, cea socialistă, a drumului Chinei către comunism va dura o sută de ani, ceea ce ar însemna că democrația va veni în China cu pași foarte înceți.

MARELE „ZID DE FOC" CHINEZESC

Nu există nici o îndoială că uimitoarea creştere a numărului de utilizatori de internet din China, a permis accesul chinezilor de rând la informaţie. Desigur că autorităţile chineze se tem că dacă ar permite accesul nelimitat la internet, populaţia ar afla prea multe lucruri nedorite. Ca atare, au făcut tot ce le-a stat în putere pentru a se asigura că oamenii vor vedea numai ceea ce este „sănătos" şi „în interesul publicului". Opiniile disidente nu sunt în interesul publicului, iar pornografia este nesănătoasă. O armată de 30000 de informaticieni stă chiar în clipa de faţă aşezată în faţa calculatoarelor, supraveghind site-urile de web şi e-mail-urile, eliminând orice informaţie nepotrivită, într-un sistem care a fost botezat **Marele Firewall** (Zid de Foc – n.red.) Chinezesc.

O parte a sistemului se ocupă de blocarea traficului dinspre site-urile străine, care intră în China prin cele cinci porţi electronice ale sale. O altă parte se ocupă de blocarea anumitor cuvinte-cheie, împiedicând populaţia să găsească, sau să intre pe acele site-uri considerate a fi nepotrivite. Cele aproximativ 110000 internet café-uri sunt atent monitorizate de numeroase sisteme de supraveghere. Autorităţile se bazează, de asemenea, pe autocenzura indivizilor, şi pentru că teama de măsurile punitive aplicate disidenţilor este foarte mare, ideea se dovedeşte a fi surprinzător de eficace. Pentru a cita din raportul organizaţiei Amnesty International pe 2006: „Amnesty International are cunoştinţă de existenţa a cel puţin 64 de „cyber-disidenţi", incarceraţi doar pentru că şi-au exprimat liber părerile pe internet." Firmele străine se autocenzurează la rândul lor, temându-se să nu-şi piardă piaţa. În 2005, când motorul de căutare american Google şi-a lansat versiunea chineză, a fost acuzat că şi-a trădat principiile fundamentale, pentru că aceasta era modificată pentru a exclude căutarea unor subiecte precum Piaţa Tiananmen şi Falun Gong. Microsoft şi Yahoo au făcut şi ele acelaşi lucru. În pofida acestor inconveniente, chinezii au totuşi acces la o mare varietate de subiecte, unii reuşind chiar să găsească modalităţi de a evita cenzura, prin intermediul blog-urilor şi al browser-elor de text, însă, până şi acestea, nu mai pot scăpa mult timp de supraveghere.

Ce mai **urmează**?

Deși există numeroase speculații asupra direcției în care se va îndrepta politica chineză în următorii cinci ani și asupra celor care vor fi aleși la viitorul Congres Național, adevărul este că nimeni din afara cercului închis al conducerii chineze nu știe nimic precis – nici măcar membrii de partid. Nimeni nu știe nici măcar când vor avea loc schimbările majore. Cu toate acestea, majoritatea observatorilor cred că Hu Jintao va conduce țara mai departe, în aceeași direcție în care a condus-o în ultimii ani.

Hu a arătat că este profund conștient de clivajul apărut între bogați și săraci din cauza *boom*-ului economic al țării și, de asemenea, de faptul că păturile de jos ale populației suferă din pricina eliminării ajutoarelor de stat, fie ele pentru sănătate, locuințe, educație, sau șomaj. Cel mai probabil este ca el să inițieze o serie de măsuri intenționate a rezolva aceste probleme și nu să întoarcă China din drumul spre o piață deschisă, așa cum le-ar conveni criticilor săi. Cu două săptămâni înainte de apariția scrisorii amintite la începutul capitolului, Hu a ținut un discurs în care a subliniat că cele două obiective cheie ale sale sunt crearea „armoniei sociale" și construirea „unei societăți a bunăstării." Pronunțate de un politician occidental, aceste expresii ar părea banale și fără sens, dar în China, ele reprezintă un mesaj cifrat, cu un înțeles extrem de specific, pe care oricare membru al partidului l-ar înțelege. Înseamnă, mai exact, că înaintarea către economia de piață va continua, pentru a produce mai multă bunăstare, dar și că partidul va lua toate măsurile necesare pentru ajutorarea celor lipsiți de mijloace, asigurându-se astfel că liniștea țării nu va fi tulburată de problemele și protestele celor dezavantajați. Drepturile democratice nu au fost menționate.

. . . .

Capitolul 3:
URBAN ŞI RURAL

„Am văzut o suferință inimaginabilă și o neajutorare de neconceput, o rezistență amestecată cu o tăcere de neînțeles și am fost mișcați dincolo de imaginație de tragedia de necrezut."

Chen Guidi și Wu Chuntao – *Țăranii Chinei: O Investigație*

În iulie 2007, World Watch făcea cunoscută lumii tragedia care se abătuse asupra unui tânăr muncitor din Guangdong. Într-o confruntare dintre muncitorii migranți și bătăușii angajați de una dintre companiile chineze, tânărul Lei Mingzhong, de 27 de ani, a fost lovit în cap cu o lopată, provocându-i leziuni cerebrale fatale. Nu se știe exact cum s-au petrecut lucrurile în cazul bietului Lei, însă muncitorii migranți devin, adesea, victime ale societății în rapidă schimbare a Chinei. Există aproximativ două sute de milioane de astfel de muncitori, majoritatea oameni extrem de săraci, din mediul rural, care și-au părăsit familiile pentru a căuta de lucru la oraș. Aceștia vor forma noua clasă de jos a Chinei.

Extraordinara creștere economică a Chinei a stimulat cea mai rapidă dezvoltare urbană din istoria lumii. În fiecare săptămână, numărul locuitorilor din orașele Chinei sporește cu încă un milion. În fiecare an, orașele Chinei cresc cu echivalentul populației din Tokyo. Cu doar un sfert de secol în urmă, patru din cinci chinezi trăiau la țară, un procent mai mare decât în orice altă țară din lume. În 2000, procentul celor care locuiau la oraș s-a dublat. În câțiva ani, mai mult de jumătate din populația Chinei, ajunsă acum la 1,3 miliarde de locuitori, va locui la oraș. În 2020 doar unul din trei chinezi va mai trăi la țară; în vreme ce, în orașele Chinei vor locui aproape un miliard de locuitori. În China există deja 60 de orașe cu peste un milion de locuitori. În următorii zece ani, vor apărea mai multe megalopolisuri, cu o populație de 30 de milioane, sau mai mult – Beijing, Shanghai, Guangzhou și Chongqing – și o duzină de orașe de mărimea Londrei (care are în jur de 7,5 milioane), cum ar fi Shenzhen și Tianjin.

Migranţi în mişcare

Cum natalitatea din mediul urban este limitată prin politica „copilului unic", este clar că cea mai mare parte a acestei expansiuni nu provine din oraşele înseşi, ci dintr-un enorm aflux de populaţie de la ţară. Cauzele acestei migraţii, cea mai mare din istoria omenirii, sunt atât atracţia reprezentată de oraşe, cu tentaţia locurilor de muncă şi a stilului de viaţă mai bun, cât şi presiunea exercitată de mediul rural, în care, în ciuda unei jumătăţi de secol de regim comunist, sărăcia este fi la fel de chinuitoare ca oriunde altundeva în lume.

Una dintre problemele migranţilor este cea a statutului provizoriu pe care îl au în oraşe. La începuturile statului comunist, semnalmentele fiecărui membru al unei familii erau înregistrate într-un dosar, numit *hukou*, păstrat la sediul local al poliţiei. În baza acestora era stabilit nu doar locul în care poţi munci, ci şi cel în care poţi cere ajutor social. Sistemul *hukou* a făcut ca mutarea din localitatea de baştină să fie un demers extrem de dificil pentru toată lumea, îndeosebi pentru cei de la ţară. Locuitorii oraşelor se mai puteau plimba de colo-colo, ajungând chiar şi în alte oraşe, însă, cei de la ţară, rareori ajungeau mai departe de câţiva kilometri de casă.

Cu toate acestea, în oraşe, începutul dezvoltării economice din anii '80 a dat naştere unei cereri imense de muncitori, care pur şi simplu nu putea fi satisfăcută la nivel local. Astfel încât guvernul a slăbit restricţiile, permiţând populaţiei să se deplaseze prin ţară şi să se mute în alte localităţi, în baza unor permise de şedere temporară pe care trebuiau să le reînnoiască în fiecare lună, la poliţie. Soluţia trebuia să fie doar una temporară, dar, în foarte scurt timp, un uriaş val de migranţi străbătea ţara de la un capăt la altul, în căutarea unor locuri de muncă şi a unei căi de a ieşi din capcana sărăciei. În anul 2000 existau în jur de 130 de milioane astfel de migranţi. Acum sunt aproape două sute de milioane. Majoritatea migranţilor se îndreptau spre sud, către Guangdong, sau spre est, către Shanghai şi Beijing. În sud, 85% din cei 10 milioane de locuitori ai oraşului Shenzhen sunt migranţi, iar în Shanghai sunt peste patru milioane.

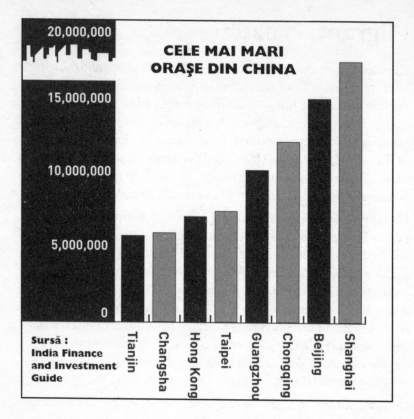

CELE MAI MARI ORAŞE DIN CHINA

20,000,000

15,000,000

10,000,000

5,000,000

0

Sursă :
India Finance
and Investment
Guide

Tianjin · Changsha · Hong Kong · Taipei · Guangzhou · Chongqing · Beijing · Shanghai

Fără eforturile acestor „nomazi", care, în general, sunt gata să muncească ore în şir pentru nişte salarii de nimic, dezvoltarea economică chineză nu ar fi fost posibilă; banii pe care aceştia i-au trimis familiilor rămase la ţară au reuşit să amelioreze condiţiile de sărăcie lucie în care trăiau sute de milioane de locuitori din mediul rural. Aproape 70% dintre muncitorii din producţie şi construcţii şi 32% dintre cei care lucrează în domeniul serviciilor nu locuiesc în oraşele în care îşi exercită profesia. Însă, din păcate, deplasarea acestor mase uriaşe de oameni a afectat profund structura socială a vieţii rurale.

. . . .

DOAR UN SINGUR COPIL

În 1980, guvernul chinez a inițiat una dintre cele mai controversate legi de planificare familială concepute vreodată. Decis să încetinească creșterea populației, pe care o considera a fi un obstacol în calea prosperității Chinei, acesta a impus respectarea unei limite de un singur copil pe familie.

Existau și categorii exceptate de la această regulă, cum ar fi minoritățile etnice, iar din 1980 au mai fost introduse și alte excepții, dar altfel, aplicarea politicii a fost aproape universală, în special în orașe. În aprilie 2007, un amănunțit studiu științific efectuat de cercetători americani și chinezi, a arătat că măsura, în ciuda zvonurilor contrare, a fost extraordinar de eficientă. Principalul autor al acestui studiu, Wang Feng, de la Universitatea Irvine din California, spunea: „în ciuda celor spuse de unii, politica nu s-a „destins" de-a lungul anilor... Sistemul de excepții seamănă, în complexitatea sa, cu codul fiscal american. Dar aceasta nu schimbă cu nimic faptul că politica „copilului unic" se aplică fără greș unei majorități semnificative (peste două treimi) din populația chineză."

Rezultatul este că mărimea medie a unei familii din China este de sub 1,5 persoane, iar populația chineză, cu ale sale 1,3 miliarde de suflete, este cu un sfert de miliard mai mică decât ar fi fost în alte condiții. Însă, deși mulți susțin că această limitare a populației a ajutat la scăderea gradului de sărăcie și foamete care apăsa odată China, politica „copilului unic" n-a fost lipsită de consecințe dureroase și alarmante, mai grave chiar decât temerea nerespectării drepturilor fundamentale ale omului.

În primul rând, eforturile de a aplica această politică au dus la tot felul de abuzuri din partea unor funcționari plini de zel. Nenumărate femei au fost forțate să facă avort, adesea în stadii înaintate ale sarcinii, în unele cazuri, la peste opt luni. Altora li s-au injectat cu forța soluții saline în uter pentru a se asigura că pruncul se va naște mort. Multe femei au fost sterilizate cu forța după nașterea primului copil. Pentru acele cupluri care se riscă să facă un al doilea copil, pedepsele pot fi extrem de severe. Amenzile sunt usturătoare, iar dacă cuplul nu le poate plăti, se poate trezi cu locuința golită, sau chiar demolată de către autorități. În mai 2007, sătenii din Guangxi au fost atât de iritați de încercările autorităților locale de a spori severitatea pedepselor, încât au atacat birourile guvernului. Potrivit unui buletin de știri al agenției *Reuters*, un sătean a declarat: „Funcționarii responsabili cu planificarea familială s-au purtat la fel ca invadatorii japonezi din timpul războiului. Au luat totul, devastând, sau distrugând casele dacă oamenii nu puteau plăti amenzile." Familiile mai bogate îşi pot, desigur, permite să plătească amenzile şi o fac, având familii numeroase şi alimentând resentimentul.

În oraşe, politica „copilului unic" este aproape universală, excepţie făcând doar cei bogaţi, dar în mediul rural, oamenii au găsit diverse căi prin care s-o ocolească. Familiile îşi pot trimite copiii la rude, pentru a evita să fie descoperiţi, sau pot pretinde că micuţii sunt, de fapt, adoptaţi, sau că le-au fost lăsaţi în grijă de un prieten. În ultimii ani, tot mai multe femei apelează la medicamente pentru fertilitate, pentru a creşte şansa unor naşteri multiple. Dacă nasc gemeni, tripleţi, sau chiar cvadrupleţi, mamele pot avea familii numeroase fără a încălca legea „copilului unic". Cum diverse medicamente pentru fertilitate ieftine şi fără prescripţie, cum ar fi clomifen citratul, sunt disponibile la farmacii, nu e de mirare că unele sate din China au avut parte de o proliferare uimitoare a gemenilor şi a tripleţilor.

Cu toate astea, în ciuda acestor excepţii, politica copilului unic a fost aplicată pe scară largă şi are cel puţin o consecinţă neprevăzută şi extrem de tristă. Din cauza preferinţei tradiţionale a chinezilor pentru băieţi, bebeluşii fetiţe au fost principalele victime. Ca rezultat al avortului fetuşilor de sex feminin, al infanticidul comis de femei şi a simplei neglijări a fetiţelor, în China raportul fete-băieţi devine din ce în ce mai nefavorabil celor dintâi. Rezultatul este că, în fiecare an, în China se nasc cu un milion mai mulţi băieţi decât fete. În 2007, pentru fiecare 100 de fete, s-au născut 117 băieţi. Dezechilibrul face ca multor bărbaţi să le fie aproape imposibil să-şi găsească soţii sau prietene, ziarele şi site-urile de internet fiind înţesate de anunţuri postate în speranţa găsirii unei partenere. Frustrarea unora este atât de mare, încât numărul abuzurilor şi al cazurilor de exploatare a femeii a crescut uimitor de mult în ultima vreme, cele mai optimiste cifre vorbind de 43000 de fete răpite în fiecare an, pentru a se prostitua sau a deveni soţii fără voie. Guvernul chinez este atât de alarmat de eventualele consecinţe ale dezechilibrului dintre numărul femeilor şi cel al bărbaţilor, încât a hotărât că orice persoană care testează sexul fătului fără acceptul autorităţilor va fi „aspru pedepsită." Guvernul a declarat, de asemenea, că îşi va spori eforturile de protejare a copiilor de sex feminin.

O altă discrepanţă cauzată de politica „copilului unic" este procentul din ce în ce mai scăzut pe care îl deţin tinerii în populaţia Chinei. Numeroşi experţi estimează că, în curând, China va avea un mai mare număr de vârstnici decât majoritatea ţărilor occidentale, şi foarte puţin din bogăţia utilizată de acestea pentru a-i susţine. Cu toate astea, guvernul rămâne la fel de ferm în ceea ce priveşte politica copilului unic, intenţionând ca, până în 2050, populaţia Chinei să nu depăşească 1,6–1,7 miliarde.

. . . .

Familii divizate

Unul dintre motivele de suferinţă ale muncitorilor este dificultatea de a se muta şi lucra la oraş. Statutul de rezidenţă temporară al muncitorilor migratori face ca acestora să le fie foarte greu să-şi aducă şi alţi membri de familie cu ei. Majoritatea trebuie să meargă în oraşe pe cont propriu, lăsându-şi în urmă familiile şi prietenii. Salariile mici şi orele lungi de muncă înseamnă că vizitele acasă sunt foarte rare. Adesea, migranţii ajung acasă doar o dată pe an, de Anul Nou chinezesc, când trenurile şi autobuzele sunt pline de muncitori care ţin cu dinţii de sacoşele lor cu dungi roşii, albe şi albastre (pungi din plastic tare, pe care occidentalii le folosesc pentru a depozita rufele murdare).

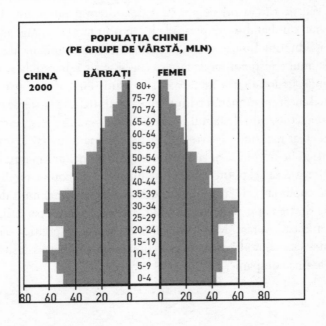

POPULAŢIA CHINEI
(PE GRUPE DE VÂRSTĂ, MLN)

CHINA
2000   BĂRBAŢI   FEMEI

80+
75-79
70-74
65-69
60-64
55-59
50-54
45-49
40-44
35-39
30-34
25-29
20-24
15-19
10-14
5-9
0-4

80 60 40 20 0   0 20 40 60 80

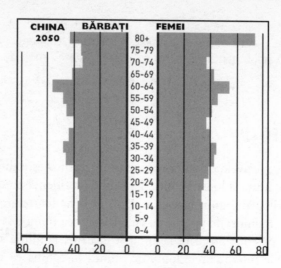

Sursă: Biroul de recensământ al SUA

Pentru muncitorii căsătoriți sau cu copii situația este și mai dificilă. Este la fel de greu și pentru zecile de milioane de cupluri care, dacă se văd de câteva ori pe an, sunt de-a dreptul norocoase. Chiar și atunci când ambii soți pleacă la lucru prin țară, ei ajung, adesea, în orașe diferite. Însă, adevărata tragedie este cea a copiilor migranților. Sistemul registrelor locale face ca copiii să aibă dreptul la școlarizare numai în localitatea în care ei și părinții lor locuiesc permanent. Astel încât, nenumărați părinți înlăcrimați trebuie să-și lase copiii în urmă, conștienți de faptul că n-o să-i mai revadă decât peste un an, sau chiar mai mult. Foarte des, greutățile financiare fac ca ambii părinți să fie nevoiți să-și lase copiii în grija bunicilor sau a rudelor. Se estimează că cel puțin 85% dintre migranții cu copii au trebuit să-și lase copiii la țară, iar în multe regiuni din țară, mai mult de jumătate dintre copii au cel puțin unul, adesea amândoi părinții, plecați la muncă în orașe. Mai trist este, însă, faptul că politica „copilului unic" face ca mulți dintre acești copii să nu aibă frați sau surori care să le țină companie.

REPRIMAREA SEXUALĂ

În 2006, un articol din **China Daily** releva frustrarea sexuală a multora dintre muncitorii migranți. O anchetă a Ministerului Sănătății arăta că 88% din migratorii de sex masculin sufereau de „depresie sexuală" – lucru deloc surprinzător.

Munca este atât de grea, iar condițiile atât de sărăcăcioase, încât muncitorii nu au niciodată ocazia să-și facă vreo prietenă, iar soții își văd soțiile, în cel mai bun caz, de câteva ori pe an. Un sondaj efectuat de **Beijing Daily Star** arăta că aproape un sfert dintre muncitorii căsătoriți nu au făcut sex de ani de zile, iar aproape jumătate nu mai făcuseră sex cu soțiile lor de cel puțin șase luni. Deși, pentru cei care și-o doresc, există suficiente prostituate, dar salariile migranților sunt atât de mici încât nu și le pot permite.

Chiar și atunci când cuplurile de muncitori au șansa nesperată să lucreze în același oraș, sau pentru aceeași companie, viața lor sexuală este cel puțin dificilă. Multe întreprinderi insistă ca lucrătorii lor să locuiască lângă șantier, dar le asigură doar dormitoare unisex. **China Daily** anunță o nouă inițiativă în Shenzhen, unde o întreprindere a finanțat construcția a zeci de apartamente ieftine denumite „cuiburi ale dragostei", care pot fi închiriate soților sau soțiilor venite în vizită. Cu toate acestea, unii dintre sociologii chinezi susțin că această soluție nu este de natură să pună capăt frustrărilor sexuale ale muncitorilor în viitorul apropiat. Ei propun, printre altele, ca muncitorilor să le fie prezentate filme „sănătoase" și să li se asigure mese de ping-pong și de cărți – sugerându-le, probabil, să mai facă, din când în când, și câte un duș rece.

Școlile **migranților**

Fiecare părinte migrant este pus în fața unei decizii cruciale atunci când se pregătește să plece la oraș. Fie își lasă copiii în urmă, ca să învețe la o școală bună, fie îi ia cu el, expunându-i greutăților vieții de la oraș, conștient fiind că s-ar putea să nu le poată oferi nici o educație. Deși mulți copii de migranți rămân acasă, în orașe numărul lor continuă să fie apreciabil. În 2003, în Shanghai erau trei sute de mii de copii de migranți, de vârstă școlară; în Shenzhen erau patru sute de mii.

Când migranții au început să sosească în orașe, le mai puteau obține, uneori, copiilor lor, un loc la o școală, însă numai dacă plăteau o taxă ce depășea mijloacele multora. Nerăbdători să găsească o soluție, unii dintre muncitori s-au unit pentru a-și întemeia propriile școli. Acestea erau ilegale, fiind frecvent închise de autorități, și chiar și atunci când nu erau, ele trebuiau să se bazeze doar pe micile taxe pe care le puteau percepe migranților. Unii dintre ei nu-și puteau permite nici măcar aceste taxe, astfel încât, potrivit estimărilor UNICEF, în 2003, 10% din copiii migranților nu au mers la nici un fel de școală. Autoritățile au încercat să rezolve problema cerând școlilor de la oraș să primească o parte dintre copii, însă, după ce clasele au ajuns să aibă chiar și 45 de elevi fiecare, metoda nu a mai funcționat.

Un sentiment de neliniște își face, actualmente, loc printre sociologii chinezi, în legătură cu o întreagă generație de zeci de milioane de copii, crescuți fie la țară, unde au fost lipsiți de dragostea și îndrumarea părinților, fie la oraș, unde au fost privați de o educație corespunzătoare. Există serioase temeri legate de o viitoare societate chineză, dominată, pe de-o parte, de „copiii pierduți" ai migranților ajunși la maturitate, și, pe de altă parte, de „micii împărați" proveniți din mediile înstărite de la oraș.

. . . .

NU PRIMIM MIGRANȚI!

În afara vieții lor personale dificile, mulți migranți trebuie să facă față unei discriminări, în numeroase feluri chiar mai dure, decât cea suferită de emigranții sosiți în orașele occidentale, la începutul secolului XX. În ciuda faptului că noii sosiți sunt chinezi, la fel ca locuitorii permanenți ai orașelor, ei pot fi imediat identificați ca „străini", după modul lor de comportament și hainele „tradiționale" – având doar statutul de rezidenți temporari.

Una dintre probleme este că nu au statut legal, ceea ce înseamnă că pot fi exploatați fără milă de către angajatori. Majoritatea muncitorilor emigranți câştigă nu doar sub salariul mediu ci, adeseori, chiar sub cel minim, lucrând ore nesfârşite în condiții mizerabile şi, de cele mai multe ori, periculoase. Şi mai grav este faptul că salariile nu le sunt plătite cu lunile şi, fiindcă nu au un contract, nu au cum să-şi obțină drepturile. Cazul lui Lei, prezentat la începutul acestui capitol, este unul tipic. Lei făcea parte dintr-un grup de muncitori migranți care au intrat în grevă după ce au muncit mai mult de 4 luni fără salariu – revendicările lor au fost întâmpinate de o bandă de bătăuşi angajați de patronii firmei. Însă, în iulie 2007, după descoperirea a sute de adulți şi de copii răpiți muncind aproape ca nişte sclavi în minele şi la cuptoarele de cărămizi din Shanxi şi Henan, guvernul a intrat în acțiune, promulgând o lege care impune angajatorilor să încheie contracte scrise cu muncitorii, începând din 2008.

Rămâne de văzut dacă aceasta va schimba ceva – însă o altă lege, pusă de curând în aplicare, a făcut-o. Până acum câțiva ani, migranții erau constant agresați de polițişti, care aveau dreptul să le ceară actele de flotant şi să-i deporteze, dacă nu le aveau. Dar în 2003, moartea unui designer din Guangzhou, pe nume Sun Zhigang, survenită în timp ce acesta se afla în custodia poliției, a stârnit un asemenea scandal, încât guvernul a schimbat legea, migranții nemaifiind nevoiți să poarte la ei actele doveditoare. Din câte se pare, această măsură a avut un impact pozitiv major în viețile migranților.

Oraşe în schimbare

Oraşele în care sosesc aceşti muncitori s-au schimbat dramatic fața de acum douăzeci de ani. Ele nu sunt doar mai mari, ci "altfel". Cu 20 de ani în urmă, majoritatea erau nişte locuri adormite, foarte puțin diferite de cele din epoca imperială. Oraşe precum Suzhou, aflat pe Marele Canal, la nord de Shanghai, s-au schimbat foarte puțin fața de vremea lui Marco Polo (secolul 13), când era descris ca o Veneție a estului, pentru canalele sale înconjurate de grădini şi ceainării străvechi. În Beijing, deşi oraşul avea cartierele sale moderne, majoritatea locuitorilor încă stăteau, aşa cum o făcusră timp de sute de ani, în cartiere de case vechi, înghesuite de-a lungul unor străduțe înguste, denumite *hutong*. Pe acolo nu se putea circula cu mașinile, iar în adăposturile dintre case, sau în curțile interioare, viața era foarte simplă și trăită în comun, cu oameni care veneau și plecau, bârfeau, găteau, se spălau, jucau șah sau, pur și simplu, priveau cum trecea lumea.

Orașul tradițional chinez dispare rapid, pe măsură ce frenezia construcțiilor continuă cu o intensitate nemaiîntâlnită, consumând jumătate din cimentul din lume și folosind mai mult de jumătate dintre macaralele existente pe glob. Cele mai spectaculoase rezultate ale acesteia pot fi văzute la Beijing și Shanghai, unde sute de noi zgârie-nori, blocuri și alte clădiri apar în fiecare an, creând cartiere centrale care fac Manhattan-ul să pară demodat, dar același lucru se produce în toate orașele Chinei, de la Wenzhou, la Shenzhen, de la Xiamen, la Chongqing. Administratorii orașelor se tem ca urbea lor să nu fie lăsată în urmă, așa că fac presiuni pentru o dezvoltare și mai accelerată.

. . . .

Mania demolărilor

Cum, în unele locuri, terenurile pentru construcție sunt extrem de rare, vechile case sunt pur și simplu demolate pentru a face loc șantierelor. Noi autostrăzi gigantice sunt croite prin străvechi cartiere de case, la fel cum șinele de cale ferată străpunseseră orașele victoriene. Din praful *hutong*-urilor demolate se înalță, în doar câteva săptămâni, turnuri falnice de sticlă și beton. Atât de mare este graba, încât demolările continuă să se desfășoare chiar dacă nu s-a stabilit ce va fi construit pe locul respectiv, multe orașe fiind împânzite de goluri pline de moloz, răspândite ca niște dinți lipsă printre noile construcții. Urbaniștii par să alerge constant prin oraș, pictând pe clădirile vechi caracterul chai, printre chinezi apărând și o glumă macabră, potrivit căreia țara a ajuns, în sfârșit, să fie vrednică de numele său străin, care, în mandarină, sună ca *chai*-ne, adică „demolează-o". În cartea sa *Mai întâi bogați* (2007), Duncan Hewitt menționează o altă glumă amară, foarte la modă în Shanghai, unde ritmul schimbărilor a fost extrem de rapid. Din câte se pare, trebuie întotdeauna să suni înainte de-a te duce la restaurantul unde plănuieşti să iei cina, nu pentru a-ţi confirma rezervarea, ci pentru a te asigura că nu a fost demolat.

Mulţi chinezi sunt fericiţi să scape de vechile case. Acestea sunt greu de modernizat, confortul lor este cât se poate de sumar, iar străduţele sunt, adesea, prea înguste pentru a permite accesul automobilelor. Cei obişnuiţi să trăiască în frig şi duhoare, adeseori fără nici un fel de instalaţii sanitare, sunt extrem de încântaţi să se mute în apartamente moderne, cu vedere asupra oraşului. De multe ori, însă, oamenii au fost evacuaţi din vechile lor locuinţe, chiar şi atunci când nu voiau să le părăsească, uneori, chiar într-o manieră brutală şi fără nici un fel de compensaţie financiară. Se zice că unii bătrâni care au refuzat să se mute au fost bătuţi de găşti de haidamaci. În plus, cei evacuaţi din casele vechi nu primesc întotdeauna o altă locuinţă.

Chiar şi acolo unde demolările decurg fără incidente, toate părţile fiind satisfăcute, există persoane care suportă cu greu să vadă cum o atât de mare parte din moştenirea culturală a Chinei este distrusă cu un zel şi o îndârjire ce amintesc de Revoluţia Culturală. Unii consideră că păstrarea *hutong*-urilor nu este altceva decât o idee romanţioasă pe care şi-o pot permite doar intelectualii şi străinii. „Este suficient să vezi o bătrânică târşâindu-şi picioarele pe gheaţa groasă, la 5 dimineaţa, pentru a ajunge la toaleta publică, ca să-ţi piară, dintr-o dată, tot cheful [de a mai păstra *hutong*-urile]," scrie Jha Aimei, într-un articol citat în *Christian Science Monitor*. Cu toate acestea, din ce în ce mai mulţi oameni încep să conştientizeze amploarea distrugerilor, chiar şi printre cei aflaţi la cele mai înalte nivele. În iunie 2007, o tânără numită Xia Jie, a purtat o campanie curajoasă pentru a-şi salva *hutong*-ul natal, din Beijing, Dongsi Batiao, ale cărui case fuseseră construite în secolul al XIII-lea. În mod cu totul surprinzător, campania lui Xia Jie a reuşit să suspende demolarea. Suspendarea se poate dovedi a fi de scurtă durată, dar ministrul adjunct al construcţiilor a vorbit presei despre „acţiunile fără sens" ale unor birocraţi care au devastat siturile arheologice şi monumentele istorice ale Chinei, afirmând că „unii oficiali locali par să nu fie conştienţi de valoarea moştenirii culturale." Şi are dreptate. Nu este vorba doar de nişte case vechi şi frumoase. Multe temple din timpul dinastiei Ming şi numeroase situri arheologice au fost strivite de lama buldozerelor. Odată, o echipă de muncitori a dărâmat chiar şi o secţiune din Marele Zid pentru a construi un drum pe care să fie transportate materialele de construcţie...

· ·

Noul **stil de viaţă**

Suferinţele muncitorilor migranţi şi distrugerea vechilor clădiri ale Chinei reprezintă reversul *boom*-ului economic chinez. Însă, pentru majoritatea chinezilor, aspectele pozitive sunt covârşitoare. Oricât de dificile ar fi vieţile muncitorilor migranţi, câştigurile pe care le trimit înapoi familiilor lor au contribuit mai mult decât orice altceva la îmbunătăţirea vieţii oamenilor de la ţară. Mulţi dintre cei care trăiau în locuinţe improvizate îşi pot acum permite case solide şi bunuri de larg consum, cum ar fi televizoare, frigidere, telefoane mobile şi chiar motociclete – lucruri care, nu cu foarte mult timp în urmă, le-ar fi fost inaccesibile. Muncitorii migranţi fac, la rândul lor, progrese. Mulţi se stabilesc în oraşele adoptive, începând să se adapteze traiului permanent la oraş şi să pună deoparte suficienţi bani pentru a-şi permite o locuinţă acceptabilă, chiar dacă sunt încă o minoritate.

Locuitorii permanenţi ai oraşelor au fost, însă, martorii celor mai dramatice schimbări ale stilului de viaţă, beneficiind cel mai mult de pe urma acestora. Salariile de la oraş sunt, în medie, de trei ori mai mari decât cele de la ţară şi, deşi costurile vieţii la oraş sunt mult mai mari, cei suficient de norocoşi au acum un stil de viaţă care, cu doar un sfert de secol în urmă, era imposibil de imaginat pentru chinezii obişnuiţi.

Pentru vizitatori, cele mai evidente semne ale noii Chine sunt zgârie-norii strălucitori, restaurantele tip fast-food, mall-urile ale căror magazine vând toate mărcile cunoscute, de la Nike la Armani, şi cele

mai noi produse de înaltă tehnologie, de la iPhone-uri până la televizoare cu plasmă. Dar cele mai profunde schimbări sunt, probabil,
cele petrecute în spatele ușilor închise.

. . . .

A **locui** pe cont propriu

Până în 1990, majoritatea locuințelor erau controlate de stat, iar cei
mai mulți muncitori trăiau în case puse la dispoziție de către companiile unde lucrau. Casele erau adesea împărțite, nu doar între
membrii unei familii extinse, ci între mai multe familii. Și totuși,
deși erau departe de a fi ideale, erau foarte ieftine, iar statul se asigura că toată lumea avea unde să stea. Dar în 1998, alături de alte
măsuri, conducerea chineză a luat dificila decizie de a renunța la
locuințele sociale ieftine. Chiriile pentru apartamentele existente
au crescut semnificativ, iar acum, orice casă nou-construită poate fi
doar cumpărată, nu și închiriată. Într-un fel, situația semăna cu cea
din Marea Britanie a anilor '80, când Margaret Thatcher a vândut
casele pe care consiliile locale le închiriau la prețuri modice, numai
că în China era mai gravă – și nu pare a fi o coincidență că iniția-
torul acestei măsuri îi făcuse o vizită doamnei Thatcher, pe care se
spune că o admira.

Odată dispărută siguranța reprezentată de locuințele sociale, oamenii și-au dat, dintr-odată, seama că, în viitor, vor trebui să-și facă
singuri rost de locuințe și, în numai câțiva ani, după ce toată lumea
înțelesese ce implica acest lucru, a deține o casă a devenit prioritatea
numărul unu a celor care trăiau la oraș. Chiar și atunci când a închi-
ria o locuință era mai simplu și mai ușor, oamenii aveau toate motivele să cumpere pentru a-și asigura viitorul – și poate că acest lucru
nici nu era surprinzător pentru vârstnicii ce se temeau de scăderea
treptată a pensiilor și pentru tinerii care s-au trezit, din senin, că nu
mai sunt „partide bune" dacă nu au o casă a lor. Deloc surprinzător,
în orașele chineze a apărut un *boom* al proprietăților imobiliare, însă
proporțiile acestuia au fost de-a dreptul copleșitoare într-o țară care,

cu numai câţiva ani în urmă, era o republică socialistă săracă. Între 1998 şi 2005, valoarea ipotecilor făcute de chinezi a crescut de 35 de ori, ajungând la aproape 130 de miliarde de lire sterline.

. . . .

Cum **se mobilează** locuinţa

Pe de-o parte, această dorinţă de a cumpăra i-a supus pe unii la o formidabilă presiune, transformându-i în sclavi ai creditelor ipotecare, sau obligându-i să părăsească cartierele în care locuiseră înainte. Pe de altă parte, mulţi tineri au putut, în sfârşit, să se mute din casele părinţilor şi să-şi găsească o casă a lor. În trecut, cuplurile tinere, chiar şi cele căsătorite, aveau foarte puţină intimitate, locuind în case pe care le împărţeau cu familiile lor, adesea fără o cameră a lor şi neavând unde să stea singuri pentru a se bucura de lucrurile (foarte diferite) de care se bucură tinerii din generaţia lor. Acum, fiecare dintre cuplurile care trăieşte la oraş doreşte să deţină propriul apartament modern, în care să-şi poată pune în valoare propriul stil.

Adeseori, acesta este stilul *Ikea*, care a avut asupra gustului chinezilor un mai mare impact chiar şi decât cel avut asupra europenilor. Aceşti tineri orăşeni chinezi nu ştiu cum să-şi aranjeze casele. A merge la giganticele magazine Ikea seamănă cu vizitarea unei excepţionale expoziţii de design interior, la care primeşti şi asistenţă din partea unor consultanţi speciali. Minimalist, cu pereţi albi şi ecrane TV uriaşe – acesta este, actualmente, stilul la modă, care se va schimba, probabil, la fel de repede cum o face şi în Europa. Mulţi dintre locuitorii mai stilaţi din Shanghai trec acum prin faza „bobo" – boemi burghezi, apartamentele lor, foste depozite restaurate, sau chiar *hutong*-uri, fiind îmbodobite cu mobilier tradiţional tibetan şi chiar cu mobilă veche chinezească, pe care majoritatea, în graba lor de a cumpăra piese moderne, o aruncaseră în stradă cu doar câţiva ani înainte.

. . . .

STILUL EUROPEAN

Ultima modă, printre cei înstăriți, este cea a locuințelor în stil american sau european. Cel mai nou curent în construcții împodobește Beijingul cu un amalgam arhitectural, de la castele, până la vile italienești. Aceste construcții au chiar și nume americane sau europene, cum ar fi, **Regent Gardens** sau **Versailles Island**. Ideea este, desigur, ca ocupanții acestora să aibă un stil de viață în ton cu locuința pe care o cumpără. Stilul californian, cel spaniol, francez și englez sunt cele mai populare, dar cel newyorkez și cel italian, au și ele adepții lor. În jurul Shanghai-ului au fost construite o serie de orașe satelit, fiecare imitând cu o acuratețe remarcabilă stilul unei țări europene. Orașul britanic a primit numele de **Orașul Tamisei** și este dotat cu piețe georgiene, telefoane publice de culoare roșie și pub-uri englezești.

· ·

Deplasările

A doua pe lista cumpărăturilor importante, după achiziționara unei case, este, bineînțeles, o mașină, iar numărul posesorilor de automobile din orașe crește cu cinci milioane în fiecare an, făcând din China una dintre cele mai mari piețe pentru autovehicule noi. În general, noile automobile sunt simboluri ale statutului social al persoanei, fiind folosite mai mult la deplasarea pe străzile aglomerate ale orașelor, decât la drumurile mai lungi. Noile autostrăzi ale Chinei sunt folosite mai mult de transportatori. Bicicleta, odinioară principalul mijloc de transport al chinezilor, a căzut acum în desuetudine.

· ·

Desproprietărirea

Un efect, probabil neprevăzut, al acestei expansiuni accelerate a orașelor a fost acoperirea unor imense suprafețe de teren arabil din cel mai fertil cu beton. Un total de aproape 7 milioane de hectare au fost pierdute în fața dezvoltării urbane din ultimii douăzeci de ani. Departe de a fi restricționată de reglementări cum sunt cele din Europa, care impun păstrarea unei centuri verzi în jurul orașelor, expansiunea urbană chineză este încurajată de dezvoltarea imobiliară și ajutată de legi care conferă autorităților locale puterea aproape dictatorială de a acapara orice teren doresc. În fiecare an ies la iveală din ce în ce mai multe povești „de groază" ale unor țărani săraci expropriați cu minime compensații, pentru a face loc proiectelor imobiliare ce căpătuiesc atât funcționarii locali, cât și antreprenorii, lăsându-i pe țărani fără nimic și lipsind China de terenuri valoroase, ce ar fi putut fi utilizate în producția agricolă. Multe dintre cele mai violente tulburări au loc, acum nu în orașe, ci la marginea lor, în zonele în care țăranilor le-a fost luată pâinea de la gură.

. . . .

Decalajul rural

În anumite privințe, fermierii chinezi au fost lăsați în urmă de *boom*-ul economic care a transformat orașele țării. Ironia faptului că, în urmă cu puțin timp, țăranii trebuiau să fie vârful de lance al revoluției lui Mao nu poate trece neobservată. Una dintre primele și cele mai dramatice schimbări pe care le-au făcut comuniștii atunci când au venit la putere, a fost să ia pământurile de la proprietari și să le dea țăranilor – o acțiune care a costat viețile a un milion sau mai mulți de proprietari. Însă, treptat, Mao a luat pământurile înapoi de la țărani, reunindu-le și transformându-le în uriașe cooperative de producție, cunoscute în anii '50 drept „colectivele poporului". Colectivele au fost un asemenea dezastru – în primul rând, din cauza unor recolte slabe și, în al doilea rând, din cauza faptului că grânele erau trimise la oraș înainte ca țăranii să fie hrăniți - încât, între anii 1958-1961, peste 30 de milioane de oameni au murit, în cea mai rea foamete din lume – cu atât mai șocantă, cu cât a fost provocată de mâna omului.

Oraşele şi regiunile Chinei	Produsul intern brut %	Propretari de telefoane mobile (mln)	Utilizatori de internet (mln)	Speranţă de viaţă	Grad de alfabetizare %
Shanghai	5.5	13.1	4.4	78.1	91.8
Beijing	3.1	13.4	4.0	76.1	94.7
Hong Kong	N/D	N/D	2.5	81.6	N/D
Shandong	11.3	19.1	8.5	73.9	88.8
Jiangsou	11.3	22.3	6.6	73.9	85.7
Guangdong	11.7	53.7	11.9	73.9	93
Sichuan	4.8	115.1	5.2	71.2	86.5
Quinghai	0.3	1.2	0.2	66	75.2
Mongolia Interioară	2.0	5.9	0.9	69.9	86.5
Xinjiang	1.6	4.9	1.2	67.9	91.8
Tibet	0.2	0.4	0.1	64.4	56.2

Sursă: Anuarul Statistic al Chinei 2005

N/D – date nedisponibile

. . . .

TRISTEŢEA FEMEILOR

China este singura ţară din lume unde femeile sunt mai predispuse la suicid decât bărbaţii. În China, o femeie se sinucide la fiecare patru minute, iar alta încearcă să o facă la fiecare douăzeci de secunde. Problema este deosebit de gravă în zonele rurale, unde rata suicidului este de trei ori mai mare decât în oraşe. Conform cercetătorului chinez Xu Rong, unul dintre motive este, pur şi simplu, larga răspândire a pesticidelor în zonele rurale. Dar ingerarea pesticidelor este un semn cât se poate de clar al vieţii grele pe care unele femei din zonele rurale sunt nevoite să o ducă.

Multe dintre atitudinile tradiţionale faţă de femei au supravieţuit revoluţiei comuniste, iar căsătoriile aranjate, în care părinţii mirelui cumpără mireasa, sunt încă la ordinea zilei. Odată căsătorită, tânăra este luată de la casa ei şi devine imediat calul de bătaie al socrilor ei. Pentru unele fete, educaţia a făcut rolul tradiţional şi mai greu de suportat, ele fiind adeseori prinse în conflicte maritale din care nu au nici o posibilitate de evadare.

Politica „copilului unic" a scos în evidenţă lipsa de importanţă a femeii, mulţi fetuşi de sex feminin fiind avortaţi, iar unele fiind ucise. Aceasta a dus la scădera numărului de femei. La fiecare 100 de fete născute în China se nasc 117 băieţi, iar până în 2020 vor fi cu 40 de milioane de băieţi mai mulţi decât fete. Xie Lihua, editor la una dintre cele mai apreciate reviste pentru femei crede că acest lucru va pune fetele într-o postură şi mai vulnerabilă, temându-se că „Răpirea şi traficul de femei vor creşte. Tot aşa se va întâmpla cu prostituţia, cu agresiunile sexuale şi violul." Diverse organizaţii din China încearcă acum să dezvolte programe pentru a înfiinţa grupuri de ajutor în sate şi cursuri de stimulare a încrederii în propriile forţe.

. . . .

„Fermierii **chinezi** arată calea"

În cele din urmă, în anii '70, conducerea a recunoscut eşecul colectivelor şi a împărţit din nou pământul familiilor individuale. Povestea oficială, bine cunoscută de majoritatea chinezilor, este că 18 fermieri din Xiaogang Anhui, disperaţi pentru a găsi un mod mai bun de a-şi hrăni familiile au decis în secret să-şi împartă pământul colectiv, astfel încât fiecare să aibă propriul lot. Ei plănuiau să plătească împreună taxa datorată colectivului pentru grâne, dar să-şi cultive pământul pentru consumul propriu şi să vândă surplusul. Aranjamentul era total ilegal şi s-ar fi putut termina cu o execuţie, dar a funcţionat şi, după cum se povesteşte, întâmplarea a ajuns la urechile lui Deng Xiaoping care, în 1980, a introdus „sistemul de responsabilitate gospodărească," conform căruia familiilor le era permis să-şi cultive propriul teren cu culturi la alegere şi să vândă surplusul.

Efectul s-a văzut imediat. Producţia agricolă a început să crească, iar mulţi fermieri nu numai că au început să-şi hrănească mai bine familiile, dar au câştigat şi bani din vânzarea produselor pe „pieţele libere", apărute în anii '80 în multe oraşe chineze. Mulţi fermieri au început să simtă o ameliorare substanţială a vieţii lor, putând să cumpere lucruri pentru prima oară, provocând o uşoară creştere a consumului şi îmbunătăţind standardele de viaţă în mediul rural.

Unii dintre fermieri au început să caute modalităţi de a investi banii, mulţi dintre ei punându-şi laolaltă economiile pentru a pune pe picioare mici făbricuţe acceptate de Deng Xiaoping, denumite „întreprinderi săteşti şi orăşeneşti." Acestea s-au răspândit în anii '80, unele fiind înfiinţate de grupuri de fermieri, altele ca investiţii private ale administraţiilor locale. Majoritatea erau mici firme cu mai puţin de zece muncitori, al căror obiect de activitate era procesarea alimentelor sau fabricarea de piese de schimb pentru utilaje agricole, dar unele au înflorit, transformându-se în mari corporaţii industriale – în special în sud, în regiunea Guangdong. Există acum un număr impresionant de 120 de milioane de asemenea întreprinderi care au jucat un rol cheie în *boom*-ul economiei chineze. Deşi majoritatea sunt întreprinderi foarte mici care produc doar cu puţin mai mult decât banii de buzunar, ele au reprezentat, totuşi, o adevărată şcoală pentru ţăranii chinezi, ajutându-i să devină oameni de afaceri şi antreprenori. Unele dintre ele îşi vând acum produsele peste tot în lume.

Săracii de la ţară

Din păcate, în ciuda succesului acestor mici întreprinderi săteşti, îmbunătăţirea veniturilor acestora nu a fost una constantă, dintr-o varietate de motive. De exemplu, majoritatea terenurilor sunt prea mici pentru mecanizare şi agricultura industrială. Multe terenuri au avut de suferit de pe urma secetei, întrucât oraşele şi producţia agricolă folosesc debite mari de apă din râurile Chinei. Altele au de suferit din cauza eroziunii solului, întrucât pământul este folosit în exces, iar despăduririle masive expun câmpurile urgiilor naturii. În 2001, când China a aderat la Organizaţia Mondială a Comerţului, fermierii chinezi s-au confruntat, de asemenea, cu concurenţa preţurilor reduse ale marilor exploatări agricole occidentale.

Deşi veniturile medii s-au îmbunătăţit în mediul rural, acestea au însă un ritm de creştere de doar 50% faţă de cele din mediul urban, reprezentând doar o treime a acestora, iar în unele zone, mediile ascund o situaţie şi mai sumbră, în special în vestul ţării. Una dintre probleme este că, în China, aproape toţi banii pentru dezvoltare au mers către oraşe şi industrie. Aproape nici un dolar nu s-a îndreptat spre agricultură.

Pentru a înrăutăţi şi mai mult lucrurile, sistemul de asistenţă socială a început să se prăbuşească atunci când guvernul a desfiinţat ajutorul social şi a concentrat toate fondurile existente în oraşe. În 1998, guvernul a desfiinţat Ministerul Educaţiei, măsura având un efect dezastruos asupra educaţiei rurale. Un raport al Băncii Mondiale a arătat că patru din zece copii din unele zone rurale sărace nu au primit nici un fel de educaţie. Îngrijirea medicală era şi mai precară. În timpul conducerii maoiste „doctorii desculţi" – oameni cu un minim de educaţie medicală – au plecat în toate colţurile ţării, asigurând servicii medicale de bază chiar şi celor mai săraci. Cu toate acestea, sistemul era concentrat în jurul colectivelor, iar când acestea au dispărut în anii '80, a dispărut şi minima îngrijire medicală pe care o asigurau. O serie de zone agricole mai bogate şi-au constituit propriul lor sistem medical. Cifrele oficiale din anul 2002 arătau că doar 7% din cei 800 de milioane de ţărani chinezi aveau asigurare medicală, comparativ cu 90% în 1979. Ministerul Sănătăţii a recunoscut că, în primii ani ai secolului XXI, două treimi din populaţia ţării care avea nevoie de tratament medical nu a beneficiat de el.

Dar poate cel mai rău lucru a fost puterea lacomilor oficiali locali asupra vieţilor ţăranilor. În decembrie 2003, soţii Chen Guidi şi Wu Chuntao au scris un reportaj şocant intitulat *Ţăranii Chinei: o investigaţie*, care a provocat un adevărat scandal atunci când a fost publicat, 200 000 de exemplare vânzându-se foarte repede şi, după ce a fost interzis de către guvern, s-au mai vândut alte 7 milioane de exemplare pe piaţa neagră. Mult mai mulţi l-au citit pe internet. Ideea cărţii s-a născut atunci când Wu Chuntao a aflat despre o ţărancă care a sângerat până la moarte după naştere, întrucât nu şi-a permis cei 360 de dolari ceruţi de spitalul local pentru tratament. Chen şi Wu au petrecut trei ani călătorind prin Anhui, în încercarea de a descoperi cauzele problemelor ţăranilor. Poveştile pe care le-au relatat erau de ajuns pentru a-i face pe mulţi dintre cititori să plângă de tristeţe sau să strige cu furie, auzind cum ţăranii sunt exploataţi şi abuzaţi de către oficialii locali corupţi şi cum sunt covârşiţi de taxele din ce în ce mai mari care reuşeau să anuleze orice creştere a profitului fermelor. Nu a fost deloc o surpriză când atât de mulţi ţărani au renunţat şi au emigrat spre oraş, adeseori lăsând pământurile bune pentru agricultură pradă buruienilor.

. . . .

Drumul spre mai bine

În 2006, guvernul chinez a conştientizat existenţa problemei, mărind cu 15% suma alocată agriculturii. Măsura a făcut ca bugetul anual pentru dezvoltare al fermelor să ajungă la 42 de miliarde de dolari. Această cifră poate părea mare, însă, din moment ce în mediul rural trăiesc 800 de milioane de oameni, creşterea nu a fost decât de 7 dolari/persoană.

. . . .

PROTESTE RURALE

Peste tot în China, expansiunea oraşelor provoacă conflicte, întrucât dezvoltarea lasă ţăranii fără pământ. Guvernul primeşte acum zeci de mii de petiţii din partea ţăranilor convinşi că este suficient ca guvernul central să audă de problemele locale, pentru ca nedreptăţile să înceteze.

Într-un articol din decembrie 2004, din **New York Times**, Jim Yardley relatează povestea sfâşietoare a ţăranilor din Sanchawan, ţinutul Shaanxi. Când oficialii din oraşul vecin, Yulin, au preluat o zonă vastă pentru dezvoltare, ţăranii au încercat să protesteze în toate felurile posibile. Oamenii din sat au plecat la Beijing pentru a încerca să găsească o rezolvare a cazului lor dar nu au putut să treacă de zidul birocraţiei. ,,De mii de ani, relaţia dintre fermieri şi pământul lor a fost la fel de densă ca şi sângele, la fel de strânsă precum buzele şi dinţii,'' au scris aceştia într-una dintre petiţiile lor, dar apelul lor nu a avut nici un efect. După ce oficialii din oraşul Yulin au acaparat şi mai mult pământ, ţăranii disperaţi au făcut o grevă, refuzând să lucreze pământul, un act provocator din moment ce oficialii aveau de îndeplinit nişte cifre de producţie. Atunci a fost trimisă poliţia să spargă greva cu o asemenea violenţă, încât sătenii au fost aduşi la tăcere.

În cartea sa **Mai întâi bogaţi**, Duncan Hewitt citează un caz la fel de cutremurător despre 25 000 de săteni care au fost pur şi simplu daţi afară din case din zona râului Taizi din nord-estul Chinei pentru a face loc unui rezervor. Unora li s-a dat nişte pământ atât de sterp, încât nu era deloc bun pentru agricultură; altora nu li s-a dat nimic şi au fost transformaţi în cerşetori. Timp de şapte ani, sătenii au luptat pentru dreptate, dar li s-a dat atenţie doar când fiecare dintre cei nouă reprezentanţi ai lor au plecat la Beijing şi au ameninţat că-şi vor tăia degetul cel mic şi-l vor aşeza în faţa sediului guvernului. În cele din urmă, cazul lor a fost revăzut, iar atunci când au primit compensaţia, acest lucru a fost întâmpinat de presă ca o reuşită, deşi această compensaţie a valorat doar 16 dolari pentru fiecare.

Totuşi, a fost un început, şi, în acelaşi an, guvernul a decis să renunţe la taxele pe produsele agricole care erau cea mai mare povară pentru fermieri, renunţând, apoi, la toate celelalte taxe rurale. Toate acestea au făcut parte dintr-un program mai larg denumit „Crearea unei noi zone agricole socialiste", ce-şi propunea să rezolve unele dintre problemele rurale, cum ar fi lipsa educaţiei şi a îngrijirii medicale. În unele zone, eliminarea acestor taxe a început deja să aibă efect, fiind vizibile mici, dar sigure, semne ale prosperităţii – atât de evidente, încât mulţi ţărani au ales să rămână la ţară pentru a lucra pământul, iar mulţi muncitori migranţi au început, în sfârşit, să se întoarcă din oraşe. Rapoartele oficiale arată că veniturile agricole sunt în creştere, existând un optimism general în ceea ce priveşte bunul mers al agriculturii chineze.

. . . .

Capitolul 4:
CHINA MURDARĂ?

„Dacă aș munci în Beijing-ul vostru mi-aș scurta viața cu cel puțin 5 ani."

Primul ministru chinez, Zhu Rongji, adresâdu-se oficialilor din Beijing în 1999

În ianuarie 2007, paznicul oficial al mediului înconjurător din Çhina, Administrația de Stat pentru Protecția Mediului (ASPM), a raportat că anul 2006 a fost cel mai poluat an din istoria Chinei. Pan Yue, vicepreședintele agenției, a recunoscut că „2006 a fost cel mai sumbru an al Chinei, din punctul de vedere al stării mediului înconjurător." Declarația fiind una destul de surprinzătoare pentru administrația chineză. Palmaresul Chinei în ceea ce privește poluarea mediului este de-a dreptul catastrofal. Îndreptându-se cu o viteză amețitoare către succesul economic, China a lăsat în urmă un adevărat munte de probleme de mediu nerezolvate.

Deșeurile industriale sunt deversate în fiecare zi în apele râurilor, numai în 2006 fiind înregistrate 161 de astfel de incidente. Nivelul de dioxid de sulf s-a dublat în ultimii zece ani, transformând China în zona cea mai poluată cu dioxid de sulf din lume – ceea ce face ca o treime din teritoriul țării să fie măcinată de ploi acide care distrug pădurile până în apropierea Japoniei. Șaisprezece dintre cele mai poluate douăzeci de orașe din lume se află în China, printre care și Linfen, cel mai grav afectat de pe glob, raportul guvernului chinez dezvăluind faptul că în două treimi dintre cele mai mari trei sute de orașe ale Chinei calitatea aerului este cu mult sub standardele acceptate de Organizația Mondială a Sănătății.

Și lista de probleme cauzate de poluare continuă. Un raport al Băncii Mondiale concluziona că 750 000 de oameni au murit prematur în orașele Chinei în 2006 din cauza poluării aerului. Alți 60 000 se crede că au murit din cauza apei alterate, care poate provoca diaree cronică, cancer de ficat și de vezică. Agenția pentru Protecția Mediului estimează că 70% din apa a cinci mari bazine hidrografice din cele șapte ale Chinei este atât de poluată, încât nu mai este bună nici măcar pentru spălat, ca să nu mai vorbim de băut. Se estimează că 90% din rezervele de apă ale orașelor sunt contaminate cu deșeuri organice și industriale. Doar jumătate din apele menajere sunt tratate înainte de a fi deversate în râuri, rezultatul fiind că în China există peste opt sute de milioane de cazuri de diaree în fiecare an. Iar cireaşa de pe tort este că, în 2006, China a devansat Statele Unite, mult mai devreme decât se aştepta, ca cel mai mare emiţător de dioxid de carbon, unul dintre gazele cu efect de seră.

PROBLEMA PUNGILOR DE PLASTIC

Când ţi se dă o pungă de plastic pentru a-ţi duce acasă cumpărăturile de la supermarket, e foarte probabil ca aceasta să fi fost confecţionată în Shenzhen, de firme precum Deluxe Arts Plastics, care produce trei sferturi de milion de pungi pe lună. Odată folosite, aceste pungi se întorc în aproape acelaşi loc din China pentru a fi „reciclate". Legislaţia Uniunii Europene interzice depozitarea deşeurilor în străinătate, dar permite transportarea lor în China pentru reciclare. În China există numeroase centre de reciclare pentru tot felul de produse, însă, la capătul întregului lanţ, se află unităţile de colectare a pungilor şi sticlelor de plastic din oraşe precum Shunde şi Heshan, în care cartiere întregi sunt pline de mormane toxice de pungi vechi şi urât mirositoare, ce aşteaptă să fie mărunţite, topite şi transformate în granule de o armată de muncitori prost plătiţi. În februarie 2007, în urma unei serii de rapoarte publicate în presa britanică, în care erau condamnate groaznicele condiţii de trai şi de muncă din satele unde se efectuează reciclări, guvernul chinez a hotărât să închidă cele mai periculoase centre şi să interzică importul deşeurilor din străinătate. Însă unora, această afacere le asigură pâinea zilnică, aşa că pur şi simplu s-au mutat în altă parte şi au găsit alte modalităţi de a obţine deşeuri.

Pământul şi apa

Din nefericire, problemele de mediu nu se termină cu poluarea. China este una dintre ţările care suferă cel mai mult din lume din cauza lipsei de apă. Aceasta a fost întotdeauna o problemă, într-o ţară în care resursele de apă pe cap de locuitor reprezintă mai puţin de un sfert din media la nivel mondial. Ministerul Apelor din China afirmă că patru sute dintre cele mai mari oraşe ale Chinei duc lipsă de apă. În zona aridă din nord, 80% din zonele umede situate de-a lungul bazinului hidrografic al marelui râu Huang Ho au secat, cotele apelor acestuia fiind, la rândul lor, atât de scăzute, încât este în pericol să sece înainte de a ajunge la mare. Mai spre sud, secetele distrug recoltele chiar şi de-a lungul râului Yangtze, principalul râu al Chinei. În Chonqing şi Sichuan, două treimi dintre râuri au secat cu totul în 2006.

Câmpurile şi pădurile Chinei dispar şi ele cu repeziciune, fiind invadate din ambele părţi de deşerturi şi oraşe. Numai în ultimul deceniu, 6 milioane de hectare din cel mai bun teren arabil al Chinei au fost îngropate sub betoane, în timp ce deşerturile se întind în toată ţara ca rezultat al supraexploatării resurselor de apă şi al păşunatului excesiv.

. . . .

Probleme ale
mediului înconjurător

Luând toate aceste lucruri în considerare, nu este deloc surprinzător că activiştii de mediu consideră China o zonă de dezastru ecologic şi solicită autorităţilor să reducă viteza expansiunii economice, temându-se că, dacă acestea nu o vor face, situaţia se va înrăutăţi. Numeroşi economişti occidentali susţin, la rândul lor, că dezastrul ecologic va face oricum ca progresul economic să nu mai poată fi susţinut, având în vedere că oraşele se sufocă, iar industriile rămân fără apa curată, esenţială sporirii producţiei, sau fără muncitori, seceraţi fiind de bolile provocate de poluare. Între timp, costurile umane sunt mari şi probabil că nu este de mirare că în China protestele publice în legătură cu problemele de mediu sunt în creştere. De fapt, problemele de mediu, cum sunt deversările toxice sau lipsa apei, incită populaţia la acţiune civică mai mult decât oricare alt subiect. În mai 2007, mii de oameni au ieşit în stradă în oraşul Xiamen, din provincia Fujiang, reuşind să oprească construirea unei uzine petrochimice. În 2005, cel puţin 3 oameni au fost ucişi de poliție în orașul Dongzhou, din provincia Guangdong, în timpul revoltelor iscate în urma anunțării proiectului de construcție al unei centrale electrice.

După această listă de dezastre, ar fi extrem de ușor să ne imaginăm că țara se îndreaptă nepăsătoare către o catastrofă ecologică, indiferentă la consecințe. Concluzie care nu ar fi departe de adevăr. Problemele sunt cunoscute, la cel mai înalt nivel al guvernului, de mai mulți ani de zile. Și nu am greși dacă am afirma că guvernul chinez a fost mai activ decât oricare altul în încercarea de a rezolva problemele de mediu. Când primul ministru Wen și-a ținut principalul discurs anual, în martie 2007, a situat problemele de mediu în fruntea priorităților guvernului. Wen a recunoscut că țara sa a eșuat în îndeplinirea unora dintre obiectivele esențiale privitoare la reducerea poluării și a consumului energetic și că, dacă nu va reuși să protejeze mai bine mediul și să eficientizeze consumul, prețioasa sa dezvoltare economică va avea mult de suferit.

Provocarea pe care Wen și guvernul chinez o au de înfruntat constă în faptul că problemele pe care le întâmpină sunt enorme, și se tem ca nu cumva să intervină prea brutal, perturbând creșterea economică pe care atât de mulți chinezi se bazează pentru a ieși din sărăcie. După cum declara Lu Xuedu, reprezentant al Ministerului Mediului la o conferință din 2006, „Nu le poți spune celor care se zbat să supraviețuiască că trebuie să-și reducă emisiile de gaze cu efect de seră."

Problemele de mediu pe care guvernul va trebui să le rezolve pot fi împărțite în patru categorii: cele energetice, cea a resurselor hidrologice, cea a lipsei terenurilor și cea a poluării propriu-zise. Cea mai presantă este problema energiei.

. . . .

Energia **poluantă**

Pentru o țară cu resurse energetice limitate, China este uimitor de risipitoare. Fabricile ineficiente și construcțiile de proastă calitate duc, în fiecare zi, la pierderi de energie uriașe. E greu de spus cu precizie câtă energie se pierde, dar câteva corelaţii de bază ne vor ajuta să ne facem o imagine: pentru fiecare dolar din PIB-ul său, China foloseşte de trei ori mai multă energie decât se foloseşte, în medie, pe glob, şi de unsprezece ori şi jumătate mai multă decât Japonia.

Situaţia devine şi mai gravă, dacă ne gândim că ţara are resurse limitate de petrol şi gaze naturale, cea mai mare parte a energiei sale provenind din cărbune. Peste 70% din energia chineză provine din cărbune, atât pentru producerea electricităţii, cât şi pentru încălzirea locuinţelor, iar China este responsabilă pentru 90% din creşterea consumului de cărbune din ultimii patru ani. Ca şi arderea petrolului, arderea cărbunelui produce importante cantităţi de dioxid de carbon, dar şi de funingine şi dioxid de sulf, gazul responsabil pentru ploile acide, mai ales dacă huila utilizată este sulfuroasă şi de proastă calitate, cum este, în general, cea chineză. China produce deja, de două ori mai mult dioxid de sulf decât SUA şi cantitatea este în creştere rapidă.

Deoarece industria chineză este în plină expansiune, necesităţile sale energetice vor creşte la rândul lor. Formidabila sete de petrol a Chinei creează, deja, tulburări majore pe piaţa mondială a petrolului, iar importarea unor cantităţi mai mari nu va rezolva nici una dintre problemele de mediu ale ţării. Mare parte din cantitatea suplimentară de combustibil va ajunge în milioanele de automobile noi ce inundă, în fiecare an, recent construitele autostrăzi ale Chinei. În urmă cu doar câteva decenii, China avea unul dintre cele mai ecologice „sisteme de transport" din lume – milioanele de biciclete. Însă acele zile au trecut de mult, iar valul de prosperitate încurajează populaţia să se alăture restului lumii în spatele volanului. Din câte se pare, în viitorul apropiat, producţia de electricitate a Chinei va continua să se bazeze pe cărbune. Pentru a face faţă nevoilor sale energetice, China construieşte capacităţi de generare echivalente cu două centrale energetice pe cărbune de 600 de megawaţi, în fiecare săptămână. Doar în 2006, China şi-a suplimentat capacitatea de generare a curentului electric cu instalaţii ce produc mai mult decât întreaga Californie – 90% din această creştere era reprezentată de centrale pe cărbune.

În China, folosirea maşinii rămâne un obicei atât de puţin răspândit, încât nu contribuie aproape deloc la gravele problemele de poluare a aerului ale ţării, însă numărul de maşini creşte cu repeziciune. Cu toate acestea, centralele pe cărbune, utilizarea cărbunelui pentru activităţile domestice şi emisiile nelimitate ale fabricilor sunt suficiente pentru a da oraşelor Chinei o atmosferă atât de îmbâcsită, încât, în multe zile ale anului, nu pot fi văzute din satelit. Numărul posesorilor de automobile din China este mic în comparaţie cu cel din lumea occidentală, doar unul din 60 de chinezi deţinând o maşină, faţă de unul din 2 americani. Ecologiştii se tem că dacă numărul de automobile din China va ajunge vreodată măcar la o zecime din cel al Statelor Unite, poluarea ar putea face unele oraşe total nelocuibile.

. . . .

CHINA ŞI ÎNCĂLZIREA GLOBALĂ

Pentru unii, refuzul Chinei de a accepta respectarea unor plafoane pentru emisiile sale de gaze cu efect de seră reprezintă una dintre cele mai mari probleme cu care se confruntă lupta împotriva încălzirii globale. Unul dintre principalele argumentele ale lui George Bush pentru retragerea din procesul de la Kyoto (Protocolul de la Kyoto este o înţelegere internaţională, semnată în 1997, care impunea ţărilor semnatare respectarea unor limite specifice a emisiilor de gaze cu efect de seră) a fost că nu impunea Chinei nici o reducere a emisiilor sale de gaze cu efect de seră. Fără implicarea reală a Chinei, considera el, protocolul nu are nici un sens. Atunci când China a depăşit Statele Unite, devenind cel mai mare emiţător de dioxid de carbon din lume, părea să confirme cele susţinute de americani.

Argumentul Chinei a fost, însă, că ea nu era responsabilă decât pentru un procent infim din gazele de seră care existau deja în atmosferă şi care produceau cea mai mare parte a efectului de încălzire. În plus, din cauza numărului mare de locuitori şi a sărăciei acestora, energia ieftină este esenţială pentru dezvoltarea ţării. „Dacă vizitaţi numai Beijingul, Shanghaiul, sau Hong Kongul, nu veţi vedea decât o singură Chină,“ a spus Lu Xuedu, directorul general adjunct al Oficiului Chinez pentru Afacerile Mediului, în faţa comisiei sino-britanice pentru studierea schimbării climatice, „însă, dacă veţi merge la ţară, sau doar la două ore de mers cu maşina de Piaţa Tiananmen, veţi vedea o cu totul altă situaţie.“

Cu toate acestea, din moment ce seceta şi lipsa apei bântuie deja ţara, guvernul chinez este perfect conştient de faptul că ar putea deveni una dintre primele victime ale schimbărilor climatice, astfel că în iunie 2007, a lansat propriul plan independent de reducere a emisiilor de gaze cu efect de seră. Planul statuează de la bun început că „ţara nu va impune limite ale emisiilor de dioxid de carbon, căci acestea ar putea dăuna grav unei naţiuni în curs de dezvoltare, ce încearcă să eradicheze sărăcia," dar include o serie de măsuri care vor ajuta la atenuarea schimbărilor climatice, cum ar fi reducerea treptată a numărului de automobile poluante produse şi plantarea de copaci pentru a creşte suprafaţa împădurită a ţării, de la 14% în anii '90, la 20% în 2010. Ecologiştii atrag atenţia asupra faptului că urgenţa situaţiei necesită acţiuni cu mult mai drastice decât acestea şi că, oricât ar fi de nedrept, China va trebui să se alăture acum restului lumii în scăderea emisiilor de gaze. Uşoara schimbare ce poate fi sesizată în atitudinea americană, ca urmare a presiunilor exercitate de Tony Blair la Sumitul G8 din 2007, ţinut la Heiligendamm, în Germania, ar putea convinge, în timp, şi China, să se alăture eforturilor internaţionale.

. . . .

Măsuri de reducere a emisiilor

Există, totuşi, o rază de speranţă, iar aceasta este dată de faptul că guvernul chinez pare a fi mult mai conştient de magnitudinea problemelor cu care se confruntă, decât sunt gata să admită mulţi dintre criticii săi occidentali.

În primul rând, guvernul încearcă să încetinească creşterea consumului de energie. China s-a angajat ca în actualul său plan cincinal, care durează până în 2010, să reducă intensitatea energetică – consumul de energie pe unitate de PIB – cu 20%. Desigur că, din moment ce PIB-ul ţării creşte cu aproape 10% pe an, asta înseamnă că speră să reducă consumul energetic cu doar 8% pe an. Până acum, aşa cum admite şi SEPA, nu au reuşit să atingă această ţintă, însă progrese există.

În al doilea rând, conducerea încearcă să limiteze emisiile centralelor bazate pe cărbune. În prezent, guvernul cheltuieşte în fiecare an 70 miliarde de dolari pentru introducerea sistemelor de filtre şi a altor măsuri similare, care să facă emisiile mai puțin poluante. Se lucrează intens pentru construirea unor centrale electrice de mare putere, mult mai eficiente decât nenumăratele centrale mai mici pe care s-a bazat China în trecut.

În al treilea rând, guvernul caută surse alternative de combustibil. Ar putea părea surprinzător, dar China este deja cel mai mare consumator de energie alternativă, căutând, în prezent, să-și extindă capacitatea eoliană de generare a curentului electric. Peste 60 de ferme eoliene uriașe au fost construite în vestul țării, și acestora, le vor urma, cu siguranță, altele. Energia hidroelectrică are și ea, problemele sale specifice (v. mai jos – *Cele Trei Strâmtori*). Din păcate, energiile regenerabile nu acoperă decât 7% din necesarul energetic al Chinei și, pe măsura creșterii consumului, expansiunea surselor de energie alternativă reușește cu greu să țină pasul.

. . . .

BARAJUL CELOR „TREI STRÂMTORI"

În 2007, uriașele ziduri ale barajului celor „Trei Strâmtori" din provincia Hubei, au fost terminate. În 2009, când generatoarele vor fi instalate și vor intra în funcțiune, ele vor reprezenta încununarea celui mai mare proiect hidroelectric din lume. Barajul cu o înălțime de 180 m, construit peste râul Yangtze, a creat un rezervor, care, atunci când va fi plin, va avea 640 km lungime și peste 100 metri adâncime.

Se speră că barajul va domoli, în sfârșit, legendarele inundații ale fluviului Yangtze, care au luat mai mult de un milion de vieți în ultimul secol. De asemenea, acesta va permite cargoboturilor oceanice de 10 000 tone, să navigheze în interiorul Chinei timp de șase luni pe an. Iar cele 26 de turbine gigant ale sale vor genera 1/9 din necesarul energetic al Chinei.

Faptul că proiectul este aproape gata și se încadrează în programul stabilit este o realizare fenomenală, însă criticii consideră că prețul său a fost și va fi prea mare. Deja, peste un milion de oameni au fost mutați din casele lor pentru a face loc barajului, iar 1 200 de sate și două orașe mari vor fi înghițite de apele sale crescânde. Activiștii de mediu susțin că apa barajului este deja puternic poluată de reziduurile provenite de la fabricile inundate, iar limitarea debitului fluviului Yangtze va înrăutăți poluarea în aval. Istoricii afirmă că 1 300 de situri arheologice importante vor fi distruse la inundarea zonei, printre care și vestigiile, vechi de peste

4 000 de ani, ale locului de baştină al populaţiei Ba. Guvernul chinez consideră că, în ciuda acestor probleme, terminarea unui asemenea proiect este un motiv de mândrie naţională, iar aportul de energie regenerabilă pe care-l aduce este nepreţuit.

. . . .

O trecere de la cărbune, la gaz, cu toate că nu la fel de bună ca una la energie regenerabilă, aduce cu sine o atmosferă mai curată. În Beijing s-au făcut eforturi imense de a trece la încălzirea pe gaz, în încercarea de a curăţa aerul poluat al oraşului înainte de Olimpiadă. China a început, încă din primii ani ai acestui secol, exploatarea zăcămintelor sale de gaz din bazinul Tarim, situat în provincia Xinjiang, în vestul ţării. Regiunea este foarte îndepărtată, aşa că livrarea gazului la destinaţie este o adevărată provocare. Pentru a alimenta cu gaz Shanghaiul, conducta de 3 900 de km, ce străbate ţara de la vest la est, a trebuit să treacă peste terenuri muntoase foarte periculoase. În 2005, conducta a început să livreze gaz centralelor electrice din Shanghai şi se speră ca, până în 2010, întregul oraş să fie alimentat numai cu gaz. În 2008, o conductă de două ori mai lungă, va purta gazul din Xinjiang către oraşul Gungdong, situat în sudul ţării.

. . . .

Iniţiative **eşuate**

Din 1998, SEPA s-a aflat în centrul eforturilor guvernului chinez de a rezolva problemele de mediu, punându-şi amprenta pe numeroase iniţiative de protecţie a mediului. Problema este că nu are nici personalul suficient, nici puterea necesară, pentru a-şi duce la îndeplinire toate planurile. Al zecelea plan cincinal al Chinei, spre exemplu, demarat în anul 2000, prevedea o reducere de 10% a emisiilor de dioxid de sulf. Însă, până în 2005, acestea crescuseră, de fapt, cu 27%.

. . . .

HARTA APELOR

În noiembrie 2006, o organizaţie nonguvernamentală din China, denumită Institutul Afacerilor Publice şi de Mediu, a făcut publică o nouă hartă de-a dreptul uimitoare. Aceasta prezenta, cu detalii în acelaşi timp elocvente şi şocante, efectele poluării apelor în China. Harta Poluării Apelor din China, opera activistului de mediu Ma Jun, a fost alcătuită folosind date guvernamentale, iar apariţia sa a fost un semnal clar al disponibilităţii actuale a guvernului de a recunoaşte adevăratele dimensiuni ale problemelor ecologice.

Harta ierarhizează oraşele şi regiunile nu doar după gradul lor de poluare, ci şi după cel al transparenţei oficialităţilor locale la aceste probleme. Chiar mai surprinzător este faptul că nominalizează şi acuză companiile responsabile de poluarea cea mai puternică. 80 dintre cele 5 500 de companii menţionate erau multinaţionale europene şi americane, precum Pepsi şi General Motors. Dacă acestea doresc ca numele lor să fie şters de pe hartă, trebuie să accepte să fie evaluate de o terţă parte. În iulie 2007, aproape 30 de companii reacţionaseră la nominalizarea lor, mai ales cele multinaţionale, iar şase dintre ele acceptaseră deja să fie evaluate, sau merseseră chiar mai departe, precum Panasonic Battery, care şi-a dotat uzina din Shanghai cu un sistem de tratare a apelor reziduale. Ma Jun crede că multinaţionalele sunt mai sensibile la presiunea publică din cauza numelui mărcii lor, aşa că, pentru a influenţa şi companiile chinezeşti, el plănuieşte să numească multinaţionalele pe care le aprovizionează, cum ar fi Wal Mart şi IBM. Următorul proiect al lui Ma Jun este o hartă a calităţii aerului.

Problema majoră este că, deşi China are acum un nou set de reglementări privitoare la mediul înconjurător, SEPA şi alte organizaţii nu au puterea reală pentru a le impune la nivel local. Proprietarii de fabrici sunt, adesea, protejaţi de relaţiile pe care le întreţin cu reprezentanţii locali ai partidului. Mulţi dintre aceştia închid ochii atunci când fabricile construiesc conducte secrete pentru a deversa chimicalele în râuri sau când eliberează toxine în aer pe timpul nopţii. În 2007, o inspecţie efectuată la 529 de fabrici situate de-a lungul Fluviului Galben a demonstrat că 44% dintre acestea încălcaseră legile de mediu. Aproape jumătate din cele 75 de staţii de tratare a apei de pe malurile râului erau complet inutile. Cu toate acestea, SEPA nu poate face aproape nimic în legătură cu aceste încălcări. Sucursalele SEPA din țară, cunoscute ca Birouri de Protecție a Mediului, se află, în cea mai mare parte, în mâinile administrațiilor locale, a căror singură grijă este să mențină dezvoltarea regiunilor lor și să elimine șomajul. Se întâmplă frecvent ca un astfel de birou să amendeze o companie pentru încălcarea legilor de mediu, apoi să înmâneze banii încasați administrațiilor locale, iar acestea să-i returneze celor amendați sub forma scutirilor de taxe.

Chiar și atunci când SEPA reușește să închidă o fabrică poluantă, aceasta pur și simplu se mută într-o zonă mai săracă, în care oficialitățile locale sunt atât de preocupate de păstrarea locurilor de muncă și de încasarea impozitelor, încât acceptă și poluarea. Acum câțiva ani, acesta a fost motivul mutării bruște a uzinelor de hârtie și produse chimice, care necesită multă apă, din regiunea costală Jiangsu, în regiunea săracă, din interiorul țării, Jiangxi.

În ciuda tuturor acestor probleme, actuala conducere a Chinei pare a fi hotărâtă să le rezolve. Spre deosebire de atitudinea din trecut a acesteia, acum este mult mai deschisă în recunoașterea acestor probleme. A încercat să facă legile de mediu mai aspre și a cerut oficialităților locale să efectueze studii de impact asupra mediului înainte de inițierea altor proiecte. În 2006, a propus introducerea unui „Produs Intern Brut verde", care să ia în considerare, în calcularea creșterii economice, costurile de mediu. Guvernul considera că, astfel, problemele de mediu nu vor mai fi date la o parte de goana după progresul economic, nici la nivel local, nici la cel național. La o evaluare a performanțelor din acest domeniu, guvernul a constatat că, numai în 2004, măsurile pentru reducerea poluării sau prevenirea ei, au costat 116 miliarde de dolari, adică aproape 5% din PIB. Mulți consideră că aceasta este o subestimare uriașă a costurilor lor reale, dar, cel puțin, a fost făcut un pas în direcția potrivită.

. . . .

Capitolul 5:
CHINA ȘI RESTUL LUMII

„Aşadar, adevăratul războinic nu este cel care câştigă o sută de bătălii, ci acela care îşi învinge adversarul fără luptă."

Sun Tzu, *Arta războiului* (sec.6 î.Hr.)

În noiembrie 2006, Beijing-ul a trecut printr-o transformare subită. Fabricile au fost închise pentru ca aerul să fie mai curat. Pentru fluidizarea traficului, în centrul oraşului a fost interzis accesul unei jumătăţi de milion de maşini. Au fost instalate panouri uriaşe, pictate cu diverse animale, care să mascheze cele mai inestetice clădiri, sau terenuri virane. S-au plantat flori şi copaci şi au fost montate bannere uriaşe cu lozinci precum: „Prietenie, pace, cooperare şi dezvoltare." Într-un fel, totul semăna cu o repetiţie pentru Olimpiada din 2008, însă era mai mult decât o simplă repetiţie. Cu toate că în media occidentală a fost receptat marginal, pentru China, evenimentul a fost uriaş. Beijing-ul a fost gazda şefilor de guvern din 48 de state africane.

Cu toate extrem de mediatizatele declaraţii de intenţie ale guvernelor occidentale, care plănuiau să scape Africa de sărăcie, nici unul dintre ele nu dăduse atâta atenţie liderilor africani, şi nici nu le oferise o şansă atât de bună de a se face auziţi de cei de-acasă. Nu este de mirare că poporul chinez a cucerit multe inimi africane. Unora dintre africani li se pare că, în timp ce lumea occidentală le vorbeşte şi îi tratează ca pe nişte copii săraci care au nevoie de îngrijire, chinezii chiar fac ceva, tratându-i, chiar dacă superficial, ca pe nişte adulţi. La summitul de la Beijing, Preşedintele Hu a promis să dubleze ajutorul dat Africii până în 2009, să ofere împrumuturi şi credite în valoare de 5 miliarde de dolari, să asigure pregătirea a 15 000 de specialişti africani din toate domeniile şi să pună bazele unui fond pentru construcţia de şcoli şi spitale. Şi mai important, summitul de la Beijing s-a axat pe încheierea a 2 000 de înţelegeri comerciale cu Africa, pentru a spori nivelul schimburilor dintre cele două ţări. Cu o valoare a contractelor de 42 de miliarde de dolari în 2006, China a înlocuit deja Statele Unite ca partener comercial principal al Africii.

Goana după **resurse a Chinei**

În aparență, atenția acordată Africii de către China are un scop evident. China are nevoie de materii prime pentru a-și susține dezvoltarea economică, iar Africa le are. Principala țintă a Chinei a fost petrolul din Sudan, Angola, Guineea Ecuatorială, Gabon și Nigeria, dar își mai dorește și platina din Zimbabwe, cuprul din Zambia, lemnul tropical din Congo-Brazzaville și minereul de fier din Africa de Sud. Iar Africa nu este singurul stat curtat de China. De-a lungul întregului său mandat, George W. Bush nu a petrecut mai mult de o săptămână la vecinii săi din America de Sud. În schimb, președintele Hu Jintao a petrecut acolo, doar în 2004, mai mult de două săptămâni, discutând asiduu cu guvernele sud americane și promițând investiții de miliarde în Argentina, Brazilia, Chile, Venezuela, Bolivia și Cuba. Modelul s-a perpetuat și liderii chinezi, considerați odinioară oarecum izolaționiști, au pornit în jurul lumii, într-o adevărată ofensivă a farmecului. În 2006, spre exemplu, premierul Wen Jiabao a vizitat 15 țări diferite, în timp ce președintele Hu își punea la lucru șarmul diplomatic în Rusia, Arabia Saudită, Maroc, Nigeria, Kenya, India și Pakistan, fără a mai pune la socoteală Vietnamul, unde s-a întâlnit cu majoritatea liderilor asiatici, summitul african de la Beijing, sau importanta vizită efectuată în SUA.

Aproape neobservată de lumea occidentală, a cărei privire era ferm ațintită asupra Orientului Mijlociu, China și-a extins atât de mult legăturile comerciale cu vecinii, încât este pe punctul de a înlocui Statele Unite ca forță dominantă în Asia de Sud-Est. În timp ce schimburile comerciale ale Americii cu această zonă a lumii au rămas, de la începutul acestui secol, aproape neschimbate, cele chineze au depășit orice așteptări. Și nu e vorba doar de schimburi de monedă. În nordul Thailandei, inginerii chinezi au aruncat în aer cataractele de pe râul Mekong, regularizându-i cursul, astfel încât vasele mari să poată naviga către fabricile chinezești de acolo. Antreprenorii chinezi construiesc mai multe autostrăzi care vor lega orașul Kunming, din China, de capitala Vietnamului, Hanoi, sau orașul Mandalay, din Myanmar, de capitala Thailandei, Bangkok.

Desigur, resursele sunt forţa motrice a acestei deschideri către lume, acesta fiind şi motivul pentru care Australia a fost, la rându-i, co-optată în cercul din ce în ce mai extins al prietenilor Chinei. Însă, în 2006, Hu a efectuat o vizită amicală în India, o ţară cu care China a fost în război, în 1962, angajându-se la dublarea volumului schimburilor comerciale şi la o participare comună la licitaţiile pentru acele proiecte de exploatare petrolieră pentru care cele două ţări concuraseră în trecut. Apoi, în primăvara lui 2007, premierul Wen a efectuat o vizită extrem de cordială în Japonia, adevărata *bête noire* a Chinei, deschizând drumul pentru o detensionare reală a relaţiilor dintre aceşti doi vechi duşmani.

O **ascensiune** paşnică?

Toate acestea par să corespundă intenţiei Chinei de a continua să-şi sporească prosperitatea pentru a-şi scoate poporul din sără-cie, fără a face valuri în lume – o intenţie sintetizată în celebra formulare a lui Zheng Bijian, preşedintele Forumului Chinez pen-tru Reformă, ca o „ascensiune paşnică". După Tiananmen, Deng Xiaoping recomanda Chinei „să urmărească cu seriozitate evoluţia evenimentelor, să-şi menţină poziţia, să facă faţă cu calm provocă-rilor şi să-şi ascundă adevăratele capacităţi în aşteptarea momen-tului prielnic, fără false ambiţii şi fără a pretinde rolul dominant." Deng considera că ţara sa nu ar trebui să-şi intimideze vecinii, sau să tulbure pacea lumii. Şi avem toate motivele să credem că aceasta este politica pe care a urmat-o China în relaţia sa cu lumea de-a lungul ultimului deceniu. În 1999, când americanii au bombar-dat din greşeală ambasada chineză de la Belgrad, capitala fostei Republici Iugoslave, autorităţile chineze au permis desfăşurarea unor manifestaţii de protest, dar numai pentru o foarte scurtă pe-rioadă. Acelaşi lucru au făcut şi în 2001, când un avion de spionaj american s-a lovit de un avion de vânătoare deasupra teritoriului chinez, ucigând pilotul.

Din punct de vedere politic, atitudinea Chinei pare a fi una rezervată, văzându-şi de propriile probleme şi aşteptându-se ca şi celelalte ţări să facă acelaşi lucru. Acesta este şi motivul pentru care nu acceptă nici un fel de amestec internaţional în chestiunea Tibetului, considerând-o a fi o problemă pur internă. Acelaşi lucru e valabil şi pentru Taiwan. Din aceleaşi raţiuni, în 1999, China a fost uşor deranjată de intervenţia NATO în Iugoslavia. De asemenea, s-a împotrivit puternic intervenţiei internaţionale în Irak şi în Afganistan.

· ·

Legături africane

Poziţia sa nonintervenţionistă a permis Chinei să iniţieze legături comerciale cu ţările africane, spre exemplu, fără a acorda prea multă atenţie politicii lor interne. Problema este că această atitudine începe să pună China în faţa unor situaţii conflictuale la care poate că nici măcar nu se aşteptase. În timp ce Occidentul oferă ajutoare şi împrumuturi în Africa, numai acelor regimuri cu care este de acord, sau celor care îndeplinesc anumite condiţii, China pare să ofere bani fără a pune întrebări sau condiţii - situaţie extrem de atractivă pentru unii lideri africani, dar care provoacă îngrijorare în Occident, în special printre organizaţiile preocupate de drepturile omului. În 2004, atunci când Fondul Monetar Internaţional a sistat un împrumut către Angola din cauza suspiciunii de corupţie la nivel înalt, chinezii au trimis, în schimb, 2 miliarde de dolari. În aceeaşi manieră, în timp ce Occidentul încerca să-l izoleze pe preşedintele Robert Mugabe din Zimbabwe, chinezii au intervenit, oferindu-i 2 miliarde de dolari în împrumuturi, în afară de armamentul chinezesc pe care-l primise deja. Iar când Uniunea Africană l-a expulzat pe François Bozizé din Republica Centrafricană, printr-o violentă lovitură de stat, China i-a oferit un împrumut uriaş şi l-a invitat să vină în vizită.

Cu toate acestea, Sudanul a fost adevăratul măr al discordiei. Acest stat a devenit ţinta atenţiei internaţionale din cauza măcelului etnic din regiunea Darfur, unde 200 000 de oameni au murit şi 2,5 milioane au fost forţaţi să-şi părăsească casele. Şi totuşi, aparent nepăsătoare la situația din Darfur și la eforturile internaționale de impunere a unor sancțiuni, China s-a implicat în construirea unei conducte necesare unei mai bune exploatări a resurselor de petrol ale Sudanului, iar acum ia două treimi din petrolul țării. Fabulosul palat al președintelui Sudanului, Omar al-Bashir, se construiește cu ajutorul unui împrumut fără dobândă, acordat de China. Însă, ceea ce a deranjat cel mai tare criticii, a fost faptul că țara asiatică și-a folosit poziția din cadrul Consiliului de Securitate al ONU, pentru a sabota rezoluțiile acestuia care făceau presiuni asupra guvernului Sudanului pentru a permite intervenția forțelor ONU în sprijinul locuitorilor din Darfur. Când a fost chestionat în legătură cu atitudinea Chinei, în 2006, ministrul de externe Zhou Wenzhong a declarat: „Afacerile sunt afaceri. Noi încercăm să separăm politica de afaceri și, oricum, situația din Sudan este o problemă internă a acestei țări, iar noi nu suntem în postura de a o influența" (citat în cartea lui Will Hutton, *Scrisul de pe Zid*, 2007).

. . . .

China cedează

Presiunile internaționale asupra Chinei în legătură cu Darfur-ul devin, pe zi ce trece, mai intense, iar aceasta pare că începe să reacționeze. În aprilie 2007, chinezii au trimis un mesager diplomatic special pentru a-l convinge pe președintele sudanez Omar al-Bashir să accepte forțele ONU de menținere a păcii, iar în iunie eforturile acestuia au fost, în sfârșit, încununate de succes. Pentru unii, acest lucru nu este suficient, dat fiind că, împotriva locuitorilor din Darfur, sunt folosite arme chinezești. Presiunile venite din partea politicienilor americani, a unor vedete de la Hollywood, cum ar fi Mia Farrow, și a grupurilor pentru drepturile omului, au împins China să-și înțețească eforturile, dar aceasta continuă să susțină că politica „pașilor mărunți" pe care o aplică, funcționează, și că este mai mult decât dispusă să coopereze. La o conferință de presă din mai 2007, purtătoarea de cuvânt a ministrului de externe chinez, doamna Jiang Yu, a ținut să sublinieze: „În chestiunea

Darfur, China și Statele Unite au același scop. Sperăm să rezolvăm problema prin mijloace politice, așa că suntem gata să facem eforturi comune, alături de comunitatea internațională, inclusiv de Statele Unite."

În sfârșit, China începe să-și dea seama că nu poate întreține legături economice cu restul lumii, fără a întreține și legături politice. Mai mult decât atât, în Africa, China are de întâmpinat critici nu numai în legătură cu guvernele dubioase pe care alege să le susțină, ci și cu propriul comportament. Pe de o parte, este vorba despre modelul comercial adoptat de China, potrivit căruia, spun unii, aceasta se folosește de resursele țărilor africane, după care le inundă cu produse ieftine, și chiar cu alimente, cu care comercianților locali le este imposibil să concureze. În decembrie 2006, președintele sud-african Thabo Mbeki a avertizat Africa că nu trebuie să permită Chinei să devină precum una dintre vechile puteri coloniale. Pe de altă parte, operațiunile miniere și exploatările petroliere chinezești din Africa încep să capete o proastă reputație prin lipsa măsurilor de siguranță, salariile execrabile și caracterul instabil al locurilor de muncă.

Alinierea internațională

Până acum, sub conducerea lui Hu și a lui Wen, China și-a jucat foarte bine rolul, reușind să potolească multe dintre temerile resimțite de unii, în epoca lui Mao în legătură cu țara. Într-adevăr, un sondaj internațional, efectuat de Centrul de Cercetari Pew în 2005, a relevat că această țară este mult mai populară și credibilă în lume decât SUA. În ciuda criticilor vizând legăturile sale cu diverse regimuri dubioase și practicile sale comerciale, China și-a văzut netulburată de treabă și, când a fost nevoie, a făcut, în general, „ceea ce trebuie." În anii '50, China a intrat în război cu SUA pentru a proteja Coreea de Nord și a pierdut milioane de soldați, dar în toamna anului 2006, când aceasta din urmă și-a efectuat testul nuclear, China nu numai că s-a alăturat SUA în condamnarea lui Kim Jong-il, dar chiar a susţinut o rezoluţie a Naţiunilor Unite care îi impunea sancţiuni.

Pe de altă parte, dacă interesul Chinei în a menţine stabilitatea în regiune coincide cu cel al Coreei de Nord, nu acelaşi lucru se poate spune despre poziţia sa faţă de Iran. China a refuzat să susţină sancţiunile dure pe care Europa şi America doresc să le impună Iranului, pentru a opri programul nuclear al acestuia. Este posibil ca liderii chinezi să considere că iranienii ar trebui lăsaţi să-şi dezvolte capacităţile nucleare în linişte, însă, ceea ce este sigur, este faptul că îşi doresc petrolul şi gazul iranian, pentru care au încheiat deja un contract în valoare de 16 miliarde de dolari.

Întrucât economia Chinei se extinde la nivel global, aceasta nu doar că se va găsi expusă unor presiuni internaţionale din ce în ce mai mari, cum au fost cele cu care s-a confruntat în problema Darfur şi a preşedintelui din Zimbabwe, ci va descoperi că impactul său asupra lumii poate produce animozitate în locuri în care nu s-ar fi aşteptat niciodată să o facă.

. . . .

Războaie comerciale?

O potenţială zonă de conflict este cea a comerţului şi a finanţelor. SUA înregistrează deja un dezechilibru comercial masiv în relaţiile sale cu China – de fapt, cel mai mare din istorie. În 2005, SUA a importat din China bunuri în valoare de 240 de miliarde de dolari, exportând doar echivalentul a 40 de miliarde dolari. Probabil că, în următorii ani, deficitul va continua să crească. Singurul motiv pentru care acesta poate fi menţinut este faptul că această ţară comunistă este bucuroasă să-şi transforme veniturile excedentare în dolari.

Mulţi dintre muncitorii şi producătorii americani sunt deranjaţi de acest dezechilibru, la fel şi politicienii, care se tem de o nouă dependenţă. Ei se plâng că produsele lor sunt boicotate de fabricile din China şi că piaţa americană este continuu invadată de produse chinezeşti ieftine. Şase dintre industriile americane – textile, îmbrăcă-

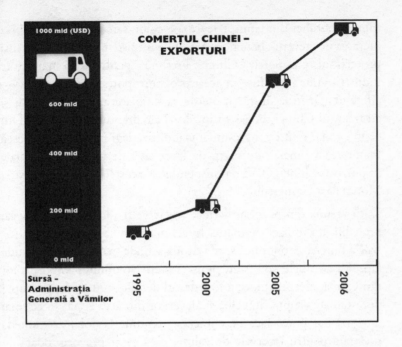

COMERȚUL CHINEI – EXPORTURI

1000 mld (USD)

600 mld

400 mld

200 mld

0 mld

1995 2000 2005 2006

Sursă –
Administrația
Generală a Vămilor

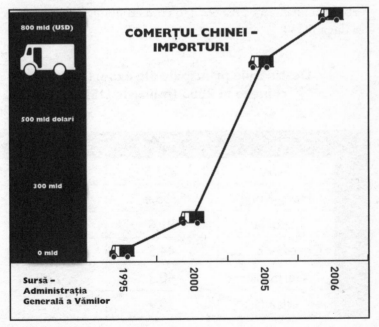

COMERȚUL CHINEI – IMPORTURI

800 mld (USD)

500 mld dolari

300 mld

0 mld

1995 2000 2005 2006

Sursă –
Administrația
Generală a Vămilor

minte, mobilier din lemn, televizoare color, semiconductori şi prelucrarea de creveţi – beneficiază deja de un sistem special de măsuri protecţioniste împotriva Chinei. Presiunea pentru ca şi mai multe industrii să fie introduse în acest program sporeşte, democraţii vociferând atât în legătură cu pierderea slujbelor americanilor, cât şi cu trecutul Chinei, bogat în încălcări ale drepturilor omului. Din ce în ce mai mulţi congresmeni elaborează legi menite să oprească înaintarea Chinei, care merg de la crearea de bariere comerciale împotriva Chinei, până la suspendarea acesteia din Organizaţia Mondială a Comerţului.

Dacă vreuna dintre măsurile mai severe va fi adoptată, ea va avea, probabil, un impact dramatic. În cel mai bun caz, China îşi va canaliza puterea economică spre Europa – unde, până acum, în ciuda faptului că unele voci s-au opus creşterii volumului importurilor din China, efectul chinez a fost destul de mic – cu efecte potenţial devastatoare asupra slujbelor şi afacerilor din acea zonă. În cel mai rău caz, i-ar putea face pe chinezi să renunţe la dolar ca monedă preferată pentru rezervele de valută, ceea ce ar provoca, odată cu prăbuşirea financiară a Americii, o criză economică mai gravă decât cea din anii '30.

Destinaţiile principale ale exporturilor chineze în 2006 (miliarde USD)

Loc	Ţară	Volum	% Schimbare*
1	SUA	203,5	24,9
2	Hong Kong	155,4	24,8
3	Japonia	91,6	9,1
4	Coreea de Sud	44,5	26,8
5	Germania	40,3	23,9
6	Olanda	30,9	19,3

7	Marea Britanie	24,2	27,3
8	Singapore	23,2	39,4
9	Taiwan	20,7	25,3
10	Italia	16	36,7

*schimbare procentuală față de 2005

Sursă: Administrația Generală a Vămilor – Statistica vamală a Chinei

Principalii importatori în China
în 2006 (miliarde USD)

Loc	Țară	Volum	% Schimbare*
1	Japonia	115,7	15,2
2	Coreea de Sud	89,8	16,9
3	Taiwan	87,1	16,6
4	SUA	59,2	21,8
5	Germania	37,9	23,3
6	Malaysia	23,6	17,3
7	Australia	19,3	19,3
8	Thailanda	18,0	28,4
9	Rusia	17,7	37,3
10	Singapore	17,7	7,0

*schimbare procentuală față de 2005

Sursă: Administrația Generală a Vămilor – Statistica vamală a Chinei

BOOM-UL CHINEZESC ÎN MAREA BRITANIE

Anglia nu a suferit încă prea mult din cauza efectului chinez. Într-adevăr, în ultimul deceniu, boom-ul chinezesc nu prea a dat bătăi de cap Marii Britanii. Unele locuri de muncă s-au pierdut în fața concurenței chinezești, cum au fost cele de la întreprinderea de automobile Rover, dar asta s-a întâmplat, cel mai adesea, cu întreprinderi care oricum erau pe ducă. Pe de altă parte, nici salariile minime și nici prețurile produselor nu au crescut. Ceea ce înseamnă că inflația și ratele dobânzilor au rămas mici, încurajând mărirea prețului proprietăților imobiliare. Cu ratele dobânzilor mici și prețurile proprietăților în creștere, consumatorii britanici și-au putut permite să facă împrumuturi ipotecare, sau, pur și simplu, credite de consum, pentru a cheltui la un nivel nemaiîntâlnit până acum. Toate aceste cheltuieli au dus la crearea multor locuri de muncă în domeniul comerțului cu amănuntul, serviciilor și a unui nou tip de industrie care se bazează pe consumul personal.

Războaiele petrolului

Mulți cred că producția de petrol și-a atins acum apogeul, că mai mare de-atât nu va mai fi niciodată. Deși sunt descoperite și dezvoltate noi zăcăminte de petrol, acestea nu pot compensa scăderea producției zăcămintelor deja existente, pe măsură ce acestea încep să sece. Nu toată lumea este de acord, dar consumul de petrol în lume este încă în creștere, iar în China, mai mult ca în orice altă parte. În 2003, China a depășit Japonia, devenind al doilea mare consumator de petrol din lume după SUA și, de atunci, este responsabilă de circa 40% din întreaga creștere a cererii mondiale de petrol. Dacă actuala tendință se menține, China va depăși SUA în 2009, chiar dacă și consumul SUA este în continuă creștere. Atunci, de unde va veni tot acest petrol?

În general, China a avut extrem de multă grijă să nu intre într-o competiție prea fățișă cu lumea occidentală. Acesta este motivul pentru care dorește să preia petrolul Iranian și pentru care a jucat un rol cheie în dezvoltarea zăcămintelor aflate la mare distanţă de Orientul Mijlociu, în Africa, în special în Sudan şi Angola, şi în America de Sud. Aceste zăcăminte s-ar putea, însă, dovedi insuficiente, iar dacă SUA intră în război cu Iranul, China ar putea fi nevoită să aleagă una dintre părţi, sau va pierde o sursă vitală de petrol.

. . . .

Acumularea de **forţe militare**

În ultimii zece ani, conform Institutului Internaţional pentru Studii Strategice de la Londra, cheltuielile militare ale Chinei s-au triplat şi par să continue să o facă, într-un ritm din ce în ce mai alert. Doar în 2006, cheltuielile pentru înarmare ale Chinei au crescut cu 15%. Pentru o ţară care insistă că îşi doreşte o dezvoltare paşnică, aceasta pare a fi o stranie contradicţie, iar oamenii au început să se întrebe care este rostul acestei acumulări de forţe militare. Unii consideră că ţinta ar putea fi Taiwanul şi au început să se întrebe ce va face America în cazul în care China atacă Taiwanul? Ar putea fi acesta începutul unui război între superputeri? Majoritatea consideră că este foarte puţin probabil, din moment ce şi China, şi SUA sunt interesate să menţină status-quo-ul în Taiwan.

Probabil, China va continua să acumuleze forţe militare până în momentul în care SUA vor decide că o intervenţie în sprijinul Taiwanului ar fi prea costisitoare. Asta cred unii dintre generalii intervenţionişti americani. Noile destinaţii ale investiţiilor militare au transformat uriaşa masă a Armatei de Eliberare a Poporului, într-o forţă mai mică, dar mai avansată din punct de vedere tehnologic, ale cărei performanţe sunt la acelaşi nivel cu cele ale forţelor americane. La rândul ei, marina militară chineză are noi rachete de croazieră şi rachete antinavale, destinate penetrării apărării electronice a vaselor americane. Cu toate acestea, bugetul de apărare al Chinei reprezintă doar o zecime din cel american, fiind chiar mai mic decât cel al Marii Britanii, aşa că este improbabil să-i permită acestei ţări să poarte un război împotriva SUA, chiar dacă şi-ar dori-o. În consecinţă, un război împotriva Taiwanului pare extrem de puţin probabil.

Dacă armele chinezilor nu sunt pentru Taiwan, atunci pentru cine ar putea fi? Poate o simplă măsură de apărare. În secolul XX, China a fost invadată de două ori, ultima oară cu efecte devastatoare. De asemenea, ea are frontiere terestre de 22 000 km lungime şi 18 000 de km de coastă care au nevoie de protecţie. S-ar putea ca aceasta să anticipeze un viitor conflict pentru resurse. Deja şi-a pus în alertă forţele navale, într-un război al voinţelor cu Japonia asupra unor câmpuri de petrol extrem de disputate.

. . . .

Un **viitor** democratic?

Pentru moment, China pare să fie mulţumită să joace un rol mai puţin reprezentativ în lume. Un sondaj desfăşurat în 2006 în China, a arătat că 87% dintre chinezi cred că ţara lor ar trebui să joace un rol mai important în afacerile mondiale, ajungând, cât se poate de curând, la acelaşi nivel cu SUA. Aceste răspunsuri veneau, probabil, din patriotism şi din credinţa, din ce în ce mai răspândită printre chinezi, că ţara lor ar trebui să-şi ocupe „locul de drept" în lume, şi nu dintr-o dorinţă imperialistă de dominare a lumii. Singura problemă este că „locul lor de drept" ar putea fi obţinut în dauna altora. Mai mult decât atât, China rămâne un stat monopartid, care suprimă aproape orice disidenţă şi care, până acum, nu a fost prea pretenţios în alegerea statelor cu care să fraternizeze. În ultimii 20 de ani, numărul democraţiilor din lume s-a dublat, astfel încât acestea reprezintă acum două treimi dintre naţiunile lumii. Există posibilitatea ca ascensiunea Chinei să însemne o încetinire, sau chiar un declin al acestui reviriment democratic – aceasta, desigur, numai în cazul în care China însăşi nu trece la democraţie.

. . . .

Capitolul 6:
CHINA ȘI TAIWANUL

„Taiwanul este o parte inalienabilă a teritoriului Chinei. Cea mai mare amenințare a păcii în Strâmtoarea Taiwan vine din partea activităților separatiste ale grupului 'Independența Taiwanului'."

Președintele Chinei – Hu Jintao, 2003

În iunie 2007, Taiwanul a primit o dureroasă lovitură din partea statului Costa Rica, țară mică, aflată în cealaltă parte a lumii. S-a dovedit că aceasta din urmă, una dintre puținele țări care recunoștea oficial Taiwanul, schimbase tabăra, trecând de partea Republicii Populare Chineze. Costaricanii, se pare, nu mai putuseră rezista atracțiilor și „stimulentelor" financiare venite din partea unei Chine din ce în ce mai mari și mai prospere. Președintele Costa Ricăi, Oscar Arias, a explicat succint decizia țării sale, intitulând-o: „un act de realism elementar." Ministrul de externe al Taiwanului, James Huang, părea extrem de abătut când a replicat: „Nici o țară care își dorește pacea și democrația n-ar trebui să facă un astfel de act, rupând legăturile cu un partener vechi de 60 de ani." Din păcate pentru Taiwan, este foarte probabil ca tot mai multe dintre țările ce alcătuiesc plăpândul său grup de susținători, cum ar fi Nicaragua, sau Panama, să facă același lucru. În prezent, scorul este 170 pentru China continentală și 24 pentru Taiwan – și cea mai mare parte a „echipei" acestuia din urmă, este formată din țări mici și sărace.

Totul s-a schimbat în comparație cu anii '50, când situația era exact inversă – fapt cu atât mai ironic, din moment ce Taiwan este, astăzi, o democrație funcțională, în timp ce atunci era o dictatură militară, condusă de generalul Chiang Kai-Shek. Acesta a fost conducătorul naționaliștilor chinezi din partidul Guomindang, care s-a refugiat pe insula Taiwan, după ce armatele sale au fost învinse de către comuniști, în 1948. Acolo i s-au alăturat aproape două milioane de partizani. Aceștia sunt denumiți „chinezi de uscat", pentru a-i distinge de majoritatea populației din Taiwan, venită tot de pe continent, în special din Fujian și Guangdong, însă cu mult timp în urmă, în epoca imperială. Mai există și un număr mic de aborigeni taiwanezi.

Grupul **Chiang**

Atunci când au ajuns în Taiwan, în 1949, Chiang şi cei care l-au urmat – în principal, foşti soldaţi din armata naţionalistă chineză – au preluat repede controlul insulei şi au înfiinţat aici Adunarea Naţională Chineză. Pentru Chiang şi Guomindang, şederea în Taiwan trebuia să fie una de scurtă durată. Republica Populară Chineză, întemeiată de comunişti pe continent, era, din punctul lui Chiang de vedere, ilegală, şi nu era decât o chestiune de timp până când s-ar fi întors, alături de trupele sale, pentru a restabili Republica Chineză(RC). Taiwanul era, pentru el, doar o provincie a Chinei, chiar dacă, de-a lungul anilor, oamenii au ajuns să-l numească Republica Chineză, pentru a-l deosebi de China continentală, cunoscută drept Republica Populară Chineză. Până una alta, Republica Populară Chineză a început, la rându-i, să pretindă că Taiwan este o parte integrantă a teritoriului său.

Până în 1971, comuniştii erau cei priviţi de restul lumii ca nişte renegaţi, iar guvernul din RC era considerat a fi singurul guvern legitim al Chinei. Însă, eforturile preşedintelui Republicii Populare, Zhou Enlai, de a câştiga recunoaşterea internaţională, conjugate cu încercarea preşedintelui american Nixon de a face din China un aliat împotriva Uniunii Sovietice, au dat, în cele din urmă, rezultate. Naţiunile Unite au încetat să mai recunoască RC, pe care au şi scos-o din organizaţie, recunoscând, în schimb, Republica Populară. De atunci, numărul ţărilor care recunosc ca legitimă Republica Chineză este într-o continuă scădere. Aceasta îşi menţine, totuşi, legăturile diplomatice cu majoritatea ţărilor lumii, însă într-o manieră neoficială, prin intermediul unor agenţii, nu al unor ambasade.

. . . .

Dezvoltarea **Taiwanului**

Relaţiile dintre China şi Taiwan au fost mereu încordate, China ameninţând mereu că, dacă va fi nevoie, va scoate Taiwanul din mâinile Guomindang-ului, chiar şi cu forţa. Cu toate acestea, de-a lungul anilor '60 şi '70, Taiwan a început să se dezvolte, transfomându-se într-o ţară prosperă şi dinamică, a cărei expanisune economică a ajutat-o să ajungă unul dintre cei „Patru tigrii asiatici" (alături de Singapore, Hong Kong şi Coreea de Sud). Un element esenţial în ascensiunea către prosperitate în Taiwan a fost, fără îndoială, şi faptul că membrii Guomindang-ului aduseseră cu sine toate rezervele de aur şi valută ale Chinei. Însă, în ciuda faptului că, din punct de vedere economic şi industrial, Taiwan începea să arate ca un stat modern, el continua să rămână o dictatură militară, aflată sub conducerea lui Chiang Kai-Shek şi a Guomindang-ului. Conducerea efectivă a ţării aparţinea chinezilor de pe continent, ce reprezentau doar 14% din populaţie.

Cu toate acestea, în 1975, Chiang a murit şi a fost urmat la conducere de către fiul său Chiang Ching-Ko, iar lucrurile au început să se schimbe. În 1984, Chiang Jr. a făcut o alegere curajoasă, numind în funcţia de vicepreşedinte o persoană din afara Guomindangului, pe taiwanezul Lee Teng-hui. Câţiva ani mai târziu şi-a făcut apariţia un partid care cerea o conducere democratică şi independenţa Taiwanului, Partidul Democratic Progresist (PDP), care, cu toate că a fost interzis, a continuat să fie tolerat. Apoi, în 1987, Chiang Ching-Ko a abolit legea marţială.

După moartea lui Chiang Ching-Ko, în 1988, democratizarea a intrat într-un ritm mai alert, odată cu alegerea ca preşedinte a lui Lee Teng-Hui. E important de remarcat, însă, că acesta nu a fost un simplu proces de democratizare, Lee iniţiind o transformare fundamentală a relaţiilor între Taiwan şi China. El a renunţat să mai pretindă că guvernul Taiwanului nu este altceva decât un guvern în exil, pregătit în orice moment să preia frâiele întregii Chine. În schimb, şi-a îndreptat întreaga atenţie asupra Taiwanului. În loc să fie emise, ca până atunci, de Banca Provinciei Taiwaneze (ceea ce implica faptul că Taiwanul era doar o provincie a Chinei), banc-notele ţării erau emise de Banca Centrală a Taiwanului. O măsură mai drastică a fost cea de desfiinţare a Adunării Naţionale Chineze, ai cărei membri, cu excepţia celor care muriseră de bătrâneţe, erau aceiaşi încă de la alegerea sa, din 1947. În 1996, Lee a fost ales preşedinte în primul scrutin democratic al ţării. Apoi, în 2000, Guomindang-ul a ieşit de la guvernare când reprezentantul PDP, Chen Shui-bian, a fost ales în fruntea primului guvern non-Guomindang din istoria ţării. În 2004, Chen Shui-bian a câştigat un al doilea mandat în fruntea coaliţiei conduse de PDP, denumită

Pan-Greens, ce luptă pentru obținerea unei independențe autentice. Coaliția adversă, *Pan-Blue*, condusă de Guomindang, se declară în favoarea unei eventuale reunificări cu China.

. . . .

Vremuri de restriște

Evoluțiile de pe scena politică a Taiwanului au pus China în fața unei dileme. După zeci de ani de ostilități, în anii '80 relațiile dintre China și Taiwan au început să se îmbunătățească. Deng Xiaoping mersese până într-acolo, încât să propună aceeași soluție aplicată în Hong Kong și în Macao, „un singur stat, două sisteme." Potrivit acesteia, Taiwanul ar fi făcut parte din Republica Populară Chineză, dar i s-ar fi permis un anume grad de autonomie și păstrarea unui guvern propriu. La începutul anilor '90, Președintele Lee a renunțat, în mod neoficial, la pretenția Republicii Chineze asupra Chinei continentale, cu toate că aceasta continuă să fie stipulată în constituția Taiwanului. Pentru observatorul obișnuit, aceasta ar putea părea o mișcare conciliatorie, însă pentru China, ea însemna o grijă în plus. Pe vremea când Republica Chineză din Taiwan încă mai ridica pretenții asupra Republicii Populare, pentru ambele părți era subînțeles că nu sunt altceva decât oponenți în războiul civil chinez și că Taiwanul este doar o provincie a Chinei. Faptul că Republica Chineză renunța la pretențiile sale asupra continentului reprezenta o intenție clară de a separa Taiwanul de China – ultimul lucru pe care aceasta și l-ar fi dorit. În 1996, când Taiwanul și-a anunțat intenția de a organiza primul său scrutin democratic, China a fost atât de alarmată, încât a ordonat efectuarea unei serii de exerciții militare navale în apropierea coastelor Taiwanului, în timpul cărora au fost trase și câteva rachete „de probă" înspre țărm, în încercarea de a-l determina pe Lee să anuleze alegerile. Imediat, președintele Bill Clinton a dispus cea mai mare desfășurare de forțe navale americane de la Răboiul din Coreea, trimițând un mesaj cât se poate de explicit autorităților chineze, sub forma a două portavioane care să patruleze Strâmtoarea Taiwan. Posibilitatea izbucnirii unui război nuclear între China și Statele Unite i-a înspăimântat pe protagonişti, făcându-i să revină la sentimente mai bune. Spiritele au fost calmate şi taiwanezii şi-au continuat alegerile. Toată agitaţia stârnită de chinezi nu făcuse altceva decât să întărească sprjinul pentru Lee, asigurându-i alegerea ca preşedinte.

. . . .

PRIETENI AMERICANI

Statele Unite sunt, fără nici o îndoială, cel mai râvnit prieten al Taiwanului, şi au fost încă de la iniţierea acestei legături, din timpul celui de-al Doilea Război Mondial şi al Războiului Rece, când SUA era pro Chiang Kai-Shek, ca stavilă împotriva comunismului. Prin urmare, în anii '70, atunci când Statele Unite au încetat să recunoască oficial Taiwanul în favoarea Chinei, prietenia celor două ţări a fost pusă la grea încercare. În ciuda acestei palme pe obrazul Taiwanului, SUA nu doreau să-l abandoneze complet, aşa încât, în 1979, Congresul american a votat Actul privind relaţia cu Taiwanul, prin care se angaja să aprovizioneze Taiwanul cu arme de apărare şi să considere orice atac asupra acestuia ca fiind o problemă „de interes maxim" a SUA.

Iar faptul că angajamentul acestora fusese unul cât se poate de serios a fost demonstrat în 1996, când preşedintele Clinton a trimis marina militară a SUA în apele Taiwanului, ca răspuns la provocatoarele teste chinezeşti cu rachete. În ciuda acestei reacţii rapide, era clar că americanii nu voiau să-şi asume prea multe obligaţii, din moment ce, doi ani mai târziu, Clinton promitea că SUA va respecta „cei trei NU" – NU independenţei Taiwanului, NU dezmembrării Chinei şi NU accederii Taiwanului în orice fel de organizaţie a cărei cerinţă de intrare ar fi recunoaşterea ţării candidate ca stat (adică, ONU). Administraţia Bush a fost poate, chiar mai fermă şi mai agresivă. BBC-ul citează dintr-un raport intern al administraţiei americane, din 2003, în care se spune: „Preşedintele le-a transmis chinezilor, într-un limbaj cât se poate de clar, că în cazul în care China încearcă să folosească constrângerea sau forţa, pentru a schimba în mod unilateral statutul Taiwanului, Statele Unite vor fi nevoite să se implice." Atitudinea SUA în problema Taiwanului este, fără nici o umbră de îndoială, una extrem de riscantă. Nu doreşte să supere China, mai ales că acum, boom-ul economic al acesteia favorizează intensificarea schimburilor comerciale dintre cele două ţări. Dar nici nu este dispusă să abandoneze Taiwanul cu totul. Rezultatul este un joc diplomatic bazat pe semnificaţia cuvintelor. Statele Unite „admit", mai degrabă decât să „recunoască" – adică, „să susţină" – pretenţia

Chinei potrivit căreia Taiwan este o parte integrantă a teritoriului său. În aceeași manieră, mai curând „nu susțin", decât să „se opună" ideii independenței Taiwanului. Statele Unite rămân, însă, cât se poate de ferme în insistența lor asupra unei soluții pașnice la această problemă.

. . . .

Ce **reprezintă** un nume?

De atunci, Taiwanul a încercat să intre din nou în ONU, de data aceasta în nume propriu și nu ca reprezentant al întregii Chine, cum fusese atunci când a fost dat afară din organizație, în 1971. Sub conducerea lui Lee, Republica Chineză s-a autointitulat Republica Chineză din Taiwan. Chen Shui-bian a mers și mai departe, denumind-o, în timpul primului său mandat ca președinte, Republica Chineză (Taiwan). După ce a fost reales, în 2004, a susținut că Taiwanul ar trebui să intre în ONU sub numele de Taiwan. Din moment ce nu este recunoscută ca națiune suverană, va participa mai întâi numai cu statutul de observator, la fel ca palestinienii, însă, bineînțeles că mulți vor percepe această mișcare ca un pas pe calea statalității. Și, evident că Republica Populară Chineză exact așa o și vede, fiind hotărâtă să blocheze reintrarea Taiwanului în ONU. Din moment ce China este membru în Consiliul de Securitate și are drept de veto, este puțin probabil ca Taiwanul să facă mari progrese.

Foarte interesant este, însă, faptul că majoritatea taiwanezilor probabil că nici nu-și doresc altceva. Cu toate că susținerea pentru Guomindang și reunificare a scăzut, chiar și pe continent, în Taiwan, doar o minoritate este de acord cu demersurile lui Chen și ale coaliției Pan-Green pentru o independență totală. Majoritatea populației vrea doar să fie lăsată să-și vadă de viața ei, din ce în ce mai prosperă în liniște, fără să-și supere nici unul dintre puternicii vecini. Deși sondajele arată că două treimi dintre taiwanezi ar lupta cu arma în mână, în cazul în care chinezii ar încerca să-i cucerească, numai 14% doresc să mărească miza până la independența deplină. Status quo-ul este perfect, cel puțin pentru taiwanezii mai înstăriți.

SCĂPĂRI TAIWANEZE

A şti cum să numeşti Taiwanul a devenit un adevărat calvar. Din când în când, chiar şi aceia pentru care contează cu adevărat mai greşesc. Enciclopedia on-line *Wikipedia* enumeră o lungă serie de gafe ale politicienilor. Ambii preşedinţi americani, Reagan şi Bush, au avut scăpări, referindu-se în mod eronat la Taiwan ca la o ţară, ceea ce, din punctul de vedere al Statelor Unite, nu este adevărat. Donald Rumsfeld a mers şi mai departe, descriind în 2005, Taiwanul, ca o „naţiune suverană". Dar nu li se întâmplă doar americanilor. Premierul Republicii Populare Chineze, Zhu Rongji, a descris în mod accidental China şi Taiwanul, ca două ţări diferite, iar atunci când Lien Chan şi Guomindang-ul au vizitat Beijingul, în 2005, au fost prezentaţi de oficialii Republicii Populare ca un partid politic al Taiwanului, deşi aceştia din urmă încercau să negocieze cu Guomindang-ul pe baza faptului că ambii vedeau China ca un întreg care includea şi Taiwanul. Se pare că în februarie 2007, Orchestra Regală a Poliţiei din insula caraibiană a Grenadei a intonat imnul naţional taiwanez pentru a întâmpina o delegaţie din Republica Populară Chineză ce finanţase construcţia unui stadion local!

Banii vorbesc

Există motive serioase pentru comportamentul pragmatic al Taiwanului, în afara dimensiunilor uriaşe şi a puterii militare a vecinilor lor de pe continent. De fapt, în ultimii douăzeci de ani, locuitorii din Taiwan au legături din ce în ce mai strânse cu cei de pe continent. După Hong Kong, Taiwanul a fost cel mai mare investitor în economia în creştere a Chinei. De la sfârşitul anilor '80, afaceriştii taiwanezi au pompat peste 100 de miliarde de dolari în China. Iar taiwanezii nu au investit numai bani; mai mult de un milion dintre ei lucrează în China. Deşi nimeni nu ştie exact, între 40 şi 80% din exporturile de electronice chinezeşti provin, probabil, din fabrici aflate în proprietate taiwaneză, iar un procent imens din exporturile Taiwanului, merge către China.

TAIWAN – STĂPÂNUL ELECTRONICELOR

Cheia prosperității taiwaneze a fost uimitorul success al insulei în domeniul industriei high-tech. Cu o populație ce numără doar 23 de milioane,
Taiwanul a ajuns să domine afacerile IT la un nivel fără precedent. Dacă
ai un calculator personal, un notebook sau un iPod, dacă te uiți la DVD
pe un ecran LCD poți fi sigur că taiwanezii au fost implicați în producerea
acestora. China a ajuns să rivalizeze cu Taiwanul ca furnizor de produse IT,
dar taiwanezii sunt aceia care asigură creierele sau banii din spatele companiilor chinezești. Foarte puține din companiile de IT taiwaneze au nume
de marcă, dar ei sunt furnizorii celor mai cunoscute mărci. De-a lungul
coastei de vest a Taiwanului se află companii precum: Asustek Computer,
proprietara fabricilor chinezești care produc iPod-uri, sau laptopurile
Apple; AU Optronics, care fabrică Playstation-ul de la Sony; Quanta, liderul mondial al producătorilor de notebook-uri; Taiwan Manufacturing Co,
care face mai multe cipuri decât orice altă companie din lume. Cu doar
zece ani în urmă, firmele de IT taiwaneze făceau bani din furnizarea unor
componente extrem de ieftine, sau a unor mașini create în altă parte.
Acum, însă, Taiwanul a trecut la alt nivel, fabricând componentele ieftine
în China și devenind, la rândul său, un inovator în domeniu. Guvernul a
jucat un rol-cheie, susținând financiar diverse inițiative, cum a fost cea de
înființare a Institutului de Cercetări Tehnologice Industriale din Hsinchu.
Rezultatul este că Taiwanul are un foarte mare număr de talente în domeniu, dar și un grad de flexibilitate în a răspunde la comenzile specifice ale
fiecărei corporații care l-au ținut cu un pas înaintea concurenței.

Într-o remarcabilă schimbare de politică, având în vedere vechea lor
dușmănie, și cu sprijinul multor oameni de afaceri de origine taiwaneză,
Guomindang-ul a început să se apropie de Republica Populară Chineză, în
încercarea de a le crea lui Chen și PDP-ului o imagine de separatiști ex-
tremiști. În aprilie 2005, Lien Chan, liderul Guomindang, a efectuat o vizită
intens mediatizată la Beijing, milioane de taiwanezi și de chinezi urmărindu-l
în direct la televizor, în timp ce lua parte la o fastuoasă recepție oferită de
președintele chinez Hu Jintao. Când Lien Chan s-a întors în Taiwan, cu doi
imenși urși panda pentru grădina zoologică din Taipei, a avut parte de o
primire călduroasă din partea elitei oamenilor de afaceri taiwanezi.

Republica Populară Chineză este conștientă de puterea pe care o deține
asupra afacerilor taiwaneze și, în afară de a curta Guomindang-ul, face
presiuni asupra firmelor cunoscute a fi pro Chen, susținându-le pe cele
pro China. Chiar înainte de vizita lui Lien Chan la Beijing, președintele
Chen a fost uimit să descopere într-un ziar din Taipei, o scrisoare deschisă
din partea unui vechi suporter, Hsu Wen-long în care eforturile sale pen-

tru obţinerea independenţei erau criticate ca fiind o reţetă pentru dez-astru. Grupul patronat de Hsu Wen-long, Chi Mei, deţinea multe afaceri în China şi era dornic să se extindă. Potrivit guvernului taiwanez, China a făcut multe presiuni asupra lui Hsu.

O **atitudine** conciliantă

În ultimii ani, Chen a urmat o linie din ce în ce mai conciliantă. Totodată, sprijinul pentru el şi pentru o poziţie fermă în favoarea inde-pendenţei au mai scăzut. În mai 2007, PDP a hotărât ca Frank Hsieh să fie candidatul său pentru alegerile prezidenţiale din 2008, respingân-du-l pe favoritul lui Chen, actualul prim-ministru, Su Tseng Chang. În timp ce Su este adeptul unei atitudini dure faţă de China, Frank Hsieh optează pentru o politică mai blândă. Schimbarea nu pare să fi impresi-onat votanţii, din moment ce candidatul Guomindang, Ma Ying-jeou, continuă să fie preferat în sondaje. Probabil că indiferent care va fi câşti-gătorul, Taiwanul va face tot ce-i stă în putinţă să nu provoace China.

În ciuda acestor evoluţii pozitive, statutul ambiguu al Taiwanului continuă să fie o problemă. Şi, cu toate că pe mulţi taiwanezi nu-i deranjează absolut deloc, el este extrem de periculos. China consideră în continuare Taiwanul ca o parte integrantă a teritoriului său, şi, la nivel internaţional, aceasta este situaţia recunoscută oficial. În plus, chinezii îşi rezervă dreptul de a folosi forţa în cazul în care Taiwanul şi-ar declara independenţa. Pe de altă parte, deşi mulţi taiwanezi au legături strânse cu China, din ce în ce mai mulţi consideră că sunt taiwanezi, nu chinezi. Şi chiar şi cei care sunt prounificare, cum ar fi Guomindang-ul, nu vor accepta apropierea de China, până ce aceasta nu va da suficiente semne că se îndreaptă către democraţie. Ambele părţi sunt puternic înarmate, iar acele arme sunt îndreptate unele spre celelalte deasupra îngustei Strâmtori Taiwan. Nu încape nici o îndo-ială cine va câştiga dacă se va ajunge la un conflict armat. Întrebarea este cât va rezista Taiwanul? Unii spun că o lună, alţii, doar şase minu-te. Va veni oare SUA în ajutorul Taiwanului şi, în caz că o va face, va ajunge la timp? Majoritatea observatorilor speră ca aceste întrebări să nu-şi primească niciodată răspunsul, însă, deşi relaţiile dintre China şi Taiwan sunt, în prezent, mai bune ca niciodată, asta nu înseamnă că situaţia nu se poate schimba peste noapte.

Capitolul 7:

RECITAL
DE HONG KONG

„Se spunea că nimeni nu a făcut vreodată bani pariind împotriva Hong Kongului. A rămas un adevăr până în ziua de azi şi aşa va fi şi în 2017."

Lordul Chris Patten, *The Guardian*, 30 iunie 2007

Pe 1 iulie 2007, populația din Hong Kong a ieşit să se distreze cu ocazia fastuoasei sărbători ce marca a zecea aniversare a predării oraşului de către britanici Chinei, iar lucrurile arătau mult mai bine pentru Hong Kong decât şi-ar fi putut închipui majoritatea celor care asistaseră la înmânarea cheilor oraşului, într-o ploioasă zi din 1997. Economia Hong Kongului este în plin avânt, iar prețurile proprietăților, întotdeauna un semn de prosperitate financiară pentru locuitorii acestuia, sunt mai ridicate ca niciodată.

Pentru ca nivelul de optimism să fie şi mai ridicat (mai ales cel al proprietarilor imobiliari), o ştire interesantă a ajuns la urechile protestatarilor care luau parte la marşul prodemocratic anual, cerând drepturi democratice depline pentru cetățenii din Hong Kong. Aceasta era că, la discursul său aniversar, preşedintele chinez Hu Jintao afirmase că progresul reformelor politice – prin care înțelegea, desigur, progresul democrației – trebuie să fie unul „ordonat şi gradual." Nu a fost precizată nici o dată anume, însă era pentru prima oară când conducerea chineză vorbea explicit despre existența unui proiect de democratizare, chiar şi parțială, a Hong Kongului.

. . . .

Saltul Hong Kongului

La zece ani după ce britanicii au predat oraşul, cel puțin la suprafață, lucrurile par să-i meargă din plin Hong Kongului. În ciuda temerilor potrivit cărora o conducere comunistă chineză ar distruge energia financiară a oraşului, subminându-i libertățile de bază, Hong Kongului pare să-i meargă chiar mai bine decât în cele mai înfloritoare perioade ale dominației coloniale. Într-adevăr, poziția Hong Kongului, aceea de cale de acces între lume şi economia cu cea mai rapidă dezvoltare şi (în curând) cea mai mare de pe glob, se dovedeşte a fi una câştigătoare.

Când Hong Kongul a fost predat Chinei, în 1997, aproape un sfert din comerţul acesteia cu lumea exterioară trecea prin mâinile sale. Această proporţie s-a mai micşorat uşor, dar în termeni absoluţi, s-a mărit enorm, din cauza faptului că economia chineză a crescut atât de repede. Din 1997, comerţul cu China continentală a crescut de patru ori, ajungând la 165 de miliarde de dolari. Într-adevăr, nivelul total al comerţului exterior al Hong Kongului a crescut cu aproape 70% în zece ani, în timp ce PIB-ul a crescut cu 7,5% în 2005 şi cu 6,9% în 2006, ajungând la 254 de miliarde de dolari. Acestea sunt nişte performanţe excelente pentru un oraş care funcţiona deja la un nivel înalt. Într-adevăr, PIB-ul său pe cap de locuitor este al şaselea din lume, ajungând la aproape 40 000 dolari. Nivelul activităţii comerciale din Hong Kong este uriaş. De asemenea, pe lângă faptul că este principalul centru financiar al Asiei, oraşul este, în prezent, al treilea mare centru de transport aerian de mărfuri din lume şi al doilea port de containere, după volumul de mărfuri tranzitate. Mai mulţi turişti ca niciodată (acum, peste 25 de milioane) vin, an de an, la Hong Kong, lasându-se copleşiţi de savoarea străzilor sale aglomerate şi pline de culoare, a peisajelor uimitoare, şi a noului Disneyland.

. . . .

PROFIL: LI KA-SHING

„Nu, nu am fost norocos. Am muncit din greu pentru a reuşi în ceea ce mi-am propus."

Nimeni nu simbolizează mai bine capacitatea Hong Kongului de a-şi îmbogăţi locuitorii, decât Li Ka-shing. Binecunoscuta sa acuitate în afaceri i-a adus o avere de mai multe miliarde de dolari, care-l face cel mai bogat om din China, situându-l pe locul nouă în lume.

Fiu al unui profesor modest din Guangdong, a ajuns în Hong Kong în 1940, la vârsta de 12 ani, fugind de groaznicele lupte interne din China. În Hong Kong, spectacolul umilitor al bogăţiei arogantului său unchi i-a insuflat dorinţa de a deveni la rândul său bogat, pentru a arăta lumii că merită atenţie. La vârsta de 15 ani, când tatăl lui a murit de tuberculoză, a fost obligat să părăsească şcoala pentru a munci într-o fabrică de mase plastice. Însă flerul său antreprenorial, hotărârea de a face lucrurile aşa cum trebuie şi foarte multă muncă i-au permis să-şi depăşească condiţia şi să-şi înfiinţeze propria fabrică de mase plastice, Cheung Kong Industries, la doar 21 de ani.

De la producerea de mase plastice, Li s-a extins la imobiliare, devenind, extrem de repede, un jucător major pe piaţa din Hong Kong. În 1972, Cheung a preluat Hutchinson Wampoa, iar în 1985, Hong Kong Electric Holdings Ltd. În prezent, afacerile lui Li se întind de la activităţile bancare la telefonia mobilă, de la confecţionarea maselor plastice la conducerea de aeroporturi. Hutchinson Wampoa este cel mai mare operator portuar, având 150 000 de angajaţi, răspândiţi pe tot globul. Firma controlează terminalele de la ambele ieşiri ale Canalului Panama, dar şi porturi precum Singapore sau Hong Kong, ceea ce face din Li un personaj incredibil de puternic.

Li a fost unul dintre cei mai mari investitori din noua Chină, având interese de afaceri aproape peste tot în această ţară. Evident că are relaţii până la vârf în Partidul Comunist, fiind, timp de un an, preşedintele CITIC (Corporaţia de Investiţii şi Trustul Internaţional Chinez), organul central de investiţii al guvernului chinez. Relaţiile sale i-au făcut pe americani să se teamă de el şi de influenţa pe care ar putea-o avea, dar acest lucru nu pare să-l deranjeze prea tare. Este un renumit filantrop, cheltuind peste un miliard de dolari pentru diferite acte de binefacere, însă donaţia de 128 de milioane de dolari făcută Academiei de Medicină din Hong Kong a stârnit o adevărată controversă atunci când aceasta a fost rebotezată, în 2006, Facultatea de Medicină Li Ka-shing. Se zvoneşte că, în 1996, când fiul său, Victor Li, a fost răpit de celebrul gangster din Hong Kong, Cheung Chi Keung Li, i-ar fi plătit acestuia o răscumpărare de 128 de milioane de dolari.

Oraşul se vopseşte în roşu

Nimeni nu s-ar fi aşteptat la toate acestea în posomorâta zi de 1 iulie 1997, când Hong Kongul a fost predat de britanici Chinei. Întreaga ceremonie a predării a fost încărcată cu tensiune. Procesul începuse din 1984, când primu-ministrul britanic Margaret Thatcher semnase acordul prin care accepta să predea Hong Kongul Chinei în anul în care expira concesiunea britanică, în 1997. Bineînţeles că englezii au semnat înţelegerea fără a se deranja să-i consulte pe locuitorii Hong Kongului, însă, potrivit formulei lui Deng Xiaoping „o ţară, două sisteme", acestora le-a fost garantată menţinerea structurilor econo-

mice şi politice fundamentale ale oraşului, inclusiv a tribunalelor independente şi a libertăţii de exprimare, printr-o lege numită Legea
Fundamentală. Masacrul din 1989, din Piaţa Tiananmen, a fost un
mare şoc pentru locuitorii Hong Kongului. Oare acesta era regimul
cărora le erau predaţi? O jumătate de milion de oameni au luat atunci
cu asalt străzile oraşului, protestând împotriva evenimentului. Înainte
de masacru, au trimis bani, medicamente şi mesaje de simpatie studenţilor din piaţă. După aceea, s-au prezentat cu sutele ca să doneze
sânge şi şi-au retras toate economiile din băncile de pe continent.

Republica Populară Chineză a respins reacţia Hong Kongului, considerând-o drept confirmare a faptului că drepturile omului nu erau
altceva decât o conspiraţie a Occidentului menită a îndepărta de la
putere conducerea comunistă. Cu toate acestea, englezii au fost nevoiţi să admită că s-ar putea să fi făcut o greşeală neacordând locuitorilor oraşului dreptul de a avea un cuvânt de spus în propria guvernare.
În mod surprinzător, Hong Kongul era singurul dominion britanic
în care nu exista nici o urmă de democraţie. Nesăbuiţi, englezii au
crezut că locuitorii din Hong Kong nu-şi doreau altceva decât să facă
bani; protestele în sprijinul studenţilor din Piaţa Tienanmen le-au
dovedit contrariul. Problema lor era cum să introducă democraţia
în Hong Kong fără a deranja Beijingul. Într-un articol din 1992,
din ziarul *Guardian*, John Gittings cita un personaj important din
ministerul de externe al cărui comentariu redă perfect atitudinea autorităţilor britanice în această problemă: „Toate aceste discuţii despre
reforma politică sunt minunate, însă, cât mai avem până în 1997?
Dacă de-abia v-aţi vândut casa, nu vă apucaţi s-o redecoraţi de sus
până jos într-o culoare pe care noul proprietar nu o agrează!"

Model pentru **democraţie**

Prim-ministrul britanic John Major s-a săturat de lipsa de acţiune
a înalţilor funcţionari din Ministerul de Externe şi, în 1992, l-a
numit pe mult mai activul Chris Patten în postul de guvernator
al Hong Kongului. Imediat ce a preluat funcţia, Patten a ţinut să

facă evident faptul că lucrurile aveau să se schimbe şi, folosindu-se de o scăpare legislativă, a accelerat eforturile de trecere la democraţie, a cărei posibilitate era doar schiţată în Legea Fundamentală. Locuitorii Hong Kongului au fost încântaţi, însă Beijingul era de-a dreptul furibund, dat fiind că planul lui Patten însemna că, în 1997, când trebuia să preia oraşul, acesta ar fi avut, practic, un guvern democratic funcţional.

Pe măsură ce Patten îşi continua planurile de democratizare, interesele de afaceri britanice erau periclitate. A-i supăra pe chinezi ar fi putut însemna să-şi ia adio de la ademenitoarele perspective ale unei pieţe chineze pe zi ce trece mai mari. Politicienii cu relaţii în lumea oamenilor de afaceri, cum erau lordul Young şi lordul Prior, au început să facă presiuni asupra lui Patten, pentru ca acesta să-şi mai strunească demersurile. În biografia sa despre Patten, Jonathan Dimbleby îl citează pe lordul Young: „Cred că unii dintre noi au văzut că oportunităţile din China erau de-a dreptul fabuloase. Că am fi putut să ne întoarcem şi să pretindem pieţele care ne-au aparţinut de-a lungul secolului trecut." Însă, Patten era hotărât să continue, în ciuda oricărei opoziţii. Evenimentele şi-au atins maximul de intensitate în 1995, atunci când Michael Heseltine, care era ministru de externe la acea dată, a condus o delegaţie comercială la Beijing, revenind cu comenzi de 1,6 miliarde de dolari şi promisiunea altor 8 miliarde de dolari – cu singura condiţie, i s-a spus, ca problema Hong Kongului să fie rezolvată într-o manieră mai acceptabilă pentru chinezi.

Cum presiunile asupra lui Patten au crescut, acesta le-a dat colegilor săi de cabinet un celebru ultimatum: „sprijiniţi-mă, sau daţi-mă afară." Atitudinea se pare că i-a înduplecat, pentru că Patten a primit undă verde să-şi continue reformele, creând, însă, şi o serie de animozităţi în rândurile conservatorilor. Patten plănuia să manipuleze Legea Fundamentală pentru a creşte numărul membrilor Consiliului Legislativ, for ales direct de populaţia din Hong Kong. Cu toate că autorităţile chineze au obiectat în faţa acestei propuneri, englezii au mers mai departe, organizând alegerile din 1995 potrivit acestui plan. Consiliul s-a dovedit a avea o viaţă foarte scurtă şi a stârnit multe nemulţumiri printre chinezi, aceştia privindu-i pe britanici ca pe nişte intriganţi ipocriţi, care încearcă să introducă democraţia în ultimul minut, după ce, timp de 150, au condus Hong Kongul fără să aibă nevoie de ea. Unii au respins iniţiativa lui Patten ca nefiind nimic altceva decât un gest provocator, care a şi eşuat, doi ani mai târziu, când chinezii au abandonat ideea consiliului lărgit. Alţii o considerau un gest esenţial, care a oferit unor oameni speriaţi de cele petrecute în Piaţa Tienanmen şi îngrijoraţi de viitorul lor sub conducerea Chinei, posibilitatea să vadă, chiar şi pentru scurt timp, ce înseamnă democraţia.

· ·

Preluarea chineză

Pe 30 iunie 1997, la miezul nopţii, a avut loc predarea oficială a Hong Kongului Chinei. Chris Patten a amintit faptul că Marea Britanie a dat Hong Kongului „domnia legii, un guvern curat şi eficient, valorile unei societăţi libere" şi, totodată, începutul unui guvernări reprezentative. Prinţul Charles, prezent, la rândul său, la eveniment, îl numea în jurnalul său, „Marea preluare chineză", descriind soldaţii ce mărşăluiau în pas de paradă şi „groaznicele figuri de ceară" ale liderilor chinezi. Orice ar fi crezut cei doi, chinezii s-au instalat foarte repede în Hong Kong, trimiţând Armata de Eliberare a Poporului exact la miezul nopţii şi declarând ilegitimă Adunarea Legislativă aleasă în 1995. Şeful executivului din Hong Kong urma să fie ales de o adunare formată din 800 de delegaţi stabiliţi de Beijing. Totuşi, în afara acestui element, chinezii păreau dispuşi, cel puţin iniţial, să lase lucrurile aşa cum erau. Până la urmă, Hong Kongul era o scenă publică pentru China şi, totodată, o valoroasă sursă de finanţare. Soldaţii au rămas în cazarmă, iar liderii de partid la Beijing. Viaţa în Hong Kong părea să se desfăşoare aproape la fel ca înainte, cu excepţia faptului că în şcoli, copiilor li se preda în chineză şi nu în engleză.

· ·

A **doua zi** de dimineață

Cu toate acestea, luna de miere a Hong Kongului a fost de scurtă durată. La momentul predării, Asia era într-o profundă criză financiară. A doua zi după predare, Thailanda a rămas fără rezerve de valută. Imediat, investitorii au început să-și retragă banii din țările asiatice. Indonezia, Malayzia și Coreea de Sud au fost primele care au căzut, iar Taiwanul, Filipinele, Singapore și Hong Kongul au fost în curând prinse în vârtej. Prețurile proprietăților din Hong Kong s-au prăbușit, mulți locuitori din clasa de mijloc trezindu-se într-o dezastruoasă situație cu capital propriu negativ. Părea că balonul financiar al Hong Kongului explodase dintr-odată. Și lucrurile avea să fie și mai grave.

În ianuarie 1999, potrivit deciziei Curții de Apel din Hong Kong, copiii din China aveau dreptul să locuiască în Hong Kong dacă unul dintre părinți era cetățean al orașului. Administrația din Hong Kong se temea de o migrație masivă a chinezilor din Guangdong, astfel încât a cerut Beijingului să „reinterpreteze" legea respectivă. Beijingul a făcut cât se poate de clar faptul că se aștepta ca guvernul din Hong Kong să ordone tribunalelor să schimbe legislația – aparent fără să-și dea seama că justiția din Hong Kong era, în principiu, una independentă. Multe familii au fost despărțite prin această hotărâre, populația Hong Kongului începând să manifeste o ostilitate clară față de guvernatorul local – Tung Chee-haw, un fost magnat al transporturilor maritime. Hotărât să nu se lase influențat de capriciile locuitorilor din Hong Kong, Beijingul l-a desemnat pe Tung pentru un al doilea mandat în 2002. Întrebat de un jurnalist din Hong Kong dacă Tung era „alegerea împăratului", președintele chinez Jiang Zemin și-a pierdut cumpătul și a transmis presei să nu fie atât de „naivă". Tung a fost ales, potrivit ordinului, dar a descoperit că era asediat din toate părțile.

. . . .

Legaţi de Tung

În primul rând, opinia publică considera că Tung a gestionat extrem de prost criza provocată de SARS (virusul gripei aviare), încercând să minimalizeze problema. Apoi a stârnit mânia locuitorilor din Hong Kong prin încercarea de a introduce o nouă lege a securităţii, denumită Articolul 23. Articolul 23 a fost ultima picătură, jumătate de milion de oameni ieşind în stradă să protesteze pe 1 iulie 2003, cu ocazia celei de-a şasea aniversări a predării oraşului, şi, din nou, un an mai târziu. Surprinzător pentru unii, Beijingul a decis să adopte o atitudine mai blândă. Nu numai că a slăbit restricţiile impuse călătoriilor din şi către marile oraşe Guangzhou, Shanghai şi Beijing, dar, în 2005, l-a şi înlocuit pe Tung cu o veche cunoştinţă colonială, Donald Tsang.

....

SARS

Poziţia Hong Kongului în China este definită legal cu titulatura de Regiune Specială Autonomă (SAR – acronim în lb.eng.), astfel că virusul SARS părea, din nefericire, să i se potrivească ca o mănuşă. Criza declanşată datorită virusului SARS a început în februarie 2003. În timp ce din Guangdong veneau tot felul de zvonuri cu privire la decesele provocate de gripa aviară, la hotelul Metropol din Hong Kong, tocmai se instala un doctor venit de pe continent. Se pare că acesta avea deja virusul, reuşind să-l transmită altor şaisprezece oameni ce locuiau la acelaşi etaj al hotelului. Printre cei infestaţi se aflau şi câţiva membri ai unor companii aeriene şi, în numai câteva zile, infecţia se răspândea în jurul lumii, cazuri grave apărând la distanţe uriaşe unele de altele, în Toronto, Frankfurt sau Hanoi.

Doctorii se temeau că acesta era începutul unei pandemii mondiale de gripă aviară, o atmosferă de frică vecină cu panica cuprinzând întreaga lume, ceea ce a transformat Hong Kongul într-un oraş interzis – toate călătoriile spre oraş au fost anulate, iar cei care puteau pleca au făcut-o. Organizaţia Mondială a Sănătăţii a emis comunicate prin care oamenii erau sfătuiţi să-şi anuleze toate călătoriile spre China, unde se credea că s-a declanşat infecţia. Chinezii, care se străduiseră să muşamalizeze totul, au lansat o uriaşă campanie de igienă în Guangdong. Potrivit rapoartelor, un număr uimitor de mare de oameni, 80 de milioane, au fost mobilizaţi pentru dezinfectarea străzilor şi a locuinţelor. Aceste măsuri draconice păreau să dea rezultate, infecţia din China părând să fie sub control.

Şi în alte părţi, eforturile de a stopa epidemia au început să-şi facă efectul, iar până în iunie 2003 aceasta părea să se fi stins. Până acum, infec-ţia fusese denumită Sindrom Respirator Acut Sever (SRAS – lb. rom., SARS – lb.eng.), după teribilele simptome pe care le provoca, dar s-a descoperit că nu fusese gripă aviară, ci un coronavirus, unul dintre viruşii care provoacă răceala. S-a stabilit că primii purtători ai virusului au fost, într-adevăr, animalele din Guangdong, precum zibeta asiatică şi dihorul domestic, folosite în medicina tradiţională chineză, în mod ironic, chiar pentru tratarea răcelilor. Hong Kongul a fost declarat, în sfârşit, în afara oricărui pericol, însă întregul episod a reprezentat o serioasă lovitură pentru moralul fostei colonii.

Donald Tsang a rămas în funcţie până la sfârşitul mandatului lui Tung şi a fost reales pentru un nou mandat de 5 ani, în 2007. Deşi era clar că Tsang va câştiga, pentru că Beijingul controla comisia electorală ai cărei 800 de membri aveau să îl aleagă, locuitorii Hong Kongului simţeau că iau şi ei parte la acest proces. Dezbaterea tele-vizată dintre Tsang şi avocatul democrat Alain Leong a avut cea mai mare audienţă din istoria Hong Kongului. Sondajele relevă faptul că 80% din locuitorii oraşului sunt satisfăcuţi de Tsang.

. . . .

Revirimentul oraşului

După momentul său nefast din 2003, Hong Kongul pare să-şi fi revenit. Beijingul considera că dacă oraşul ar ajunge din nou să pros-pere, nemulţumirea legată de situaţia politică ar putea fi disipată. Astfel încât, nu doar că a anunţat construirea unui pod de 2 miliarde de dolari şi a unui tunel care urma să lege Hong Kongul de delta Râului Perlelor, ci a pus şi bazele unei înţelegeri comerciale prin care firmelor din oraş le era acordat acces preferenţial pe continent. Era ca şi cum afaceriştii din Hong Kong ar fi obţinut un permis de in-trare la cel mai mare spectacol din oraş. Hong Kongul era deja unul dintre investorii principali din China, dar această favoare punea cu-adevărat lucrurile în mişcare.

În 2005, Hong Kongul investise mai mult de 240 de miliarde de do-lari în companiile de pe continent şi avea 12 milioane de angajaţi în China, cei mai mulţi în delta Râului Perlelor. Acest acces privilegiat la economia cu cea mai rapidă dezvoltare din lume a permis lumii să capete din nou încredere în Hong Kong. În 2004, produsul intern brut al oraşului a crescut, dintr-o dată, cu peste 8%. De la mijlocul anului 2004 până la jumătatea lui 2005, indicele bursei Hang Sheng din Hong Kong, a crescut cu 22%. Şomajul, care atinsese aproape 9% în 2003, a scăzut, în numai doi ani, la doar 5%. Şi preţuri-le proprietăţilor au început să crească. Acum, aproape nimeni din Hong Hong nu se găsea în situaţia de a avea capital propriu negativ, principala temere fiind că începătorii vor fi eliminaţi de pe piaţă de preţurile concurenţei. De fapt, între toamna lui 2003 şi toamna lui 2006, preţurile proprietăţilor din centrul oraşului au crescut cu 290%, ceea ce făcea din Hong Kong, oraşul cu cele mai scumpe proprietăţi centrale din lume.

Astăzi, viitorul pare mult mai luminos decât şi-ar fi putut cineva închipui în 1997, cu toate că unele zone sunt încă în umbră. În primul rând, este vorba de problema democraţiei. China a promis că se va ajunge şi la ea, dar nu a spus când. Teama că Beijingul ar putea, în orice moment, limita libertatea economică a Hong Kongului, continuă să persiste. În cel mai rău caz, criticii se tem că ar putea exista un alt episod Tiananmen, Hong Kongul nemaiputând primi, acum, sprijin internaţional. Hong Kongul se bucură, însă, de libertatea cuvântului, de tribunale independente, de o bună structură de menţinere a ordinii publice şi o administraţie eficien-tă – într-adevăr, toate cele necesare unei guvernări democratice cu excepţia votului. Iar atâta timp cât lucrurile merg bine, majoritatea locuitorilor de rând ai oraşului nu se arată chiar atât de nerăbdători să-l obţină. Donald Tsang susţine că o democratizare prea rapidă ar putea provoca un haos similar celui adus de *perestroika* în Rusia, şi mulţi sunt de acord cu el.

. . . .

Hong Kong sau China?

Între Hong Kong şi China continentală există şi alte probleme, mai puţin tangibile. Cum este, spre exemplu, cea a identităţii. Spiritul antreprenorial entuziast din Hong Kong nu pare a fi deloc compatibil cu sobrietatea şi autoritarismul guvernului de la Beijing. Astfel încât, întrebarea este: oare Beijingul va trage Hong Kongul în jos, sau acesta va reuşi să schimbe China? Locuitorii mai vârstnici ai oraşului se consideră mai întâi cetăţeni ai Hong Kongului, şi de-abia apoi, ai Chinei, fiind hotărâţi să nu renunţe la sălbatica lor independenţă. În iunie 2007, revista *Time* îl cita pe Yan Xuetong, de la Universitatea Tsinghua din Beijing: „Reîntoarcerea Hong Kongului la China s-a realizat doar pe jumătate. Hong Kongul este acel loc aparte din China care continuă să fie privit ca o ţară străină. Hong Kongul s-a întors cu numele, dar nu şi în realitate."

Interesant, totuşi, acest lucru s-ar putea schimba mai repede şi mai uşor decât şi-ar fi putut imagina cineva. În prezent, tânăra generaţie de locuitori ai Hong Kongului creşte cunoscând doar regulile chineze şi învăţând după programa impusă de Beijing. Mulţi dintre aceşti copii sunt chiar mândri că sunt chinezi, aşteptând să-şi primească valorile din partea Chinei şi nu a Occidentului, aşa cum făcuseră părinţii lor. Ei sunt mai mult decât dispuşi să se considere atât chinezi, cât şi locuitori ai Hong Kongului. Şi într-adevăr, majoritatea vorbesc doar chineză, mai degrabă decât engleză, iar în opinia generaţiilor mai vârstnice, aceasta ar putea constitui o problemă în viitor. Succesul afacerilor din Hong Kong, argumentează ei, depinde de abilitatea de a acţiona ca o poartă spre lumea din afara Chinei dar, în special, de fluenţa englezei vorbite în cadrul comunităţii de afaceri a oraşului. Dacă cei din Hong Kong îşi pierd engleza, oraşul şi-ar putea pierde atuul în afaceri. Mai rău, se îngrijorează aceştia, copiii învaţă cantoneza, nu mandarina, aşa că ar putea avea parte de cele mai rele lucruri din ambele lumi, nefiind capabili să comunice fluent nici în limba engleză, care ar putea fi folosită în toată lumea, nici în mandarină, care le-ar fi utilă pe continent. Deloc surprinzător, locurile din şcolile private internaţionale, unde se predă în engleză, sunt la mare căutare. Însă, chiar dacă copiii familiilor înstărite vor privi spre vechea putere colonială, viitorul Hong Kong-ului este chinez.

Capitolul 8:
CHINA ȘI JAPONIA

„O veche zicală japoneză spune: Muntele nu se clinteşte, oricât ar bate vântul. Relaţiile dintre ţările noastre au trecut prin furtuni şi vijelii, dar fundaţia prieteniei nostre este de nezdruncinat, precum muntele Tai şi muntele Fuji."

Premierul chinez Wen Jiabao, adresându-se parlamentului japonez, 12.04.2007

În aprilie 2007, premierul Wen Jiabao a efectuat o remarcabilă vizită în Japonia, calificată de organele oficiale de presă drept un "dezgheţ". A fost prima vizită efectuată de un lider chinez în Japonia în ultimii 7 ani, petre-cându-se la mai puţin de 18 luni după cel mai tensionat moment al rela-ţiilor sino-nipone din ultimele câteva decenii. Pe parcursul acesteia, Wen s-a lansat într-o campanie de câştigare a simpatiei, jucând baseball, luând parte la o sesiune de *tai-chi* şi plantând un răsad de roşie alături de un ţăran japonez. În timp ce-şi făcea alergarea de dimineaţă în parcul Yoyogi din Tokyo, s-a oprit să dea mâna cu un alt alergător, căruia i-a spus că, dacă va veni vreodată în Beijing, va fi primit cu braţele deschise. În Osaka, a avut o întâlnire neprotocolară cu diverşi reprezentanţi ai comunităţii de afaceri şi politicieni, la care a recitat un poem în care îşi rezuma vizita: "A venit primăvara. Soarele străluceşte cu putere. Cireşul a înmugurit mândru, iar zăpada şi gheaţa s-au topit."

Totuşi, punctul culminant al vizitei lui Wen a fost cel în care s-a adresat parlamentului japonez, prima oară când un lider chinez a făcut acest lucru. Tonul lui a fost direct, dar remarcabil de concili-ant. Vorbind despre problema atrocităţilor uriaşe comise de japonezi în China, în 1937, el a declarat: „Invaziile japoneze au provocat pagube uriaşe Chinei. Rănile adânci rămase în inimile chinezilor nu pot fi redate în cuvinte." Cu toate acestea, a continuat într-o tur-nură fără precedent, învinuind o elită extremistă pentru agresiunea japoneză şi admiţând că şi japonezii au avut partea lor de suferinţe. Un răspuns pe măsură la gestul conciliatoriu reprezentat de vizita efectuată de Shinzo Abe în China, în octombrie 2006, la doar două săptămâni după alegerea sa ca premier al Japoniei.

Rănile **istoriei**

Problemele actuale dintre China şi Japonia datează din timpul războiului sino-japonez din 1894-95, în care Japonia a reuşit să iasă din umbra Chinei, provocându-i vecinei sale o înfrângere umilitoare şi anunţându-şi prin aceasta ieşirea pe scena lumii ca putere mondială. Prin acordurile de pace care au urmat, Japoniei i-a revenit Formosa (cunoscută acum ca Taiwan), un act care încă stârneşte amintiri dureroase, cu toate că Formosa a fost retrocedată imediat după înfrângerea japonezilor, la sfârşitul celui de-al Doilea Război Mondial.

Gustul cel mai amar l-a lăsat, însă, invadarea Chinei de Nord de către Japonia, în 1931. După ce, timp de şase ani de zile, şi-au consolidat puterea în nord, forţele japoneze au pornit către sud, capturând oraşul Nanjing, capitala regimului naţionalist al lui Chiang Kai-shek. Cele întâmplate în continuare rămân un subiect de aprigă dispută între China şi Japonia, cel puţin la nivel oficial, însă, cea mai probabilă versiune a faptelor este aceea potrivit căreia soldaţii japonezi au pornit o campanie sistematică de măcelărire, violuri şi jaf, în care peste un sfert de milion de civili au fost ucişi şi aproape douăzeci de mii de femei au fost violate. Pentru ca situaţia să fie şi mai gravă, zeci de mii de chinezoaice au fost transformate într-un adevărat „sistem de recreere" al soldaţilor japonezi. Chinezii susţin că acest lucru nu însemna nimic altceva decât că erau obligate să fie sclave sexuale. Poziţia oficială a lui Shinzo Abe a fost că nu există dovezi în acest sens, dar la scurt timp după vizita lui Wen Jiabao în Japonia, un grup alcătuit din academicieni japonezi de renume a demonstrat că existau dovezi cât se poate de veridice ale faptului că femeile din China fuseseră obligate să se prostitueze.

În timpul ocupaţiei lor în China, japonezii au testat diverse tipuri de arme biologice şi chimice, adesea pe prizonieri de război şi civili. Când s-au retras definitiv, în 1945, se crede că au lăsat aproape trei sferturi de milion de arme chimice împrăştiate prin China.

Rivali economici

După cel de-al Doilea Război Mondial, în ciuda faptului că a fost
învinsă, Japonia şi-a revenit, devenind cea mai importantă putere
economică din Asia, în timp ce China, deşi fusese de partea învingă-
torilor, a lâncezit multă vreme în umbra ei. În prezent, însă, China
ajunge cu repeziciune Japonia din urmă, cele două ţări urmând, în
curând, să fie a doua şi a treia economie din lume.

Din anumite puncte de vedere, acest lucru este benefic pentru
Japonia, din moment ce China a luat locul Americii, devenind cea
mai mare piaţă de desfacere a Japoniei şi cel mai mare furnizor al său
de produse manufacturate. Ambele ţări sunt, însă, mari consuma-
toare de resurse energetice. În ciuda economiilor lor gigant, ele au
foarte puţin petrol propriu şi, în curând, vor intra în conflict pentru
rezervele de petrol. A existat, deja, o neînţelegere în ceea ce priveşte
petrolul iranian. Iar în 2004, au existat dispute asupra traseului unei
conducte care aducea petrol din Siberia, întrebarea fiind dacă aceasta ar trebui să se termine în zona de coastă a Japoniei sau să ajungă
până în China. Japonia a câştigat.

Adevăratul punct nevralgic îl constituie, însă, câmpurile petrolifere şi
cele de gaze din Marea Chinei de Est, un teritoriu aflat încă în dispută,
pentru care, în primii ani ai acestui secol, cele două ţări au început să
se certe ca doi elevi neastâmpăraţi. În 2004, un submarin chinez s-a
aventurat „din întâmplare" în apele teritoriale japoneze de lângă insulele
Sakishima, din apropierea Okinawei. Apoi, în februarie 2005, Japonia a
luat în posesie disputatele Insule Diaoyu (cunoscute ca insulele Senkaku
în Japonia), ceea ce le va da controlul asupra unora dintre cele mai mari
câmpuri petrolifere. Câteva săptămâni mai târziu, chinezii au avertizat Japonia să se retragă sau să „îşi asume întreaga responsabilitate"
pentru orice fel de consecinţe. Japonia a făcut planuri pentru a trimite
55 000 de soldaţi în insulele Diaoyu în cazul unei debarcări chineze în
zonă. În timpul confruntării dintre cele două ţări, China a trimis 5 nave,
printre care şi un distrugător înarmat cu rachete teleghidate, spre un alt
teritoriu disputat, câmpul gazifer Chunxiao. În cele din urmă, ambele
părţi şi-au retras forţele, dar tensiunea a continuat să fie mare.

Să nu vorbim despre **război**

Cu toate acestea, în spatele acestei rivalități politice și militare se află tot chestiunea amară a trecutului război. Japonia crede că a ispășit destul pentru distrugerile provocate. A plătit reparații de război substanțiale Chinei și a asigurat o mare parte din investițiile-cheie care au dat startul economiei chineze. De asemenea, a adresat 17 scrisori oficiale de scuze.

Pentru China, însă, nici una dintre aceste acțiuni nu este suficientă. Japonezii nu și-au cerut scuze niciodată pentru masacrul de la Nanjing, iar naționaliștii lor neagă că femeile chineze ar fi fost vreodată sclave sexuale. Pentru a pune sare pe rană, cred chinezii, premierii japonezi și-au făcut un obicei din a vizita frecvent monumentul de la Yasukuni, care preamărește trecutul militar al Japoniei, comemorând, pe lângă o jumătate de milion de soldați obișnuiți, și 1 000 de criminali de război (dintre care 14, executați pentru crime de război după încheierea păcii de tribunalele aliate).

Fără îndoială, China suflă în ceafa Japoniei ca putere economică dominantă în Asia, însă Japonia dorește să se impună ca putere mondială. Constituția Japoniei, concepută de americani la sfârșitul celui de-al Doilea Război Mondial, interzice în mod expres Japoniei să poarte război și-i permite să aibă doar forțe defensive. Pentru naționaliștii japonezi, constituția a lăsat Japonia „castrată". În opinia acestora, țara și-a ispășit sentința și este pregătită să devină. din nou. o putere militară. Japonia caută să obțină un loc în Consiliul de Securitate al ONU, la fel ca și China – idee pe care chinezii o resping cu hotărâre.

. . . .

Cum se predă **istoria**

În 2004 și 2005, aceste presiuni au început să capete formă deținută. Prim-ministrul japonez, Junichiro Koizumi, a reinterpretat constituția pentru a permite trupelor japoneze să se alăture americanilor în Irak. În acelaşi timp, media conservatoare din Japonia a început o campanie pentru revizuirea constituţiei, publicând, în paralel, o serie de articole în care demoniza puterea militară a Chinei.

În preajma celei de-a şaizecea aniversări a masacrului de la Nanjing, acesta a devenit centrul atenţiei, cele două ţări pornind un adevărat război mediatic asupra acestei probleme. În China, sala memorialului Nanjing a beneficiat de o cosmetizare costisitoare, iar la televiziunea publică au început să fie difuzate o serie întreagă de programe în care se vorbea despre rezistenţa Chinei în faţa Imperiului Japonez. Oraşul Eroilor, spre exemplu, povestea cum oraşele din China „au luptat cu vitejie împotriva Japoniei, sub comanda partidului comunist."

Între timp, în Japonia se făceau eforturi pentru a controla felul în care tinerii priveau acest eveniment. Un serial de desene animate despre invazia japoneză, numit *Ţara arde*, pe parcursul căruia erau prezentate imagini cu cadavre chineze, a fost retras rapid, în urma protestelor politicienilor. Apoi, 291 de profesori din Tokyo au fost concediaţi pentru că nu au luat poziţie de drepţi în timpul imnului naţional cântat la ceremoniile şcolare.

Cea mai supărătoare pentru chinezi a fost, însă, o serie de manuale apărute în şcolile japoneze. Cărţile erau distribuite de editura naţionalistă Fushosha şi minimalizau atrocităţile comise de japonezi în China, descriind masacrul de la Nanjing doar ca un simplu „incident" şi omiţând să menţioneze numărul victimelor chineze. Manualele erau, de fapt, o reeditare a celor publicate în 2001, dar apoi retrase, după ce guvernul japonez ceruse schimbări ca răspuns la protestele Chinei şi ale altor ţări asiatice afectate de invaziile japoneze. Schimbările cerute fuseseră făcute, dar nu au fost de ajuns pentru chinezi. Când ştirea despre reeditarea acestora a ajuns la Beijing, mii de chinezi au ieşit în stradă pentru a protesta, Ambasada Japoniei din Beijing a fost atacată cu pietre şi 25 de milioane de oameni au semnat o petiţie împotriva cererii Japoniei de aderare la Consiliul de securitate al ONU. Unii cred că Partidul Comunist a orchestrat aceste proteste, însă, nu există nici o îndoială că invazia japoneză rămâne o problemă amară pentru China, cel puţin pentru generaţia mai în vârstă.

. . . .

Să stăm de **vorbă**

În timp ce tensiunile erau încă mari între cele două țări, preşedintele chinez Hu Jintao şi premierul japonez, Junichiro Koizumi, s-au întâlnit în aprilie 2005, la Djakarta, la summitul Africa – Asia. Africa trebuia să fie în centrul discuțiilor, dar subiectul războiului a dominat atmosfera. Hu şi Koizumi s-au întâlnit în particular, iar Koizumi şi-a încă o dată scuze pentru rolul Japoniei în război. „Japonia, prin maniera sa colonială şi agresivă de conducere," a admis Koizumi, „a provocat multe suferințe." Nu a mers atât de departe pe cât şi-ar fi dorit chinezii, dar tensiunile au început să scadă, cele două țări acceptând să se întâlnească pentru a discuta problema câmpurilor de petrol şi gaze.

Divergențele dintre cele două părți în problema câmpurilor petrolifere şi gazifere, s-au dovedit a fi greu de soluționat, iar la începutul lui 2006, discuțiile s-au împotmolit. Japonezii l-au invitat pe Hu Jintao în Japonia pentru discuții, însă acesta a refuzat, iar Koizumi continua să facă vizite regulate la monumentul Yasukuni. Cu toate acestea, în vara anului 2006, Hu a dat de înțeles că ar putea să vină dacă „condițiile se îmbunătățeau". Deşi nu a fost decât o deschidere extrem de timidă, atunci când Shinzo Abe l-a înlocuit pe Koizumi în postul de premier, a profitat de ea, călătorind la Beijing şi invitându-şi omologul, Wen Jiabao, să viziteze Tokyo. Abe făcuse parte din guvernul lui Koizumi şi, asemenea lui, vizita monumentul, dar atâta timp cât nu o făcuse ca premier, Wen, probabil mai lipsit de prejudecăți decât preşedintele Hu, putea merge în Japonia fără a-şi pierde onoarea.

. . . .

Relații înfloritoare

Interesant este faptul că partea chineză le-a transmis japonezilor că singura perioadă în care Wen le putea vizita țara era în luna aprilie. Acesta nu este doar cel mai prielnic moment pentru a admira cireşii în floare, ci şi perioada favorită de vizitare a monumentului Yasukuni. Abe nu ar fi putut merge la monument decât dacă şi-ar fi dorit să-i insulte cu-adevărat pe chinezi şi, bineînţeles, nu a făcut-o. Un alt moment propice pentru vizitarea monumentului era în august, exact în timpul vizitei programate a ministrului chinez al apărării. Iar când cele două ţări au fost de acord cu o vizită a preşedintelui chinez Hu, în 2008, singura dată liberă în calendarul ocupat al acestuia era aprilie.

Vizita lui Wen, din aprilie 2007, ar fi putut fi un moment de răscruce pentru relaţiile sino-nipone. Discursul lui Wen a plăcut parlamentarilor japonezi, iar farmecul lui ofensiv a câştigat inimile multor japonezi. Ca un rezultat direct al vizitei, China şi Japonia au pus bazele unui plan de cooperare economică la nivel înalt, semnând chiar un acord comun de încetinire a încălzirii globale care să intre în vigoare după sfârşitul acordului de la Kyoto, în 2012. Japonezii au fost invitaţi să contribuie cu *know-how* (şi investiţii) în diverse proiecte de mediu, iar firmelor japoneze li s-a oferit posibilitatea de a participa la licitaţiile pentru construirea unor centrale nucleare şi a unor linii de cale ferată de mare viteză, cum ar fi cea dintre Beijing şi Shanghai. Şi mai important, China a fost de acord cu propunerea japonezilor ca zăcămintele de petrol şi gaze să fie exploatate împreună de ambele ţări. La prima vedere, singurul lucru care mai rămânea de stabilit era care dintre câmpuri să fie exploatat primul.

Ca şi cum toate acestea nu erau de ajuns, cele două ţări au tatonat posibilitatea înfiinţării unor linii de comunicare directă între ele, pentru a coordona misiunile de căutare şi salvare din Marea Japoniei, care le desparte, şi a unor legături de comunicaţii între marinele lor, pentru a se evita accidentele dintre vasele acestora. Există chiar posibilitatea ca marina chineză să fie invitată într-o vizită de prietenie la Tokyo. Între timp, guvernul chinez a început să restricţioneze site-urile de Internet antijaponeze, lansând un program de schimburi interacademice pentru studenţii chinezi şi japonezi.

În ciuda acestei manifestări bruşte de simpatie, neînţelegerile dintre cele două ţări sunt departe de a fi rezolvate. În China, spre exemplu, refuzul lui Abe de a recunoaşte că tinerele asiatice au fost sclave sexuale în „sistemul de recreere" japonez din anii '30, continuă să provoace nemulțumire. În Japonia, știrile despre faptul că țara vecină a început deja să foreze pentru petrol în câmpul de la Chunxiao, înaintea termenului stabilit în acord, este pe cale de a stârni tensiuni. În plus, reputațiile politice ale lui Abe și Wen sunt în joc. Dacă Abe mai face o vizită la monumentul de la Yasukuni, imaginea lui Wen ar avea de suferit. Însă, Abe ar putea fi supus, la rândul său, presiunilor venite din partea naționaliștilor din guvernul său, cerându-i să nu se ploconească în fața chinezilor. Cu toate astea, din moment ce o nouă generație de chinezi crește urmărind vedetele japoneze la televizor, citind benzile desenate nipone și aflând despre război doar din cărțile de istorie, tensiunea dintre cele două națiuni ar putea începe să scadă din intensitate, indiferent de ceea ce fac sau spun politicienii. Un curent de gândire susține că americanii au cultivat prietenia cu Japonia ca un stat tampon împotriva ascensiunii Chinei, în special în relația acesteia din urmă cu Taiwanul. Dacă Japonia și China sfârșesc prin a deveni prietene, SUA s-ar putea confrunta cu o problemă cu totul diferită.

. . . .

Capitolul 9:
CHINA OLIMPICĂ

„Construim un nou Beijing – Fiţi bineveniţi la Olimpiadă!"
Afiş în Beijing

În martie 2007, locuitorii din Beijing au învăţat un nou cuvânt: **mai**. Unele ziare din Beijing, dornice să fie de ajutor populaţiei, au publicat şi transcrieri fonetice, pentru a se asigura că locuitorii din Beijing vor şti cum să-l pronunţe. **Mai** înseamnă *smog* şi a fost cuvântul pe care oficialii oraşului au dorit să-l folosească pentru a descrie murdara ceaţă cenuşie care adastă deasupra Beijingului, în cea mai mare parte a anului, unul dintre cele mai poluate oraşe din lume. În trecut, oficialii se referiseră doar eufemistic la acest fenomen, numindu-l **Wu**, un termen mai blând, care înseamnă ceaţă, ca şi cum a-i da un nume mai delicat ar fi făcut ca efectele sale să fie mai puţin grave, distrăgând atenţia de la adevăratele sale cauze – fumul eliberat în atmosferă de fabricile din Beijing, praful stârnit de cele opt mii de şantiere ale oraşului şi gazele de eşapament emise de numărul din ce în ce mai mare de automobile de pe străzile sale. A recunoaşte că **wu** este, de fapt, **mai**, arată cât de mult îşi doreşte China să facă o impresie bună la Jocurile Olimpice din 2008.

Desemnarea sa, în 2001, ca ţară organizatoare a Olimpiadei a fost un eveniment istoric pentru China. Atunci când Comitetul Olimpic Internaţional (COI) a anunţat Beijingul că a fost preferat în faţa unor oraşe precum Toronto, Paris, Istanbul sau Osaka, străzile din Beijing au fost cuprinse de febra Olimpiadei. Pentru locuitorii obişnuiţi a fost, într-un fel, ca o ieşire din întuneric. În sfârşit, zilele „de tristă amintire" erau lăsate în urmă şi China era recunoscută ca o ţară mare, în plină expansiune. De-a lungul şi de-a latul ţării, internetul şi blog-urile s-au umplut de texte, în special din partea tinerilor, cu acelaşi mesaj: „Iubesc China!"

Fără îndoială că Partidul Comunist a fost cuprins şi el de o atmosferă sărbătorească. Deşi Comitetul Olimpic nu-şi bazează alegerea pe reputaţia economică a unei ţări, el ia, bineînţeles, în considerare capacitatea gazdei de a organiza corespunzător evenimentul. Când oraşul Tokyo a fost desemnat organizator al Olimpiadei din 1964, aceasta părea a fi o recunoaştere a uimitoarei dezvoltări economice a Japoniei şi a ieşirii sale definitive din perioada sumbră de după război. La fel, când oraşul Seoul a fost ales organizator al Jocurilor

Olimpice din 1988, părea a fi o binemeritată încununare a recentei prosperități a Coreei de Sud. Astfel încât, numirea Beijingului ca organizator al Olimpiadei din 2008 a fost văzută ca un fel de petrecere de „ieșire în lume" a Chinei – recunoașterea internațională a dezvoltării economice chineze.

. . . .

PROFIL: DENG YAPING

Deng Yaping este o legendă în China. Această femeie micuță, ce măsoară doar 1,49 m înălțime, a fost votată de chinezi, în 2003, ca atleta secolului XX, și pe bună dreptate, pentru că este una dintre cele mai bune jucătoare de tenis de masă din toate timpurile. S-a născut pe 5 februarie 1973, în orașul Zhengzhou, din provincia Henan. La vârsta de 9 ani a câștigat un campionat provincial de juniori, dar nu i s-a permis să joace în echipă fiindcă era prea scundă. La 13 ani, Deng a câștigat campionatul național, dar din nou nu i s-a permis să joace în echipa națională, neavând înălțimea corespunzătoare. Însă, când a împlinit 16 ani, antrenorii au cedat în sfârșit și au lăsat-o să joace, iar ea a câștigat imediat titlul mondial la dublu, alături de Qiao Hong. Doi ani mai târziu, în 1991, l-a bătut pe nord-coreeanul Li Bun-Hui, câștigând titlul la simplu. Anul următor, la Jocurile Olimpice de la Barcelona, și-a învins toți adversarii, câștigând medalia de aur, atât la simplu cât și la dublu. A repetat performanța și la Olimpiada din 1996. Deloc surprinzător, a fost numărul unu mondial feminin din 1990 până în 1997. Când s-a retras în acel an, la 24 de ani, câștigase mai multe titluri decât orice alt jucător din istoria tenisului de masă. De atunci, a jucat un rol cheie în mișcarea olimpică și a condus echipa care a obținut desemnarea Beijing-ului ca organizator al Olimpiadei, în 2008. Nu este de mirare că este un fel de vedetă la Beijing.

. . . .

Dinamul Beijingului

În foarte multe privințe, Olimpiada de la Beijing este cel mai bun (și cel mai de amploare) lucru care i s-a întâmplat Chinei de foarte, foarte mult timp, iar partidul s-a lansat în organizarea ei cu un entuziasm și o energie uimitoare. Rămâne de văzut dacă și chinezii obișnuiți simt același lucru, însă asupra implicării la vârf nu poate plana nici o îndoială. Bugetul pentru organizarea Olimpiadei este de 40 de miliarde de dolari, de două ori şi jumătate bugetul Londrei pentru Jocurile din 2012, iar acesta este, probabil, doar o fracţiune din suma imensă cheltuită pentru cosmetizarea Beijing-ului în aşteptarea jocurilor.

Beijing-ul trece acum printr-o tranformare mult mai radicală decât cea iniţiată în Shanghai, la începutul anilor '90. Cei care au vizitat oraşul în 1990 nu l-ar mai recunoaşte. Într-adevăr, chiar şi localnicii îşi găsesc cu greu drumul, atât de multe s-au schimbat şi atât de multe locuri familiare au dispărut înghiţite de mania dezvoltării. Beijingul nu a avut nici una dintre problemele şi grijile locuitorilor Londrei pentru găsirea unui loc bun de amplasare a satului olimpic. Pentru a crea satul olimpic, primăria a evacuat, pur şi simplu, locuitorii unui cartier sărac, ce adăpostea zeci de mii de oameni, dărâmându-le vechile locuinţe cu buldozerul. Atât de hotărâţi sunt constructorii să dea oraşului o înfăţişare modernă, încât par a fi gata să răstoarne cerul şi pământul şi, odată cu ele, şi Beijingul, pentru a o face.

În piaţa Tienanmen se află un cronometru care ţine socoteala zilelor rămase până la deschiderea Jocurilor, fiecare dintre ele fiind cât se poate de importantă. Beijingul şi-a propus să construiască sau să renoveze 72 de stadioane şi arene de antrenament, 59 de noi şosele şi 3 noi poduri, fără a mai menţiona o nouă linie de metrou, un nou aeroport, o sumedenie de birouri pentru presă, noi case, hoteluri şi multe altele. Cu toate acestea, Beijingul pare să fi abordat această sarcină colosală cu o mare însufleţire, convocând armate uriaşe de muncitori de la ţară, pentru a munci în ture de şase luni. Singurul comentariu pe care vizitatorii îl pot face, văzând 40 de mii de oameni muncind la noul aeroport şi 7 mii la stadionul naţional, este că aşa trebuie să fi arătat şi lucrările de construcţie la Marele Zid. Cu un an înaintea evenimentului, grosul muncii a fost terminat şi mulţi dintre muncitori au fost trimişi înapoi, în satele lor - lăsând, din câte se spune, străinii şi elita oraşului să se bucure de strălucitorul Beijing pe care l-au construit.

Spectacolul arhitectural

Beijingul este un oraş uriaş, aglomerat, murdar, dar nu există nici o îndoială că organizatorii Olimpiadei fac totul pentru a pune în scenă un spectacol strălucitor. Ei au angajat cei mai prestigioşi arhitecţi şi le-au dat undă verde. Expertul în design, Deyan Sudjic, susţine că ţara se foloseşte de Olimpiadă, considerând-o „o şansă de a face o declaraţie sfidătoare şi fără echivoc că ţara şi-a ocupat, în sfârşit, locul de drept în lume." Faimosul arhitect englez, Norman Foster, a fost adus pentru a proiecta noul aeroport internaţional al Beijing-ului, o clădire uimitoare, ultra-modernă, de forma unui dragon. Controversatul arhitect olandez, Rem Koolhaas, a dat centrului de televiziune naţional un nou sediu, care a fost descris ca „un zgârie nori care se dă peste cap," „o persoană care îngenunchează," sau chiar, ca „o gogoaşă". Koolhaas a făcut, de asemenea, parte din comitetul de designeri care au acordat contractul pentru proiectarea principalului stadion asociaţilor elveţieni, Herzog şi de Meuron, care au modernizat galeria Tate Modern, din Londra. Stadionul Naţional al lui Herzog şi de Meuron este, cu siguranţă, o creaţie uimitoare, formată dintr-o reţea de coloane şi grinzi din oţel. Acesta a fost, deja, poreclit de localnici, cuibul păsărilor. Numele este unul norocos, din moment ce cuibul de pasăre este atât o armonioasă creaţie a naturii, cât şi o delicatesă extrem de costisitoare. Cu toate acestea, unul dintre proiecte a primit porecla răutăcioasă „Oul", – antipatizatul proiect al lui Paul Andreu pentru Marele Teatru Naţional, aflat în apropierea Pieţei Tiananmen.

. . . .

CENTRUL NAŢIONAL ACVATIC DIN BEIJING

Noul Stadion Naţional, construit pentru Olimpiada din 2008, din Beijing, poreclit „Cuibul de păsări", a atras destul de multă atenţie prin design-ul său foarte original. Dar în imediata lui apropiere, cei din echipa olimpică au construit un alt loc de întâlnire, care va fi cel puţin la fel de uimitor: Centrul Naţional Acvatic, creat de parteneriatul australian Arup-PTW, Corporaţia Chineză a Construcţiilor de Stat şi Institutul de Design din Shenzhen. Poreclit deja „Cubul de apă," această clădire foarte originală a fost inspirată de bulele de apă şi arată ca o „felie" tăiată dintr-o cadă plină cu spumă de baie. Structura metalică a pereţilor centrului este alcătuită din diverse forme inspirate din modul de compunere al moleculelor balonaşelor de săpun, plantelor, sau cristalelor. Intersitiţiile acestor forme sunt acoperite cu o membrană extrem de subţire de fluorocarbon. Aceasta este ataşată structurii, apoi este umplută cu aer. Potrivit intenţiei arhitecţilor, „Cubul de apă" trebuie să fie corespondentul răcoros, feminin (*yin*), al înfocatului Stadion Naţional, masculin (*yang*) – însă, membrana de fluorocarbon, a cărui culoare obişnuită este albastru-deschis, se poate transforma într-un roşu aprins, la o simplă schimbare de lumină.

. . . .

Transformarea **manciuriană**

Cosmetizarea Beijingului nu se va opri la clădiri. Autorităţile sunt hotărâte să cureţe oraşul, pentru a-l prezenta lumii în cea mai favorabilă lumină posibilă. Poluarea aerului este, într-adevăr, o problemă fundamentală, fapt relevat şi de adoptarea cuvântului *mai* pentru a o descrie. Beijingul nu doreşte ca atleţii să se plângă că nu pot concura din cauza calităţii aerului. Potrivit Cotidianului Poporului, Beijingul a cheltuit, numai în 2007, aproximativ 3 miliarde de dolari pentru reducerea poluării înaintea jocurilor. Nu doar că automobilelor le-au fost impuse niveluri de emisii mai severe, montându-li-se aparate de control al noxelor, dar una dintre cele mai poluante fabrici din oraş, o oţelărie dintr-un cartier vestic al acestuia, a fost mutată la periferie. Unele dintre măsurile pe care se crede că le vor lua autorităţile în vederea Olimpiadei relevă faptul că mare parte din această agitaţie nu este motivată de o reală precupare pentru mediu, ci, mai mult, de grija pentru imaginea Chinei. Se pare că administraţia intenţionează să închidă toate fabricile poluante (dar numai pe durata Olimpiadei) şi să interzică circulaţia multor maşini în oraş (tot pe durata jocurilor). Conform viceprimarului Beijingului, Ji Lin: „Controlul maşinilor, adică interzicerea temporară a circulaţiei unora dintre ele, este necesar atât pentru administrarea traficului, cât şi pentru controlul poluării."

Aproape toată lumea crede că autoritățile vor curăța străzile orașului de cerșetori și vagabonzi pe parcursul Jocurilor, însă acestea au negat orice zvonuri potrivit cărora ar intenționa să evacueze trei milioane de muncitori migranți din oraș, să strângă prostituatele de pe străzi sau să închidă persoanele alienate mintal în instituții medicale. Totuși, pentru a se asigura că străzile sunt curate, chiar și străinilor li se oferă acum pungi pentru gunoi, la sosire, iar zeci de oameni au fost deja amendați pentru că au scuipat pe stradă, un obicei local, pe care autoritățile sunt dornice să-l facă să dispară înaintea Jocurilor. La data de 11, în fiecare lună, în Beijing este Ziua Cozii, o zi în care oamenii învață cum să formeze cozi ordonate, sub supravegherea unor voluntari cu banderole de mătase, la acestea asistând, uneori, și funcționari care oferă un trandafir celui mai ordonat om de la coadă.

MENIUL ÎN LIMBA ENGLEZĂ

Autoritățile din Beijing sunt hotărâte a nu se face de râs în niciun fel cu ocazia Jocurilor Olimpice din 2008. Așa se face că au fost de-a dreptul îngrozite când și-au dat seama că traducerile engleze de pe semnele de circulație și meniurile din tot Beijingul, intenționate a fi de ajutor străinilor veniți în vizită, le puteau părea acestora comice. Potrivit unui articol al lui Jim Yardley, publicat în New York Times, o serie de profesori universitari au fost însărcinați să meargă prin oraș pentru a descoperi traducerile greșite și a le corecta. Aceștia au găsit câteva „opere" de traducere de-a dreptul incredibile. Spre exemplu, turiștii din Beijing sunt invitați să viziteze Parcul Rasist, un parc tematic despre minoritățile etnice din China. Meniul unui restaurant îi tentează, apoi, cu delicatesa locală – crab, scrisă cu „p", în loc de „b" (crap – lb.eng. orig – porcărie, mizerie – n.tr.). Una dintre cele mai des întâlnite specialități este „pullet", adică o găină tânără, tradusă, se pare, ca „pui fără experiență sexuală." Din fericire, unele dintre acestea au fost deja schimbate. Spitalul de Anus Dongda este cunoscut acum ca Spitalul de Proctologie Dongda.

Nimeni nu se îndoieşte de faptul că, din punct de vedere economic, Jocurile Olimpice au reprezentat un câştig pentru Beijing. În prezent, întreaga economie chineză creşte într-un ritm accelerat, însă Beijingul pare s-o depăşească. În timp ce economia Chinei creşte cu aproximativ 10% pe an, economia Beijingului a crescut cu 12% în perioada premergătoare Jocurilor Olimpice. Există, însă, şi unii care se tem că, odată terminate Jocurile Olimpice, prosperitatea oraşului ar putea să scadă. Doi profesori universitari din Beijing, Liu Qiyun şi Wang Junping, susţin că, din cauza faptului că Beijingul a cheltuit atât de mult cu organizarea jocurilor – jumătate din totalitatea fondurilor cheltuite pentru toate cele opt olimpiade anterioare – efectele ulterioare ale unei astfel de investiţii ar putea fi neobişnuit de grave, lăsând oraşul într-un adevărat dezastru economic.

. . . .

Criticii **Jocurilor Olimpice**

Există oameni care, din diverse motive, critică Jocurile din Beijing. Beijingul a fost întotdeauna o alegere controversată pentru aceste Jocuri, din cauza trecutului său presărat cu încălcări ale drepturilor omului. Unii au asemănat decizia cu cea din 1936, prin care organizarea Jocurilor Olimpice era oferită Berlinului nazist. Deşi majoritatea criticilor nu merg atât de departe, China va fi, fără îndoială, ţinută sub o atentă observaţie. Unii observatori au sugerat că atribuirea Jocurilor Chinei, ar putea-o stimula să facă progrese în privinţa drepturilor omului, punând-o în centrul atenţiei mondiale. Într-un articol din *Business Week*, Laura D'Andrea Tyson, o fostă consilieră a lui Bill Clinton, scria: „În mod paradoxal, găzduirea Jocurilor va fi un avantaj pentru cetăţenii chinezi şi o durere de cap pentru conducerea chineză." Cu toate acestea, alte voci susţin că acordarea Jocurilor Olimpice Chinei n-a făcut altceva decât să dea suficientă încredere autorităţilor pentru a nu mai ţine cont absolut deloc de condamnarea morală a Occidentului. Rolul extrem de controversat al Chinei în masacrul de la Darfur i-a determinat pe unii să nu-mească aceste Jocuri „Jocurile Genocidului", însă, chestiuni precum soarta Tibetului, cea a prizonierilor politici, condiţiile de lucru din fabricile chineze şi problemele de mediu ale Chinei stârnesc, la rân-dul lor, extrem de multe critici.

Interesant este faptul că această situaţie creează un adevărat coşmar al relaţiilor publice pentru corporaţiile multinaţionale care spon-sorizează Jocurile, cum ar fi Adidas, Coca Cola, General Electric, McDonald şi Kodak. Dacă aceste companii ar ignora complet criti-cile activiştilor pentru drepturile omului, şi-ar putea pierde clienţii din ţările lor de origine. Însă, dacă i-ar critica pe chinezi, şi-ar putea pune în pericol viitorul pe această piaţă extrem de profitabilă. În tre-cut, autorităţile chineze au fost foarte prompte în a interzice licenţe-le, sau permisele de funcţionare ale companiilor străine pe care nu le agreau. Acum, însă, companii precum Coca Cola şi Mc Donalds se confruntă chiar acasă la ele cu nişte critici acerbe. Se spune că actriţa Mia Farrow, preşedinta unui grup denumit Vis pentru Darfur, ar fi scris un e-mail în care concluziona: „Reputaţia Jocurilor Olimpice va fi pătată pentru totdeauna, în cazul în care China nu intervine pe lângă Khartoum [în problema Darfurului]; mărcile sponsorilor acestora vor fi şi ele defăimate prin asociere." Departamentele de re-laţii publice ale corporaţiilor încearcă să îşi asigure spatele, susţinând că acestea nu au nici o putere de a influenţa guvernele suverane şi subliniindu-şi celelalte proiecte umanitare, însă aceste probleme vor continua, cu siguranţă, să agite spiritele.

. . . .

MARŞUL TORŢEI OLIMPICE

Pentru a începe jocurile din 2008, Beijingul plănuieşte cel mai lung tra-seu din istorie al torţei olimpice. Flacăra va fi aprinsă, ca de obicei, în localitatea Olympia, din Grecia, pe 25 martie 2008, iar apoi, va călători 137 000 km, pe 5 continente, până va ajunge, într-un final, pe Stadionul Naţional din Beijing, pentru a da startul jocurilor. Flacăra va merge de-a lungul vechiului drum al mătăsii, prin oraşe precum Samarkand şi

Taşkent din Uzbekistan, simbolizând vechimea relaţiilor dintre China şi restul lumii. Traseul a fost intitulat Călătoria Armoniei, dar parcurgerea sa nu a fost complet armonioasă. Una dintre escalele propuse era oraşul Taipei, din Taiwan, însă guvernul taiwanez nu este încântat deloc de idee, susţinând că, din moment ce Taiwanul nu este o parte a Chinei, chinezii nu pot, pur şi simplu, decide unilateral să treacă prin Taiwan. O altă parte litigioasă a planului este de a purta torţa pe vârful muntelui Chomolungma (Everest). Problema care-i deranjează pe ecologişti şi pe activiştii pentru drepturile tibetanilor nu este atât purtarea torţei pe munte, ci porţiunea de 108 km de autostradă pe care chinezii îi construiesc până la tabăra de la baza muntelui. Pe durata maratonului torţei, autostrada Everest va permite accesul presei, însă, după aceea, drumul va deveni principala cale de acces pentru turiştii şi alpiniştii care vor să ajungă pe munte fără efort.

. . . .

Oricare va fi rezultatul Olimpiadei, nu există nici o îndoială că aceasta va aşeza noua Chină pe hartă. Miliarde de oameni din lume vor vedea pentru prima oară uimitoarele schimbări prin care a trecut China, admirând pe micul lor ecran arhitectura ultramodernă a oraşelor chineze şi văzând pe străzi o populaţie îmbrăcată cu haine la fel de moderne ca şi cele din Occident. Nimeni nu-i va mai putea considera vreodată pe chinezi nişte năpăstuiţi care poartă faimoasele pijamale din epoca lui Mao.

. . . .

Capitolul 10:
TÂNĂRA **CHINĂ**

„Poate în trecut, toată lumea era supusă şi asculta bunicuţele care ţineau lecţii despre cine era persoana potrivită cu care să faci sex şi în ce poziţie. Dar noi nu avem timp să ascultăm. Suntem prea ocupaţi să facem sex!"

Li, un tânăr blogger citat de revista *Time*, decembrie 2005

Spre sfârşitul anilor '90, în media chineză au început să apară relatări despre apariţia unui nou fenomen. Câţiva tineri chinezi din oraşe precum Shanghai-ul, începuseră să arate şi să se poarte curios. Poate că în Occident, nimeni nu le-ar fi acordat prea mare atenţie. Cu hainele lor negre, machiajul strident şi smocurile de păr vopsit, aceşti tineri nu păreau a fi altceva decât nişte adepţi mai cuminţi ai curentului *Gotic*. Cu gustul lor pentru fumatul intens şi muzica *heavy rock*, à la Kurt Cobain sau grupuri chineze, precum *Brain Failure*, erau un fel de amestec de culturi occidentale ale tinerilor – de la *punk*, la Generaţia X – cu un strop de cultură chineză. Occidentul este obişnuit, acum, cu aceste transformări ale tinerilor rebeli, dar pentru chinezi a fost un şoc extraordinar.

Presa i-a denumit pe aceşti tineri boemi, aflaţi în jurul vârstei de 20 de ani, Generaţia *Weiku*. *Weiku* combina cuvintele chineze *wei* şi *ku* care înseamnă mare şi extrem, dar era şi un joc de cuvinte construit în jurul expresiei americane, folosite în mediul tinerilor, *way cool* – „foarte *cool*." Cuvântul era deja cam perimat printre tinerii chinezi care îl foloseau, dar eticheta a prins. Generaţia *Weiku* era născută în anii '70, după revoluţia culturală, iar China în care crescuse nu mai era cea a lui Mao şi a comuniştilor duri. În timpul copilăriei tinerilor *Weiku*, în China aveau loc primele reforme care aveau să deschidă ţara către restul lumii. În timpul adolescenţei acestora, influenţele occidentale începuseră să pătrundă prin diverse canale, astfel încât ei au început să respingă o parte dintre valorile părinţilor lor.

. . . .

Lansarea **Web**-ului

Interesant este faptul că mulţi dintre chinezii care erau cu doar zece ani mai mari decât cei din generaţia *Weiku* – cei care aveau în jur de 30 de ani în anii '90 – părăsiseră China pentru a studia în America, înainte ca efectele reformelor să poată fi simţite. Aceşti emigranţi s-au întors, dornici să facă accesibile tinerilor chinezi minunile internetului, dând naştere, între anii 1999-2000, unui balon chinezesc al *dot.com*-urilor. Finanţaţi, adesea, de americani, au lansat o puzderie de noi portaluri şi motoare de căutare, pentru a lansa Generaţia Galbenă, cum o numeau ei, în epoca internetului. *Site*-uri precum E-Tang, Sohu.com, Sina.com şi Netease au dat proaspătului *web* chinez noi afaceri de viitor, iar finanţatorii americani, aşteptându-se la realizări măreţe din partea acestora, au investit masiv.

Aceste investiţii au dat, fără îndoială, naştere *web*-ului chinez, dar antreprenorii chinezi ai *dot.com*-urilor, întorcându-se plini de speranţă din America, nu erau conştienţi de amploarea schimbărilor petrecute în lipsa lor, în China. Crezând că erau la curent, atât cu ultimele tendinţe din lumea occidentală, cât şi cu propria lor cultură, nu au înţeles cât de puţine aveau în comun cu compatrioţii lor cu doar zece ani mai mici. Aceşti copii ai anilor '60 erau, adesea, optimişti şi idealişti, într-un total contrast cu cei din generaţia *Weiku*, denumiţi uneori, *kuadiao yi dai*, „generaţia căzută," din cauza cinismului şi a obsesiei lor faţă de propria persoană.

. . . .

TĂRÂMUL FANTEZIEI

Toate lucrurile care vin din Japonia sunt considerate foarte la modă de către tinerii chinezi, în ciuda duşmăniei faţă de Japonia ca ţară, iar benzile desenate şi desenele animate japoneze au numeroşi fani. Cel mai la modă, în ultimii ani, a fost jocul de roluri Cosplay, importat tot din Japonia. În Cosplay, adolescenţii se costumează şi joacă diverse poveşti din desenele animate sau din jocurile lor favorite pe computer. Pentru unii tineri, Cosplay a devenit mai mult un mod de viaţă decât un joc, însă atracţia pe care o reprezintă pentru aceştia nu poate fi pusă la îndoială. Într-o lume aflată într-o permanentă schimbare şi lipsiţi de o îndrumare reală, aceste jocuri fanteziste constituie o evadare binevenită. Întregul concept al Cosplay se potriveşte perfect nevoii din ce în ce mai presante a tinerilor chinezi de a ieşi în evidenţă. În timpurile în care baza societăţii chineze era reprezentată de spiritul comunitar sau în epoca imperială, era uşor să-ţi găseşti locul în viaţă, dar acum, tinerii din China sunt nevoiţi să se descurce, într-o măsură din ce în ce mai mare, pe cont propriu – şi s-o facă într-o ţară cu peste 2 miliarde de locuitori. Nu e de mirare atunci că mulți copii chinezi spun că visul lor este să *zuo xiu* (adică să se dea în spectacol) şi să-şi construiască gaşca lor de *fen-si* – textual, fen-si înseamnă „tăiței de orez", însă expresia este un joc de cuvinte extrem de răspândit printre tinerii chinezi, pornind de la cuvântul englezesc *fans* (fani – n.tr.). Cosplay reuşeşte să le ducă idealul la îndeplinire fără multă bătaie de cap, evenimentele cărora acesta le dă naştere fiind uneori colosale, cu zeci de mii de adolescenți îmbrăcați aproape scandalos gata să se dea în spectacol sau doar să ia parte la distracție.

. . . .

Rezultatul a fost că aceste noi *site*-uri de internet şi-au ratat segmentul țintă de piață aproape în totalitate. Erau portaluri de *site*-uri – adică *site*-uri care acționau doar ca puncte de intrare – şi aveau foarte puțin conținut, iar *site*-urile la care te trimiteau erau prea generaliste şi necombative pentru adolescenți şi cei de douăzeci şi ceva de ani care se puteau conecta la internet. Rapperul taiwanez Zhang Zhenyu a spus cât se poate de explicit care este atitudinea celor din generația Weiku față de aceşti repatriați chinezi, în melodia sa *Bullshit*, în care le spune: „Spuneți că aveți o diplomă americană; eu zic că trageți vânturi." În scurt timp, marile *site*-uri chinezeşti de-abia mai reuşeau să supraviețuiască.

Revoluția comunicațiilor

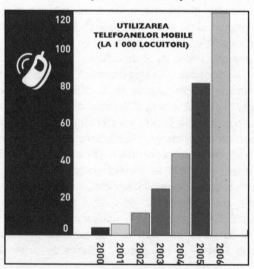

UTILIZAREA
TELEFOANELOR MOBILE
(LA 1 000 LOCUITORI)

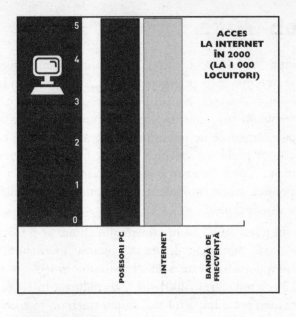

ACCES
LA INTERNET
ÎN 2000
(LA 1 000
LOCUITORI)

POSESORI PC

INTERNET

BANDĂ DE
FRECVENȚĂ

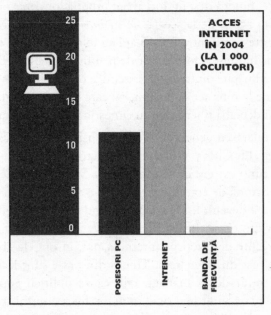

ACCES
INTERNET
ÎN 2004
(LA 1 000
LOCUITORI)

POSESORI PC

INTERNET

BANDĂ DE
FRECVENȚĂ

Web-ul alternativ

Generația Weiku a fost, totuşi, prima dintre generațiile de tineri chinezi cu o mai mare pricepere tehnică. Astfel încât, în loc să folosească binecunoscutele *site*-uri portal, aceştia au început să-şi creeze propriile *site*-uri – uneori, *site*-uri străine traduse, alteori, *site*-uri personale. *Site*-urile de nişă, precum Menkou.com, se concentrau asupra unor probleme specifice, cum ar fi grafica, literatura dură, sau muzica. Totul era *underground* şi alternativ şi, deşi rareori avea tentă politică, fenomenul internet a început să se răspândească rapid printre tinerii chinezi.

Impactul internetului asupra tineretului chinez ar fi foarte greu de supraestimat. Statisticile despre dezvoltarea internetului în China sunt impresionante – câteva mii de utilizatori în 1994, 4 milioane în 1999, 21 de milioane în 2001 şi 137 de milioane în 2006. Dar aceste cifre maschează impactul real asupra tinerilor, în special al celor din oraşe, fiindcă deşi nu toți aveau propria lor conexiune, aproape toți aveau acces, fie la şcoală, fie în *internet café*-uri. Mai mult de 70% dintre copiii între 7 şi 15 ani au folosit cel puțin o dată internetul, iar în oraşe a fost folosit de mai mult de 87%. De fapt, mai mult de jumătate dintre copiii născuți la oraş locuiesc în case care au conexiune la internet şi, desigur, cei care folosesc această conexiune sunt mai degrabă tinerii care au cunoştințe IT, decât părinții lor.

Totuşi, odată cu generația Weiku, considerată deja cam depăşită de tinerii din China, utilizarea internetului a făcut un drum lung într-un timp extrem de scurt. În zilele Weiku, internetul era, mai ales, o metodă de comunicare pentru o cultură alternativă limitată. Acum a devenit un loc comun, fiind o parte integrantă a vieții tinerilor din oraşe. În Occident, suntem familiarizați cu zecile de ore petrecute de tineri pe internet, însă, în oraşele chineze, acest obicei a fost dus la extrem. Tinerii din oraşe sunt lăsați de capul lor mai mult decât altădată. Din cauza politicii copilului unic, implementată mult mai rigid în oraşe, foarte puțini copii au frați, iar presiunile din ce în ce mai mari asupra veniturilor înseamnă că ambii părinți trebuie să muncească. Lăsați de capul lor, tinerii, adeseori singuratici, găsesc în internet o resursă fantastică pentru a lua legătura cu alții cu ajutorul *chat-room*-rilor și pentru a-și urmări interesele. (În ultimul timp, pentru tineri contează din ce în ce mai mult prietenii, și nu familia).

. . . .

TINERE VEDETE CHINEZE

Rapida dezvoltare a mijloacelor media printre tinerii chinezi a dus la apariția unei sumedenii de vedete care, deși puțin cunoscute în restul lumii, sunt notorii în China. Există staruri pop și vedete de film, cum ar fi cele din Hong Kong - Edison Chen, Cecilia Chung și Nic Tse, al cărui cântec Jade Butterfly – Fluturele de Jad, a fost un succes uriaș. Există și *web-writeri* extrem de controversați, precum Han Han. Sunt și sportivi-vedetă, precum uriașul de 2.30m înălțime, Yao Ming, care joacă acum pentru echipa Houston Rockets, în cadrul Ligii Naționale de Basket americane, sau aruncătorul de greutăți, câștigător la Olimpiada de la Atena, Liu Xiang. Cel mai mare star este, totuși, vedeta pop Jay Chou, din Taiwan, situat de societatea Chatham House din Anglia, în 2007, în topul celor mai influenți 50 de oameni din China. Denumit Yu Tsun (prost) de către profesorii săi la școală și considerat urât de către colegii de clasă, Jay Chou a învins soarta, compunând cântece de suflet care par să fure inimile fanelor. Firma Panasonic are o fotografie a lui Jay Chou marcată pe telefoanele sale mobile, iar revista Time i-a dedicat un întreg editorial în 2003.

. . . .

Diferențe culturale

În mod interesant, internetul a contribuit la apariția unei diferențe uriașe între nivelul de cunoștințe al adulților și cel al tinerilor. După cum declară Sun Yun Xiao, de la Centrul de Cercetări pentru Tineri și Copii: „Internetul a dat aripi copiilor din China." Internetul oferă tinerilor un grad de contact cu și o cunoaștere asupra lumii din afară inimaginabilă pentru părinții acestora. Ei pot urmări evoluția echipei de baseball *Miami Heat* din SUA, pot asculta ultimele noutăți R&B de la New York, sau se pot conecta la *chat-room*-uri alături de tineri din toată lumea. Faptul că interesul lor este la fel de superficial ca al tuturor celorlalţi tineri de pe glob nu pare a fi foarte revoluţionar, dar poate că însăşi asemănarea lor este cea esenţială. Poate chiar această transformare culturală din rândul tinerilor este cea care forţează China să se deschidă, într-o mai mare măsură decât ar putea-o face vreodată orice fel de discurs politic.

Generaţia mai în vârstă simte deja răceala vântului schimbării. La şcoală, profesorii au început să se simtă ameninţaţi, nu numai din cauza cunoştinţelor pe care copiii le-au acumulat în afara controlului lor, ci şi de atitudinea lor mult mai provocatoare. În trecut, copiii chinezi acceptau ce le spuneau profesorii lor fără să crâcnească, iar respectul pentru cei mai în vârstă era unul dintre reperele milenare ale societăţii chineze. Acum, copiii nu numai că sunt mai dornici să întrebe „de ce", dar pot fi chiar duri atunci când descoperă că profesorii lor sunt prost informaţi, iar unii profesori găsesc acest lucru enervant.

Şocul tinerilor

Părinţii sunt şi mai îngrijoraţi. Lumea din jur se schimbă într-un ritm ameţitor – totuşi, copiii lor acceptă acest lucru într-o manieră de-a dreptul deconcertantă. Prea mulţi părinţi trebuie să se bazeze pe copiii lor să le spună ce trebuie să cumpere când merg la cumpărături în noile malluri, ţinându-se după ei umili în timp ce precocele lor odrasle le arată cele mai bune mărci. O cercetare a arătat că în discuţiile familiale din China, copiii vorbesc mai mult de jumătate din timp, părinţii o treime, iar bunicii stau în tăcere majoritatea timpului – o completă răsturnare a modelului tradiţional.

Se dovedeşte că prăpastia dintre generaţii este mult mai profundă decât simplele sfaturi în privinţa cumpărăturilor sau discuţiile de la masă. Prin contactul pe care-l au cu lumea dinafară, nu doar pe internet, dar şi la televizor, adolescenţii chinezi sunt, adesea, mult mai detaşaţi decât părinţii lor de vechile duşmănii naţionale. Japonia şi

Taiwanul continuă să se afle pe lista neagră a Chinei, dar acest lucru nu reprezintă un obstacol pentru tinerii chinezi, pentru care majoritatea lucrurilor celor mai la modă vin din Japonia şi din Taiwan. Multe dintre trupele şi desenele animate japoneze sunt foarte îndrăgite de adolescenţii chinezi, iar muzica şi emisiunile TV taiwaneze sunt atât de populare în China încât foarte mulţi adolescenţi din Shanghai şi Beijing au început, spre iritarea părinţilor lor, să folosească în locul mandarinei rigide şi formale din nord, accentul mult mai dulce, mai degajat, din Taiwan.

SPRE TIBET

Ca orice ţară occidentală, China are parte de proprii săi tineri visători aflaţi în căutarea unui alt mod de viaţă. Pentru generaţia Weiku, Tibetul este cel mai tare loc de pământ. Totul a început pe la mijocul anilor '90, atunci când cântăreţul Zheng Jun a filmat un videoclip pentru cântecul Hui Dao Lhasa (Înapoi în Lhasa), în care mergea cu motocicleta sa de-a lungul platoului tibetan. La vremea aceea, Tibetul reprezenta o destinaţie turistică pentru doar câteva zeci de mii de oameni, majoritatea străini. Însă, după şlagărul lui Zheng Jun, călătorii care se întorceau din Tibet erau priviţi ca nişte vedete, cei mai tari din oraş, cei care aveau spirit de exploratori. Nu după mult timp, din ce în ce mai mulţi tineri chinezi începuseră să meargă în Tibet pentru a-şi demonstra spiritul de aventură şi independenţa, iar în 2004, mai mult de un milion se îndreptau spre vest, în fiecare an, spre munte. Odată cu construcţia noii şosele spre Everest se aşteaptă ca aceste cifre să crească şi mai mult. Însă nu doar numărul celor care călătoresc în Tibet a luat amploare. Din moment ce generaţia Weiku a ajuns la maturitate şi are bani de cheltuit, a început să cumpere tot ce este tibetan. Bijuterii tibetane, haine şi chiar mobilă, toate acestea se vând în magazine „oraganice", în stil tibetan, aflate în cele mai moderne malluri din Beijing, cum ar fi Wangfujing. Există acum chiar şi restaurante în stil tibetan care servesc delicatese cum ar fi ceai din unt de iac. Muzica folclorică tibetană, sau cea inspirată de acest gen, a devenit fundalul liniştitor folosit de mulţi dintre tinerii designeri chinezi la prezentările lor de modă, iar melodii precum Sister Drum (Toba Soră) a lui Dadawa şi Voices from the Sky (Voci din cer), au ajuns adevărate hituri.

Virusul **F4**

În 2002, stațiile de televiziune chineze, dornice să atragă telespectatori tineri, au început să difuzeze un serial taiwanez, inspirat de niște desene animate japoneze. Intitulat *Meteor Garden* - Grădina Meteor, acesta spunea povestea a patru studenți aroganți, bogați, arătoși, jucători de baseball și rockeri, și a unei tinere fete sărace care nu se lasă impresionată de șarmul lor nonșalant. Adolescenților chinezi le-a plăcut la nebunie, iar cele patru tinere vedete ale serialului, poreclite F4, au furat inimile adolescentelor din toată țara. Pe măsură ce serialul capta și mai multă atenție, părinții și presa au început să se plângă de el: de personajele sale agresive, de găștile sale, de lipsa de respect față de profesori și de accentul pe care-l punea pe dragostea fizică.

Când în ziare au început să apară titluri precum: *Este F4 un virus?*, organele de control al presei au decis să oprească difuzarea acestuia, demonstrându-și lipsa de conectare la realitate. În secunda următoare, DVD-urile pirat cu serialul *Meteor Garden* au început să se vândă cu milioanele, pe *site*-uri au început să apară bârfe și informații, iar revistele au scris nenumărate articole despre cei patru tineri F4. Într-un final, F4 au lansat un album pop care a devenit, imediat, *best seller*. Mania F4 cuprinsese toată țara – numai până la următorul hit de senzație, desigur.

. . . .

VOCEA TINERILOR

Cel mai mare hit al anului 2005 a fost serialul numit *Supergirl*. *Supergirl* era echivalentul chinezesc al *show*-ului Pop Idol (Idolul Pop). Supergirl atrăgea audiențe amețitoare, de peste o sută de milioane. Succesul acestui show a fost atât de mare încât a dus la apariția mai multor imitații cum ar fi *My Hero* (Eroul meu) și *My Show* (Spectacolul meu). Televiziunile din China se chinuie acum să introducă „conținut" pentru tineret, de la *reality-show*-uri, până la telenovelele în stil taiwanez, sau chinez. Chiar și canalele de stat își dau seama acum că trebuie să înceapă să atragă tinerii, dacă nu doresc să-și piardă audiența. Cu adevărat interesant, însă, la Supergirl, a fost interacțiunea pe care a creat-o cu publicul său.

În primul rând, câştigătoarea *show*-ului a fost o tânără de 21 de ani – Li Yuchun. Li Yuchun nu era o frumuseţe convenţională chineză care interpreta unul dintre şlagărele ,,consacrate'', ci o băieţoasă deşirată, cu păr ţepos, care-şi alesese *single*-ul oarecum alternativ, *Zombies*, al faimosului grup irlandez *Cranberries*. Li Yuchun a devenit o celebritate naţională, alături de la fel de neconvenţionalul concurent Zhou Bichang, iar cei doi au început să apară împreună în numeroase spectacole şi reclame. Poşta Chineză a emis chiar şi o serie de timbre cu chipul lui Li Yuchun.

Cel de-al doilea aspect interesant al *show*-ului, în ceea ce priveşte interacţiunea cu audienţa, a fost că zeci de milioane de tineri chinezi au votat prin SMS pentru ea. Acum toate show-urile pentru tineri au acest element de participare a audienţei şi de votare. Nu este nimic surprinzător pentru o generaţie care aşteaptă acelaşi gen de implicare pe care i-l oferă internetul, însă mulţi au început să se întrebe cât va mai fi lipsită această generaţie, obişnuită să-şi expună punctul de vedere în cele mai ,,triviale'' chestiuni, de posibilitatea de a se exprima în chestiuni politice de mai mare importanţă. Mulţi tineri susţin că nu sunt interesaţi de politică şi vor doar să-şi vadă de viaţa lor, dar, dacă nu sunt interesaţi de problemele politice care-i preocupau pe părinţii lor, aproape toţi îşi declară interesul acut pentru problemele de mediu.

. . . .

Dragoste de **adolescenţi**

În Occident, ideea unor adolescente care devin isterice din cauza unei trupe de băieţi nu este deloc nouă, dar pentru părinţii chinezi întregul fenomen creat de trupa F4 a fost de-a dreptul şocant. Revoluţia sexuală a fost o problemă în Occident, deşi s-a întins aproape pe perioada unui secol întreg, dar în China ea a fost comprimată într-un singur deceniu. Nu este vorba doar de faptul că sexul premarital era de neconceput pentru generaţia mai în vârstă – ci însăşi ideea de a avea un prieten sau o prietenă era total străină. Părinţii chinezi consideră că a le permite copiilor lor să aibă chiar şi o relaţie platonică este total inacceptabil. Totuşi, printre tineri atitudinile se schimbă şi nenumăraţi băieţi şi fete au relaţii de dragoste ascunse de părinţii lor, ajutaţi, în special, de telefonul mobil, care le dă un grad de intimitate necunoscut în tinereţea acestora din urmă.

Spre îngrijorarea generaţiei mai în vârstă, mulţi adolescenţi chinezi, în special fete, sunt cuprinşi de un val de romantism. Adolescentele înfulecă romane de dragoste pe pâine, iar ziua Sfântului Valentin, numită Ziua Îndrăgostiţilor în China, a devenit un eveniment popular printre tineri. Totul a fost de-a dreptul şocant pentru mulţi chinezi vârstnici, care acum trebuie să se obişnuiască cu ideea cuplurilor sărutându-se şi ţinându-se de mână în public, ceva inimaginabil în tinereţile lor colectiviste.

. . . .

Sexul

Până de curând, poveştile de dragoste erau limita maximă a îndrăznelii adolescenţilor chinezi. În 1989, doar 15% dintre locuitorii Beijingului avuseseră relaţii sexuale înainte de căsătorie. În 2004, procentul ajunsese la 60-70%. Iar aceştia nu doar că aveau relaţii sexuale premaritale, ci le aveau la o vârstă mai fragedă decât înainte. În 2000 o anchetă făcută printre tinerii chinezi de ambe sexe arăta că 43% dintre ei îşi păstraseră virginitatea până la 22 de ani şi doar 6% şi-o pierduseră înainte de 19 ani. În 2005, a putut fi observată o schimbare dramatică, în momentul în care jumătate dintre respondenţi au admis că făcuseră sex la 17 ani, iar mulţi dintre ei chiar şi mai devreme. Chiar şi cei din generaţia Weiku aveau, în medie, în jur de 24 de ani când făcuseră prima dată sex, astfel încât schimbarea a fost cu adevărat uimitoare.

Acum, că adevărul a ieşit la lumină, mulţi tineri se aruncă în iureşul sexual, poate din dorinţa de a afla ce au pierdut. Cu câţiva ani în urmă s-a produs o adevărată explozie de confesiuni sexuale feminine, care au sfârşit ca *bestsell*-uri sau *site*-uri de *web* foarte vizitate. Primele au fost lascivele romane *Shanghai Baby*, de Zhou Weihui şi *Candy*, de Mian Mian. Apoi a apărut *Beijing Doll* a lui Chun Sue, care s-a vândut în doar câteva săptămâni de la lansarea sa, în mai

2002, în 100 000 de exemplare. La vremea respectivă, Chun Sue avea doar 17 ani şi istorisea povestea semiautobiografică a unui şir de relaţii sexuale dezamăgitoare, începute la doar 14 ani. *Beijing Doll* (Păpuşa din Beijing) a dat naştere unui cult printre tinerii chinezi mai puţin sociabili care se identificau cu viziunea sumbră şi fascinaţia autoarei pentru sex şi muzica rock occidentală. Apoi, în 2003, a apărut jurnalul *on-line* al lui Muzi Mei în care îşi relata întâlnirile sexuale, care includea, printre altele, şi o înregistrare cu gemetele ei de la finalul unui act, care a fost atât de accesată, încât a dus la căderea reţelei. Autorităţile chineze au interzis înregistrările, însă fără prea mult efect, din moment ce copii ale cărţii circulau pe piaţa neagră, iar tinerii cunoscători de IT au găsit modalitatea de a le materializa pe alte site-uri.

În 2002, arestarea unui grup de fete de gimnaziu din Kunming a provocat uimirea cetăţenilor Chinei. Fetele erau acuzate că practicau prostituţia în grup cu 50 dintre colegii de clasă, unii în vârstă de numai 13 ani. Fetele nu au fost constrânse să facă asta, nici nu au fost împinse de sărăcie sau depresie. Se pare că erau doar curioase şi flatate de atenţia bărbaţilor şi de cadouri. A fost un eveniment şocant, însă, probabil, doar cea mai gravă dintre defulările provocate de îndelungata perioadă de reprimare sexuală.

· ·

DEPRINDEREA MODULUI DE A FI CHINEZESC

Chinezii au pus întotdeauna mare preţ pe valoarea educaţiei. Încă din timpul lui Confucius, era clar că trebuie să înveţi mult pentru a reuşi în viaţă. În ultimele decenii, a devenit o adevărată obsesie. Din moment ce vechile slujbe şi viaţa familială au fost spulberate de iureşul reformelor, părinţi şi copii sunt convinşi că singurul mod de a-şi asigura o poziţie mai bună în ierarhia socială este o bună educaţie.

Încă dinainte de a merge la şcoală, copiii sunt îndopaţi cu lecţii despre orice, de la limba engleză la caligrafie, iar în momentul în care încep şcoala ritmul lucrului ar speria de moarte un copil occidental. Chiar şi şcolile obişnuite cer multe ore de lucru acasă din momentul în care copiii încep şcoala, la vârsta de 6 ani. Unele dintre şcolile de top, care solicită şi mai mult elevii, devin din ce în ce mai populare printre copiii familiilor înstărite.

Pe măsură ce cresc, ritmul se accelerează, atingând apogeul în ultimii 3 ani de liceu. Aceştia sunt anii în care elevii se pregătesc pentru neplăcuta *Gaokao* – examenul de bacalaureat pe care orice elev care doreşte să meargă la universitate trebuie să-l treacă. Importanţa acestor examene de 3 zile şi teroarea pe care o inspiră este atât de mare, încât părinţii aşteaptă în faţa şcolii precum antrenorii din Turul Franţei, gata să-şi aprovizioneze copiii cu gustări energizante ori de câte ori ies în pauza dintre examene.

Presiunea a atins un punct maxim la sfârşitul anilor '90, când 5 milioane de elevi au trecut prin teroarea acestor examene *gaokao* pentru a ocupa doar un milion şi jumătate de locuri la universităţi. Guvernul chinez s-a trezit pus dintr-o dată în faţa acestei probleme şi a declanşat un masiv program universitar care a făcut deja ca numărul locurilor în universităţi să ajungă la 4 milioane. Este o realizare uimitoare, dar nu a reuşit să elibereze decât foarte puţin din presiunea exercitată asupra sistemului, dat fiind că solicitările pentru locurile din învăţământul universitar au crescut dramatic – iar 4 milioane reprezintă doar un procent infim din numărul tinerilor care au vârsta facultăţii.

În ultimii ani, pentru a satisface cererea atât la nivel universitar, cât şi la nivelul instituţiilor şcolare de mare performanţă, au apărut o sumedenie de şcoli şi colegii particulare, la care oamenii sunt pregătiţi să plătească adevărate averi pentru a le obţine odraslelor lor un loc. Interesant este faptul că unele dintre aceste colegii particulare au propus o abordare cu totul nouă pentru învăţământul chinezesc. S-a considerat că sistemul rigid, bazat pe acumularea de fapte învăţate pe de rost, norma din şcolile chinezeşti nu se potrivesc deloc cu minţile din ce în ce mai iscoditoare ale tinerilor chinezi. Poate că acesta era bun în trecut, dar nu va produce creativitatea de care mulţi cred că ar avea nevoie China pentru a-şi susţine progresul economic. În cartea sa Mai întâi bogaţi, Duncan Hewitt descrie Institutul Particular Jianqiao, dintr-o suburbie a Shanghai-ului, unde profesorii încurajează o atitudine mai creativă din partea studenţilor, în acelaşi timp cu o implicare activă a acestora în afacerile şi proiectele locale. Se pare că acest tip de abordare va prinde.

. . . .

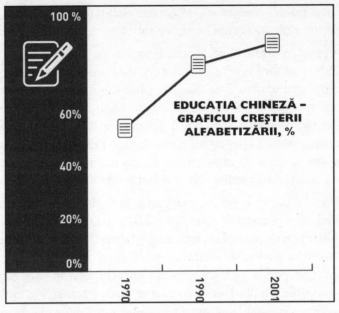

EDUCAȚIA CHINEZĂ –
GRAFICUL CREȘTERII
ALFABETIZĂRII, %

Sursă: Anuarul Statistic Chinez 2005

Lăsați **în urmă**?

Deși grupul vicios al școlărițelor din Kunming a fost cel mai extraordinar caz, este clar că între tinerii chinezi și părinții lor a apărut o profundă segregare generațională, iar schimbările au loc foarte rapid. Generația Weiku a fost deja înlocuită de generația celor din anii '80 care, la rândul ei, face loc generației anilor '90, a copiilor care nu au cunoscut decât viața de după reformele din 1991.

Cea mai pronunțată este, poate, diferența dintre generația anilor '90 și cea a părinților lor. Părinții acestor copii erau, la rândul lor, copii în timpul Revoluției Culturale. Copii fiind, au fost influențați de cele mai rele excese ale Revoluției și ale mișcării Gărzilor Roșii, iar când Revoluția a luat sfârșit, au fost trimiși de acasă pentru a munci în colective, fiind privați de educație. Această întreagă generație nu doar că știe extrem de puține lucruri despre lume, dar poartă povara unei tristeţi şi a unor aşteptări pentru copiii săi, la înălţimea cărora aceştia nu se pot ridica.

Din păcate, aceste aşteptări apasă, adesea, asupra unui singur copil, fiindcă membrii generaţiei anilor '90 sunt produsul politicii copilului unic, ce se manifesta atunci în plină forţă. Părinţii trebuie să-şi pună speranţele şi visele doar într-un singur copil. Nu e de mirare că aceşti copii au devenit rebeli şi închişi în sine, nefiind capabili să împartă povara aşteptărilor părinţilor lor. Presiunea asupra reuşitei lor este enormă şi mulţi dintre ei iau nenumărate lecţii de pian, caligrafie şi limbi străine, chiar şi înainte de a începe şcoala.

Pe de altă parte, aceşti copii singuri la părinţi, mai ales mult-doriţii băieţi, sunt răsfăţaţi de către părinţii lor şi nu doar de aceştia, ci şi de ambele perechi de bunici, care au grijă de ei cât părinţii sunt plecaţi la serviciu. Deloc surprinzător, aceşti copii sunt extrem de răsfăţaţi, fiind porecliţi „micii împăraţi" pentru felul în care comandă în propriile familii. Într-o oarecare măsură, internetul şi mijloacele moderne de presă le-au pus în faţă orizonturi mult mai largi decât cele pe care şi le puteau imagina părinţii sau bunicii lor, însă grija excesivă de care au avut parte îi face extrem de prost pregătiţi pentru a înfrunta chiar şi cele mai banale încercări ale vieţii.

. . . .

Generaţia „**Eu**"

Câteodată, tinerii din China de azi sunt caracterizaţi ca generaţia EU. Sunt adesea criticaţi pentru faptul că sunt obsedaţi de sine, egoişti şi orientaţi în totalitate spre bunuri de consum şi autosatisfacţie. Este adevărat că mulţi cred că propriile lor nevoi sunt pe primul loc. În serialul BBC World Service *Young In China* (Tânăr în China), un tânăr muzician, Long Kuan, declară: „Cel mai important lucru pentru mine sunt chiar eu. Consider că prima responsabilitate pe care o am este faţă de mine. Apoi te gândeşti la ceilalţi. Poţi face orice doreşti atâta vreme cât nu-i răneşti pe ceilalţi."

Concentrarea pe nevoile personale şi o atitudine de tip *laissez-faire* faţă de alţii pare, la început, diferită de ideile colectiviste şi foarte rigide ale părinţilor acestor tineri chinezi. Pare egoist şi revendicativ, în comparaţie cu spiritul comunitar al vechii generaţii. Dar, într-un anume fel, poate fi vorba de faptul că sunt prima generaţie de la revoluţia comunistă care a trebuit să stea pe propriile picioare. Pe vremea părinţilor lor, oamenii erau, cel puţin în anumite privinţe, asistaţi de la naştere până la moarte, li se oferea un loc de muncă, hrană şi o locuinţă pe viaţă. Dar în anii '90, „vasul de orez din oţel" al sprijinului le-a fost smuls cu violenţă. Tinerii de astăzi trăiesc într-o lume unde sunt singurii responsabili pentru asigurarea unei locuinţe, a hranei, a sănătăţii şi a unui loc de muncă, fiind, probabil, conştienţi că trebuie să aibă un talent de a supravieţui pe care părinţii lor nu l-au avut.

PORECLE

Îngrijoraţi, probabil, să nu se rătăcească printre sutele de milioane de contemporani ce poartă nume comune, cei mai cool adolescenţi au, toţi, porecle. Tinerii chinezi iubesc numele englezeşti care exprimă cu totul altceva în chineză, sau viceversa. Dar şi numele japoneze sunt populare, fiind adesea inspirate de protagoniştii unor desene animate favorite.

Unii dintre tineri sunt, fără îndoială, înspăimântaţi de lumea care se deschide în faţa lor. Alţii se simt prinşi ca într-o cuşcă de restricţiile lumii autoritare care încă încearcă să le modeleze gândurile şi viaţa. Deloc surprinzător, unii dintre ei au luat-o pe căi greşite, devenind depresivi sau dependenţi de droguri. Cu toate acestea, cei mai mulţi tineri chinezi par să fie plini de energie, excitaţi de noile posibilităţi care apar în viaţa lor şi hotărâţi să profite din plin de ele. Viitorul nu va fi deloc uşor, societatea chineză devenind din ce în ce mai profund divizată între cei care au totul şi cei care nu au nimic, însă, pentru cei care ajung unde trebuie, ambiţia fără limite şi hotărârea tinerilor ar putea schimba China pentru totdeauna.

Capitolul 11:
CHINA – ÎNCOTRO?

„Când nu voi mai fi cine sunt, voi deveni ceea ce aş putea fi."
Lao Tzu, filozof taoist (sec. VI î.Hr.)

China este o ţară de o complexitate extremă, care a reuşit, de-a lungul timpului, să-i surprindă de nenumărate ori pe observatorii occidentali, astfel încât a face previziuni pentru viitor sau chiar şi a descrie prea în amănunt situaţia actuală a ţării, ar fi o greşeală. Totuşi, câteva lucruri sunt foarte clare. China pare să se schimbe, şi încă repede.

Oraşele chineze se dezvoltă într-un ritm fantastic, fiind transformate de o dinamică explozivă în domeniul construcţiilor, ce înalţă peste noapte malluri şi zgârie-nori care ar face majoritatea oraşelor occidentale să pară desuete. În aceste oraşe creşte o nouă generaţie de tineri, a căror educaţie nu este dată nici de învăţăturile lui Confucius, nici de Cartea Roşie a lui Mao, ci de internet şi televizor. În aceste oraşe, există oameni care acumulează mai multă bogăţie decât ar fi putut visa strămoşii lor vreodată şi care o folosesc pentru a-şi cumpăra întreaga gamă de bunuri de consum, de la DVD-uri, la genţi Gucci. Mulţi chinezi obişnuiţi au început să călătorească în străinătate şi să vadă lumea. În acelaşi timp, sute de milioane de oameni de la ţară au fost scoşi din acea stare de sărăcie lucie, ce caracteriza odinioară majoritatea ţăranilor chinezi. Şi ei încep să se familiarizeze cu tipul de existenţă comodă pe care cei mai mulţi dintre noi, locuitorii Occidentului, o considerăm a fi un dat, iar majoritatea sunt mai educaţi şi mai sănătoşi decât locuitorii altor ţări aflate de atât de puţină vreme pe calea dezvoltării.

Chinezii şi liderii lor pot fi foarte mândri de toate acestea. Este o reuşită extraordinară, iar energia şi freamătul multora dintre oraşele chineze arată că ei sunt conştienţi de acest lucru şi ştiu că pot realiza chiar mai multe. Nu există nici o îndoială că mulţi dintre ei simt că a sosit, în sfârşit, şi vremea lor şi că îşi vor ocupa locul binemeritat pe scena lumii.

Republică **populară**?

Pe de altă parte, nici una dintre aceste realizări nu pare să fi deschis drumul spre democrație și nici să fi oferit acea libertate de exprimare pe care mulți occidentali o consideră esențială pentru o societate sănătoasă. Presa este încă puternic monitorizată, internetul este cenzurat, iar știrile din afară continuă să fie filtrate de o armată devotată de polițiști de informații. În plus, nonconformiștii trăiesc cu teama structurilor de represiune ale statului. Cu toate că, în ultima vreme, nu au mai existat evenimente atât de traumatizante precum cele din Piața Tienanmen, protestatarii sunt, adesea, tratați cu brutalitate, dacă manifestările lor deviază chiar și extrem de puțin de la programul stabilit.

Proteste au existat cu siguranță, iar numărul lor este în continuă creștere. Însă acestea nu au fost pentru democrație, ci pentru chestiuni locale, precum poluarea mediului înconjurător sau confiscarea pământurilor. În fiecare zi, există sute de mici proteste de acest fel. Niciunul nu implică mai mult de câteva mii de oameni, dar aceștia sunt foarte înverșunați și se întâmplă destul de frecvent ca un număr de oameni să fie uciși de forțele de ordine, în încercarea de a ține lucrurile sub control. Este greu de spus dacă acest val de proteste în creștere se referă doar la plângerile locale, cum susține majoritatea analiștilor, sau dacă este vorba de un curent subteran, a cărui singură cale de manifestare sunt aceste probleme mai mărunte – și a cărui acumulare ar putea duce la o presiune mult mai substanțială pentru schimbare, până când, în cele din urmă, aceasta ar deveni de neoprit.

Nu este deloc întâmplător că majoritatea acestor proteste se desfășoară în mediul rural, acolo unde oamenii au beneficiat cel mai puțin de bogăția care s-a revărsat în țară, în ultimii cinsprezece ani. În China rurală există sute de milioane de oameni pentru care viața continuă să fie extrem de grea și care se confruntă cu abuzuri și nedreptăți greu de imaginat din partea funcționarilor lacomi și a antreprenorilor hrăpăreți. Dacă cineva are vreun motiv să se ridice împotriva sistemului, atunci este vorba despre acești oameni. Deși există mulţi oameni săraci şi obidiţi şi în oraşe, aceştia pot vedea că viaţa se schimbă în jurul lor, în timp ce mulţi alţii sunt fie prea ocupaţi încercând să-şi câştige existenţa, fie le e prea bine pentru a se mai preocupa de problemele politice.

. . . .

În fruntea **schimbării**?

Unii s-ar putea întreba de ce se teme atât de tare Partidul Comunist de introducerea libertăţilor democratice, dacă, aşa cum susţine acesta, oamenii sunt atât de mulţumiţi de felul în care merg lucrurile şi de prosperitatea pe care partidul a reuşit s-o aducă ţării. N-ar fi, cumva, aceasta chiar cireaşa de pe tort, adevărata încununare a revoluţiei populare? Există, desigur, o mulţime de motive de ordin ideologic din pricina cărora răspunsul ar fi unul negativ. Poate că în afara acestora există, însă, şi alte motive, mai pragmatice. Partidul se află la putere de atât de multă vreme, încât multitudinea de grupuri de interese dezvoltate împrejurul său nu şi-ar dori cu nici un chip o schimbare a statutului acestuia. Prea mulţi oficiali s-au obişnuit cu puterea şi cu privilegiile pe care aceasta le oferă, iar China este o ţară atât de mare încât, chiar dacă conducerea centrală ar dori să facă schimbări, nu există nici o garanţie că liderii locali nu ar încerca să le zădărnicească. Mulţi lideri chinezi simt că trecerea la democraţie ar deschide o adevărată cutie a Pandorei, dând naştere unei societăţi crude, în care cei slabi sunt exploataţi, şi nu unei societăţi stabile şi libere.

În preşedintele Hu şi în premierul Wen, China pare să aibă doi conducători conştienţi de problemele unei societăţi divizate. Ei au implementat o serie de măsuri care îşi propun să direcţioneze o parte din noua bogăţie a Chinei şi către săraci, să rezolve problemele de mediu şi să creeze o formă de guvernare mai raţională şi mai transparentă. Ar putea fi doar o iluzie, dar pare improbabil ca aceşti doi oameni să fie de acord cu genul de reprimare extremă la care am asistat în Piaţa Tienanmen. Într-un fel, pentru prima oară în isto-

ria Republicii Populare, ei dau impresia că țara este în mâini sigure, moderate și raționale. Deși ar putea-o nega, viziunea „societății
armonioase" spre care se îndreaptă nu pare să fie mult diferită de
viziunea socialistă a vechiului partid laburist britanic, cu industriile
sale naționalizate și confortul său minimal, reprezentat de ajutorul
social pentru cei mai săraci. Diferența este că ei sunt sprijiniți de o
întreagă mașinărie fortificată de represiuni ale statului și de cea mai
mare armată permanentă din lume.

. . . .

China iese în lume

În timpul perioadei lui Mao, China a păstrat majoritatea imenselor
sale probleme pentru sine. După sfârșitul Războiului din Coreea,
forța militară chineză nu prea s-a manifestat vizibil, iar interacțiuni-
le comerciale ale Chinei cu restul lumii au fost aproape inexistente.
Într-adevăr, atât de puține lucruri se știau despre China, încât studenții occidentali din anii '60 s-au putut lăsa seduși de farmecul
Cărții Roșii a lui Mao, fără a fi conștienți de adevărata teroare reprezentată de Revoluția Culturală. Acum, însă, China începe să interacționeze cu lumea într-un fel chiar dramatic. Din punct de vedere
politic, se pare că încearcă să se păstreze pentru sine. Hu și Wen par
să fi făcut minuni în crearea unei imagini a Chinei care nu intențio-
nează să facă vreun rău și se va dezvolta în mod pașnic. Unii încă se
tem că probleme precum cea a Taiwanului ar putea fi scânteia care
va trezi dragonul adormit, făcându-l să scuipe foc. Însă, cel puțin
pentru moment, acest scenariu este puțin probabil.

Mai îngrijorător este, însă, impactul expansiunii economice chineze
asupra restului lumii. Pe de o parte, în lumea occidentală și, în special în SUA, se face din ce în ce mai mult simțită temerea potrivit căreia industriile mamut ale Chinei le vor fura muncitorilor occidentali
locurile de muncă și vor face imposibilă supraviețuirea propriilor
industrii. În iulie 2007, între SUA și China a izbucnit un adevărat
război verbal cu privire la calitatea produselor chineze. Este posibil,

însă, ca intensificarea atacurilor la adresa calității pastei de dinți și a altor produse chinezești să nu fie altceva decât un simptom al ostilității americane crescânde față de puterea comercială a Chinei. Pe de altă parte, cererea de resurse a Chinei sporește exponențial. China nu pare să-și dorească să intre în competiție directă cu lumea occidentală pentru resurse precum petrolul, ceea ce a determinat-o, spre marea îngrijorare și iritare a multor guverne occidentale, să stabilească legături cu niște regimuri extrem de antipatizate, cum este cel al lui Mugabe, din Zimbabwe.

Fapt interesant, totuși, conducerea chineză pare să recunoască aceste probleme și să caute soluții pentru rezolvarea lor. Într-un fel, China pare să fi ajuns la un grad de stabilitate politică sub conducerea lui Wen și a lui Hu ce va permite sporirea prosperității țării și o mai bună distribuție a bunăstării în rândul populației. S-ar putea ca cel mai mare obstacol pe acest drum să nu fie unul politic, ci unul de mediu – nu doar pentru că țara are o varietate la fel de mare de probleme ecologice ca oricare alta din lume, ci, mai ales, pentru că dezvoltarea sa continuă va solicita resursele mondiale până la limită.

În 2008, Olimpiada de la Beijing va permite lumii să vadă mai limpede ca niciodată ce se întâmplă în China, asistând, mai ales, la uimitoarele schimbări petrecute în acel oraș. Rămâne de văzut dacă adevărata Chină va deveni mai transparentă.

CADRU ISTORIC

Istorie

Unul dintre cele mai uimitoare lucruri la civilizaţia chineză este persisten-
ţa sa. Nu există nici o îndoială că este o civilizaţie străveche – mai veche
decât islamul, decât creştinismul sau budismul, chiar şi decât hinduismul,
considerată cea mai veche religie din lume. Într-adevăr, primii împăraţi
chinezi au venit la putere cu secole înaintea primilor împăraţi romani
şi, în timp ce Imperiul Roman dispărea cu totul de pe hartă, împăraţii
chinezi au continuat să conducă, până când au fost, în sfârşit, detronaţi
de proprii supuşi, cu mai puţin de un secol în urmă. Revoluţia a dezvăluit
adevărata vârstă a civilizaţiei chineze.

Cât timp a supravieţuit imperiul, singurele cunoştinţe despre trecutul antic al Chinei proveneau din istoriile imperiale – scrise cu
mii de ani în urmă, dar pline deja de mituri şi adevăruri amintite
pe jumătate. Imaginea originilor chineze, aşa cum era ea zugrăvită
de aceşti istorici, era cea a unei civilizaţii apărute în mod miraculos,
în trecutul îndepărtat, fără a trece prin stadiile de dezvoltare treptată prin care trecuseră alte civilizaţii. Doar cu prilejul Revoluţiei
au început arheologii şi paleontologii să caute dovezi palpabile în
pământ, făcând descoperiri cheie, cum ar fi aşezarea preistorică de la
Banpo din Shaanxi, care au început să dezvăluie adevărul. Într-adevăr, multe dintre acele descoperiri care ne dezvăluie, în sfârşit, cum a
apărut China în trecutul îndepărtat, au fost făcute de arheologi doar
în ultimii 30 de ani.

China preistorică

Cu 2 milioane de ani în urmă – anul 2000 î.Hr.

A devenit evident că ţara a fost locuită încă de la începuturile preistoriei.
În 1995 au fost descoperite oase de hominizi datând de acum 1,9 milioane de ani, cu mult mai devreme decât ar fi crezut cineva posibil. Apoi,
în 2004, în localitatea Majuangou, din nordul Chinei au fost descoperite unelte de piatră datând de acum 1,66 milioane de ani. Majoritatea
palentologilor nu mai au acum nicio îndoială că *Homo erectus*, primul
umanoid care a plecat din Africa, a ajuns în China mai devreme decât
se crezuse înainte.

După *Homo erectus* au mai apărut şi alţi hominizi, cum ar fi faimosul „om din Beijing", *Sinanthropus pekinensis*, ale cărui oase vechi de jumătate de milion de ani au fost găsite într-o peşteră de lângă Beijing, în 1923, şi „omul din Lantian", *Sinanthropus lantianensis*, ale cărui oase, vechi de şase sute de mii de ani, au fost descoperite în 1923, în Shaanxi. Alte descoperiri sugerează că cei mai evoluaţi oameni, *Homo sapiens*, au apărut în China la fel de devreme ca şi în restul lumii – cu cel puţin 80 000 de ani în urmă sau poate mult mai devreme. Nu se ştie exact când au apărut caracteristicile distinctive ale rasei chineze, însă acestea s-ar putea să nu fie mai vechi de 20 000 de ani.

La un moment dat, se credea că strămoşii noştri vânători-culegători au descoperit agricultura în Orientul Mijlociu, cu aproximativ 10 000 de ani în urmă, şi că aceasta s-a răspândit, încet, către est, de-a lungul mai multor milenii. Însă, pe măsură ce numărul descoperirilor arheologice creşte, devine evident nu doar că agricultura a apărut simultan în mai multe locuri de pe Terra, printre care şi China, ci şi că, în această ţară, ea a avut mai multe centre de răspândire distincte, care au dat naştere la trei sau mai multe culturi diferite. Dar cum din ce în ce mai multe dovezi arheologice sunt dezgropate, devine clar nu doar faptul că agricultura s-a dezvoltat independent şi dintr-o dată în China, dar s-a mai dezvoltat şi în alte trei sau mai multe regiuni separate, din China, independent şi în diferite moduri. Fiecare dintre aceste regiuni avea propria sa cultură distinctă.

Prima dovadă a existenţei uneia dintre aceste culturi a fost descoperită la Yangshao, în provincia Henan, în 1920, primind astfel numele de cultura Yangshao. Populaţia Yangshao cultiva mei în solurile argiloase, bătute de vânturi din Shaanxi, de-a lungul albiei râului Wi şi a Fluviului Galben. Reprezentanţii culturii Yangshao creau, de asemenea, produse de olărit împodobite cu modele specifice şi unelte agricole de piatră, crescând câini şi porci pentru hrană. Cultura Longshan îşi avea centrul mai spre sud, pe văile râurilor Yangtze şi Huai, unde, în urmă cu aproximativ 10 000 de ani, cultiva orez şi creştea câini, porci şi bivoli de apă. Cultura sud-estică a înflorit, cu cel puţin 11 000 de ani în urmă, în câmpiile costiere de sud şi de est, cultivând plante tuberculifere, cum ar fi ignamele şi taro (plantă tropicală comestibilă).

Care dintre aceste culturi a fost cultura chineză originară continuă să fie un subiect ce dă naştere la aprige dezbateri printre cercetătorii chinezi. Una dintre probleme este că unele dintre siturile Logshan mai târzii se găsesc în regiunea Yanshao, şi viceversa. Adevărul este că se produceau, probabil, întrepătrunderi substanţiale, fiecare dintre aceste culturi având contribuţia sa la apariţia a ceea ce acum numim civilizaţie chineză. Totuşi, în 1987, o remarcabilă descoperire arheologică a fost făcută la Puyang, la 500 de km sud de Beijing, pe malul Fluviului Galben. Era vorba despre mormântul unui şef de trib Yangshao, dar acesta nu era deloc unul obişnuit. De-o parte şi de cealaltă a scheletului se aflau două reprezentări animaliere de doi metri lungime, alcătuite din scoici de moluşte – una înfăţişa un tigru, iar cealaltă, un dragon. Mormântul are 6460 de ani vechime, ceea ce demonstrează că tigrul şi dragonul au fost simboluri importante în cultura chineză de mai mult de 6 milenii. Atât de important este dragonul în cultura chineză, încât oraşul Puyang se laudă că adăposteşte „Primul Dragon al Chinei", iar în 2007, şi-a anunţat planul de a construi un uriaş parc tematic „al dragonului"..

Epoca Bronzului în China

2000–1046 î.Hr.

Chinezii din antichitate nu ştiau totuşi nimic despre strămoşii lor din Epoca de Piatră, a căror existenţă a fost dezvăluită doar de arheologi. Istoricii din vremurile străvechi, cum ar fi Sima Qian, care şi-a scris celebra istorie a Chinei, denumită *Shiji*, în preajma anului 100 î.Hr., şi-au bazat scrierile despre originile Chinei pe legende, cum ar fi aceea a lui Shen Nong, care se presupune că a inventat medicina pe bază de plante sau cea a Împăratului Galben, căruia i se atribuie crearea tuturor trăsăturilor esenţiale ale civilizaţiei – agricultura, organizarea familială, calendarul, mătasea, vasele, hărţile şi arta tirului cu arcul – sau pe legenda lui Yu cel Mare, care controla cursurile de apă ale Chinei. Despre Yu cel Mare se spune că ar fi întemeiat prima dintre cele trei dinastii antice ale Chinei – Xia, Shang şi Zhou.

Acum un secol, experţii credeau că majoritatea acestor istorii erau doar fabulaţii. Însă descoperirile arheologice au demonstrat că dinastiile Zhou şi Shang au existat cu certitudine şi poate chiar şi dinastia Xia. Dacă dinastia Xia se dovedeşte a fi una reală, atunci este posibil să fi ajuns la putere în Shanxi, sau în Henan, în jurul anilor 2100-2000 î.Hr. În acea epocă, după cum demonstrează arheologii, cultura din nordul Chinei începuse să fie mult mai stabilă şi mai structurată. Satele se transformau în oraşe înconjurate de ziduri, iar societatea se diviza în clase – conducători, fermieri, negustori, meşteşugari, etc. Apoi chinezii au descoperit maniera de prelucrare a bronzului, inaugurându-şi astfel propria Epocă a Bronzului. Unii istorici cred că prelucrarea bronzului a fost preluată din Occident, dar chinezii prelucrau bronzul într-un mod atât de diferit, folosind matriţe de lut, în locul ciocanului şi al nicovalei, încât este foarte posibil ca producerea bronzului să se fi dezvoltat independent şi aici.

Oricare ar fi adevărul, în momentul în care dinastia Shang preia puterea, în jurul anilor 1600-1500 î.Hr., chinezii demonstrau deja un talent deosebit în confecţionarea uriaşelor urne de bronz, atât de specifice acelei perioade istorice. Cea mai mare dintre acestea a fost descoperită la Anyang, lângă Fluviul Galben, în Henan, pe locul sitului ce demonstra existenţa dinastiei Shang. Anyang a fost capitala dinastiei Shang, iar puterea acesteia este atestată nu doar de giganticele topitorii de bronz, ci şi de dimensiunile monumentelor funerare regale. Pe lângă care, arme şi obiecte din bronz, aceste morminte conţineau şi rămăşiţele a sute de trupuri – sclavi sau soldaţi sacrificaţi în onoarea regelui mort. Un alt oraş al dinastiei Shang, Zhengzhou, este înconjurat de un zid de 9 metri înălţime şi 36 de metri lăţime, pentru ridicarea căruia se crede că au fost folosiţi zece mii de oameni, timp de 18 ani.

Cea mai relevantă descoperire din epoca Shang a fost, totuşi, cea a „oaselor de dragon". Aceste oase au început să apară la sfârşitul secolului XIX în magazinele de produse farmaceutice tradiţionale. Erau vândute ca leacuri magice pentru boli, fiindcă erau acoperite cu simboluri misterioase. Mii de astfel de oase au fost descoperite cu ocazia excavaţiilor arheologice din anii '20, de la Anyang, iar istoricii au început să descifreze simbolurile. După multă muncă, cercetătorii au ajuns la concluzia că aceste simboluri erau versiuni rudimentare ale caracterelor chinezeşti. Există 5 000 de semne diferite pe oase, iar până în prezent au fost descifrate în jur de 1 500. Studiindu-le, cercetătorii au constatat că oasele erau folosite pentru a cere sfaturi zeilor. Pe fiecare os – de obicei, un omoplat de bivol sau o carapace de broască ţestoasă – era notată o întrebare, iar răspunsul era aflat prin interpretarea crăpăturilor apărute pe suprafaţa acestuia după ce era încins în foc. Din moment ce unele dintre acestea amintesc supuşilor că trebuie să-şi venereze strămoşii, adică pe Xia, este greu de crezut că această populaţie nu a existat.

Dinastia Zhou

1045–221 î.Hr.

În secolul XI î.Hr., după cinci secole de dominaţie a dinastiei Shang, un popor războinic denumit Zhou, a pătruns în valea Fluviului Galben dinspre Valea Wei spre vest, condus de regele Wen, de regele Wu şi de fratele acestuia, ducele Zhou. Atât de zdrobitor a fost atacul lor, încât a reuşit să alunge dinastia Shang de la putere, preluând controlul asupra unei mari părţi din nordul Chinei. Destul de interesant este faptul că, printre chinezi, exista un sentiment de nelinişte asupra moralităţii preluării puterii prin mijloace militare. Astfel încât, dinastia Zhou a venit cu ideea „mandatului cerului", idee cu un impact fundamental asupra tuturor conducătorilor chinezi care i-au urmat. Aceasta se referă la faptul că regii chinezi îşi primesc dreptul de a domni de la Divinitate – însă, dacă nu conduc aşa cum se cuvine, li se retrage mandatul şi sunt daţi jos de pe tron. Evident că dinastia Zhou voia să sublinieze bunătatea, cumpătarea şi altruismul regilor Wen şi Wu şi al ducelui de Zhou.

Dinastia Zhou este, cu siguranţă, cea mai longevivă din istoria Chinei, supravieţuind timp de opt sute de ani, însă domnia sa se împarte în mai multe perioade. Prima, care a durat trei secole, denumită Dinastia Zhou Occidentală, a fost perioada de maximă expansiune a acesteia, stăpânind din cetăţile lor de la Xi'an şi Luoyang, peste Shaanxi, Shanxi şi Hebei. Dar în anul 771 î.Hr., un trib de nomazi călare a pătruns dinspre vest, probabil ajutat de supuşi nemulţumiţi, a preluat Xi'an-ul şi l-a ucis pe You, regele dinastiei Zhou. Nobilii l-au încoronat atunci pe unul din fiii săi, Ping, în capitala din est, Luoyang.

Prăbuşirea Dinastiei Zhou de Vest a declanşat o lungă perioadă în care China a fost divizată în nenumărate mici state. Dinastia Zhou a continuat să existe, fiind denumită dinastia Zhou de Est, dar puterea ei nu mai era aceeaşi. Războiul era o constantă, ţara nemaiavând nici stabilitatea epocilor anterioare, nici liniştea rigidă a celor ce vor urma. Cu toate acestea, perioada a fost una de efervescenţă intelectuală şi de inovaţie tehnologică. Într-adevăr, multe dintre ideile esenţiale ale culturii chineze şi multe dintre primele sale invenţii au apărut acum. Într-un fel, chiar această instabilitate era cea care îi îmboldea pe chinezi să gândească, să inventeze şi să facă negoţ, căutând să găsească o insulă fermă în marea agitată care-i înconjura. În mod cât se poate de interesant, cea mai mare parte a descoperirilor tehnice uimitoare, cum ar fi cea a oţelului, nu a venit din partea statelor mai „rafinate" din centru, precum Zhou, Song sau Lu, ci din zonele periferice mai „barbare", din state precum Qi, în est, Chi, la sud, sau Qin, înspre vest. Însă nu invenţiile au făcut ca această epocă să fie una atât de preţuită, ci marile idei filozofice care au apărut în aceste vremuri zbuciumate, în care gânditorii încercau să-şi dea seama de ce lucrurile sunt atât de tulburi şi de fără sens.

Gândirea Zhou

În perioada regatului Zhou de Est au apărut patru mari curente filozofice. Cel mai faimos a fost confucianismul, denumit astfel după Confucius, numele roman dat de iezuiţi, în sec. XVII, omului pe care discipolii îl cunoşteau ca Kong Fuzi (maestrul Kong). Ideile lui Confucius s-au transmis mai ales sub forma unor proverbe, strânse de către discipolii săi într-un tratat denumit *Analecte*. Credinţa sa fundamentală era că trebuie să încercăm să ne trăim viaţa bine, purtându-ne întotdeauna cu respect şi curtoazie, muncind harnic şi onorându-ne familia şi conducătorii. El se considera un conservator, pentru că amintea mereu cu respect de „Calea foştilor Regi" din Epoca de aur, dar, în anumite privinţe, a fost aproape revoluţionar, prin insistenţa sa că poziţia socială trebuie să fie întotdeauna câştigată printr-un comportament moral adecvat şi nu prin ereditate. Din punct de vedere politic, confucianismul susţinea o societate puternic ierarhizată.

Al doilea mare filozof al vremii a fost Mo Zi. Acesta considera că accentul pus de Confucius asupra familiei putea da naştere nepotismelor şi luptei între clanuri. El susţinea teza Iubirii universale – a iubi şi onora pe toată lumea şi a-i îngriji pe ceilalţi în aceeaşi manieră în care ţi-ai dori să fii şi tu îngrijit. În opinia sa, acesta nu era un vis idealist, ci singura modalitate practică în care o societate poate funcţiona fără lupte intestine.

Al treilea curent filozofic a fost daoismul (scris uneori Taoism), al cărui text fundamental era *Dao De Jing* (Cartea Căii). Potrivit legendei, a fost scrisă de cineva numit Lao Zi, dar Lao Zi înseamnă, pur şi simplu, Bătrânul Maestru, aceasta fiind, probabil, o operă colectivă. Soluţia lui Lao Zi la toate problemele lumii este de a nu face nimic. Credinţa sa era că luptele apar fiindcă oamenii se agită în permanenţă, confruntându-se astfel cu opoziţia şi cu obstacolele. Intenţia lui nu era aceea de a nu face cu-adevărat nimic, ci de a te lăsa purtat de curent, aidoma unui râu ce se îndreaptă către mare. „Calea", spune textul, „nu acţionează niciodată şi, totuşi, nimic nu rămâne nefăcut". Deşi occidentalii de astăzi asociază Calea cu o stare de serenitate absolută, fără nici o legătură cu politicul, nu aceasta era intenţia sa iniţială. Dao De Jing spune că liderii trebuie să continue să conducă fără a ţine cont de supuşii lor, lăsându-i în ignoranţă şi tratându-i ca pe nişte „oameni de paie" – acesta ar putea fi unul dintre motivele pentru care mulţi conducători au adoptat daoismul. Nu implica nici o responsabilitate de a avea grijă de populaţie.

A patra doctrină filozofică din perioada Zhou era, în multe privinţe, o contrazicere a Daoismului politic. Era vorba de ideea Legalismului. Aceasta propovăduia crearea unui cadru de legi atât de atotcuprinzător şi de rigid, încât nimeni să nu poată greşi. Dar, pentru ca acest lucru să fie posibil, era necesar ca legiuitorii să pună stăpânire pe întreaga Chină. Dacă atât daoismul cât şi legalismul au influenţat modul de gândire al împăraţilor chinezi de-a lungul veacurilor, este posibil ca ele să fi avut un impact şi asupra conducătorilor comunişti ai ţării.

Primăvară şi Toamnă

Aşa cum dinastia Zhou a fost împărţită în două perioade, Dinastia Zhou de Est a fost şi ea împărţită tot în două perioade, denumite Primăvara şi Toamna (770-464 î.Hr.), şi Statele combatante (463-222 î.Hr.), după principalele cronici istorice ale epocii, cunoscute ca Analele Primăverii şi Toamnei şi Strategiile Statelor Combatante.

De-a lungul ambelor perioade, nenumăratele state în care era divizată China erau într-o stare de permanent conflict. La începutul dinastiei Zhou de Est existau 170 de state, fiecare dintre ele luptându-se cu celelalte cel puţin pentru propria supravieţuire, dacă nu mai mult. Cea mai fragmentată zonă era cea din centrul Chinei. Pe măsură ce perioada Zhou înainta în timp, aceste mici state centrale se simţeau din ce în ce mai ameninţate de statele mai mari aflate la periferia Chinei, cum ar fi Chu, Wu şi Qin. Ele considerau că purtau flacăra civilizaţiei chineze împotriva acestor barbari de la marginea hotarelor şi se autointitulau Zhongguo, Regatele Centrale, aşa cum îşi denumesc astăzi chinezii ţara. Totuşi, aceste Regate Centrale au fost atât de absorbite de propriile conflicte încât nici măcar nu au remarcat că aceşti străini nechlipiţi începuseră să câştige teren.

Războaiele erau o caracteristică definitorie a acestei epoci, în special în Regatele Centrale, şi, pe măsură ce acestea se luptau pentru supremaţie, numărul lor a scăzut, treptat, până când rămăseseră numai câteva astfel de state. Între timp, un exilat din statul Wei, un funcţionar de rang înalt pe nume Shang Yang, descoperind că ideile sale nu găsesc ascultare acasă, a decis să propovăduiască Legalismul în statul Qin. A intrat repede în graţiile conducătorul statului Qin, punând bazele unei ierarhii rigide bazată pe funcţie şi ale unui cadru legal extrem de strict care să reglementeze dreptul de proprietate şi îndatoririle fiecărei persoane. Reformele lui Shang Yang au transformat statul Qin într-un stat centralizat, incredibil de bine organizat, cu o armată pe măsură. Treptat, după anul 318 î.Hr., statul Qin a devenit atât de puternic, încât a înglobat din ce în ce mai multe state. În anul 221 î.Hr., Qin cucerise toate statele din nord, iar regele Zheng şi-a schimbat numele în Shi Huangdi, Primul Împărat, China fiind, pentru prima dată, unificată sub un singur sceptru.

Shi Huangdi şi statul Qin

221–206 î.Hr.

Shi Huangdi era în mod clar un om carismatic şi puternic, care s-a implicat în conducerea noului său imperiu cu o forţă nemaiîntâlnită. A coagula diverse culturi şi state într-un tot unitar necesita o oarecare asprime, iar Shi Huangdi era exact omul potrivit pentru această sarcină. În câţiva ani, reuşise să impună un cadru legal uniform pe tot teritoriul imperiului, divizându-l în 36 (mai târziu 48) de districte militare, conduse de o ierarhie fixă de funcţionari. Greutăţile, măsurile şi, mai ales, scrisul au fost modernizate şi standardizate, stabilindu-se ideogramele care mai sunt şi astăzi folosite.

În acelaşi timp, Shi Huangdi era hotărât să-şi păzească imperiul atât împotriva ameninţărilor din afară, cât şi a haosului din interior. Cea mai mare ameninţare externă venea din partea nomazilor din stepele nordice. Mici valuri de pământ asigurau oarecare protecţie, dar Shi Huangdi a decis să le unească într-un mare zid care să se întindă de-a lungul graniţei nordice a imperiului. Prin intermediul muncii forţate a zeci de mii de ţărani, acest prim Mare Zid, construit din pământ bătătorit, a fost înălţat în numai cinci ani.

Dar în ciuda tuturor eforturilor lui Shi Huangdi, neînţelegerile continuau să persiste, iar cărturarii au început să protesteze împotriva jugului aspru al legalismului. Certurile cărturarilor deveniseră atât de zgomotoase şi deranjante, încât împăratul a decis să ardă toate cărţile, în afara celor din propria bibliotecă şi a celor referitoare la probleme practice, cum ar fi agricultura, sau medicina. Măsura i-a adus lui Shi Huangdi ura nesfârşită a învăţaţilor adepţi ai confucianismului şi nu a reuşit să reprime rezistenţa la ideile legaliste.

În anul 210 î.Hr., Shi Huangdi a murit şi i s-au organizat funeralii pe măsura imensei sale puteri. În 1974, muncitorii care săpau un puţ în Lintong, în afara Xianului, au descoperit mai multe statui de teracotă, în mărime naturală, ale unor războinici de demult. Când arheologii au început să exploreze situl au găsit a vastă necropolă sub un deal artificial. De atunci, s-a descoperit o armată de şapte mii de asemenea războinici din teracotă, fiecare cu trăsături unice, alături de cai din bronz, care de luptă şi multe altele. Uimitor este, însă, că acesta este doar începutul, arheologii mai având de explorat camera mortuară a lui Shi Huangdi, în care se presupune că se află multe alte comori nedescoperite.

Odată cu moartea lui Shi Huangdi, imperiul Qin a fost cuprins de haos, în timp ce lorzii Qin se luptau pentru a prelua puterea. După ce un ţăran pe nume Chen She a refuzat să se lase recrutat în armata imperială s-au stârnit o serie de revolte populare împotriva stăpânirii Qin, iar opoziţia nobiliară a readus la viaţă statul Chu, rivalul dintotdeauna al imperiului Qin. În anul 206 î.Hr., un locotenent din statul Chu pe nume Liu Bang, o fostă căpetenie de bandiţi, a condus o armată împotriva celui de-al treilea (şi ultimul) împărat Qin, iar apoi, aidoma unui Oliver Cromwell chinez, şi-a trădat propriul stăpân şi s-a autodeclarat Împăratul Gao Zu, primul împărat al unei noi dinastii, dinastia Han, care avea să conducă China pe parcursul următoarelor patru secole.

Dinastia Han

206 î.Hr.–220

Gao Zu era un om din popor, care şi-a păstrat modul de comportament necizelat chiar şi în timpul vieţii sale la curte. Zu era chiar mândru de felul lui de a fi simplu şi direct. Puterea vechii aristocraţii, care triumfase sub Zhou, a dispărut pentru totdeauna, iar totalitarismul dur al statului Qin a fost abandonat în favoarea unei filozofii confucianiste mai blânde, care a devenit baza doctrinară a noului imperiu. În conformitate cu idealurile confucianiste, povara taxelor, cu excepţia celor aplicate negustorilor, a fost redusă, iar intervenţia statului în tranzacţiile comerciale a scăzut.

Treptat, vechea nobilime feudală a fost îndepărtată de la putere, fiind înlocuită de o clasă meritocratică.

Dar Gao Zu era un pragmatic, nu un idealist, mulţumindu-se să menţină mare parte din standardizarea statului Qin şi din puterea sa centralizată. Pentru a preîntâmpina o lovitură de stat militară, cum fusese cea prin care ajunsese el la putere, Zu şi-a înzestrat rudele cu mari suprafeţe de teren.

Melanjul de legalism şi confucianism părea să funcţioneze, în timpul dinastiei Han, China cunoscând prima sa perioadă de înflorire a culturii şi artelor. Recăpătându-şi încrederea în sine, chinezii au început să-şi extindă frontierele şi să facă negoţ în jurul lumii, atât cu mărfuri, cât şi cu idei. Şi într-adevăr, atât de definitorie a fost această perioadă pentru cultura chineză, încât şi astăzi numele grupului etnic şi cultural din care fac parte majoritatea chinezilor se numeşte Han.

După proclamarea sa ca împărat, Liu Bang a mai trăit doar zece ani, dar regulile stabilite de el s-au dovedit a fi atât de durabile, încât au supravieţuit multor povocări şi câtorva împăraţi care au domnit mai puţin, până la domnia celui de-al şaselea împărat Han, instaurată în 141 î.Hr. Wu Di este cunoscut ca Împăratul marţial, meritându-şi pe drept numele. Era energic, aspru şi foarte ambiţios. Una dintre primele sale acţiuni a fost să facă curăţenie în guvern. În locul numeroşilor mari demnitari, el a înfiinţat un birou de scribi imperiali sau funcţionari, care urmau să emită edicte către toate ramurile guvernului şi să decidă care dintre numeroasele documente primite de guvern ajung la împărat. De asemenea, a dus ideea confucianistă a numirii demnitarilor în funcţie de meritele lor la concluzia sa logică, înfiinţând o universitate naţională pentru pregătirea acestora, în care admiterea se făcea printr-un examen deschis. El a emis această faimoasă proclamaţie:

> „Se caută eroi!
>
> O Proclamaţie!

O muncă excepţională are nevoie de oameni excepţionali. Un cal care loveşte poate deveni câteodată un animal de mare valoare. Un om care este obiectul dezaprobării lumii poate ajunge să facă lucruri extraordinare. Asemenea unui cal dificil de mânuit, aşa se întâmplă şi cu omul detestat – este doar o chestiune de educaţie.

Aşadar, ordonăm oficialilor districtelor să caute oameni străluciţi şi talentaţi, care să devină generalii Noştri, miniştrii Noştri şi trimişii Noştri în statele îndepărtate."

Citat din Giles, *Podoabe ale Literaturii chineze*.

Nemulțumit doar cu înființarea unei administrații care continuă să fie un model chiar și în zilele noastre, Wu Di a hotărât să extindă granițele imperiului. În momentul morții sale, în anul 87 î.Hr., după 54 de ani de domnie, Wu Di nu numai că reușise să extindă granițele imperiului, înglobând multe state vestice și sud-vestice, dar trimisese o faimoasă expediție militară, sub conducerea generalului Li Guangli, care ajunsese până în îndepărtatul teritoriu al Kazahstanului de astăzi. Sub atenta supraveghere a armatelor Hanului au fost puse bazele legendarei rute comerciale numite Drumul Mătăsii, ce permitea negustorilor să transporte mătasea chinezească, mirodeniile și ceaiul prin toată Asia Centrală, până la Roma.

Cu toate acestea, în secolul ce a urmat morții lui Wu Di, imperiul Han începuse să ducă lipsa resurselor necesare menținerii puterii sale, iar curtea era măcinată de intrigi politice. În anul 9 d.Hr., Wang Mang a luat tronul de la cei din dinastia Han. Wang Mang era un adept înfocat al confucianismului, restabilind ceea ce considera el că fuseseră titlurile nobiliare și instituțiile din „epoca de aur" Zhou. Uimitor, printr-o mișcare care-l anticipa cu aproape 2 000 de ani pe Mao, el a decis să naționalizeze pământul și să-l redistribuie țăranilor. Din păcate, mișcarea s-a lovit de puternica opoziție a proprietarilor de pământuri. Înainte ca Wang Mang să fi găsit o cale de a distribui pământul, niște inundații catastrofale au distrus recoltele, iar un grup de țărani, cunoscut sub numele de Sprâncenele Roșii (fiindcă își vopseau fețele în roșu precum demonii), s-a revoltat. Opoziția atât din partea aristocrației cât și a țărănimii s-a dovedit a fi prea mult pentru Wang Mang, care a fost alungat de la putere de un alt leader Han puternic, Guang Wu Di (Împăratul Războinic Strălucitor).

Domnia dinastiei Han a fost restabilită, dar zilele bune ale imperiului se sfârșiseră. Treptat, imperiul a început să se destrame, iar generalii și nobilii locali au început să-și traseze propriile domenii. China era măcinată de războaie civile și revolte țărănești cum au fost cele ale Turbanelor Galbene și ale celor Cinci Banițe de Orez, din Sichuan și Shaanxi, care au încercat să abolească proprietatea particulară. În ciuda acestor tulburări, cultura chineză a înflorit.

Atât confucianismul cât şi daoismul au cunoscut o dezvoltare puternică, acestora alăturându-li-se budismul, care a îmbogăţit viaţa şi artele cu un nou mod de gândire. Tehnologia a progresat la rândul ei, în această perioadă făcându-şi apariţia invenţii precum morile de apă, roaba, ceasurile de apă, seismografele pentru înregistrarea cutremurelor şi sferele armilare care urmăreau mişcarea astrelor şi a planetelor.

Perioada Celor Trei Regate şi Sui

220–618

În anul 220, imperiul Han s-a prăbuşit, iar în următoarele patru secole China a fost măcinată de războaie nesfârşite între cele trei state rivale, Wei, Wu şi Shu, care şi-au câştigat numele de cele Trei Regate. Totuşi, în ciuda acestor conflicte, cultura chineză a continuat să înflorească la fel ca în timpul imperiului Han, iar în 581, când generalul Yang Jian a unificat în sfârşit China, devenind împărat, sub numele de Wen, şi punând bazele dinastiei Sui, ţara era prosperă şi cu o bogată cultură.

Wen şi-a stabilit capitala la Chang, în nordul Chinei, însă grânarul Chinei era acum de-a lungul râului Yangtze, la peste 2 000 km distanţă. Mutarea unor cantităţi uriaşe de cereale, cu ajutorul carelor, pe drumuri proaste, s-a dovedit a fi nepractică, astfel încât succesorul lui Wen Sui, Yang Di, a demarat un proiect şi mai grandios decât Marele Zid, şi anume Marele Canal, care făcea legătura între Yangtze şi Fluviul Galben. Acest proiect măreţ s-a realizat într-un an, cu ajutorul muncii forţate a cinci milioane şi jumătate de oameni. Însă, pe parcursul lucrărilor, au murit mai mult de două milioane de oameni şi, ca şi cum asta nu ar fi fost suficient, Yang Di a decis să sfideze suferinţa acestora plimbându-se, alături de concubine, în susul şi în josul canalului, în fruntea „flotei dragonului", lungă de 100 de km, pe care o conducea din giganticul său palat plutitor, cu patru niveluri, tras de 80 000 de ţărani. Deloc surprinzător, Yang Di nu era prea iubit, iar în anul 618 a fost asasinat în revolta condusă de generalul Li Yuan, care a devenit primul împărat din dinastia Tang, Gao Zu, acelaşi nume pe care Liu Bang şi-l alesese când a devenit primul împărat Han.

China Medievală: Tang și Song

618–1278

Dinastia Tang a reprezentat, probabil, momentul de vârf al vechii culturi chineze. În timp ce Europa era scufundată în întunecatul Ev Mediu, China a înflorit ca niciodată. Într-o vreme în care doar câteva orașe din Europa aveau o populație de peste câteva zeci de mii de locuitori, iar cele mai multe clădiri ale acestora nu erau decât niște colibe sărăcăcioase, China se mândrea cu câteva zeci de orașe cu peste jumătate de milion de locuitori, multe dintre ele centre cosmopolite și sofisticate, cu grădini, ceainării, restaurante și case elegante pentru cei din clasa de mijloc. Cu o agricultură productivă, foametea era aproape inexistentă, iar cei bogați duceau o viață de plăceri, delectându-se cu bidivii lor de rasă, șoimii pentru vânătoare, jocurile de polo și de șah, mătăsurile, mirodeniile, parfumurile și minunatele lor porțelanuri.

Era o societate cosmopolită și aproape 25 000 de străini locuiau în capitala Xi'an, care se estimează că avea o populație de 2 milioane de locuitori – performanță atinsă în Europa, de-abia în secolul XIX, de Londra. Încrederea chinezilor în propriile forțe atinsese cote maxime, aceștia trimițând comercianți și călători peste tot în lume, pentru a aduna idei noi care să le îmbogățească propria societate. Drumul mătăsii era cel mai folosit, dar calea maritimă către vest prospera și ea, iar vasele comerciale persane și arabe acostau adesea în Gaungzhou, în timp ce vasele chinezești navigau spre Golful Persic. Călătorul Xuan Zang a petrecut 16 ani vizitând India și s-a întors cu numeroase informații noi despre budism, care, la acea vreme, era o forță puternică în societatea chineză.

Punctul de maximă dezvoltare a inovațiilor tehnice chineze se regăsește tot în această perioadă. De-a lungul acestei perioade medievale, cărțile au început să fie tipărite cu ajutorul tiparniței mobile. Praful de pușcă era folosit pentru crearea unor arme distrugătoare. Petrolul era extras din puțuri de mare adâncime și pompat prin conducte din bambus. Magneții erau folosiți la confecționarea busolelor, dar și pentru previziuni astrologice. Iar, în timp ce europenii încă mai navigau în vase mici, cu un singur

catarg şi o singură velă, chinezii construiau nave uriaşe, cu numeroase catarge şi vele, jonci mai mari decât tot ce se va construi în
Europa, în următorii 500 de ani.

Interesant, dinastia Tang a dat singura împărăteasă a Chinei, pe
Wu Zetian, care a condus China cu o mână de fier timp de 50 de
ani, din 655 până în 705. Wu a iniţiat un număr de reforme importante, cum ar fi admiterea cărturarilor săraci în administraţie
sau a femeilor la ritualuri rezervate înainte exclusiv bărbaţilor, şi
a vegheat la construirea multor monumente budiste, printre care
şi celebrele sculpturi Longmen, de la Luoyang. Îşi crease, însă, o
reputaţie de suveran nemilos, astfel încât, în 705, pusă în faţa unei
opoziţii covârşitoare, a fost nevoită să abdice.

Odată cu Wu, pare să fi dispărut şi încrederea în dinastia Tang. În
următoarele două secole, ţara a fost divizată între diverse alianţe
politice şi regionale, devenind din ce în ce mai vulnerabilă în faţa
atacurilor din nord. Până în anul 907, domnia dinastiei Tang luase
sfârşit. În următoarea jumătate de secol, puterea a pendulat între
cele Cinci Dinastii din nord şi cele Zece Regate din sud, până în
anul 960, când armata a numit, în sfârşit, un general, Song Tai Zu,
pe tronul imperial, întemeind dinastia Song, care a domnit până
în 1278. Prima jumătate a dinastiei Song este cunoscută sub numele de Dinastia Song de Nord, din cauza împăraţilor care au condus ţara din oraşul Kaifeng, situat pe râul Galben, în nord. Dar în
1115, tribul Jurched, din Manciuria, i-a gonit pe împăraţii Song
din Nord restabilind una dintre cele Cinci Dinastii, dinastia Jin.
Dinastia Song s-a mutat spre sud şi a condus din Huangzhou.

Pierderea teritoriilor din nord a reprezentat o mare lovitură pentru
dinastia Song, dar nu un dezastru absolut, fiindcă, de această dată,
sudul era la fel de dezvoltat ca şi nordul, iar terenurile arabile din
valea fluviului Yangtze şi din delta Râului Perlelor erau cele mai
roditoare din întreaga Chină. Huangzhou s-a dezvoltat, devenind
un oraş la fel de mare ca şi Xi'an sub dinastia Tang, pentru aceasta
mărturie stând şi jurnalul lui Marco Polo, care a trecut pe-acolo în
secolul XIII, mult după dispariţia dinastiei Song.

Hanatul

1278–1368

Cum dinastiile Jin şi Song erau ocupate să se războiască între ele, probabil că nu şi-au dat seama ce se întâmpla la graniţa lor de nord, printre mongoli. După ce, multă vreme, au fost împărţiţi în numeroase fiefuri, mongolii s-au unit, în 1206, sub conducerea lui Temujin, care a devenit apoi Genghis-Han, însemnând Conducătorul Suprem. Genghis-Han s-a dovedit a fi un lider militar uimitor de eficient care, cu ajutorul minunaţilor săi călăreţi, s-a lansat într-o mare expediţie de cucerire, ce a eclipsat-o până şi pe cea a lui Alexandru cel Mare, unul dintre cei mai renumiţi comandanţi militari din istorie. Tibetul şi bazinul Tarim au căzut sub atacul hoardelor mongole. În 1209, aceştia au cucerit regiunea Uigur. Apoi, în 1210, au pătruns în China de nord a dinastiei Jin şi au devastat-o cu cruzimea lor binecunoscută. În sud, dinastia Song se bucura de situaţia grea a rivalilor săi, gândindu-se, probabil, prea puţin la ce însemna acest lucru pe termen lung. În 1234, mongolii conduşi de Ogedai Han, fiul lui Genghis-Han, au cucerit oraşul Kaifeng, ceea ce le punea, practic, în mână toată China dinastiei Jin, iar în urma acestei înfrângeri, ultimul împărat Jin s-a sinucis.

Pentru o vreme, incursiunile mongole în China s-au mai domolit, în timp ce Ogedai îşi concentra eforturile asupra Vietnamului şi Europei, aici mongolii reuşind să ajungă până în Polonia şi Ungaria. Dar momentul de răgaz a fost scurt. Când nepotul lui Genghis-Han, Kubilai-Han, a devenit Han, în anul 1250, asaltul mongolilor asupra Chinei a fost reluat. Kubilai a devenit Marele Han, a construit un oraş nou, „oraşul Tartar" din Beijing şi s-a autoproclamat împăratul Chinei, întemeind dinastia Yuan. În câţiva ani, dinastia Song s-a prăbuşit, iar Kubilai-Han a devenit conducătorul unui vast imperiu, ce cuprindea aproape toată Asia, de la Moscova la Ind şi de la Marea Mediterană la Oceanul Pacific.

China a cunoscut din nou pacea sub Kubilai-Han şi urmaşii lui. În mod surprinzător, în China mongolii şi-au pierdut obiceiurile sângeroase, preluând din obiceiurile chineze, iar dinastia Yuan s-a dovedit a avea conducători la fel de eficienţi pe cât fuseseră şi ceilalţi conducători ai Chinei. Dimensiunile imperiului au făcut ca vizitatorilor străini, printre care şi Marco Polo, să le fie mai uşor să admire splendorile noului oraş, Beijing. Un amănunt interesat: în 1341, un rus a ieşit pe primul loc la examenul pentru intrarea în administraţia imperială. Întotdeauna au existat, însă, resentimente mocnite, nu doar din partea oficialilor chinezi, care se retrăgeau în locuinţele lor pentru a picta şi citi, dar şi din partea oamenilor obişnuiţi, care considerau puterea mongolă mult mai represivă decât cea a împăraţilor chinezi. Pe tot parcursul secolului XIV, revoltele au devenit din ce în ce mai dese, iar în 1368, în urma unei răscoale în Yangtze, călugărul devenit conducător de bandiţi, Zhu Yuanzhang, autointitulat Prinţul Wu, a luat tronul de la ultimul împărat Yuan, încă un copil.

Ming şi Qing

1368–1840

Wu a devenit primul împărat al dinastiei Ming, care a condus de la Nanjing (capitala de astăzi a provinciei Jiangsu). Dinastia Ming a unificat, din nou, China sub o conducere chineză, întâia oară de la prăbuşirea dinastiei Tang, dar împăratul Wu s-a dovedit a fi mult mai nemilos decât oricare dintre împăraţii Yuan, ucigând mii de funcţionari şi de cărturari într-o serie de epurări. Impactul acestor atrocităţi, după un secol de dominaţie străină, i-a făcut pe chinezi să-şi piardă încrederea în sine, cultura lor devenind din ce în ce mai închisă şi mai conservatoare, tendinţă ce a devenit şi mai pronunţată în timpul dinastiei Qing, care a ajuns la putere în 1644.

Într-adevăr, China a devenit atât de introvertită, încât nici n-a băgat de seamă că exploratorii europeni navigau în jurul lumii şi că ştiinţa europeană nu doar că ajunsese din urmă descoperirile chineze, dar le depăşea cu mult. Astfel că, în 1793, când lordul englez MacCartney a ajuns în China, alături de o numeroasă delegaţie comercială, pentru a negocia un parteneriat, a fost refuzat de împăratul Qing, care considera că restul lumii nu avea nimic de oferit şi că nu putea încheia o alianţă cu o naţiune pe care o considera minoră.

Din păcate pentru Qing, europenii nu erau pregătiţi să accepte un refuz, considerând că o naţiune atât de numeroasă şi bogată cum se spunea despre China că ar fi, avea, cu siguranţă, de oferit nenumărate posibilităţi de comerţ. Din secolul XVII, în China crescuse cererea pentru opiu. Mare parte era cultivat pe plan local, dar comercianţii britanici aveau în India o sursă de opiu gata pregătită şi, în curând, au început să transporte vase întregi de opiu indian în China pentru a satisface cererea de aici. Comerţul era ilegal, bineînţeles, nu din cauza unei dezaprobări morale a consumului de droguri, ci din pricina restricţiilor comerciale asupra bunurilor de import. Acest lucru nu i-a oprit pe englezi, care acostau pur şi simplu în Guangzhou şi vindeau marfa traficanţilor locali, ale căror bărci rapide o transportau la mal cu binecuvântarea tacită a autorităţilor. Între timp, vasele englezeşti duceau acasă ceai, mătase şi porţelan, pentru a satisface apetitul în creştere al englezilor pentru ceai şi chinezării.

Câţiva înalţi funcţionari imperiali, dintre care mulţi erau fumători de opiu, au încercat să legalizeze comerţul cu opiu. Dar împăratul Qing considera că opiul lăsa ţara fără banii pe care ceaiul şi alte exporturi îi puteau aduce, iar din 1837 a ordonat oficialilor să pună cu orice preţ capăt comerţului cu opiu. În 1839, Lin Xexu, guvernatorul provinciei Guangzhou, a confiscat tot opiul ţinut de negustorii europeni în vasele ancorate în largul coastei – în afara jurisdicţiei chineze. Ministrul de externe britanic, Lordul Palmerston, a trimis imediat o flotă britanică şi 4 000 de soldaţi către China, inaugurând, astfel, primul Război al Opiului. După doi ani de bombardament continuu din partea flotei engleze, chinezii au fost obligaţi să accepte deschiderea porturilor pentru comerţul internaţional şi cedarea Hong Kongului către Marea Britanie, urmând ca acesta să fie baza de operaţiuni a comercianţilor englezi.

Sfârşitul Imperiului

1840–1911

Umilinţa reprezentată de înfrângerea străină şi greutăţile economice din ce în ce mai mari au subminat autoritatea dinastiei Qing. În afară, China ceda din ce în ce mai multe teritorii şi influenţă puterilor europene. În interior, populaţia, confruntată cu prăbuşirea ierarhiilor tradiţionale şi o sărăcie în creştere, a început să conteste dreptul dinastiei de a conduce. Ultima picătură a fost înfrângerea ţării în 1895, în război cu Japonia. Ca răspuns, tinerii radicali au început nişte campanii numite ,,Reînvierea Chinei'' şi ,,Întărirea ţării'', iar în luna octombrie a aceluiaşi an, Societatea pentru Renaşterea Chinei, o societate republicană întemeiată în 1894, de doctorul Sun Iat-sen, din Guandong, a pus la cale un complot pentru instaurarea unui guvern republican la Guangzhou. Complotul a eşuat şi mulţi membri ai societăţii au fost ucişi sau aruncaţi în închisoare. Sun Iat-sen a fugit la Londra, unde a fost răpit de oficiali ai dinastiei Qing, apoi eliberat în urma presiunilor exercitate de guvernul englez.

Între timp, în anul 1899, o extrem de xenofobă sectă de arte marţiale, numită Boxerii, a decis că tot ce se întâmpla rău în ţară se datorează străinilor. Boxerii au început să atace şi să dărâme tot ce putea fi de origine străină, de la misiuni creştine până la linii de cale ferată construite de companii europene. Împărăteasa Cixi din dinastia Qing şovăia, apoi s-a decis să sprijine secta boxerilor. Străinii erau asediaţi în Beijing, astfel încât o forţă internaţională a fost trimisă să-i protejeze. Cixi a scăpat din Beijing fugind într-o şaretă, deghizată în ţărancă.

Dinastia Qing nu mai avea nici o autoritate, iar când împărăteasa Cixi s-a întors la Beijing, în 1902, nu a fost decât o chestiune de timp până să-şi găsească sfârşitul. În 1908, împărăteasa a murit, lăsându-l ca moştenitor pe nepotul său în vârstă de doi ani, Puyi Xuantong, ultimul împărat. În 1911, rezistenţa populară faţă de deţinerea căilor ferate de către străini a atins cote maxime, iar o răscoală stârnită în Wuchang, provincia Hubei, a condus la o revoltă populară, care, într-un final, a dărâmat definitiv un imperiu pe moarte. Pe data de 29 decembrie a acelui an, revoluționarul republican Sun Iat-sen a fost ales președinte interimar al noii Republici Chineze, de către un congres de delegați din 16 adunări regionale.

Republica Chineză

1911–1921

Cu toate acestea, nu Sun Iat-sen era cel care deținea puterea în China. În acel moment, adevăratul conducător al Chinei era generalul Yuan Shikai. Yuan avea în spate toată armata, iar în octombrie 1911, curtenii dinastiei Qing l-au numit premier. Acum, toate condițiile erau întrunite pentru un război civil între Yuan și Qing, pe de-o parte, și republicanii revoluționari, pe de alta. Pentru a evita lupta, ambele părți au început negocierile, principala propunere fiind ca, în cazul în care Yuan ar fi de acord să fie numit președinte, va sprijini Republica și-l va forța pe împăratul-copil Qing să abdice. Atunci când Sun Iat-sen a fost ales președinte, Yuan s-a retras imediat de la negocieri. Pus în fața unei alegeri imposibile, Sun Iat-sen s-a retras, la Beijing formându-se un alt guvern republican, cu Yuan ca președinte.

Deși guvernul adoptase o constituție, Yuan trăgea, de fapt, toate sforile și nu a ezitat să le folosească. Pentru a încerca să-i țină puterea în frâu, revoluționarii au format un partid politic, Guomindang (GMD sau partidul naționalist). Dar când acest partid a câștigat, la alegerile din 1912, Yuan a dizolvat parlamentul, a scos Guomindang-ul în afara legii și a instituit o dictatură militară. În vara anului 1913, șapte provincii din sud și-au declarat independența, iar Yuan și-a trimis armata pentru a nimici această „A doua Revoluție," forțându-l pe Sun Iat-sen să plece în exil.

Cert este faptul că Yuan avea ambiții mai mari decât aceea de a fi președinte. Cum mai făcuseră și alți lideri militari în istoria Chinei, Yuan plănuia să se înscăuneze ca împărat al unei noi dinastii. Dar a murit înainte de a fi proclamat. Sun Iat-sen s-a reîntors pentru a forma un guvern naționalist în sudul provinciei Guangzhou, în timp ce spiritele războinice şi generalii îşi făceau de cap în nord şi în alte provincii. Însă, în această perioadă în care China era divizată, iar puterile occidentale erau preocupate de Primul Război Mondial, Japonia a profitat de situaţie pentru a emite Cele 21 de cereri către China, prin care Shandong urma să fie cedat Japoniei, China devenind, practic, un protectorat japonez. În 1915, aflat într-o postură nefavorabilă, Yuan fusese forţat să accepte o versiune modificată a acestora, dar, la sfârşitul Primului Război Mondial, chinezii au sperat că Occidentul va face presiuni asupra Japoniei pentru a renunţa la cererile sale. În schimb, prin Tratatul de la Versailles, din 1919, Franţa şi SUA, care semnaseră deja pacte secrete cu Japonia, şi-au retras sprijinul acordat Chinei. În deceniul precedent, tinerii fuseseră cuprinşi de o adevărată frenezie intelectuală şi de un entuziasm profund faţă de idealurile politice ale Occidentului. Pentru ei, tratatul de la Versailles a fost o lovitură cumplită. Când veştile au ajuns în China, pe 4 Mai 1919, 3 000 de studenţi de la Universitatea din Beijing au ieşit în stradă să protesteze. Autorităţile de la Beijing au suprimat revolta, trimiţându-i la închisoare pe liderii acesteia, dar măsură nu a făcut altceva decât să dea naştere unui val de proteste în toată ţara.

Rebeliunea Roşie

1921–1949

În 1921, inspiraţi de evenimentele din Rusia, unii dintre protestatari s-au unit şi au format Partidul Comunist Chinez (PCC), cu lideri ca Mao Zedong şi Zhou Enlai. Încurajaţi de activiştii ruşi, care, la fel ca Marx, susţineau că înainte de a avea o revoluţie proletară, China trebuie să aibă o revoluţie burgheză, cei din PCC s-au alăturat Guomindang-ului în lupta împotriva conducătorilor militari din nord. Dar când Sun Iat-sen a murit, în 1925, la conducerea Guomindang-ului i-a urmat cumnatul său, tânărul căpitan de armată, Chiang Kaishek. Spre deosebire de socialistul Sun Iat-sen, Chiang Kaishek avea prea puţin timp pentru comunişti, fiind chiar suspicios faţă de sprijinul primit de aceştia de la ruşi. Expulzat din Guomindang, Partidul Comunist a fost nevoit să intre în ilegalitate. În 1928, PCC-ul a organizat o grevă în Shanghai, a cărei reprimare violentă de către trupele lui Chiang Kaishek a dus la moartea a 5 000 de muncitori şi comunişti. Guomindang-ul a început să fie considerat de partea „asupritoarei" elite chineze.

În timp ce majoritatea comuniştilor muncea în oraşe pentru a organiza opoziţia, Mao a plecat la ţară pentru a mobiliza ţăranii, pe care-i simţea a fi cheia revoluţiei. El a organizat prima armată populară, denumită Armata Roşie în provincia Jiangxi. La început, Armata Roşie a avut oarecare succes, folosind lovituri de gherilă în afara munţilor. Atunci Chiang Kaishek i-a înconjurat în Jingging Shan cu o armată de jumătate de milion de oameni. Armata Roşie, care avea doar 80 000 de oameni şi un echipament sărac nu ar fi avut nici o şansă în luptă astfel încât în Octombrie 1934, Mao a organizat o legendară retragere care urma să traverseze 9 500 de km prin munţi şi care a ajuns să fie cunoscută ca Marşul cel lung. La momentul când Armata roşie a ajuns la baza lor din nord de la Yan'an din Shaanxi, un an mai târziu, ei pierduseră trei sferturi din efective din cauza frigului, foametei şi dezertărilor. Dar această epopee a câştigat pentru Partidul comunist respectul multor oameni şi l-a transformat pe Mao în liderul de necontestat al comuniştilor.

Între timp, japonezii au devenit din ce în ce mai agresivi iar în iulie 1937 au pornit un atac asupra Beijingului. Chiang Kaishek a insistat că prima sa prioritate era să-i învingă pe comunişti, dar subordonaţii lui nu au fost de acord şi l-au forţat să se unească cu Partidul comunist în Frontul Unit împotriva japonezilor. Dar chiar şi împreună, GMD-ul şi Partidul comunist nu au făcut faţă japonezilor care au ocupat foarte repede estul Chinei, de la Beijing la Guangzhou. Frontul Unit s-a retras la Chongqing, în Sichuan unde unitatea lor s-a destrămat.

După atacul de la Pearl Harbor, Japonia a devenit inamicul SUA şi a trimis America de partea chinezilor. Când Japonia a fost definitiv învinsă în 1945, japonezii au fost forţaţi să se retragă din China, lăsând în urmă o situaţie haotică. În timpul războiului, nenumăraţi oameni s-au înrolat în Armata roșie pentru a-i alunga pe japonezi, astfel că, atunci când aceștia au plecat, majoritatea teritoriilor pe care le ocupaseră s-au numit Zone Eliberate, aflate sub controlul comuniștilor iar Armata roșie a devenit mai puternică cu un milion de oameni. Scena era pregătită pentru un spectacol uriaș între GMD și partidul comunist.

În Manciuria a izbucnit războiul civil și, cu toate că generalul SUA George Marshall a instaurat o pace temporară, aceasta a fost de scurtă durată. Lucrurile se întorseseră în favoarea comuniștilor. În 1948, armata comunistă, redenumită acum Armata de eliberare populară (PLA) a învins GMD-ul într-o mare bătălie la Huai Huai. În timp ce Armata de eliberare avansa spre Shanghai, Chiang Kaishek a înțeles că pierduse bătălia și a plecat în Taiwan pentru a forma Republica Chineză, așteptând acolo cu 2 000 000 de soldați și refugiați care s-au unit cu el mai târziu în speranța că, într-o bună zi, vor elibera China continentală. În octombrie 1949, Mao a proclamat înființarea Republicii Populare Chineze, transformând China în cea mai populată țară comunistă de până atunci.

China în perioada lui Mao

1949–1976

Majoritatea chinezilor au întâmpinat cu căldură Republica Populară, nu neapărat fiindcă erau comuniști, dar fiindcă țara era, în sfârșit, unită sub un singur conducător și fiindcă războaiele civile luaseră sfârșit. Dar conform abordării staliniștilor în Rusia, Partidul comunist chinez s-a mișcat repede în neutralizarea opoziției. Zeci de mii de suporteri ai GMD-ului au fost executați sau trimiși în lagăre de muncă, intelectualii au fost înrolați forțat în clasele criticismului și autocriticismului, presa și exprimarea opiniei în public erau reduse la tăcere, misionarii străini au fost forțați să părăsească țara și un milion sau după opinia altora, două milioane de proprietari au fost uciși astfel încât pământul să poată fi redistribuit. În mod semnificativ, eliminarea proprietarilor a distrus nobilimea, clasa care dominase întotdeauna guvernul chinez. Acum era foarte clar cine era la comandă.

La început, pământul nu a fost rechiziționat din proprietatea particulară, ci pur și simplu împărțit printre țăranii cărora li se dăduse o
bucată în proprietate. Țăranii au continuat să-și muncească pământul cu un entuziasm extraordinar iar în câțiva ani producția agricolă
era mai mare ca niciodată. În același timp, partidul comunist nați-
onalizase industria și i-a înrolat pe foștii proprietari să preia conducerea companiilor de stat. Primul dintr-o serie de Planuri cincinale,
cel din 1953-1958 a pus accentul pe industria grea iar producția
industrială a crescut simțitor.

Pe la miijlocul anilor 1950, o parte din această euforie s-a mai pierdut. Existau numeroase dezbateri despre ce ar trebuie să se facă pentru a merge înainte. Ei au fost de acord că ultima țintă era o țară comunistă, dar nu au putut fi de acord asupra modului în care puteau
ajunge acolo. Primul plan cincinal a acceptat o abordare treptată și
a fost denumit apoi Micul salt înainte. Gospodăriile țărănești au
fost forțate să se unească în cooperative de producție mai mari, care
asigurau un ajutor mutual, mai întâi 20 până la 40 de unități gospodărești, ajungându-se la 300 de cooperative.

Totuși Mao era nerăbdător și hotărât să împingă lucrurile înainte.
În 1957 a slăbit restricțiile în ceea ce privea exprimarea opiniilor și
a încurajat plângerile cu sloganul: Lăsați 100 de flori să înflorească
și 100 de școli de gândire să se întreacă. Mao a spus după aceea că
el se aștepta ca oamenii să arate cine erau oficialii ineficienți pentru
a face ca lucrurile să meargă. În schimb, campania celor 100 de flori
a deschis calea intelectualilor pentru a critica partidul comunist.
Aparent înfuriat, Mao a lansat o campanie împotriva orientărilor
„deviante", de dreapta, sub conducerea lui Deng Xiaoping, pentru
a reduce criticii la tăcere. O jumătate de milion de oameni sau mai
mulți au fost executați, exilați în lagărele de muncă sau obligați
la autocritică. Unii comentatori cred acum că această campania a
celor 100 de flori a lui Mao a fost doar un mod de a alunga criticile
ce vizau următorul său plan.

Marele Salt Înainte

1958–1961

Idea grandioasă a lui Mao a fost Marele Salt Înainte. Acesta a fost numele dat celui de-al doilea plan cincinal, care a durat din 1958 până în1963, deși acum se făcea referire doar la primii trei ani, 1958-1961. Mao credea că prin ajutorul unui efort masiv concertat atât în agricultură cât și în industrie, China va putea face Marele Salt Înainte spre o prosperitate economică și comunism. Mao era convins că cei doi stâlpi ai dezvoltării economice erau oțelul și grânele, astfel încât planul s-a axat pe o producție crescută de oțel și grâne care urma să fie obținută de toată lumea printr-o colectivizare masivă.

În august 1958, Biroul politic al partidului comunist a decis că nu mai trebuia să existe proprietate particulară a pământului. În schimb, trebuia să fie admisă în colectivele conduse de membri ai partidului, fiecare bazat pe o medie de 5000 de gospodării. Ideea era să se transforme fermele țărănești de mici dimensiuni în unități agricole eficiente. Țăranii au fost mutați din casele lor și înregimentați în brigăzi de producție și echipe unde munceau fără plată, pentru unități de muncă. Copiii trebuiau îngrijiți separat în timp ce părinții lor trăiau și munceau la comun. A existat chiar și un plan de a muta toată lumea în dormitoare imense și cantine, dar această idee a fost dată uitării destul de repede în fața unei opoziții largi. În mod surprinzător în câteva luni 25 000 de colective au fost înființate pe tot teritoriul țării.

În același timp, Mao a inițiat un plan de creștere a producției industriale prin efortul comun. Producția de oțel, cărbune și electricitate trebuia să crească cu mai mult de o treime în fiecare an astfel încât, a argumentat Mao, în 10 ani producția industrială a Chinei să fie comparabilă cu a Angliei iar în 15 ani să o depășească pe cea a SUA. Muncitorii sezonieri erau cooptați cu milioanele pentru a construi uriașe uzine, pentru a săpa canale și a seca mlaștini. Centrul planului lui Mao era ca fiecare colectiv să aibă propria sa oțelărie pentru a produce oțel din resturi de fier.

„Marele salt înainte" s-a dovedit a fi o catastrofă. Producțiile agricole au scăzut în toate fermele comunale. Una dintre probleme era faptul că aici li s-a indicat cultivarea grânelor în locuri potrivite pentru alt tip de culturi. O altă problemă au fost directivele, provenite de la pseudo omul de știință sovietic Trofim Lîsenko, de a planta cereale fără spațiu între ele și de-a ara adânc, iar rezultatul a fost că aceste culturi s-au sufocat, conducând la înnăbușirea pământului fertil. Aproape în fiecare colectivă membrii de partid fără experiență au încercat să organizeze țăranii fără entuziasm pentru această sarcină. Pentru a înrăutăți și mai mult lucrurile, lucrătorii de la ferme erau forțați să muncească în oțelării în momentul recoltărilor, lăsând recoltele să putrezească îm pământ. Pentru a încununa toate acestea, o mare parte din cerealele recoltate erau expediate spre orașe pentru a îndeplini cotele de producție, indiferent dacă lucrătorii de la țară aveau ce să mănânce. Toate astea au coincis cu o perioadă de inundații și secete. Rezultatul a fost cea mai mare foamete cunoscută vreodată în rândul populației de la țară. Deși estimările variază, se crede că aproximativ 30 de milioane de oameni sau mai mulți au murit în perioada „marelui salt înainte". După aceasta, Partidul comunist a decis că foametea a fost, în proporție de 70%, un eșec politic și 30% din cauza dezastrelor naturale.

În industrie s-a înregistrat un eșec la fel de dezastruos din punct de vedere economic, dar nu și din punct de vedere uman. Concentrarea pe producția de oțel a însemnat că toate celelalte industrii au avut de suferit, iar producția industrială a Chinei a scăzut la jumătate între anii 1958 și 1959. Dar și oțelul din furnale era atât de impur încât era aproape inutilizabil.

Mao a acceptat faptul că el era responsabil pentru dezastrul „marelui salt înainte" și a demisionat din funcția de Președinte al Republicii, lăsând locul lui Liu Shaoqi ca președinte iar Zhou Enlai a devenit premier și Deng Xiaoping secretar. Mao a rămas totuși președinte al Partidului Comunist, dar a fost doar o problemă de timp înainte de a se întoarce.

Revoluția Culturală

1966–1971

Dacă Mao a creat un şoc Chinei cu „marele sas înainte, Marea Revoluție Culturală Proletară a fost un şoc şi mai mare. Scopul recunoscut de Mao era să scape țara de ideile burgheze şi să reaprindă zelul comunist anterior prin mobilizarea tineretului țării, dar era clar că totodată dorea să scape de oponenții săi din partid. Îndemnați de Mao, studenții universității din Beijing au început să se agite împotriva oficialilor Universității şi ai guvernului care, pretindeau ei, ar fi prea burghezi. Când Liu Shaoqi a încercat să potolească agitația, imediat Mao a lansat un atac public înțepător şi a îndrumat studenții să-şi organizeze propra lor miliție politică, Garda Roşie. În acelaşi timp, suporterii lui Mao au încurajat dezvoltarea cultului personalității lui Mao prin distribuirea de copii ale citatelor sale din Cărțulia roşie.

Garda Roşie s-a extins nebănuit de mult, iar şcolile şi universitățile din China s-au închis în timp ce tinerii membri ai Gărzii au ieşit în stradă pentru a lupta împotriva Celor Patru – idei vechi, cultură veche, obiceiuri vechi şi tradiții vechi. Academiile au fost asaltate, cărțile arse, templele şi monumentele au fost atacate, magazinele care vindeau produse occidentale arse din temelii, iar grădinile burghezilor au fost distruse. Oficialii guvernului până la vârf, inclusiv Liu Shaoqi şi Deng Xiaoping au fost goniți din sedii. Zeci de mii de oameni au fost bătuți, abuzați, ucişi sau conduşi la sinucidere în timp ce campania mergea înainte. Când facțiunile Gărzii Roşii au început să se războiască între ele, iar în țară domnea haosul, Mao a cedat în sfârşit presiunii. El a trimis armata care a preluat controlul şi a strâns milioane de tineri membri ai Gărzii Roşii pe care i-a trimis în țară, pentru a predica comunității rurale mesajul comunist.

În 1969, Mao a fost reales în calitate de Preşedinte al Republicii cu mare fast, iar Lin Biao a fost desemnat succesorul lui. Lin a fost alegerea personală a lui Mao şi cel mai bun student al său şi totuşi, el s-a răzvrătit imediat împotriva lui Mao, complotând fără succes pentru a-l asasina, murind ulterior într-un accident aviatic când zbura deasupra Mongoliei în timp ce încerca să fugă în Rusia.

Moartea lui Zhou şi a lui Mao şi ascensiunea lui Deng

1971–1978

În timpul Revoluţiei Culturale s-a remarcat totuşi o figură care se pare că a rezistat, mult iubitul Zhou Enlai. Se crede că acesta şi-a folosit influenţa pentru a modera cele mai rele efecte ale Revoluţiei Culturale şi pentru a îngriji unele dintre rănile rămase. Se crede, de asemenea, că ar fi fost în spatele noii mişcări orientate spre prietenia cu SUA care a culminat cu faimoasa vizită a preşedintelui Richard Nixon în 1971 şi 1972 în China, fapt ce a ajutat la recunoaşterea statului chinez, înlocuind Taiwanul lâ Naţiunile Unite. Zhou Enlai credea că este esenţial pentru China să-şi ia locul important între statele lumii şi de a obţine un statut egal printr-o dezvoltare internă reală, care implica patru modernizări – agricultura, industria, ştiinţa şi tehnologia şi apărarea.

Mao l-a atacat pe Zhou, acuzându-l că are orientare de dreapta. Zhou a supravieţuit, dar în 1973 a fost diagnosticat cu o formă gravă de cancer. Cu acordul lui Mao, Deng Xiaoping a preluat puterea de la Zhou şi a continuat cele patru modernizări. Dar când Zhou a murit în ianuarie 1976, imediat Deng a suferit atacuri pline de insulte din partea celor patru figuri importante ale partidului, cunoscute ca Banda celor Patru – Jiang Qing, soţia lui Mao, împreună cu Wang Hongwen, Zhang Qunqiao şi Yao Wenyuan. Deng a fost dat jos din toate poziţiile oficiale, iar Mao l-a ales pe relativ necunoscutul Hua Goafeng pentru a deveni premier. Timp de o lună şi ceva părea că Banda celor Patru va răsturna toate reformele lui Zhou. Pe 5 aprilie 1976 două milioane de oameni s-au adunat în Piaţa Tiananmen din Beijing pentru a ţine un moment de reculegere pentru moartea lui Zhou Enlai, iar adunarea s-a transformat într-un protest împotriva Bandei celor Patru.

Pe 9 septembrie în acelaşi an, Mao a murit şi el, iar pe patul de moarte se pare că i-a scris lui Hua: „Cu tine la putere pot muri liniştit". Hua a devenit preşedinte al partidului şi împreună cu Deng şi susţinerea armatei a arestat Banda celor Patru. Doi ani mai târziu,

Deng s-a întors din nou la conducere. După câte se pare era vicepremierul protejatului său Hu Yaobang, dar era foarte clar cine conducea cu adevărat China. Dintre primii trei lideri inițiali din timpul revoluției culturale comuniste, Mao, Zhou și Deng, cel din urmă a supraviețuit îndrumând China pe drumul pe care merge acum.

. . . .

Peisajul

China este o țară foarte mare, a treia din lume după Canada și Rusia, și cuprinde o vastă paletă de peisaje, de la deșerturi sterpe în nord până la coaste tropicale, luxuriante în sud. În termeni mai simpli, țara pășește de la munții giganți și vastele platouri din vest, prin dealurile centrale și bazinele din mijloc spre câmpiile joase și coastă spre est. Din munți izvorăsc trei mari fluvii care curg spre Pacific în est – Huang He sau Fluviul Galben în nord, Yangtze în mijloc și mai micul Xia Jiang – Râul Perlelor în sud. În cadrul acestei scheme simple există totuși o varietate imensă.

China de nord – est cunoscută odată ca Manciuria, este formată din trei provincii – Heilongjiang, Jilin și Liaoning. Aici munții împăduriți în formă de potcoavă înconjoară o câmpie fertilă. Spre vest sunt munții Da Hinggan Ling, care se arcuiesc în jurul platoului Xiao Hinggan Ling și al Changbai Shan în est. Aproape toți munții sunt acoperiți de păduri bogate, una dintre puținele zone din China care au rămas așa, care încă asigură rezervele cele mai bogate de cherestea ale țării. Pământurile negre ale câmpiilor sunt terenuri mănoase, bune pentru agricultură, care au fost lucrate de mii de ani. Iernile din Manciuria, cu o temperatură medie care scade sub −20 grade C și verile scurte caniculare, cu multe ploi, permit culturilor de grâu, floarea soarelui, mei și în special soia să fie foarte bogate.

Antica inimă a Chinei este partea de nord, înconjurată de faimosul Zid Chinezesc în nord și dominată de Beijing. În vestul regiunii, în nordul provinciei Shaanxi, se află Huangtu Gaoyuan, un platou vast care a fost format în mai multe milioane de ani de vântul care aducea praful fin din deșertul Mongoliei, devenit celebru în filmul *Yellow Earth* (Pământul Galben). În timp, pământul galben sau loesul a fost străbătut de canale adânci și drumuri înfundate, dar irigațiile au permis cultivarea terenului, dezvoltarea fermelor și a împăduririlor. În sudul platoului de loes se află dens populata Câmpie Weihe unde se cultivă faimosul ceai chinezesc și trestia de zahăr. Spre est se întind vastele câmpii Huabei Pingyuan, traversate de Fluviul Galben. Oamenii au trăit și muncit aici de atâta timp încât mare parte din peisaj este creat de mâna omului, cu aproape fiecare inch terasat și cultivat cu excepția dealurilor unde pădurile de copaci cu frunze căzătoare încă supraviețuiesc precum insulele într-o mare întunecată. Dar aici viața a fost adesea marcată de tragediile cauzate de inundațiile provocate de revărsările Fluviului Galben, denumit câteodată „tristețea Chinei", din cauza suferințelor pe care le aduce adesea.

La nord de Marele Zid se întind stepele Mongoliei Interioare, pe mai bine de o mie de mile de la munții Da Hinggan Lind în Heilongjiang spre platoul Helan Shan în vest. O parte din acest platou vast este acoperită de iarbă. În alte părți plouă atât de puțin încât pământul se transformă în Gobi sau deșert pietrificat. Peste tot este un peisaj dur, bătut de vânturi și uscat în timpul verii, foarte friguros pe timpul iernii. Recolte, precum cele de bumbac sunt cultivate în oaze, unde sălciile și plopii, oferă o bogăție de culori de toamnă. Sus, în zona stepei de nord, păstorii tradiționali mongoli încă cresc oi, vite, cămile și cai. În spatele platoului Helan Shan pământurile uscate dar fertile de lângă Fluviul Galben pătrund imperceptibil în terenurile acoperite de iarbă și apoi în vastitatea aridă a deșertului mongolian Gobi, una dintre cele mai dure zone de pe glob, cu temperaturi foarte ridicate pe timpul verii și geruri cumplite iarna. Mai departe spre vest se întind vastele bazine ale Xinjiang-ului înconjurate în totalitate de munți înalți încât puținele râuri din regiune nu găsesc o ieșire spre mare, formând în schimb lacuri și mlaștini. Există acolo trei mari bazine principale numite Pendi – Junggar, Tarim și Turpan. De-a lungul poalelor munților și a râurilor în Jungar Pendi și Turpan Pendi, pământul este suficient de fertil pentru a permite cultivarea sa, dar apa trebuie adusă din munți prin canale subterane pentru a preveni evaporarea sub soarele fierbinte. Turpan care la punctul cel mai jos se află la 160 de m sub nivelul mării, este renumit pentru pepenii și strugurii săi. Tarim Pendi însă este atât de uscat, încât este aproape acoperit în totalitate de o mare vastă de dune de nisip care se ridică la 100 de m, formând deșertul Takla Makan – cea mai uscată regiune din toată Asia.

În sudul Taklan Makan se ridică vârfurile înalte acoperite de zăpadă ale munților Kunlun Shan. Dacă urcați pe ei veți ajunge în locul denumit câteodată „acoperișul Lumii", platoul Qinghai–Tibet. Cu o înălțime medie de aproximativ 4 000 de m, este cel mai mare platou muntos din lume. Din toate părțile este înconjurat de cele mai înalte vârfuri din lume, culminând cu gloriosul Himalaya în sud, unde se află Chomolungma, muntele cu o înălțime impresionantă de 8 850 m. Mare parte din peisaj este arid și gol, acoperit de stânci, punctat din loc în loc de lacuri cu apă sărată și mlaștini. Aici clima este rece și uscată în cea mai mare parte a anului, cu vânturi reci și aer rarefiat pe care doar locuitorii învățați cu clima îl pot respira. Doar în văile din sud de lângă râul Yarlung Zangbo clima este mai blândă și mai umedă, aici fiind locul unde trăiesc și practică agricultura majoritatea tibetanilor.

Platoul Qinghai-Tibet este sursa izvoarelor multora dintre cele mai mari râuri din Asia, inclusiv Indul, Gangele, Brahmaputra, Mekong, și Yangtze – Fluviul Galben. Din Qinghai, Yangtze curge spre est în jos pe o lungime de 6 000 de km, pentru a ajunge la mare lângă Shanghai, fiind cel mai mare râu din Asia. Yangtze și afluenții săi udă mai mult de o cincime din pământul Chinei iar valea Yangtze este, în multe privințe, inima Chinei. În drumul său spre mare el curge printre munți de-o frumusețe sălbatică, strâmtori și bazine largi, inclusiv cea a bazinului Roșu al Sichuanului, denumit aşa pentru pământurile sale bogate, roşii. Spre sud, Yunnan şi Guizhou formează un platou vast tăiat în insule de vârfuri şi văi abrupte. În Guizhou, calcarul a fost dizolvat timp de milenii de ploaie şi transformat într-un peisaj magic de vârfuri ridicate spre cer, turle şi strâmtori adânci, care emit ecouri tăcute.

Mai departe pe Yangtze spre est se află zona de jos a Chinei, intens cultivată şi dens populată. De mii de ani, aici a fost cultivat orezul pe terase joase. Ceaiul este cultivat pe dealuri blânde, care apar ici şi colo deasupra câmpiei. Câmpiile sunt traversate de nenumărate ape, inclusiv de Marele Canal, care curge dinspre Hangzhou în nord spre Beijing, existând acolo nenumărate lacuri, multe acoperite în fiecare primăvară de zăpezile care se topesc şi sunt purtate aici de Yangtze. Rămâne de văzut ce se va întâmpla când se va închide Barajul celor Trei Strâmtori în 2008.

Sudul Chinei este subtropical, iar pe insula Hainan este o climă tropicală. Climatul este umed, cu veri lungi, călduroase şi ierni blânde. Musonul de vară aduce multe ploi iar temperaturile sunt suficient de ridicate pentru a avea două sau mai multe recolte pe an. Dar regiunile de coastă sunt frecvent bătute de taifunurile de vară care pot provoca dezastre cu vânturi puternice şi inundaţii. Mare parte din zona de coastă este franjurată de munţi stâncoşi care coboară spre mare într-o multitudine de golfuri naturale şi insuliţe în larg. Totuşi acolo unde râurile pătrund, pământul este adesea format din câmpii largi, fertile, dintre care cea mai mare este delta largă a lui Xi Jiang – Râul Perlelor, din Guangdong. În trecut, delta Râului Perlelor era una dintre cele mai productive regiuni agricole ale Chinei, unde se înregistrau producţii uriaşe de orez, tuberculi şi în special trestie de zahăr, fără a menţiona o abundenţă de fructe precum tangerine, ananas şi banane. Acum este mai cunoscut ca zone de interes ale revoluţiei industriale chineze şi ca locul cel mai rapid de dezvoltare al megaoraşelor.

. . . .

Viaţa sălbatică

Bogata paletă climatică, pământurile şi înălţimile din China, precum şi vasta sa suprafaţă, fac ca ţara să fie leagănul unui varietăţi mai mari de plante sălbatice şi animale decât oricare alta din lume.

Flora

În China există aproximativ 32 800 de specii de plante, o zecime din toate speciile de plante cunoscute, jumătate dintre ele fiind specifice Chinei. În nord şi vest se află deşerturi şi stepe în care cresc nenumărate plante şi flori, dar şi multe specii de iarbă. În locurile mai umede cresc, din loc în loc, arbuşti şi chiar copaci. Însă sudul şi nordul sunt zonele cu flora cea mai variată.

Cu aproape 8 000 de ani în urmă, copacii acopereau mare parte din estul şi din sudul ţării, formând o pădure neîntreruptă, care se întindea de la Heinan, în sud-est, până la Heilonjiang, în nord-est. Copacii se schimbau treptat ca varietate, pe măsură ce înaintai dinspre sud-vestul tropical, spre nord-estul rece, şi dinspre pământurile joase, înspre piscurile golaşe ale Chinei. În clima tropicală din sud-est, au existat păduri tropicale luxuriante, pline de o mare varietate de copaci tropicali, inclusiv palmieri. Dar pe măsură ce înaintai spre nord-est, sau urcai mai sus pe pantele abrupte ale munţilor, copacii se transformau trecând de la verdele intens al pădurii tropicale, la verdele peren al celei sub-tropicale şi ajungând la culoarea mai palidă a stejarului, ulmului şi frasinului, peisaj nu foarte diferit de cel întâlnit în Noua Anglie, din SUA, sau în sudul Marii Britanii. Mai sus, spre nord-est, copacii cu frunze căzătoare făceau loc coniferelor, cum ar fi zada.

În nici o ţară împădurită culturile agricole nu există din timpuri atât de îndepărtate precum în China, iar chinezii au avut mii de ani la dispoziţie ca să defrişeze codrii pentru a face loc terenurilor agricole şi a-şi asigura provizia de lemne de foc şi de contrucţii. Aproape toate pădurile străvechi din zonele de şes au dispărut, în picioare rămânând doar cele de pe pantele abrupte şi din alte locuri mai puţin accesibile.

Practicarea medicinei pe bază de plante este o mărturie a valorii pe care chinezii au atribuit-o întotdeauna diversității speciilor de plante din aceste păduri străvechi și, acum aproximativ patruzeci de ani – poate chiar mai devreme decât în majoritatea țărilor occidentale – au început să-și dea seama de amploarea eforturilor pe care trebuie să le facă pentru a le păstra. Peste cinci mii de specii sunt acum pe cale de dispariție. Într-o inițiativă științifică cu adevărat remarcabilă pentru o țară comunistă, guvernul chinez a început să înregistreze speciile de plante existente în fiecare dintre provincii la sfârșitul anilor '60. Treizeci de ani mai târziu, aceste cercetări au fost strânse într-un studiu uriaș, alcătuit din 255 de volume, intitulat *Flora Sinica* (acompaniat de un alt studiu similar, referitor la speciile animale - *Fauna Sinica*). Pe lângă o extindere sistematică a rezervațiilor naturale, China încearcă să înființeze depozite de semințe și grădini botanice, în care vor fi conservate optsprezece mii de exemplare de plante sălbatice. În plus, cercetătorii chinezi au început să crească sute de specii de plante rare, sau pe cale de dispariție, precum *Cathaya argyronhylla* (un soi de pin), *Metasequoia glyptostroboides* (un tip de conifer) și *Davidia involucrate*. În iunie 2007, guvernul chinez a anunțat un plan de cedare a 15 milioane de hectare folosite în agricultură pentru a fi reîmpădurite până în 2010, în vederea protejării biodiversității.

Botaniștii au fost mereu conștienți de comoara pe care o reprezintă China. În ultimii 200 de ani, nenumărați botaniști europeni și americani, precum Reginald Farrar, sau George Forest, au cutreierat zonele rurale chineze, în special Gansu, Sichuan, Yunnan și Tibet, în căutarea de plante pentru a le răsădi și a le aduce acasă. Speciile de plante aduse de aceștia s-au adaptat atât de bine în noile case, încât multe dintre plantele de grădină pe care acum le considerăm obișnuite au fost, de fapt, răsaduri aduse din China. Cireșul, prunul și plantele din familia Gingko provin toate din China, la fel ca și arbuștii de rododendron, azaleele și cameliile, fără să uităm de flori precum deutzia, filadelphus, daphne, arbustul de bumbac, forsyhtia, clopoțelul și trandafirul. Chiar și delicatele gențiene, primulele, irișii și saxifragii sunt emigrante chineze. Dacă veți merge pe dealurile din Sichiuan, veți găsi majoritatea acestor plante de grădină crescând în sălbăticie, din abundență.

Fauna

Diversitatea faunei din China este şi mai bogată în comparaţie cu cea a florei. Marele tom dedicat faunei ţării, *Fauna Sinica*, a înregistrat 104 500 de specii diferite de animale, mai multe decât în oricare altă ţară de pe glob. Aceasta nu cuprinde doar minusculele nevertebrate, ci şi specii mai spectaculoase de vertebrate. China este locul de baştină al cel puţin 450 de specii de mamifere(13,5% din totalul de pe glob) 1 195 de specii de păsări (11,2% din totalul pe glob), 460 de specii de reptile şi amfibieni şi aproximativ 2 000 de specii de peşti.

Peste tot, în ţară, există numeroase carnivore mai mici, cum ar fi lupi, ratoni, vulpi şi zibete. În unele zone continuă să trăiască carnivore mari - leoparzi şi tigri Amur în pădurile din nord-est, leoparzi de zăpadă, în Tibet şi leoparzi negri şi tigri bengalezi în sudul tropical. Pădurile din nord-est, unde iernile sunt adesea foarte aspre sunt unele dintre puţinele zone din China rămase neatinse de mâna omului şi, pe lângă leoparzi şi tigri, aici îşi mai au sălaşul şi urşi bruni, hermine, cerbi roşii şi lincşi. Totuşi, cea mai uimitoare zonă faunistică este, probabil, Xishuangbanna, partea cea mai de sud a Yunnanului. În pădurile tropicale de aici trăiesc 253 de specii de mamifere, mai mult de jumătate din mamiferele Chinei. Pe lângă leoparzii negri şi tigrii bengalezi, aici mai trăiesc elefanţi indieni, giboni, macaci şi rarele maimuţe aurii.

Simbolul vieţii sălbatice din China este ursul panda uriaş, care mai trăieşte acum doar în Sichuan, Gansu şi Shaanxi, unde se fac eforturi deosebite pentru a împiedica dispariţia sa, dar cu un succes moderat. La fiecare nivel de altitudine al munţilor din Sichuan se găsesc diferite specii de animale. În pădurile veşnic verzi şi în pădurile de copaci cu frunze căzătoare de la poalele dealurilor, trăieşte cea mai rară specie de tigru, tigrul din China de sud, alături de maimuţe aurii şi creaturi asemănătoare caprelor, cum ar fi *capricornis sumatraensis*. Puţin mai sus, printre arbuştii de bambus acoperiţi de ceaţă şi crângurile de pini şi brazi trăiesc uriaşii panda, alături de caprele sălbatice. Şi mai sus, acolo unde pădurea de bambus face loc, în aerul mai rece dintre pini, tufelor de rododendroni şi azalee, este sălaşul urşilor negri asiatici, al lincşilor, căprioarelor muntjac şi al antilopelor *Genus budorcas*. La o altitudine mai mare de 3 000 de metri, unde este prea frig chiar şi pentru pini, trăiesc doar animalele mari precum linxul şi căprioara muntjac, printre cuiburile unor păsări precum fazanul lui Reeves. Doar căprioarele muntjac îşi mai croiesc drum până la fineţele îngheţate situate la peste 4 000 de metri altitudine, unde li se alătură păsări cum ar fi fazanul monal şi cocorul cu gât negru.

Animale pe cale de dispariţie

Un număr imens de specii din China se află, în prezent, pe cale de dispariţie. Cea mai mare ameninţare a fost pierderea habitatului, însă apetitul chinezilor pentru animale exotice, atât ca hrană, cât şi ca leacuri în medicina tradiţională, le-a redus şi el numărul. Deşi comerţul cu organe de tigru a fost interzis încă din 1993, acest animal a avut cel mai mult de suferit de pe urma unor astfel de practici „tradiţionale". Au existat, chiar, unele apeluri care cereau lichidarea celor 5 000 de tigri captivi din China şi utilizarea oaselor acestora pentru producerea vinului de tigru şi a altor poţiuni „dătătoare de sănătate." Aceasta, susţin numeroşi chinezi, ar reprezenta o soluţie pentru salvarea tigrilor sălbatici, reducând necesitatea braconajului. Cu toate acestea, ecologiştii din Occident privesc o asemenea posibilitate ca pe un dezastru total, care n-ar face altceva decât să dea forţe noi pieţei de organe, încurajând braconajul – mai ales că tigrii sălbatici sunt consideraţi a fi mai „scumpi." Cum în China n-au mai rămas decât 500 de tigri adulţi în libertate, orice creştere a braconajului ar duce la o dispariţie rapidă a acestora. Din moment ce, încă din anii '70, n-a mai fost reperat nici un exemplar de tigru sudic, s-ar putea ca acesta să fi dispărut deja din sălbăticie. Ultimele exemplare de tigru sudic sunt, probabil, cele 68 ţinute în captivitate în grădinile zoologice, urmaşii a doar doi masculi şi patru femele. Ursul panda uriaş nu suferă aceleaşi ameninţări din partea medicinei tradiţionale ca tigrul, dar pădurea sa de bambus a fost distrusă de fermieri şi de tăietori de lemne, iar rata scăzută a natalităţii sale l-a făcut foarte vulnerabil. În sălbăticie mai există numai câteva mii de urşi panda, pentru salvarea acestora luându-se cele mai drastice măsuri. Chiar mai rar, deşi mai puţin iubit este aligatorul chinezesc, un locuitor antic al râului Yangtze şi al altor câteva fluvii. Pe măsură ce dezvoltarea industrială de-a lungul râurilor se accelerează, iar apele acestora devin din ce în ce mai poluate, supravieţuirea aligatorului este ameninţată. În prezent, există mai puţin de 500 de aligatori chinezi în apele ţării.

. . . .

Cultura

Limba

Peste 90% dintre chinezi vorbesc limba chineză, limba poporului Han (grupul etnic dominant în China), care este cea mai vorbită limbă de pe glob. Cu toate acestea, limba Han are o multitudine de dialecte, iar acestea sunt atât de diferite încât, în trecut, unei persoane care vorbea dialectul de la Beijing i-ar fi părut la fel de dificil să o înţeleagă pe alta, care îl vorbea pe cel din Guangzhou, pe cât i-ar fi fost unui portughez să înţeleagă un român – deşi atât portugheza, cât şi româna, sunt limbi „romanice", de origine latină. Adesea, dialectele chineze au aceleaşi cuvinte, dar atât intonaţia cu care sunt pronunţate, cât şi ordinea acestora pot fi atât de diferite, încât le fac de neînţeles. În dialectul de nord chinezesc (mandarin), spre exemplu, există patru intonaţii diferite, care diferenţiază cuvintele care altfel ar suna la fel. Chineza vorbită în sud are nouă asemenea intonaţii. Limba Han are şapte dialecte principale. Şase dintre ele sunt vorbite de mai puţin de 20% dintre chinezi, printre acestea aflându-se dialectul Wu, din Shanghai şi din împrejurimi (aprox. 8%), dialectul Kejia (sau Hakka) din Fujian (4%), sau dialectul Yue (cantonez), din Hong Kong şi din Gunanzhou (5%). Mulţi dintre chinezii din vasta diasporă răspândită în toată lumea, în special cei din Asia de Sud-Est vorbesc, de asemenea, cantoneza, sau dialectul Min Nan. Totuşi, cel mai răspândit dialect din China continentală este cel mandarin, vorbit de 70% din populaţie.

În trecut, mandarina era limba oficialităţilor, primindu-şi denumirea din partea portughezilor, care foloseau cuvântul pentru a descrie limba „mandarinilor" (adică a cârmuitorilor) din Beijing.

Utilizarea sa a devenit din ce în ce mai răspândită, pe măsură ce funcționarii guvernamentali se deplasau în țară și plăteau localnicii de peste tot să învețe mandarina pentru a se putea înțelege cu ei. În anii '50, guvernul a decis să institue folosirea ei ca limbă națională, denumind-o *putonghua* (ceea ce înseamnă „vorbire comună"), în locul termenului străin *mandarină*. *Putonghua* este forma de limbă chineză predată străinilor, fiind, de asemenea, limba pe care o învață copiii la școală, cea folosită de autorități și de mijloacele de comunicare în pasă, precum presa scrisă și internetul. În marile orașe, aproape toți tinerii pot citi *putonghua*, pentru că au învățat-o la școală. Nu toată lumea care o citește o poate și vorbi, iar în zonele rurale, cunoștințele de *putonghua* sunt reduse.

Ideogramele chineze

Interesant, multe dintre diferențele existente între variatele dialecte chineze se șterg atunci când acestea apar în varianta scrisă. Dialectele pot suna foarte variat, dar cuvintele sunt scrise cu multe dintre aceleași caractere, astfel încât fraza va însemna același lucru chiar dacă cititorul provine din Beijing sau Shenzhen. Datorită funcționalității caracterelor, acestea înseamnă același lucru indiferent de felul în care sună, după cum cifra patru scrisă semnifică același lucru chiar dacă ești francez sau neamț. Totuși, majoritatea caracterelor scrise chineze sunt în forma *putonghua*. Este o raritate să încerci să scrii în orice dialect, cu excepția cantonezei.

Chineza este limba cea mai complexă din punct de vedere al scrierii. În timp ce mulți dintre noi, occidentalii, avem la dispoziție 26 de litere, plus câteva semne pentru accente, chinezii au peste 50 000 de caractere. Persoanele cu o educație solidă sunt familiarizați, probabil, cu 10 000 dintre acestea, iar oricine este școlit va cunoaște cel puțin 2 500, minimul necesar pentru a citi un ziar.

Motivul pentru care există atâtea caractere scrise este faptul că limba chineză nu funcționează fonetic, astfel încât cuvintele nu pot fi alcătuite din sunete singulare. În schimb, există câte un caracter pentru fiecare cuvânt sau silabă. La origine, scrierea chineză se baza pe simple imagini grafice (pictograme) ale obiectelor naturale. Pictograme ca acestea datează încă din secolul XI î.Hr. Multe dintre limbile scrise au început aşa şi s-au îndreptat către un alfabet fonetic, dar caracterele chineze oferă doar puţine indicii asupra modului de pronunţare. În schimb, chinezii au dezvoltat limba prin combinarea pictogramelor pentru crearea unor noi sensuri abstracte sau a ideogramelor. Astfel, combinaţia de imagini pentru soare şi lună înseamnă „strălucitor", în timp ce o femeie şi un copil înseamnă „fericire". Picturile a trei femei împreună înseamnă trădare. Caracterele chineze dezvoltate ca picturi au ajuns să fie folosite pentru cuvinte care sunau la fel ca atunci când erau vorbite. Ca exemplu, caracterul imaginii pentru porumb s-a transformat în caracterul verbului „a veni", întrucât ambele cuvinte sunau la fel atunci când erau pronunţate.

Câteva stiluri diferite de scriere s-au dezvoltat în timp ce China s-a împărţit în diferite regate, între secolele VII şi III î.Hr., dar atunci când ţara s-a unificat sub dinastia Qin în anul 221 î.Hr., stilul Qin a fost impus peste tot. Stilul Qin a fost modificat substanţial sub dominaţia Han în 206-220 î.Hr., iar caracterele moderne chineze nu sunt mai mult decât o dezvoltare a vechilor caractere Han.

Caracterele chineze par imposibil de complexe la început, dar ele sunt întotdeauna alcătuite dintr-un anumit număr de mişcări ale peniţei, într-o ordine specială. Astfel, caracterul pentru „gură", care este de fapt un pătrat, este scris din trei linii: prima în partea stângă, apoi partea de sus şi partea dreaptă dintr-o singură trăsătură, iar ultima reprezintă baza. În mod obişnuit, caracterul are două părţi, partea din dreapta semnificând cumva înţelesul, iar cea din stânga, denumită radical, semnificând sunetul. În cel mai răspândit sistem există circa 214 radicali, ei fiind cei mai apropiaţi de alfabetul occidental.

Chineza scrisă este dificilă chiar şi pentru şcolari, iar în anii '50 acest fapt a fost resimţit ca o piedică împotriva educaţiei. Aşa că guvernul a introdus atunci două măsuri controversate. Prima era să simplifice cele mai uzuale câteva mii de caractere, făcându-le mai uşor de învăţat şi mai rapid de scris. Aceste caractere simplificate sunt folosite acum pe scară largă în China continentală, deşi în locuri precum Hong Kong sunt încă uzitate caracterele tradiţionale, care, de altfel, au revenit şi în scrierea intelectualilor chinezi de pe continent, fiind considerate mai sofisticate. A doua măsură, mult mai drastică, a fost aceea de a se renunța la caracterele chinezești, și, în schimb, să se adopte o scriere în alfabetul roman. Chineza „romanizată" a fost denumită *pinyin* și implica folosirea a 25 de litere ale alfabetului latin (excluzând litera V) pentru a crea sunetele din chineza mandarină, și a unor accente care, puse deasupra fiecărei silabe, redau cele patru intonații diferite. *Pinyin* nu a prins niciodată în China, iar curând s-a renunțat la idee, dar *pinyin* este foarte utilă străinilor, permițând oricărui occidental, după o instruire de bază, să citească și să pronunțe cuvinte chinezești fără a cunoaște vreun caracter chinez. Adoptarea pe scară largă a *pinyin*-ului a condus la schimbarea Peking-ului în Beijing și a lui Mao Tse-tung în Mao Zedong. Versiunea *pinyin* este mult mai apropiată de modul în care vorbesc chinezii, iar indicatoarele stradale sunt adeseori scrise atât în *pinyin*, cât și cu caractere chinezești.

. . . .

Literatura

Literatura clasică

China are una dintre cele mai vechi tradiții literare, datând de mai bine de trei mii de ani. Una dintre primele lucrări literare a fost *Shi Jing* (Cartea Cântecelor), care datează din secolele XI-VI î.Hr., fiind o colecție de cântece populare , unele dintre ele cu temă politică, și de imnuri rituale, despre care se spune că au fost culese de Confucius (551-479 î.Hr.). *Shi Jing* face parte dintr-o colecție de texte venerate asociate cu Confucius, denumite *Clasicii Confucieni*, deși, probabil, acesta nu a scris niciunul dintre ele. Filozofia confuciană a fost păstrată (sau creată) în *Analecte*, de către discipolii săi, cum ar fi Mencius, multe secole mai târziu. Din aceeași perioadă datează și faimoasa carte a lui Sun Zi, *Arta Războiului* „care oferă sfaturi asupra strategiei și tacticilor de luptă într-un mod foarte explicit, fiind una dintre cărțile preferate ale oamenilor de afaceri care călătoresc astăzi în China.

De foarte timpuriu poezia a fost considerată drept una dintre cele mai înalte forme artistice și o caracteristică a omului educat. Se aștepta de la un funcționar guvernamental să fie bun nu doar în ceea ce făcea, ci să fie şi poet. Natura distinctivă, aluzivă, enigmatică a poeziei chineze s-a evidenţiat încă din timpul dinastiei Han (206 î.Hr.-220) ,însă apogeul acesteia a fost atins de-a lungul dinastiei Tang (618-907) odată cu mari poeţi Li Bai, Du Fu şi Bai Juyi. Marca distinctivă a poemelor Tang este forma *shi*, cu versuri de 5-7 caractere şi cu rima căzând pe versurile pare. Poemele sunt încărcate de dor şi melancolie, exprimând tristeţea despărţirii sau exilul. Noi forme de poezie au fost inspirate de cântece populare în timpul dinastiei Song (960-1279). În perioada dinastiei Ming (1368-1644) au trăit multe poete faimoase.

Nuvelele au început să se afirme tot în perioada Tang, ca şi poezia. Multe dintre ele au supravieţuit, relatând întâmplări triste ale unor îndrăgostiţi despărţiţi de soartă sau de părinţi neîndurători, ori despre studenţi zeloşi care se zbat să-şi croiască o carieră, dar sunt continuu împiedicaţi de seducătoarele zâne–vulpi (spirite care-şi schimbă forma şi care fură inimile pământenilor, lăsându-i apoi pradă deznădejdii). Treptat, micile povestiri s-au transformat în romane, iar la mijlocul perioadei Ming se scriau deja mari cărţi de aventuri, cum ar fi *Sanguozhi yanyi* (Romanul celor trei regate), un captivant roman istoric despre războinici şi luptele care au avut loc în China în timpul turbulentei perioade a celor Trei Regate, cu 1 200 de ani în urmă; *Shui hu Zhuan* (Toţi bărbaţii sunt fraţi, sau Malul Apei), este o poveste trepidantă despre bandiţi asemănătoare cu cea a lui Robin Hood; *Jin ping mei* (Lotusul de aur) este un portret al vieţii de zi cu zi dintr-o familie bogată. Totuşi cel mai mare roman chinezesc a fost, probabil, *Hong lou meng* (Visul camerei roşii), apărut în timpul dinastiei Ming (1644-1911). Această operă masivă, extrem de elaborată, scrisă de Cao Zhan şi publicată postum în 1792, este o adevărată saga familială, centrată pe măreţia şi declinul familiei Jia. Este în acelaşi timp o satiră şi un roman de mistere, care urmăreşte urcuşurile şi coborâşurile din viaţa uşuraticului adolescent Jia Baoyu şi a tinerelor sale verişoare Lin Daiyu şi Xue Baochai.

Drama a apărut în timpul împăraţilor mongoli Yuan (1279-1368), iar piesele de teatru erau scrise atât pentru a fi citite, cât şi jucate. Dar cel mai mare autor de piese de teatru a fost Tang Xianzu, care a scris drame epice romantice.

Romanul modern

În secolul XX, mulţi scriitori chinezi au început să respingă stilul pompos, prea elaborat al clasicilor, iar în 1919 o parte dintre aceştia s-au unit formând *Mişcarea Patru Mai*. Scriitorii *Patru Mai*, ca Lu Xun, au militat pentru o abordare mai pragmatică care să reflecte vorbirea chineză de zi cu zi. În 1930, Shen Congwen a început să scrie despre oameni obişnuiţi, cu o asemenea sensibilitate şi intuiţie încât a fost comparat cu scrierile marelui maestru rus Ivan Turgheniev. Venirea comunismului la putere a sufocat aproape toată literatura adevărată, întrucât partidul a refuzat să publice altceva în afara realismului socialist, cu poveştile sale entuziaste despre eroi care luptă pentru patrie, împotriva corupţiei forţelor imperialiste. În această perioadă au fost scrise mari romane, ca cel al lui Zhang Ailing (*Eileen Chang*), în care se demască ororile socialismului, publicat în China abia în anii 1990. Lao She, unul dintre cei mai mari scriitori din ultimul secol, a fost împins spre suicid în timpul Revoluţiei Culturale.

Libertatea sosită odată cu sfârşitul Revoluţiei Culturale, în 1976, a reuşit, totuşi, să scoată la lumină multă suferinţă reprimată. Poveşti personale dureroase, care au ajuns să fie denumite *„literatura celor răniţi"*, au început să vorbească despre teribilele încercări ale ultimilor ani. Reacţia oficială faţă de aceste lucrări a fost, adesea, de tăgadă indignată. Poliţiştii care investigau operele acestor scriitori „răniţi", i-au spus autorului Bei Dao, că este imposibil ca acestea să fie scrise de către ei înşişi, şi că, cel mai probabil, au fost copiate din literatura străină. Totuşi, acest lucru nu a putut opri ca romanul lui Wang Shuo, *Cel care tânjeşte*, să fie transpus, în 1989, într-un serial de televiziune de 50 de episoade.

Acum, literatura chineză se scrie într-o multitudine de stiluri, ca şi cea occidentală, dar orice carte care ar critica făţiş conducătorii sau partidul va găsi cu greu o editură care să o publice în China. Cărţi precum poveştile dure ale lui Mo Yan despre viaţa la ţară, *Baladele Usturoiului*, sunt încă interzise în China. Şi cărţile obscene sunt ţinute sub obroc de către autorităţi, cum ar fi *Shanghai Baby*, a lui Wei Hui, care era cât pe ce să fie interzisă, sau *Păpuşa din Beijing*, de Chun Sue, jurnalul unei adolescente care povesteşte despre aventurile ei sexuale sordide. În Occident, mulţi autori, în special femei, au început să se facă cunoscuți cu cercetările lor asupra greutăților vieții din China secolului 20, cum ar fi cartea lui Adeline Yen Mah, *Frunze Căzătoare*, sau a lui Jung Chang *Lebede sălbatice*. Totuși cel mai bine vândut autor din China, astăzi, este Guo Jingming, care scrie romane de factură sentimentală pentru adolescenți.

Arta

Pictura clasică

Pictura și caligrafia au fost dintotdeauna cele mai apreciate arte în China. Ele au rezultat din căutările pasionate ale celor mai venerați oameni, nobilii eruditi, care cultivau acest talent pentru satisfacție intelectuală și estetică, nu pentru a trăi din asta.

Există multe diferențe între pictura chineză și cea occidentală, dar, în primul rând, trebuie remarcată simplitatea ei extremă. Mulți artiști folosesc puțină culoare, sau deloc, însă lucrările sunt executate în cerneluri de nuanțe diferite. Chiar și în cele mai colorate, se folosesc acuarele cu nuanțe subtile, fiind pictate pe hârtie subțire, mătase sau ceramică. În mod tradițional, picturile chineze nu erau înrămate. În schimb, ele sunt pictate pe evantaie, suluri de hârtie sau pergament, în albume sau pe ceramică. Astfel încât, compoziția are întotdeauna forma unor delicate camee, mai degrabă, decât a unei picturi înrămate.

Subiectele sunt, de asemenea, simple. Abstracțiunile originale sunt rare, iar subiectele se abat rareori de la temele tradiționale: peisaje, figuri umane, păsări și flori. În ciuda varietății reduse a acestora, artiștii chinezi reușesc să obțină o impresionantă diversitate, iar simbolistica fiecărui subiect conține adesea un sens suplimentar, pe care contemplatorul occidental, de cele mai multe ori, îl pierde. Florile celor patru anotimpuri, de exemplu: lotusul simbolizează vară și puritate; bujorul evocă primăvara, bogăția și onoarea; crizantema înseamnă toamnă şi vârsta înaintată; foarea de prun, cais, migdal şi cireş înseamnă iarnă şi frumuseţe. Bambusul, prunul şi pinul, cei trei prieteni ai iernii simbolizează cele trei religii principalele chineze: budismul, taoismul şi confucianismul.

Pictura a început să se dezvolte, probabil, sub dinastia Han (206-220 î.Hr), iar manuscrisul de la Mawangdui, prima pictură pe mătase cunoscută, a fost descoperit într-un mormânt din perioada Han. Dar prea puţine au supravieţuit din acea perioadă – în parte şi pentru că uriaşa colecţie imperială a fost distrusă în timpul războiului civil de către soldaţi, care foloseau mătasea pentru a-şi confecţiona corturi şi genţi din mătase, ceea ce trebuie să fi fost foarte la modă! Abia în timpul dinastiei Tang pictura a început să capete amploare, odată cu apariţia marii tradiţii a portetelor, artiştii începând să picteze cu ocazia marilor evenimente de stat, când împăratul primea oaspeţi, sau când elegantele doamne de la curte se preumblau de colo-colo. Peisajul a înflorit sub dinastia Song, iar stilul peisagistic al pictorilor din acea epocă, cum a fost Su Dongpo, a influenţat mulţi artişti chinezi de atunci încoace. Hui Zong, ultimul împărat Song, era el însuşi un pictor talentat. Există, totuşi o abordare diferită între perioada Song de nord (960-1126) şi Song de sud (1126-1279). În picturile din perioada Song de nord, cum ar fi cele ale lui Xu Daoning, natura este dominatoare, cu munţi monumentali care dau personajelor umane alura unor pigmei. În schimb, în picturile din perioada Song de sud, omului i se permite un rol mai proeminent, ca în lucrarea *Plimbare pe o potecă de munte primăvara*, din secolul XII, în care toate elementele neesenţiale ale peisajului sunt eliminate.

Ideea de artist amator a atins apogeul sub împăraţii mongoli Yuan. Mulţi oficiali chinezi nu erau dornici să servească sub conducerea mongolilor străini Yuan sau, pur si simplu, nu erau doriţi. Aşa că s-au retras la casele lor, începând să picteze în stilul *literati*, exemplificat de maeştri precum Zhao Mengfu, Huang Gongwang şi Wu Zhen. Aceşti pictori amatori au cultivat ce-a fost mai bun din Tang şi Song, creînd compoziţii alese cu cele mai simple subiecte posibile, cum ar fi florile de prun. Ni Can, unul dintre cei mai mari pictori ai epocii, s-a specializat în rafinate picturi în cerneală ale bambusului. Interesant, dar simbolistica acestor picturi poate ascunde mesaje cu încărcătură politică. În 1306, Zheng Sixiao a pictat o simplă orhidee care simboliza înaltele principii ale unui nobil. Dar el a pictat-o fără rădăcini – o aluzie subtilă la furtul pământurilor sale de către mongolii Yuan.

Abordarea *literati* a continuat şi sub dinastiile Ming şi Qing, din această perioadă supravieţuind nenumărate picturi, desăvârşit executate, ale florilor de bambus şi prun, păsări şi peisaje. Însă, în timpul dinastiei Qing, au început să-şi facă simţită prezenţa şi influenţele occidentale, cum ar fi cea a italianului Castiglione (Lang Shi-Ning), preocupat, în lucrările sale, de cai, câini şi flori. Cel mai faimos artist al vremii a fost Qi Baishi (1863-1956), ale cărui splendide picturi cu animale, plante şi insecte sunt atât de populare în Occident.

Epoca modernă

Începând cu anii '50, arta chineză, la fel ca şi literatura, a fost silită să facă propagandă în stilul realismului socialist. Artistul Han Xin, spre exemplu, a realizat faimoasa pictură omniprezentă a Preşedintelui Mao. Persecuţia artiştilor a atins intensitatea maximă în timpul Revoluţiei Culturale, la sfârşitul căreia şi-a făcut apariţia o generaţie de tineri artişti care de-abia aşteptau să-şi exprime puternicele sentimentele legate de suferinţele provocate de persecuţii şi speranţele pentru un viitor mai bun. Un grup de tineri artişti care se autointitulau *Stelele*, au renunţat la toate tradiţiile artei chineze începând să experimenteze cu o paletă largă de stiluri occidentale, de la minimalism la cubism. Unii dintre membri *Stelelor* erau tineri studenţi la arte, dar alţii fuseseră forţaţi să meargă la muncă în fabrici. Din moment ce nici o galerie de artă nu dorea să le expună lucrările, şi-au creat propria expoziţie agăţându-şi lucrările pe gardul unui mic parc de lângă Muzeul Naţional de Artă din Beijing. Autorităţile au fost atât de şocate, încât au trimis poliţia să le dea jos, dar *Stelele* îşi făcuseră cunoscut punctul de vedere.

Anii '80 au fost martorii unei perioade de mari experimente artistice, în special în arta abstractă, ca o sfidare la adresa definirii acesteia de către Partidul Comunist ca „poluare spirituală." Majoritatea acestor eforturi radicale erau de inspirație occidentală, însă, în anii '90, pictorii chinezi au început să-şi definească propriile viziuni artistice. Pictori precum Liu Wei, Zhang Xiaogang şi Fang Lijun au început să picteze într-un stil sumbru, adesea grotesc, pe care chiar faimosul critic de artă Li Xianting l-a etichetat ca „realism cinic," în timp ce alţii au început să se joace pe marginea stilului realismului socialist. Wang Guangyi a subliniat pericolele noului capitalism prin împletirea imaginii eroilor realismului socialist cu logo-uri ale multinaţionalelor care se mută în China, în timp ce alţi artişti pictează imagini ale Preşedintelui Mao în stilul artei pop. Când artiştii au început să-şi dea seama cât de bine se vindea această artă politică în Occident, stilul pop-art a devenit aproape un clişeu. În prezent, arta chineză se îndreaptă din ce în ce mai mult spre mainstream-ul internaţional, cu vernisaje în galerii elegante din centrul Beijingului, sau al Shanghaiului şi cu artişti care primesc onorarii la fel de mari cu ale celor mai bine vânduţi creatori din Occident.

· ·

Filmul

Istoria cinematografului din China începe în 1896, odată cu prezentarea primei pelicule „mişcătoare" într-o ceainărie din Shanghai, acest oraş devenind, în anii '30, o prosperă scenă cinematografică, pe care rulau mai ales filme importate din Occident, spre delectarea numeroşilor străini ce locuiau în China, dar şi un număr de filme produse în studiouri locale, precum Mingxin, sau Lianhua. Filmele din Shanghai nu au avut totuşi un impact prea mare în afara elitelor oraşului. Sub Mao a fost produsă, desigur, o întreagă serie de filme „memorabile", a căror singură calitate era că au făcut cunoscut populaţiei, pentru prima oară, cinematograful. Vânzările de bilete au crescut de la 47 de milioane, în 1949, la uimitoarea cifră de 4 miliarde, zece ani mai târziu, când cinematografele şi studiourile de film începuseră să apară în fiecare oraş. La sfârşitul anilor '50, când Mao se retrăsese de la conducerea statului, guvernul a început să relaxeze regulile privind subiectele potrivite pentru filme, în această perioadă realizându-se unele filme remarcabile precum *Lin Zexu*. Însă, în 1966, Revoluția Culturală a ucis încă din faşă această uşoară înflorire a cinematografului chinez.

Odată cu sfârşitul revoluției, Academia de Film din Beijing s-a redeschis, iar absolvenții săi au inițiat curentul numit *A cincea generație de creație cinematografică*, care a oferit cinematografiei chineze recunoaşterea internațională. Regizorii din *Generația a cincea* au abandonat realismul socialist pentru a explora, într-un stil grandios, tradițiile şi peisajele Chinei prerevoluționare. Primul a fost uimitorul film al lui Chen Kaige şi al cameramanului său Zhang Yimou, *Pământul galben* (1982), cu peisajele sale superbe din Shaanxi, ce aminteau de picturile chinezeşti. Acesta a fost urmat de filmul lui Zhang Yimou – *Sorgul roşu* (1987) şi de cel al lui Tian Zhuanzhuang – *Hoțul de cai*. *Sorgul Roşu*, ce relatează povestea unor țărani eroici care au luptat împotriva armatei japoneze în anii '40, a cucerit peste noapte spectatorii chinezi, transformându-l pe actorul principal, Jiang Wen, într-o vedetă națională. În străinătate, filmul a câştigat aprecierea unanimă a publicului şi criticilor, vestind spectatorilor occidentali apariția unei noi stele - cinematograful chinez. Actrița principală, Gong Li, a câştigat inimile multor bărbați din Occident. Zhang Yimou şi Gong Li au devenit un cuplu şi au făcut mai multe filme de succes împreună, printre care şi *Judou, Povestea lui Qiu Ju* şi *Ridicarea Lanternei Roşii*, care au cimentat reputația crescândă a filmului chinez în străinătate. Atât Zhang Yimou, cât şi Chen Kaige par să-şi fi atins punctul culminant al carierei în 1994, Zhang, cu filmul *Pentru Viață*, iar Chen cu *Adio concubina mea*, amândouă provocatoare şi profund emoționante, a căror acțiune nu se desfăşoară în trecutul îndepărtat, ci în secolul XX. Ambii regizori au fost atât de bine primiți de autorități, încât mulți critici consideră că acesta este şi motivul epuizării talentului lor. Chen Kaige a continuat prin a face cel mai scump film chinez, *Promisiunea*, pe care mulți îl consideră un eşec monumental extrem de costisitor, în timp ce Zhang Yimou a realizat o serie de filme pe care majoritatea criticilor le consideră superficiale, cum ar fi povestea eroică, asezonată cu secvențe de arte marțiale – *Casa pumnalelor zburătoare* (2004).

Problema regizorilor chinezi este că cenzura are o influență uriașă asupra deciziei de a realiza sau nu un film, controlând nu doar sursele de finanțare, ci și variantele de scenariu și diferitele scene filmate. Regizorii mai provocatori au de ales între a-și lăsa rolele pe seama foarfecelor cenzorilor, sau a le trimite în străinătate fără aprobarea organelor, numai pentru a fi interzise în cinematografele de acasă. O modalitate de a ocoli cenzura este lansarea ilegală a filmelor pe DVD-uri. Așa și-a câștigat audiența filmul lui Jia Zhangke – *Xiao Wu* (Hoții de buzunare). Alte filme interzise ce pot fi vizionate în acest format sunt cele ale lui Jia – *Lumea* (2004), despre luptele muncitorilor din Beijing, și cel al lui Yang Li – *Săgeata oarbă* (2003), despre primejdiile capitalismului sălbatic, ce prezintă un caz de mușamalizare a unei crime dintr-o mină de cărbune. Interesant, în 2006, Jia Zhangke a fost reabilitat și angajat de stat pentru a realiza reclame pentru compania de stat de telefonie mobilă – cu clipuri din filmele sale interzise.

Între timp, peste mare, în Hong Kong, s-a dezvoltat o industrie a filmului a cărei productivitate este depășită doar de Hollywood și de Bollywood. Aceasta este, oarecum, în afara razei de acțiune a cenzorilor, dar, pe de altă parte, nici n-a făcut niciodată filme care să le dea acestora mari bătăi de cap. Producătorii din Hong Kong au adus genul filmelor de acțiune cu arte marțiale și vedete precum Jackie Chan la un asemena nivel de perfecțiune, încât regizori occidentali mai pretențioși, precum Ang Lee (*Tigrul ghemuit, Dragonul ascuns*) și Quentin Tarantino au simțit nevoia să le aducă un omagiu. Un regizor din Hong Kong care ales o altă cale de exprimare este Wong Kar-wai, filmele sale, cum ar fi *Expresul de Chungking* și *Dornic de dragoste*, fiind pătrunzătoare și caustice.

· ·

Noul dicționar universal al limbii române

Cuprinde 81.000 de intrări, dintre care 73.000 de articole propriu-zise.

Copertă cartonată
- 193 x 255mm
- 1680 pagini
- ISBN 978-973-675-307-7

● Fiecare definiție este ilustrată prin citate sugestive din literatura cultă sau populară, după modelul promovat de Lazăr Șăineanu.

● Valorifică și îmbogățește tradiția lexicografică românească, introducând noi cuvinte și sensuri ale vorbirii contemporane, adaptând sau completând definițiile din dicționarele deja existente.

● Conține numeroase neologisme, arhaisme culturale, regionalisme, termeni speciali (economici, tehnici, sociali, medicali, juridici etc.), concepte filozofice și teologice, curente culturale și politice.

● Explicațiile cuvintelor conțin forme flexionare, variante lexicale și fonetice, construcții fixe și sinonime.

▶ **Dicționar vizual
5 limbi**

engleză
franceză
germană
spaniolă
română

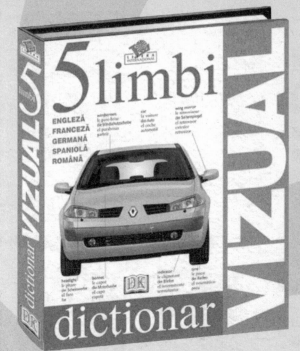

▼ **Dicționare
vizuale
bilingve**

LITERA INTERNAȚIONAL

AU MAI APĂRUT

» **GHIDURI TURISTICE VIZUALE**

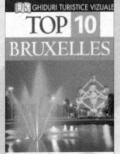

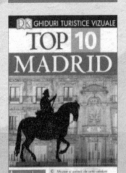

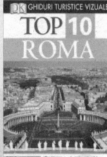

 **LITERA INTERNAȚIONAL**

AU MAI APĂRUT

▶▶ **DICȚIONARE
ȘI ENCICLOPEDII
PENTRU COPII**

MAREA CARTE
despre
PERSONALITĂȚI

DeAGOSTINI

MAREA CARTE
despre
EXPERIMENTE

DeAGOSTINI

MAREA
CARTE:
Întrebări
ȘI
RĂSPUNSURI

TESTE
RECORDURI
CURIOZITĂȚI
INFORMAȚII UTILE

INTERNAȚIONAL

MAREA
CARTE
DESPRE
Invenții

UTILE
DE VIITOR
INDISPENSABILE
REVOLUȚIONARE

INTERNAȚIONAL

AU MAI APĂRUT

▶ ÎN COLABORARE
CU REVISTA
"FELICIA"